Disability Insurance and Other Living Benefits

3rd Edition

CCH
a Wolters Kluwer business

Jacqueline E. Figas

CCH Canadian Limited
300-90 Sheppard Avenue East
Toronto Ontario
M2N 6X1
1 800 268 4522
www.cch.ca

Published by CCH Canadian Limited

Edited by: Anne-Marie Zapf-Belanger

Library and Archives Canada Cataloguing in Publication

Figas, Jacqueline E., 1952-
Disability insurance and other living benefits / Jacqueline E. Figas. — 3rd ed.

First ed. published under title Evaluating disability insurance.
ISBN 978-1-55496-489-5

1. Disability insurance — Canada. I. Title.

HD7105.25.C3 F53 2012 368.38'2 C2009-900707-X

ISBN: 978-1-55496-489-5

Typeset by CCH Canadian Limited.
Printed in the United States.

PREFACE

Today's workers are likely to change jobs or career paths five to six times during their working years. This is two to three times more frequently than in the past. The worker will initiate some of these changes, but the employer is just as likely to be the trigger. The new economy has forced employers to rethink the way they conduct business, and the workplace has become less product-oriented and more project-oriented. Today's workers must be multi-skilled and can expect to perform a variety of tasks throughout their careers.

Lifelong learning is fundamental. In the past, education followed a linear path and occurred before the worker entered the working world. Now education is in the future tense, no longer linear, and instead of preceding the worker's career, education is intertwined with it.

Globalization has affected companies in many ways. One such way is that they can no longer afford to have full-time permanent employees doing all the work that needs to be done. Many companies rely on temporary workers to fill gaps as they occur. These workers are known as the just-in-time workforce. They span a wide variety of occupations, from blue-collar to white-collar, from low-paid positions to executive positions with six-digit salaries.

Non-standard work is rapidly becoming the norm. While workers enjoy more flexible work schedules, independence, and the opportunity for many different work experiences, the flip side is that they often lack work security, company pensions, and health benefits, and they cannot predict the timing of work transitions.

Computerization has caused many traditional jobs to disappear or change. It has also created new types of work, such as telecommuting and teleworking. Working from a home office has become popular. The world has become smaller, with call centres providing global service. Workers must keep up to date with world trends and quickly changing events that can affect both employers and workers in businesses of any size.

The 21st-century workplace has brought many opportunities, but many worries too. Stability has been replaced with instability, and events no longer occur in a predictable order. There is a sense of continuing transformation that permeates work and home life. What we know today becomes irrelevant tomorrow in a rapidly changing environment. The real business imperative is to solve problems and exceptions, because routine functions can be systematized and therefore automated.

The 21st-century worker has to move to the complex and chaotic edge where value exists to the organization. We live in a high-tech and supercharged environment, with laptops, Skype, cellphones, and Blackberries creating a 24/7 work environment. Work and home life have little separation. Constant change is the disease of the 21st century and many workers are afflicted by it. The disease manifests itself as stress disguised as headaches, hypertension, heart disease, and depression.

Age 65 is no longer a marker of retirement. Workers may transition to retirement because of a personal desire to lessen stress or because they are forced to retire. These retired workers are still seeking income, status, personal achievement, structure, and interpersonal relationships. This changes what they pursue when their career has ended. The 20th-century retirement was the end stage of a linear career. Now the linear career has been replaced by a cyclical living and working model in which participation in the workforce never ceases, and is interspersed with periods of leisure and learning. Often called the "hobby job", this second, post-retirement career is punctuated by flexible arrangements such as part-time, seasonal, occasional, and project work.

Thirty years from now, will full-time employment and upward mobility just be a fond memory? Perhaps the dual-income trend will be a past phenomenon, not because societal values dictate that one parent should stay home, but because the way in which companies employ human resources has created unstable work patterns, leaving families less financially secure than the generation before them. It is a documented fact that unemployment and underemployment lead to lower self-esteem, family breakdown, and rising crime rates.

Perhaps financial planning based on career trajectories measured today in years should instead be thought of in terms of "lifetime career hours". By the end of this century, it is possible that lifetime career hours may not exceed 40,000. This would represent a mere 20 years of full-time work by today's standards.

These trends have many implications for the insurance industry. Insurers are responding with broader health insurance portfolios, new product design, and changes in underwriting protocols and claims management. So too must advisers approach financial and benefits planning differently. Disability insurance, along with other health insurance products, must meet the needs of an evolving workforce and adapt to societal changes. Advisers should review their clients' programs periodically to ensure that these programs continue to fit with their clients' life and career transitions.

May this book serve you well in this respect as a resource in your practice!

TABLE OF CONTENTS

Chapter 1

Disability Statistics

STATISTICS

Statistics are often used as evidence by speakers, writers, people in sales, large corporations, and non-profit organizations. Drug companies use them to support their claims that a new medication works. Companies quote them to demonstrate their corporate strength and industry growth. Governments use them to plan public programs such as health care and pensions for seniors. Statistics can be extremely valuable in supporting conclusions.

Scan your morning newspaper and what are you likely to find? Statistics! "New study links vitamin B with reduction in cancer rates." One week later, "Experts warn too much vitamin B causes cancer". How can two studies come to such opposite conclusions? Is one right and the other wrong?

No doubt when you hear some statistics, you wonder if a study was ever really conducted. It is good to be skeptical, because some statistics can be misleading, misquoted, or misused.

Most people believe numbers more readily than they believe words. Statistics are powerful evidence that can effectively strengthen any argument. But most people accept them at face value without question because they think that the numbers speak for themselves. However, statistics can be ambiguous, and for this reason there are some important questions you need to ask yourself about the information behind the numbers.

Did the Survey Include All the Results?

Assume you set out to prove that four out of five teenagers prefer the colour black. You might ask your first group of five teenagers, but if only three out of five picked black, you could go on to another group, and another, until you found a group of five teenagers in which four chose the colour black. In reality, you might have talked to 250 teenagers before you got the results you were looking for. In surveys you encounter, there may be reasons that seem legitimate why the results were thrown out in the first tests, but the bottom line is that all data must be included or the results are not credible.

How Large Was the Sampling?

A seniors' centre tries a new procedure designed to reduce the incidence of colds amongst the group. They announce the success of their program: they have achieved an amazing 60% reduction in the incidence of colds over the prior winter season. If last year there were 800 cases and this year there were only 640, the incidence of colds has been reduced by 160 cases, and this is statistically significant because the likelihood that this would happen by random fluctuation ("chance") is extremely low. But if last year there were only five seniors with colds and this year the incidence dropped to two (a reduction of only three cases), then while it is true that there were 60% fewer colds, the result is not statistically significant because there is a high probability that this could have happened by random fluctuation. A percentage is meaningful only if you know the base. A population must be large enough to yield results that are credible.

Who Conducted the Study?

Suppose you see a headline that reads, "New study proves cigarette smoking is not bad for your health". The first question you need to ask yourself is, who conducted the study? What do they have to gain by the results? If the Canadian Cancer Society conducted the study, we might have more confidence in the results than if the study was conducted by an affiliate of the tobacco industry. (But we should still ask ourselves what the Canadian Cancer Society stands to gain by these results; perhaps a large funding contribution depended on a favourable outcome on the survey.) When bias exists, then results can get skewed. There may be problems with how the questions were asked, who the researchers included in their study, how they interpreted the results, or what they chose to compare.

What Is Being Measured?

There is a saying that goes, "You can't compare apples with oranges". But in reality, you can if you know what it is you are measuring. For example, while you cannot measure their colour, you can measure their sugar, vitamin, and fat content. When looking at statistics, you must therefore ask, what is it that is being measured?

Has Information Been Interpreted Correctly?

Sometimes people mistakenly assume that because two things vary together, one is causing the other. In reality, it could simply be a coincidence, or both things could be caused by a third factor. Here is a classic example given to illustrate this: the larger the number of firefighters called in to fight a fire, the more damage the fire does. The explanation, of course, is that a third factor is responsible, namely, the size of the fire. A larger fire causes more firefighters to be called in, and a larger fire also causes more damage. Correlation does not equal causation.

What Is the Source of the Statistic?

Sometimes statistics are quoted from a third party rather than from the original source. Suppose you read in the newspaper, "Life expectancy in Canada drops to 61.7 years — is our water to blame?" Then upon examining the story closer, you discover that the writer interviewed someone who mistakenly quoted the life expectancy in Cambodia from a world listing found on the Internet. People have a tendency to believe that if a fact is in print, particularly in the newspaper, then it must be accurate. (After all, aren't reporters supposed to verify their stories before they are published?) But this is not always the case. Look for statistics that are from sources that are both primary and reliable, such as Statistics Canada.

Are Comparisons Based on Equivalent Standards?

Suppose an article is comparing the incidence of 911 calls by seniors in one city with the incidence in another. In one month, City A had 5 calls, while City B had 50 calls. On the surface, it appears that City A is the place you would want to retire. But we don't have all the information here — we need to be comparing equivalent measurements. We must look at the per capita rate, which is usually measured per 100,000. If City A has 2,500 residents while City B has 550,000 residents, then City A has a seniors emergency call rate of 200 per 100,000 people, and City B has a rate of only 9 per 100,000. Better rethink those retirement plans.

The Human Factor

Some studies are based on "soft" facts asked during interviews, as opposed to "hard" facts obtained in a laboratory. Such studies are subject not only to the usual biases, but also to error due to factors such as how the question was asked, by whom the question was asked, and how the respondent was feeling that day. Some studies conducted by the government are based on answers from respondents, for example, those collecting opinions from seniors on the questions, "Do you have any activity limitations?" and "Are you afraid to live on your own?" In these examples, respondents might overstate or understate their healthiness based on how they feel the day the interview is conducted, or they might not want to admit their true feelings about living alone. Pride and self-esteem affect how one responds. And of course, some people might lie outright because they feel their privacy is being invaded. So the results of such a survey may erroneously conclude, for example, that 90% of seniors have activity limitations and are very afraid of living alone.

Therefore, it is important to ask yourself whether the statistics were derived from a survey that collected soft facts or hard facts. Were questions asked in a leading way? What issue prompted the survey? What policy or action depends on the results of the survey? Who stands to gain from particular interpretations? Were the results replicated in a follow-up study or only achieved once? What was the margin of error used in interpreting results of the study? Statistics derived from soft studies are more often misused (sometimes unintentionally) than those derived from hard studies. Soft studies are often neither repeatable nor predictive, because they are based on people, not nature. People may not say or do the same thing twice, and their responses rely upon their own interpretation of what they are being asked.

In Conclusion

Many people use statistics to support their point of view; it is up to individuals to come to their own conclusions by examining what is behind the numbers. Statistics are always the product of research, and it is important to understand where they came from. When you use statistics as evidence for your argument, make sure the statistics actually apply to the point you are making. Choose your statistics wisely and they can be persuasive and powerful pieces of evidence.

SOME COMMON DISABILITY STATISTICS

The Commissioners' Disability Table (1985), produced by the Society of Actuaries, is the source of several commonly used disability statistics even today. These statistics are derived from the actual experience of a large number of U.S. companies over an extended period of time. They are used by actuaries in calculating reserves, and they measure the incidence and duration of disabilities based on factors such as elimination period, occupation, age, gender, and cause of disability. These statistics are based on insured lives, not the general population.

Another source of statistics that is often quoted is the Participation and Activity Limitation Survey, conducted by Statistics Canada. This survey was conducted between October 30, 2006, and February 28, 2007. The purpose of the survey was to gather information about Canadians who live with limitations, including those who were born with limitations, in order to assist the government in planning services and programs that enable persons with disabilities to participate more fully in society. The survey measures prevalence, not incidence. It differs from the Commissioners' Disability Table (1985) in that the results are based on the general population rather than insured lives. This survey was conducted by telephone interviewers, and the respondents included individuals who may have been answering on behalf of someone else. While its results are not predictive, the information speaks to the lifelong need to protect one's health using disability, critical illness, health, and long-term care insurance.

Likelihood of a Disability

The table below shows the likelihood of having at least one disability that lasts longer than 90 days before you reach age 65. It reveals that below age 35, the chance of becoming disabled is greater than 50%. This does not mean people get healthier as they get older; it is just that there are fewer working years remaining so the exposure is less. While the risk of having a disability decreases with age, the average duration of a disability increases. In fact, the older the person is, the less likely it is that he or she will totally recover, and the more likely it is that the disability will be permanent.

Age	Probability*	Duration†
25	58%	2.4 years
30	54%	3.0 years
35	50%	3.5 years
40	45%	3.9 years
45	40%	4.3 years
50	33%	4.6 years
55	23%	5.0 years

* Probability of having at least one disability before age 65 that will last 90 days or more
† Average duration of a disability that occurs before age 65 and lasts at least 90 days
Source: 1985 Commissioner's Disability Table, Society of Actuaries

Risk of Disability Compared with Risk of Death

The risk of becoming disabled prior to age 65 is quite high. When compared to mortality statistics, there is a greater chance that clients will become disabled than that they will die in a given year. The chart below compares the probability of having a disability lasting longer than 90 days versus dying in any given year.

Age	Probability
25	3.6 times
35	2.2 times
45	1.4 times

Source: 1985 Commissioner's Disability Table, Society of Actuaries

Risk of Disability Within a Group

The chart below shows the probability that at least one disability of more than 90 days will occur before age 65 within a small group.

	Number of Men in a Group		
Age	2	3	4
40	67.3%	81.3%	89.3%
45	62.5%	77.1%	86.0%
50	55.9%	70.7%	80.6%

Source: Commissioner's Individual Disability Table A, 1985 (Disability Insurance)

Your small business clients need protection because the risk of disability is higher than they realize.

Activity Limitations Increase with Age

Not surprisingly, when we consider the population as a whole, including people over age 65, and look at how many people have some type of activity limitation, we see that the risk of having activity limitations increases as we get older, as illustrated in the chart that follows:

Activity Limitations Increase with Age		
Age	**Males** **Percentage of Age Group Reporting Limitation**	**Females** **Percentage of Age Group Reporting Limitation**
0–14	4.6	2.7
15–24	4.8	4.7
25–44	7.7	8.3
45–64	17.3	19.3
65–74	41.3	45.1
75 and over	54.0	57.8

The Canada total excludes the Yukon, Northwest Territories, and Nunavut. The sum of the values for each category may differ from the total due to rounding.

Source: Statistics Canada, Participation and Activity Limitation Survey, 2006

This speaks to the lifelong need to protect one's health using disability insurance, critical illness insurance, health insurance, and long-term care insurance.

Accidents and Injuries

In 1993, roughly 3.9 million Canadians reported that they had collectively been involved in 4.8 million accidents in the previous 12 months. The most frequent causes are shown below.

Cause of Accidents Reported	1993
Motor vehicle accidents	27%
Sports accidents	27%
Accidents at work	21%
Accidents at home	14%

Source: Statistics Canada, Health Reports 1995, *Accidents in Canada, 1998 and 1993*, Vol. 7, No. 2, Cat. No. 82-003

Age and Gender

The accident rate reported was 223 per 1,000 people, but the distribution by age indicated that men generally have higher rates than women and that accident rates tend to decline with age. The highest accident rate was among men aged 15 to 24 (514 accidents per 1,000, compared with 306 per 1,000 among women in the same age group). However, women aged 65 and over had a higher rate than men in the same age group (94 versus 70 accidents per 1,000). To some extent, the higher accident rate among younger people as compared with older people is attributable to the greater tendency for younger people to have more than one accident in a year.

Percentage of Total Population Who Reported Having One or More Accidents in 1993

Age	Men	Women
15–24	38%	23%
25–44	24%	16%
45–64	13%	11%
65+	6%	8%

Source: Statistics Canada, Health Reports 1995, *Accidents in Canada*, 1998 and 1993, Vol 7, No. 2, Cat. No. 82-003

Personal Injury, Medical Care, and Financial Loss

Roughly 80% of the accidents reported caused personal injury, but the incidence varied based on the type of accident. For instance, while just under half (45%) of motor vehicle accidents resulted in personal injury, 90% of accidents related to sports, work, and the home resulted in injury.

Medical care in a hospital was required for 46% of all accidents; patients generally required outpatient care, but about 5% required in-patient care. About 62% of accidents caused restrictions in normal daily activities, and 29% required confinement to bed during a disability. About one-third of all accidents caused financial loss.[1]

Disability insurance plays an important role in protecting people against the financial impacts of injury.

Issues Facing Female Clients

Women's life expectancy at birth exceeds men's: the life expectancy for Canadian women is 83.1 years, while the expectancy for men is 78.5 years.[2] The risk of widowhood increases with age, and older men are more likely to remarry than older women.[3]

Both the incidence rates and the duration of disability are higher for women than they are for men. These facts underscore the need for women to ensure they adequately plan for income security in the event of a disability.

Insuring the Need

Disability insurance has traditionally been one of the most overlooked elements of financial planning. Yet statistics suggest that it is one of the most important areas. Some people argue that life insurance is more

[1] Bung, V.P. Overview of the General Social Survey on Personal Risk (GSS-8), Statistics Canada, 1993. Working Paper No. 7.

[2] Statistics Canada (2008 Data)

[3] Canada Pension Plan Reforms: Issues for Women (May 1998).

important, since death is a certainty for all of us whereas disability is not. However, when someone becomes disabled, it is not just that the person ceases to be an income-generating asset to the family unit — the person becomes a financial liability. The costs can add up quickly for diagnosis, treatment, and ongoing care.

No one thinks that disability will affect them. Yet everyone knows at least one person who has suffered a heart attack, lived with cancer, or undergone major surgery. Car accidents happen daily. The risk of disability is always present, whether as a result of accident or sickness. A permanently disabled client will go through a functional and emotional adjustment as they adapt to a new norm. During this transition, financial pressures can affect how well the person adapts. Disability insurance helps by reducing financial pressures. Advisers play an important role in making clients aware of this need and helping them plan for continued income.

Chapter 2

Sources of Income During a Disability

INTRODUCTION

For most adults under age 65, working is a daily ritual and having a regular paycheque is taken for granted. It pays our bills, funds our yearly vacation, and contributes to our future retirement. Intuitively we know that if the paycheques stopped, our savings would begin to dissolve. Assets might have to be liquidated, and if the current economy is not good, they might be worth considerably less than they were when the initial investment was made. Earnings can cease without warning when disability strikes. Professionals and executives are just as likely as lower-paid workers to suffer financially from a period of income loss. Living standards cannot be adjusted overnight. The family home and the children's education are more than simply financial obligations; they represent memories, dreams, and life goals. Having capital does not necessarily eliminate the need for protecting earned income.

Earned income is the foundation upon which all assets are built. While the largest asset investment is generally the family home, the asset with the greatest *value* is the ability to earn an income, as it enables the client to acquire and maintain everything else. A projection of future earnings, referred to as "capitalization of income", demonstrates that even clients who earn $75,000 per year will be "millionaires" during their lifetimes.

Capitalization of Income Based on $75,000 Annual Earnings to Age 65

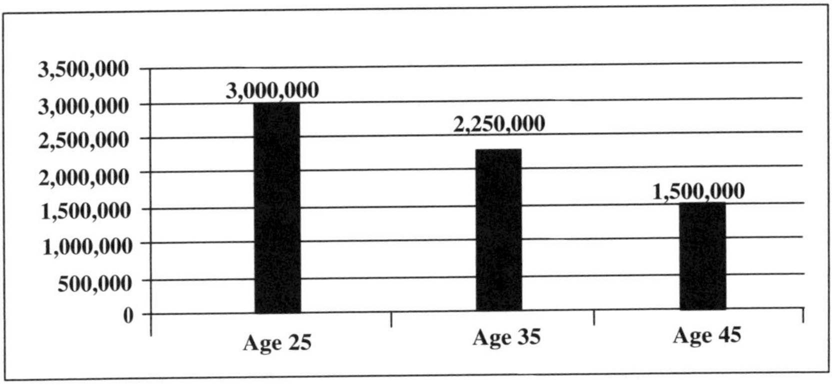

Financial planning for disability begins with assessing the potential sources a client may have available and determining whether the alternate sources will be both reliable and adequate.

NON-INSURED INCOME SOURCES

Spousal Earnings

Members of dual-income families may think that the non-disabled spouse will assume the financial responsibility in the case of a disability. Yet they generally adopt lifestyles and make financial commitments based upon their joint income, and obligations cannot be restructured as instantaneously as disability occurs. In single-income families in which a spouse is at home with small children, having that spouse carry the financial load alone may be an impractical solution, particularly when the cost of child care and career retraining is considered. Furthermore, the added stress increases the chance that the second spouse will also become disabled.

A comprehensive financial plan includes both working spouses and does not rely upon the return to work of a non-working spouse.

Sale of Assets

Clients who think that assets could serve as a source of income while they are disabled should be cautioned about the desirability of such a plan. Young families generally require today's earnings for today's expenses, with little remaining to set aside for wealth accumulation. A six-month disability could leave them in financial difficulty. Even clients who have a systematic savings program, such as mutual funds, are unlikely to have amassed sufficient resources to carry them through a sustained period of income loss.

As a couple reaches age 45, the accumulation of cash reserves and retirement savings should have grown considerably. Now in their peak earning years, they will be focusing on maximizing registered retirement savings plans (RRSPs) and other wealth accumulation plans. The effect of a disability will be twofold. First, contributions will cease — they will lose not only the immediate deposits, but also the compound growth on the earnings. Second, if the disability lasts for a long time, the couple will be forced to liquidate their RRSPs. This triggers taxation upon the disposition and, depending upon the nature of the investment, may also result in penalty charges for early surrender or market losses for untimely liquidation. Assets such as real estate require time to sell. Current values may be significantly depressed due to current market conditions.

Loans

A client who has no income may find it difficult to qualify for a loan; the bank will expect collateral and evidence of the ability to repay. Even if the bank agrees to extend the loan on the basis of the client's good credit rating and collateral backing the loan, using borrowed funds as a source of income during a disability can be quite expensive. If the client can manage to meet living expenses on $3,000 per month, a disability that lasts five years would result in a debt of over $180,000, without factoring in the cost of interest. This essentially creates a mortgage against future earnings.

province. Income benefits begin on the first day following the day the injury occurs. Half of the provinces require the employer to pay the worker for the day of the injury (Alberta, Manitoba, Newfoundland and Labrador, Ontario, Quebec, and Yukon), while the remaining provinces do not. Benefits are paid until the injured worker returns to work, no longer has an earnings loss, or reaches age 65. Benefits are tax-free.

Benefits are intended primarily for workplace injuries, but some sicknesses deemed to be work-related diseases are also covered.

More information regarding workers' compensation is included in Chapter 14, "Public Health Insurance". The table below shows the annual maximum gross earnings covered by each province in 2011.[4]

Maximum Covered Earnings		
Province	**Maximum Gross Earnings**	**Percentage of Earnings Covered**
British Columbia	$71,700	90% net
Alberta	$82,800	90% net
Saskatchewan	$55,000	90% net
Manitoba	No Maximum (max. assessable earnings for employer premiums is $96,000)	90% net (100% if average earnings equal $19,760 or less)
Ontario	$79,600	85% net
Quebec	$64,000	90% net
New Brunswick	$56,700	85% net
Nova Scotia	$52,000	75% net first 26 weeks, then 85% net on balance
Prince Edward Island	$47,800	80% net first 38 weeks, then 85% net on balance
Newfoundland and Labrador	$51,595	80% net
Northwest Territories	$75,200	90% net
Yukon	$77,920	75% gross (100% if earnings are less than the minimum compensation amount, i.e., 25% of the maximum wage rate)
Nunavut	$75,200	90% net

4 Association of Workers' Compensation Boards of Canada Web site, awcbc.org (accessed September 15, 2011).

GROUP LONG-TERM DISABILITY PROTECTION

A client who is a member of a group insurance program must determine whether the plan includes long-term disability (LTD) protection. The comprehensiveness of LTD protection varies from plan to plan. The benefit booklet shows the terms and conditions under which a client can claim benefits, as well as the formula used to determine the benefit amount payable. This formula consists of a percentage and a stated benefit maximum, such as 67% to a maximum of $5,000. It also describes the limitations and exclusions that apply when determining eligibility for benefits.

When Coverage Becomes Effective

Employees are required to fulfill a waiting period upon commencement of employment. This is a stated period of time of active employment, such as 30 days, that must pass before the employee's coverage takes effect. The waiting period is not related to the elimination period, which refers to the number of days of disability that must pass from the date of its commencement before the benefit becomes payable. If a disability occurs during the waiting period, no benefit is payable regardless of the elimination period, because coverage has not yet taken effect.

The employee may be required to submit evidence of insurability if the amount of coverage exceeds the plan's non-evidence maximum or if the employee enrolls late into the plan. The "non-evidence maximum" refers to the amount of coverage that the insurer will provide regardless of the employee's current state of health. This amount varies based upon the demographics of the group, the nature of the industry, and the insurer's underwriting guidelines. Employees whose coverage entitlement falls below the non-evidence maximum are not required to submit medical information to the company. Those who are eligible for higher amounts will be covered for the excess above the non-evidence maximum only upon submission and approval of medical information. The employee may be denied the additional coverage due to medical conditions. In this instance, the employee will still receive the non-evidence maximum amount. The employee must be active at work and not absent from the business in order for the coverage to take effect. If the employee is absent from work at the time that he or she would otherwise become eligible, coverage commences immediately upon the date of return.

When Coverage Terminates

Employees cease to be covered on the date the master contract terminates, the date they cease to be a member of an eligible class, or the date of retirement.

Eligibility

The master contract stipulates a minimum number of hours that the employee must be working in order to be eligible for coverage, such as

30 hours per week. However, some companies may have special arrangements in place whereby part-time employees who work a minimum of 20 hours per week are also covered. The waiting period must have passed, and the employee must be actively employed. Occasionally, the company may waive the waiting period for a new employee. This requires the written approval of both the employer and the insurer.

Determining the Benefit Amount

The benefit amount payable is the least of:

- a stipulated percentage of earnings
- the stated maximum benefit
- the plan's all-source maximum.

Percentage of Earnings

Standard earnings percentage amounts are 60%, 66⅔%, 70%, and 75%. The applicable percentage is applied to pre-tax monthly earnings. The lower percentages are generally non-taxable benefit amounts (e.g., the 60% formula). The higher benefit amounts are generally taxable (e.g., 70%, 75%). A 66⅔% formula may be either taxable or non-taxable, and the benefits booklet will normally indicate this. If the booklet does not specify the taxability of the benefits, then refer to guidelines contained in the Canada Revenue Agency's Interpretation Bulletin IT-428, which provides that where the employer has paid the premiums for the LTD plan, benefits during a claim will be taxable as income to the covered employee. If the employee has paid the premium, the benefit will be tax-free at the time of claim. Under a shared contribution plan, the first dollars paid out are deemed to be a return of the employee's contributions and are tax-free. All benefits in excess of this sum are taxable as income. This calculation is based upon the employee's contributions commencing after 1967. For a subsequent claim, the deduction of personal contributions by the employee from taxable benefits is restricted to contributions made since the last taxation year in which a benefit was received. There are no carryforward privileges of excess contributions as a deduction against the benefits for a future claim.

Defining the Term "Earnings"

The term "earnings" may be defined in many different ways, and the employer selects a definition from those offered by the insurer. As this affects the amount of benefit and, therefore, the cost of the plan, the employer may opt for the most common definition, such as the "base salary" definition. A more comprehensive plan may define earnings to include bonuses, commissions, overtime pay, or other profit-sharing compensation, at an additional cost. These broader earnings definitions are generally offered only to preferred-risk occupational groups.

The Stated Maximum Benefit

The benefits booklet will indicate a maximum monthly benefit, such as $5,000 or $10,000. Smaller-sized groups may have a maximum of around $2,500, while large corporations may have maximums as high as $15,000. Some insurers will average the earnings of the three highest-paid employees when considering the maximum benefit they are willing to offer the group. The employer may elect a smaller maximum even though the group qualifies for a larger amount, as a means of cost containment. Higher levels can result in a load (i.e., increase) to the premium rate and may not be necessary.

The All-Source Maximum

The benefits booklet will stipulate a percentage maximum that the employee can receive from all sources during a disability. The definition of "sources" will be described in the booklet, along with the percentage maximum allowed. There are two categories of sources that must be considered along with the benefit amount under the LTD plan; the first is "direct offsets" and the second is "indirect offsets". A standard percentage used in this calculation is 85%, though lower levels are also found. Direct offsets are more limited and include deduction of amounts from sources directly paid to and for the employee, such as the primary benefit paid under the CPP to the disabled contributor. They may also include benefits received under the provincial workers' compensation or similar legislation. When the group includes many blue-collar workers, the integration of this benefit is often effected by means of the insurer issuing the contract as "non-occupational coverage". This means that the LTD plan does not cover work-related injuries.

Most LTD plans do not require the deduction of benefits received from individual disability insurance plans. However, some insurers may offset individual disability plans that have been purchased under an employer-sponsored wage loss replacement plan.

The second category of sources that must be considered, "indirect offsets", includes a much broader range of deductions, such as amounts paid or entitled to be paid under the CPP to the disabled contributor for his or her spouse and dependent children, automobile liability insurance, and disability payments under a retirement plan.

Benefit Calculation

The employee determines the amount of the benefit by first multiplying the pre-tax earnings by the applicable earnings percentage and comparing this amount to the stated maximum benefit. The lesser of the two is the gross benefit amount. This amount is further reduced by income that the employee would receive from other sources, such as the CPP. This net benefit is then compared to the amount obtained under the all-source maximum calculation, and the employee entitlement will be the lesser amount.

Assumptions

$100,000 annual pre-tax earnings

Taxable formula of 67% basic earnings to $5,000 maximum

85% all-source maximum with primary and secondary offsets

The amount of benefit payable is the lesser of

a) a stipulated percentage of earnings:	⇒	67% ($100,000 / 12) less direct CPP-D benefit of $1,153.37* = $4,429.96
b) the stated maximum benefit:	⇒	$5,000 less direct CPP-D benefit of $1,153.37* = $3,846.63
c) the plan's all-source maximum	⇒	85% ($100,000 / 12) minus direct and indirect CPP-D benefit of ($1,153.37* + $218.50*) = $5,711.46

The benefit payable under the LTD plan is $3,846.63 as this is the least of the three.

*(2011)

Defining "Disability"

The definition of "disability" acts as the gateway to claiming benefits. Consequently, it is one of the most important provisions. The definitions available vary based on the company's industry sector. Within this range of offerings, the employer selects the one that will apply to all employees. Alternatively, the employer may divide the employees into two or more classes of employees and select a different definition for each class. Employees within a class must have commonality, such as executive officers, managers, salaried employees, or hourly workers.

The standard definition in a group LTD contract is a 24-month "own occupation" definition. This means that disability is measured based upon employees' inability to work at their regular occupation during the first 24 months of disability. During this period, employees may be able to work at other employment, but this will not affect entitlement to benefits as long as they do not participate in other work. In other words, employees have the right during this period not to seek alternate employment.

"Gainful" Versus "Scheduled Benefit" Definitions

After the own-occupation period has expired, disability is measured based on employees' inability to work at "any gainful occupation" for which they are reasonably qualified on the basis of their education, training, and experience. An income test is often used to determine whether an occupation should be considered "gainful". This eliminates from consideration occupations that could be expected to generate only a nominal income level. In this instance, "any gainful occupation" would be considered one for which they are reasonably qualified only if it could be expected to generate income within a specified earnings range, such as 60% or more of prior earnings. This percentage may be specified in the master contract or may be simply an administrative guideline applied by the insurance company's benefits examiner. An alternative to this measure is one where the earnings are expected to be equal to or greater than the scheduled monthly benefit in the contract. This is referred to as a "scheduled benefit" definition. Generally, the emphasis of the contract is not on whether the insured *is* working, but on whether the insured *can* work now or can be *expected* to work within the next few months but chooses not to do so.

A "scheduled benefit" definition will allow for a higher amount for an employee whose benefit amount falls below the plan's maximum (refer to Employee A in the example below), while the earnings percentage version will allow for a higher amount for employees whose entitlement is limited by the maximum (refer to Employee B in the example below).

Illustrative Chart

Formula -- 67% to $5,000

				Gainful Definitions Comparison	
Employee	Annual Earnings	Monthly Earnings	Monthly LTD Benefit Amount	*Scheduled Benefit	*Earnings Percentage @60%
A	$50,000	$4,167	$2,792	$2,792	$2,500
B	$120,000	$10,000	$5,000	$5,000	$6,000

**If occupation can be expected to generate income level of at least this amount, then benefit terminates.*

"Own Occupation" — Group LTD Versus Individual Disability

The term "own occupation", when contained in a group LTD contract, has a different meaning from when it is applied to an individual disability contract. Within the context of a group LTD contract, as indicated above, it means that the employee must be unable to work at the regular occupation *and is not employed elsewhere*. If the employee is working in a new occupation, the benefit ceases. In an individual disability contract, however, the term "own occupation" has a more liberal interpretation. In this instance, a true "own occupation" definition would allow the insured to be completely unable to work at the regular occupation yet be employed in a new occupation, and continue to receive full benefits under the policy without reduction. Consequently, when comparing definitions between contract forms,

Limitations and Exclusions

The following are examples of exclusions that may be found in a group LTD contract. Note that they vary from company to company. An insurer may be willing to remove one or more of the exclusions listed below, subject to an additional load to the LTD rate.

- War, whether declared or undeclared
- Riots or insurrection
- Attempting to commit a felony
- Attempting to commit suicide
- Travel outside Canada unless return is within 12 months
- Participation in the armed forces or reserves
- Normal pregnancy
- Pre-existing conditions that occur within the first 12 months where medication or treatment was received within three months prior to joining the plan.

There are variations of the pre-existing condition exclusion. The more restrictive the definition, the greater the cost savings that are afforded to the employer's rate.

Other Provisions and Features

Conversion upon Termination

The employee may have the right to convert LTD coverage to a personally owned plan upon termination of employment. Where offered, the conversion must occur within 30 days of leaving the plan. Regardless of the length of the own-occupation period contained in the LTD plan, the converted plan is usually a 24-month own-occupation contract. Rates are generally pooled with all converted contracts and are subject to rate adjustment if the experience of the pool necessitates it. This is an excellent method for employees who are otherwise uninsurable to ensure continuity of protection upon leaving the group. Advisers should check with the plan administrator to determine if the departing employee has this option, and to determine the process for taking advantage of it. As personal disability insurance can normally take up to two months to fully underwrite, the adviser should ensure that the departing employee has submitted written intent to exercise this privilege immediately upon leaving the employer. If subsequent personal coverage is approved and offers better provisions and coverage amounts, the converted policy may then be cancelled in favour of the more comprehensive plan. However, if the client is found to be uninsurable at the end of a two-month underwriting process, it will be too late to take advantage of the conversion privilege under the group LTD that was left behind.

Chapter 3

Determining Insurable Earnings

NEEDS EVALUATION

Introduction

To determine the income required, calculate the total fixed expenses minus any existing sources. The following chart illustrates sources and expenses to consider. Note that when considering a client's current income, any bonuses and commissions should generally be calculated over a three-year period to derive an average receipt. Self-employed people should use net income after business expenses plus salary taken from the business.

Needs Evaluation Chart

Monthly Earnings		
Base annual salary/12	$_______	
Total bonus received past 3 years/36	$_______	
Total commissions received past 3 years/36	$_______	
Total Earnings	=======	
Monthly Expenses		
Taxes	$_______	
Food	$_______	
Clothing	$_______	
Accommodations	$_______	
Transportation	$_______	
Health — Medical and Dental	$_______	
Utilities, Telephone, Cable	$_______	
Insurance (Home, Auto, Life, Health)	$_______	
Pension	$_______	
Education	$_______	
Loan Payments	$_______	
Total Expenses		=======
Minus: Existing Monthly Sources		
Net after-tax government benefits (EI, WCB, CPP)	$_______	
Net after-tax group LTD	$_______	
Unearned sources (dividends, rental income, etc.)	$_______	
Individual disability plans in force	$_______	
Total Existing Monthly Sources		=======
Expenses Minus Sources		=======
		Income Shortage

Government Benefits

The adviser should review the guidelines for claiming benefits under any government programs that the client may be eligible for. These limitations may make it unwise for the client to rely too heavily on these benefits. For example, while the benefit amount under the workers' compensation programs may be in the range of 80% to 90% of net earnings, the risks covered are work-related injuries and diseases only. This leaves exposure when travelling to and from work, for accidents that occur outside of work, and for sicknesses such as cancer and heart attacks. As age rises, the percentage of claims that are accident-related decreases, while those that are sickness-related increase.

The Canada Pension Plan and its Quebec counterpart pay in the range of $1,100 per month at the maximum level. (There may be additional dependant benefits.) However, benefits do not commence until the disability has been approved, a process which could take several months. As there is a three-month elimination period, there may be a considerable gap prior to the commencement of income. Benefits are taxable and the net benefit should be considered, not the gross benefit. Above all, the definition of disability is a strict one, and reflects the fact that the benefit is intended for permanent disabilities, not temporary or partial disabilities.

Employment Insurance (EI) benefits pay for a maximum of four months only. These should be integrated into the disability plan by use of elimination periods, not in place of coverage altogether.

Group Long-Term Disability

Group long-term disability (LTD) benefits are employer-linked. Consider the mobility of your client, and the probability of future changes in employers. Not all group LTD plans provide conversion options upon termination of employment. Furthermore, upon commencement of employment with a new employer, there is generally a waiting period for LTD benefits. The group LTD plan will contain a pre-existing condition limitation, which may limit benefits in the first 6, 12, or 24 months if the client had received treatment or exhibited symptoms just prior to joining the new employer's plan.

The group LTD plan must be thoroughly reviewed regarding the definition of "insurable earnings", taking into account the nature of the client's compensation. Gaps may exist in protection if the plan is based upon salary and if the client is an executive with a substantial portion of earnings derived from bonus payments. A shareholder-employee may be taking large sums of income in forms other than salary, and this can lead to an underinsured situation.

Adviser's Checklist of Sources

As can be seen from the above, not all existing sources should be used to reduce the amount of disability insurance required, as they may be unreliable sources. The following checklist can help to determine which to use in the needs evaluation chart:

❒ Does the benefit pay to age 65?

❒ Does the benefit cover both accident and sickness?

❒ Will a partial disability be covered?

❒ How soon does the benefit begin following a disability?

❒ Does the benefit exclude any specific conditions?

❒ Will the plan terminate before the client reaches age 65?

❒ Is the benefit that is payable during a claim taxable or non-taxable?

❒ Will current sources provide at least 80% replacement of net earnings?

❒ Are current benefits indexed for inflation protection?

❒ Is coverage subject to termination by a third party without the client's consent?

ISSUE LIMITS AND THE INCOME RATIO GUIDE

Insurers want to be certain that it is more financially advantageous for people to work than to be disabled. This is commonly referred to as maintaining the "incentive gap". This gap generally equates to 20% to 25% of net earnings, enabling individuals to ensure the continuation of 75% to 80% of their net income during disability. Regardless of how much a person earns, however, there are maximum limits that insurers are willing to offer — alone or in conjunction with another insurer. These are referred to as the issue and participation limits.

Issue and Participation Limits

The maximum insurance available is based upon the age and occupation class of the applicant. The coverage amount may be further limited based upon the specific product. An insurer may offer an applicant who is in a high-risk occupation a larger amount of coverage if the product applied for is more restrictive.

Insurers may also have separate charts for "issue limits" and "participation limits". The issue limit refers to the maximum the insurer will issue, and the participation limit refers to the maximum in combination with other insurers that the insured can have. Thus, an insurer might offer to cover up to $25,000, but only if this amount, in combination with coverage from other insurers, does not surpass $35,000. These amounts are still subject to an earnings ratio, as described later in this chapter under the "Income Ratio Guide" section.

An insurer may set a higher issue limit for plans that will be taxable, and a lower limit for non-taxable benefits. This reflects the fact that the net benefit after tax will equate roughly to the non-taxable limit. For example, the non-taxable maximum issue limit may be $25,000, and the taxable maximum issue limit may be $50,000. Below is a sample of what an issue limits chart may look like.

Sample Issue and Participation Limits Chart

Standard Disability Income Plan

Ages	4A	3A	2A	A*	B*
18–50	$25,000	$15,000	$10,000	$5,000	$4,000
51–55	$15,000	$10,000	$ 8,000	$4,000	$3,000
56–60	$10,000	$ 8,000	$ 6,000	$3,500	$2,500

*Applicants under "risk-reduced plan" add $500

Reinsurance

In the past, a small number of insurers did not set a maximum within the top occupational group and, instead, based coverage on the overall financial circumstances of the applicant with regards to the earned and unearned income, net worth, occupational stability, and state of health. Today, most insurers offer no more than $25,000 for their lowest-risk class. Companies work in conjunction with a reinsurer on larger amounts of coverage. By sharing the risk with the reinsurer, a company is able to control their amount of exposure per insured person. For instance, there is less risk to the company if 20 clients each have benefits of $1,000 per month than if one client has benefits of $20,000 per month, even if his or her earnings qualified for this amount. When the client "goes on claim", the insurer must immediately set aside a reserve for payment of future benefits. This impacts the insurer's financial results in the current year of claim. Consequently, the insurer will set a maximum retention limit of monthly benefit, with amounts that exceed it being reinsured through a third party. The process of reinsurance is invisible to the client, and all transactions the client has remain with the primary insurer.

Income Ratio Guide

After the maximum has been determined by age, occupation, and product type using the maximum issue and participation limits chart, the earnings-related maximum can then be determined by using an Income

Ratio Guide. The coverage applied for cannot exceed the lesser of these two charts.

An Income Ratio Guide contains maximums based upon the taxability of the plan as well as the earnings level. The non-taxable amounts are further affected by whether the applicant is covered by EI. The following chart displays a sample Income Ratio Guide. Most companies provide software that performs this calculation based on the earnings level entered.

Sample Income Ratio Guide Chart

Applicant's Earned Income		Non-Taxable Benefits		Taxable Benefits
Annual	Monthly	Total Monthly Benefit (All Sources)	Amount Available with 120-Day EP if Covered by EI	Total Monthly Benefit (All Sources)
$30,000	$ 2,500	$1,775	$ 950	$ 2,150
$40,000	$ 3,333	$2,300	$1,200	$ 2,750
$50,000	$ 4,167	$2,675	$1,150	$ 3,550
$85,000	$ 7,083	$4,025	$1,050	$ 5,725
$140,000	$11,667	$5,775	$ 900	$ 8,325
$240,000	$20,000	$8,125	$ 850	$12,550

Group Combo Limits

Some insurers have a separate chart with higher limits for the client who has existing group LTD and is purchasing individual disability insurance to complement it. These limits are sometimes referred to as "combo limits". The higher limits apply to individuals with substantial earnings, such as incomes above $160,000 (under taxable scales) or above $190,000 (under non-taxable scales). The topics of "supplement plans" and "second-payer plans" are covered in Chapter 9, "Individual Disability Insurance in the Workplace".

APPLICANT'S EARNED INCOME

The amount of monthly benefit available to an insured person is based on earned income. Income includes salary, bonuses, a sole proprietor's or partner's share of net earnings in a business or practice, and the net income before tax but after business expenses for shareholder-employees of a corporation.

Bonuses and Commissions

In order for a bonus to be included as income, the applicant must have consistently received it for at least the past three years. As bonuses are not guaranteed, the insurer generally uses an average of the bonus over this period, instead of the specific sum paid in the last bonus period. This is consistent with the principle of using conservative income assumptions, based on stable, historical patterns.

Commissions can also fluctuate. The insurer may ask for evidence of the commissions paid over a period of two or three years in order to establish an average annual rate. Individuals who receive part or all of their earnings in the form of commissions usually have expenses they write off as income tax deductions. The commissions must first be reduced by the deductible business expenses, and the remaining "net income before tax" is then used as the earned income figure on the Income Ratio Guide.

Dividends Paid to Shareholder-Employees

Dividends paid to shareholder-employees from their corporation are not considered income for the purpose of calculating earned income for individual disability insurance. This is because dividends are paid from the retained earnings of the business and can represent an accumulation of earnings over a period of several years. Instead, the net income before taxes for the year ended is used, as it represents the earnings of the business in the fiscal year. As this figure can fluctuate widely from year to year, the insurer will request evidence of two or three years and base the amount on an average over this period. To this figure is added any salary the shareholder-employee is receiving from the business. When the business shows a net loss instead of a net income, the loss must be deducted from the salary, and the difference is the earned income figure that is applied to the Income Ratio Guide. If a loss remains after deduction from the salary, or if the difference falls below the company's minimum earned income level, the client will not be insurable for individual disability insurance until a positive, stable pattern can be shown, in the form of an earned income that is above the company's minimum for at least the past two or three years.

Perquisites as a Form of Income

Most companies will acknowledge the perquisites (perks) that self-employed people and shareholder-employees enjoy as a benefit of business ownership. These include expenses that are recognized by the Canada Revenue Agency and for which individuals control the ability to elect a lower salary in favour of the benefit. Some examples are company cars, pension contributions, and parking. As these benefits form part of the individuals' earnings, and as the individuals can control whether the benefits are paid as salary or as perks, insurance companies will generally allow a 10% to 15% (sometimes as high as 20%) increase in the earned income calculation for determining their eligible benefit amount. An upper cap is usually stipulated for this gross-up. This is not normally made available to individuals who have employee status.

Spousal Earnings Under Income Splitting

Where a business owner is paying part of his or her income to a spouse as a means of income splitting for tax purposes, a portion or all of the spouse's income may be attributed back to the business owner for inclusion in the earned income calculation. This is generally permitted when the spouse is inactive in the business or when the spouse is being paid an inflated salary for the work performed as compared to the rate paid in the general economy. A fundamental test is whether the spouse's income would cease if the business owner were disabled.

NON-TAXABLE AND TAXABLE BENEFITS

Non-Taxable Benefits

The following chart shows the maximum amount available where the individual will be purchasing the insurance as a non-taxable plan. The two subsections labelled "Basic" and "Additional" reflect the fact that an applicant who is covered by EI must program coverage around this government benefit. This is essential, because EI will pay in addition to personally owned disability insurance and the result would be overinsurance during the initial period of the claim. Step 1 shows the maximum available to the insured from all sources. Step 2 reflects the EI integration amount requiring a 120-day elimination period. It is subtracted from the Step 1 amount, with the difference being available with any elimination period the client prefers. "Elimination period" refers to the number of days that must pass from the time that the disability occurs after which the insurer becomes responsible for payment. It is similar to a deductible, which is found in other forms of insurance.

Illustration

The client earns $240,000 and has EI coverage. The client wishes to have the maximum coverage possible on a non-taxable basis, with a 90-day elimination period. The client does not have any other coverage in force.

Step 1:
Calculate total available from all sources
$8,125

Step 2:
Subtract amount subject to 120-day elimination period
$8,125 - $850 = $7,275

Step 3:
Select appropriate elimination periods

90-Day EP	$7,275
120-Day EP	$ 850

Total Benefits:	$8,125

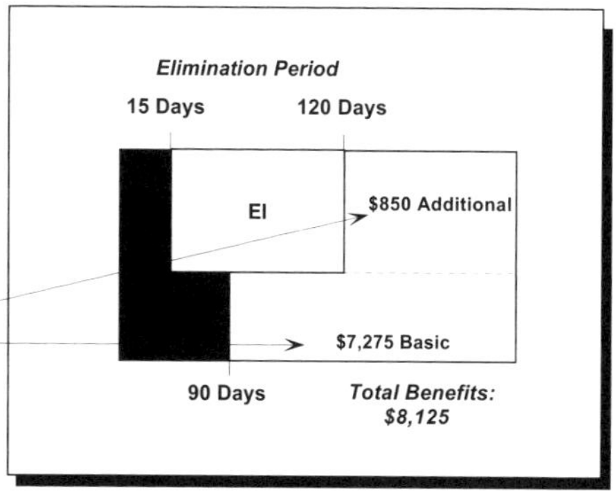

A self-employed person would not be eligible for EI and, consequently, would apply for the full benefit amount of $8,125, with the 90-day elimination period on the full benefit amount.

Taxable Benefits

This column of the Income Ratio Guide shows the maximum amount available when the client is purchasing a taxable benefit plan. The higher amount reflects the fact that tax must be paid on the benefit when it is received. After payment of the tax, the net benefit will be equivalent to the non-taxable benefit amount. Integration is not required with EI on a taxable plan. This is because EI is a second payer to employer-paid benefits, and as such, no EI benefit would be received. Therefore, on taxable plans, regardless of whether the client is an employee or self-employed, no EI integration is required, because overinsurance will not result.

Departing Employees

Some companies insure employees through a "grouped" method that involves taxable individual disability policies. There is a risk to the insurer that the policy will be given to the departing employee. This results in a change in the tax status of the policy to non-taxable benefits at such time as the employee begins to personally pay the premium. This change in tax status may result in overinsurance. To protect against this possibility, most insurers reserve the right, on taxable plans, to re-underwrite the amount of coverage in the event that the plan changes tax status from taxable to non-taxable. The purpose is to reduce the amount of coverage to the equivalent amount that would have been issued had the plan been originally purchased on a non-taxable basis. At the same time, the insurer may change the elimination period on a portion of the coverage to integrate with EI, since the insured will be able to claim for both benefits during a disability.

OTHER CONSIDERATIONS

Existing Disability Coverage

The amounts contained in the Income Ratio Guide represent the maximum benefit based upon earnings that the applicant can have from all sources. Therefore, it is necessary to deduct from this amount any existing group LTD and personal disability policies that will be kept in force. This does not include benefits payable under government sources, as these are integrated through the use of elimination periods for EI, and through policy limitation provisions in the case of the CPP and workers' compensation.

Unearned Income

Unearned income refers to income that would continue even when the insured is disabled. Insurers treat it as a form of self-insurance. Examples of unearned income include dividends from a stock portfolio, interest earnings from bonds and other investments, rental income, royalties, residuals, renewal commissions, and pension income.

The method of adjustment depends upon the amount of unearned income in proportion to earned income, and varies from insurer to insurer. One method employed is to ignore unearned income that is less than a stated percentage of earned income. The percentage that insurers are willing to ignore varies by company and can range from 15% to 25%. Some insurers go a step further and also set a cap beyond which the full amount must be taken into consideration (such as $1,250). Amounts above this are treated as existing coverage and reduce the issue limit dollar for dollar. Some insurers consider any applicant who has unearned income that is greater than 50% of earned income as fully self-insured and, therefore, ineligible for any disability coverage.

Net Worth Considerations

Insurers avoid overinsurance by setting maximum limits for net worth. Substantial net worth is generally associated with a high level of unearned income or the ability to reposition assets from capital appreciation to income generation. This can result in overinsurance.

Most insurers consider a person whose net worth exceeds $5 million to be uninsurable (some insurers go as high as $6 million). Always of interest is whether the assets are of such a nature that they can be used to generate income. The client may be required to provide additional information when net worth falls between $3 million and the company's stated upper maximum ($5 million or $6 million). Generally, a net worth of less than $3 million will not impact the amount of coverage available.

Chapter 4

Disability Insurance Policies and Provisions

POLICY SERIES

Disability insurance (DI) policies can be grouped into four different series based on the promises contained in the contract for two features: the yearly renewal privilege and the rate guarantee. These four series, progressing from those that most favour the insured to those that most favour the insurer, are as follows:

- Non-cancellable
- Guaranteed renewable
- Conditionally renewable
- Cancellable.

Non-Cancellable Policies

This series offers the highest level of guarantees favouring the insured. For this reason, it is made available to applicants who fall within the lowest risk occupation class, such as professionals and executives.

Renewal Privilege. The insured can renew the policy through to a specified age, normally age 65. Throughout this time, the insurer promises not to change the terms of the policy by adding conditions that restrict or reduce benefits. After the non-cancellable period ends, the policy may offer a further renewal period, subject to certain conditions and under an altered plan of coverage. At this point, it becomes "conditionally renewable". Most policies list an end point after which it cannot be renewed, such as age 72 or 75. A few companies promise lifetime renewal if the insured continues to meet the conditions outlined, subject to a further-reduced benefit period. The conditions for renewal include the following:

- The insured must provide evidence of continued full-time employment.
- The insured cannot be disabled at the time of renewal.

The insured does not have to provide evidence of good health, and exclusions for medical conditions cannot be added. In other words, the promise of renewal is that the insured can continue the policy without evidence of good health if the listed conditions are met.

The policy normally continues the same elimination period as the original plan. The maximum benefit period becomes two years, or may further "step down" to one year if renewed beyond a certain age, such as age 75 (in policies that promise lifetime renewal). The definition of disability may also change, and the policy may cover only total (not partial) disability.

Rate Guarantee. A further advantage favouring the insured is the promise that rates will not be changed throughout the non-cancellable period. If the insured continues the policy in force after this period ends under the conditionally renewable privilege, the rates will then be based upon attained age using the company's rate scale in effect at the renewal date. As the company cannot adjust future premiums during the non-cancellable period, the rate charged is higher than rates would be for the same insured buying equivalent coverage under a different series. This safety margin helps to protect the company against differences between actual experience and assumptions for morbidity, interest, and expenses used in establishing the non-cancellable rate.

Guaranteed Renewable Policies

Guaranteed renewable contracts were once thought of as policies only for higher-risk occupations. Today, they are a viable alternative for all occupations, offering a lower-cost premium alternative to low-risk occupations that may not value the rate guarantees associated with higher-cost non-cancellable policies.

Renewal Privilege. The renewal privileges under guaranteed renewable contracts are the same as those found in non-cancellable policies. The difference is in the rate guarantee.

Rate Guarantee. The company reserves the right to make future premium changes for all insured individuals within a particular class on any renewal date. The rate change is likely to occur if the company identifies a negative trend over a period of time, as opposed to a singular year of poor experience within the block. Adjustments in premiums cannot be applied to a sole insured, but must be applied to all members of the same class. The term "class" can refer to a particular occupational group or a subgroup within the group. It is not restricted to occupational relationships only: any grouping that is not discriminatory in nature may be defined by the company as a class for rate adjustment purposes. However, the group must be large enough for the experience to be statistically credible. Other examples of categories include geographically defined groups, groups based upon year of issuance of the policy, and groups with a common elimination or benefit period.

As the insured may incur a change in future rates, the premium charged is less than the premium charged for a contract that is non-cancellable.

Conditionally Renewable Policies

This series is one of the oldest forms of disability coverage. In recent years, insurers have been challenged to find ways of offering DI to a changing labour force with growing numbers of part-time workers, home-based workers, and contract workers. Also, with the rise in immigration, some people lack the local history (verifiable medical history, stable work experience, and lifestyle information) for insurers to investigate during the underwriting process — an important part of risk evaluation. In the past, this meant that they had to wait until a satisfactory length of time had passed before applying for coverage. Now, insurers utilize this product form to give more sectors of the labour force access to DI protection. More information about this is contained in Chapter 6, "Plans and Options for Contract Workers".

Renewal Privilege. This series allows the insurer the right to refuse to renew the policy for reasons specified in the policy at the end of a premium payment period. The following are examples of reasons that might be listed in the policy:

- Change of occupation
- No longer working full-time
- Relocation of the insured outside a defined territory (such as the province, the country, or the continent).

Rate Guarantee. The rate guarantee mirrors the provision found in the guaranteed renewable series.

Cancellable Policies

A cancellable policy is one in which the insurer has the right to change premiums on a class basis if the claims experience for that group of insured individuals deteriorates, or to cancel the contract for the class altogether. Coverage may also be cancelled by the insurer if the insured becomes a member of an ineligible risk class or if the risk class itself is no longer eligible for insurance. A client who is insured under this type of product should contact the insurance company in the event of a change of occupation to determine whether the new occupation falls within an eligible class for coverage. Lacking this, in the event of a claim, if the insured's new occupation is ineligible for coverage, the individual will only be entitled to a refund of premiums for a limited period of time, such as the past 12 months.

DEFINITIONS OF DISABILITY

The Concept of Defining "Disability"

The word "disability" has a range of meanings, from a very broad definition requiring a lack of some capacity that prevents action to a very narrow definition requiring a limitation that is both severe and permanent.

Consequently, every disability policy contains a definition of what constitutes "disability". This provision is the gateway to benefits under the policy. Individuals may be unable to perform the duties of their regular job but are able to work in a new occupation. Or they may be able to work at their regular occupation, but for less time. They may even be able to work for as long as usual but less effectively because they can perform only certain elements of the job, not all the main duties.

There are two approaches to defining "disability":

- **Occupational approach.** This is a category of time- and duties-based definitions that deals with the inability to work at an occupation. The focus is on time and duties and total disability.
- **Earnings approach.** This is a category of earnings-based definitions that deals with the inability to earn at a certain income level.

The more generous definitions place the insurer at greater risk and, consequently, are offered only to the top occupational classes, while riskier occupations will be given more restrictive definitions. All require that the insured be under the care of a physician. Some insurers, however, may waive this requirement if it would be of no benefit medically to the client's condition.

OCCUPATIONAL APPROACH

There are three basic occupational definitions from which variables are derived. These are:

- Pure own occupation
- Regular occupation and not working
- Any occupation for which qualified.

Most definitions use a combination of more than one of these three.

"Own Occupation"

This definition, also known as "*pure* own occupation", is the most liberal one used and is primarily available only to occupations with low claims experience. The focus is on the occupation itself. The definition protects clients from the inability to perform their regular duties, regardless of whether they pursue a new unrelated occupation or not. There is no penalty, and no benefit reduction, if clients begin a new career, provided it is outside the field in which they worked prior to their disability. Benefits would cease at the earlier of the end of the benefit period or when the client is no longer deemed to be disabled in terms of the occupation he or she had at the time of claim. The primary advantage of a pure own-occupation definition is that the client stands to collect not only full disability benefits, but also earnings in a new occupation, without those earnings reducing the disability benefits. The cost of insurance is higher for this type of definition.

Sample Definition:

"Total Disability" means that because of sickness or accident:

(*a*) you are unable to perform the primary duties of your regular occupation; and

(*b*) you are under the regular and personal care of a physician.

"Regular Occupation" is defined as the occupation in which you were working at the time of your disability.

Specialties and Subspecialties

Some insurers used to recognize a client's specialty as defining his or her "own occupation". This applied to professionals who had an industry-recognized degree authorizing them to work within a specific segment of a broader field. A surgeon, for example, would qualify as eligible for specialty protection, because specific training and certification are required to practice this skill. "Surgery", in this respect, is a specialty within the broader field of "the practice of medicine". In this example, if the surgeon suffered a disease such as arthritis and could no longer hold surgical instruments, the fact that the surgeon could still run a private practice would not prevent the payment of benefits. The earnings level would be irrelevant, as the focus was on primary duties and the inability to perform them. The absence of specialty protection would mean that the surgeon would not be deemed to be totally disabled, because the surgeon was still able to run a private practice.

To recognize this, some insurers included an endorsement in the policy, while others simply issued a separate letter outlining the company's administrative practice regarding interpretation of the client's occupation. An administrative letter is not a legal obligation, only a reflection of the company's current administrative practice. A policy endorsement, by contrast, is a documented interpretation concerning how the benefits examiner will interpret "occupation" during the claims process for that specific policy.

For the endorsement to apply at the time of claim, the client must still be practising the same occupational specialty, and this specialty must make up the primary duties of the client's occupation. All DI contracts specify that what constitutes "occupation" is "the occupation in which the insured was working *at the time of claim*", not the one in which he or she worked at the time of application. Therefore, in the surgeon example above, if the client's principal business evolved to a private practice with minimal or no surgical responsibilities, then the client will be deemed to be a "general practitioner" and not a "surgeon", regardless of the endorsement. This would also be true if he or she became a real estate agent or a professor. Referring back to the base own-occupation definition, in this example, surgery has ceased to be a primary duty. Instead, the client has replaced surgical duties with those of running a general practice, so the general practice becomes the "regular occupation". In evaluating this change, the claims examiner will look at both time and income to assist in the evaluation of whether the duty that can no longer be performed is still primary.

In short, clients who ceased to practice their specialty before a claim occurs — not because of a disability, but by personal choice — cannot declare a loss of that specialty during a claim for benefits.

Insurers have not generally recognized subspecialties, that is, a preferred area of practice within a broader field. An example of a subspecialty is an optometrist who has built a clientele of contact lens users. This represents a preferred area of practice and is referred to as a subspecialty.

The trend among insurers to move away from offering policies containing specialty protection was largely driven by poor claims experience, with overinsurance being a contributing factor. When reviewing existing coverage, advisers should check for a specialty endorsement before making any recommendations to update coverage through replacement, to ensure that the client is not unknowingly forfeiting a specialty definition for a broader, more general one.

As indicated, the primary advantage of a pure own-occupation definition is that clients stand to collect not only full disability benefits, but also equivalent predisability earnings, if they are able to work in a new occupation. The more critical issue to consider, however, is whether the contract will pay a benefit when the client is able to work in his or her own occupation, but only at a reduced level of earnings. This may be due to either being less effective, not working as many hours, or not being able to perform all regular duties. A contract that contains a pure own-occupation definition does not necessarily contain benefits for reduced disability.

"Regular Occupation and Not Working"

This definition also offers protection to the client against the inability to perform the primary duties of the regular occupation, but it stipulates that if the client does pursue a new occupation, benefits would cease. The decision to pursue a new occupation would belong to the client. There is no forced rehabilitation for the client to retrain for a new and different occupation. This definition eliminates the overinsurance aspect associated with the pure own-occupation definition, under which benefits would not be reduced by earnings from a different occupation. The cost is lower, as a result of the insurance company's lower risk exposure.

Sample Definition:

"Total Disability" means that because of sickness or accident:

(*a*) you are unable to perform the primary duties of your regular occupation;

(*b*) you are not engaged in another occupation; and

(*c*) you are under the regular and personal care of a physician.

"Regular Occupation" is defined as the occupation in which you were working at the time of your disability.

"Any Occupation for Which Qualified"

The "any occupation" definition is the most restrictive of the three and is associated with higher-risk occupations. By controlling the degree of risk, insurers are able to offer some form of coverage where otherwise no DI protection would be available.

Sample Definition:

"Total Disability" means that because of sickness or accident:

(*a*) you are unable to perform some or all of the duties of your regular occupation; and

(*b*) you are also unable to perform another gainful occupation for which you are qualified based upon your education, training, and prior experience, or for which you may be expected to become qualified;

(*c*) you are not currently engaged in any gainful occupation; and

(*d*) you are under the regular and personal care of a physician.

"Regular Occupation" is defined as the occupation in which you were working at the time of your disability.

The emphasis in this definition shifts to rehabilitation. If there is work that the client is able to perform, or can reasonably be expected to learn to perform, then a benefit is not payable. This strict definition enables the insurer to gently nudge the client back into the mainstream of life, by partnering with the client to create a plan of medical rehabilitation and/or occupational retraining. In practice, definitions are generally not this restrictive overall, but combine more than one type of definition to create a hybrid definition.

Hybrid Definitions

In theory, occupation-based definitions fall into the three categories discussed — "pure own occupation", "regular occupation and not working", and "any occupation for which qualified". However, most insurers balance risk containment and market attraction by offering a limited-period definition, under which disability is more liberally defined for the first few years of claim, after which time the definition changes to incorporate more restrictive criteria.

Sample Definition:

"Total Disability" means that because of sickness or accident:

(*a*) you are unable to perform the primary duties of your regular occupation;

(*b*) you are not engaged in another occupation; and

(*c*) you are under the regular and personal care of a physician.

"Regular Occupation" is defined as the occupation in which you were working at the time of your disability.

After benefits have been paid for 60 months, "Total Disability" means:

(*a*) you are unable to perform some or all of the duties of your regular occupation;

(*b*) you are unable to perform another gainful occupation for which you are qualified based upon your education, training, and prior experience, or for which you may be expected to become qualified;

(*c*) you are not engaged currently in any gainful occupation; and

(*d*) you are under the regular and personal care of a physician.

"Regular Occupation" is defined as the occupation in which you were working at the time of your disability.

The use of limited-period definitions is often found in individual disability policies for the blue-collar market and in group LTD contracts.

Most insurers today offer regular occupation definitions to even their top occupation class, with the option to add an own-occupation rider. This flexibility provides cost-conscious buyers with cost-containment options, while those who value the pure own-occupation option can still incorporate it into their policy. It also functions as an underwriting tool, enabling the head office underwriter to evaluate the eligibility of each applicant based on that applicant's occupational circumstances.

EARNINGS APPROACH

Central to this approach is insuring the client's ability to earn income at a certain level, regardless of the nature of the occupation performed to generate it. A residual disability definition falls within this category. Some companies originally adopted this definition as a means of offering a reasonable alternative to own-occupation coverage where earnings level superseded the nature of work performed to earn it. It filled the gap created by occupation-based definitions that left the client exposed to risk when disability was partial rather than total. Under an occupation-based definition, return to work in a reduced capacity resulted in the termination of benefits, even though the client still experienced a loss of earnings. This deficiency was resolved by changing the focus from loss of duties to loss of earnings.

Residual Definition

Residual disability protection provides income replacement in proportion to the client's lost earnings. The benefits are adjusted as the client's level of earnings changes. This type of protection recognizes that recovery is usually a gradual process and that the provision of some level of ongoing disability income facilitates an early return to work. This is an advantage to both the client and the insurer.

The definition itself addresses how benefits will be payable during a period of total disability and how benefits will be payable during a period of reduced disability.

Sample Definition:

"Total Disability" means that because of sickness or accident:

(*a*) you are unable to perform the primary duties of your regular occupation;

(*b*) you are not engaged in another occupation; and

(*c*) you are under the regular and personal care of a physician.

"Regular Occupation" is defined as the occupation in which you were working at the time of your disability.

"Residual Disability" means:

You are not totally disabled, but because of an accident or a sickness you have a reduction in your earned income of at least 20% and you are under the regular and personal care of a physician and are either:

(*a*) able to perform one or more of the primary activities of your regular occupation and earning an amount that is reduced; or

(*b*) engaged in a different occupation and your monthly earned income from this occupation is at least 20% less than your previous average monthly earned income

The client is protected during periods of partial disability, as well as during periods of total disability. However, in the event that the client enters a new occupation as a result of being totally disabled from the current occupation, benefits will be prorated in accordance with the new earnings level. The client cannot be forced to participate in a rehabilitation program; however, as the insurer benefits by the client's return to a new occupation, the company will generally encourage and assist in both medical rehabilitation and occupational retraining if the client wishes to pursue such a plan.

Some companies do not require the client to be "under the care of a physician" in order to satisfy the definition of disability, if ongoing care would be of no benefit to their condition. This may be the case when the disability is a permanent impairment with no expected improvement.

Dual Definition

A dual definition combines both own-occupation and residual protection. Clients who fall into low-risk occupational categories, such as accountants, executives, and lawyers, may be able to purchase a policy that contains a dual definition. Under this type of contract, when clients experience a total disability that prevents them from working in their regular occupation, the full benefit is payable regardless of earnings from a new occupation. Benefits are being paid under the own-occupation portion of the definition. However, when the client suffers a partial disability and is still able to work on a partial basis in his or her regular occupation, benefits will continue under the residual portion of the definition for as long as the loss continues.

There are two methods used by insurers to achieve a dual-definition contract:

Integrated Definition

The integrated definition method is one in which the definition of "disability" simply contains two parts. The first part defines what will be payable when clients are unable to work at all within their own occupation (i.e., own-occupation benefit). The second part defines disability benefits that will be payable when clients have reduced earnings within their own occupation (i.e., residual benefit).

Optional Rider

The optional rider approach is one in which the insurer starts with a base contract, such as an own-occupation contract, that covers total disability only, and amends it by attaching a rider for residual benefits. The client pays an additional premium for the rider. The company may alternatively use a residual policy as the base contract, to which is added an optional own-occupation rider at an additional cost.

The optional rider approach enables the company to decide, during the underwriting process, whether the specific client qualifies for the rider addition, based upon his or her own individual underwriting profile, and for this reason it is the preferred method used by insurers today. For example, an executive client who has recently become a self-employed consultant and works from a home office may be restricted to a total-disability-only provision, until such time as the office is moved outside the residence. In theory, the rider approach may enable the client to later alter the contract without the need to fully replace the base protection, while the integrated approach would require the client to completely replace the contract with a new dual definition. The rider method could mean that the insured would maintain the original age on the base policy, and the attained age on the rider only. The trend among insurers is to move away from pure own-occupation definitions as a means of reducing the overinsurance associated with this definition. Consequently, the list of eligible occupations for this type of definition is narrowing, and some companies now offer the own-occupation option through to age 55 only.

Residual Provisions

The Elimination Period

As with all disability policies, the client must satisfy the elimination period before benefits will be payable. This refers to the number of days that must pass from the day the disability occurs after which benefits may begin. The standard elimination periods are 30, 60, 90, 120, 180, and 365 days.

The Qualification Period

Some residual disability definitions stipulate that the client must satisfy a qualification period. This is independent of the standard elimination period contained in all disability income policies. The qualification period indicates a specified number of days of total disability that must precede a period of reduced disability. If this is not satisfied, then no benefits are payable during the period of reduced or partial disability. When the policy contains this provision, it runs consecutively with the elimination period. Generally, this provision is found only in older contracts, purchased around the time when residual policies first became available. In some policies, it is stated as a period that is equal to the elimination period. In such cases, as long as the client was totally disabled throughout the elimination period, benefits would be payable for reduced disability immediately thereafter.

Calculation of the Reduced Benefit

The benefit amount is calculated by determining the current earnings in relation to the prior average earnings.

Illustration

Prior Average Earnings:	\$5,000 per month
Current Earnings:	\$1,500 per month
Benefit Purchased:	\$2,500 per month
Earnings Loss:	100 - (Current Earnings/Prior Average Earnings × 100) = 100 - (1,500/5,000 × 100) = 70% earnings loss
Benefit Payable:	Monthly Benefit Purchased × Earnings Loss = \$2,500 × 70% = \$1,750 reduced monthly benefit payable

Prior Average Earnings

The client's earnings may have been reduced gradually over a period just prior to the onset of disability, or the client may have experienced a fluctuation in earnings over the past few years. Therefore, the insurer generally provides two methods for determining the prior average earnings. The first method uses a more current calculation, such as averaging the prior income over the past six months. The second method uses a longer time frame, such as the highest average from any successive two fiscal years of the last three years. (Older policies were more generous and included the average of the best 24 consecutive months out of the last 60 months.) The higher of the two will be the basis of the calculation against which earnings reduction is measured. When using the average over the past six months, some insurers now limit this calculation to 125% of average monthly earnings for the last fiscal year prior to disability. This cap is not found in older policies. This discussion again underscores that it is important for advisers to conduct a thorough policy analysis prior to replacing older policies that may be more generous.

Often, the highest earnings are the more recent earnings, because a person's income usually goes up as the years go by. However, there are many reasons that a person's income just prior to a claim may not be an accurate reflection of his or her true earnings. For instance, the illness may have been gradually reducing the person's effectiveness and, therefore, his or her recent earnings. Alternatively, the client's business may have suffered through a recent and short-lived economic downturn, which represents a temporary blip in earnings, not an ongoing trend.

Illustration:

Gillian Brown has a $6,000 residual policy, and her income history is contained in the chart below. Following a disability, she returns to work at a reduced capacity and earns $7,200.

INCOME HISTORY	
Period	**Monthy Income**
2007	$13,000
2008	$13,500
2009	$11,000
February 2010	$13,500
March 2010	$10,200
April 2010	$12,400
May 2010	$11,400
June 2010	$ 8,000
July 2010	$ 8,700
August 1: disability commenced	

If we base her predisability earnings on the six-month period prior to her disability, her benefit would be based on the average of February to July earnings: $64,200/6 = $10,700.

Predisability earnings:	$10,700
Current earnings:	$7,200
Earnings reduction:	32.7%
Benefit entitlement:	32.7% of $6,000 = $1,962 per month

If we base her predisability earnings on the best two consecutive of the last three fiscal years prior to her disability, her benefit would be based on $13,000 (2007) plus $13,500 (2008), for an average of $13,250.

Predisability earnings:	$13,250
Current earnings:	$7,200
Earnings reduction:	46%
Benefit entitlement:	46% of $6,000 = $2,760 per month

Gillian's earnings reduction is at least 20% (a requirement for receiving residual benefits). Some policies have a guarantee that during the first six months of a residual claim, the client will receive a minimum of 50% of the benefit. Regardless, as can be seen by the above illustration, the calculation of the prior average earnings has a significant effect on the benefits. By basing her earnings on the best two consecutive of the last three fiscal years, instead of the immediate six-month period prior to disability, she receives significantly higher benefits.

Minimum and Maximum Earnings Loss

For a benefit to be payable, the earnings loss must be at least 20%. Benefits will cease once the client's income reaches 80% of prior earnings. The client receives full benefits, however, when the earnings loss is between 80% and 100%.

Many residual policies provide a further guarantee that during the first six months (or 12 months) of reduced disability, the client will receive at least 50% of prior earnings. This gives the client and the insurance company time to determine the actual loss. The advantage to the client is that a larger benefit may be payable than the proportional formula would generate. If, however, the actual loss is greater, the client will receive the larger benefit amount.

Partial Disability for Loss of Time or Loss of Duties

Some policies include a provision defining a state of partial disability. This refers to a period when the client is unable to do one or more significant duties, or when the client can perform all the significant duties but for only half the normal time, and he or she is under the care of a physician. The insured can receive 50% for up to two (or three) years, and then 25% thereafter as long as partial disability continues. Some insurers provide that if the insured is collecting benefits under this provision, there may be an option to make a one-time election to have benefits calculated under the residual formula instead, if this would be more beneficial. Another approach used by insurers is to allow the client to switch back and forth during a limited period of time, such as the first 12 months, after which no further changes can be made. Once elected, the decision cannot later be reversed. When the conversion to the new method of calculation occurs, the insurer recalculates the benefits using the residual formula for the prior year and pays the difference if it is greater.

Indexing of Prior Average Earnings

During a long-term claim for reduced benefits, the client's earnings may increase as a result of the general rise in the cost of goods and services, rather than because the client returned to work. This may result in a reduction in the benefit payable under the residual policy, even though the client is no less disabled. To prevent this occurrence, many companies index the prior average earnings by a percentage equal to the Consumer Price Index. This keeps the benefit level. During periods of low inflation, this provision is not a major advantage. However, as the client may be on claim for 10 or 20 years, an average inflation rate of 4% can have a significant benefit over an extended term. The example below shows the effect of 4% inflation over a five-year period of reduced disability.

4% Inflation and $3,000 Policy Benefit Amount for Total Disability

Without Indexing Prior Average Earnings				
Year	**Prior Average Earnings**	**Current Earnings**	**% of Loss**	**Monthly Benefit**
1	$ 6,000	$ 2,400	60%	$ 1,800
2	$ 6,000	$ 2,496	58%	$ 1,740
3	$ 6,000	$ 2,596	57%	$ 1,710
4	$ 6,000	$ 2,700	55%	$ 1,650
5	$ 6,000	$ 2,808	53%	$ 1,590

Indexing of Prior Average Earnings				
Year	**Prior Average Earnings**	**Current Earnings**	**% of Loss**	**Monthly Benefit**
1	$6,000	$2,400	60%	$1,800
2	$6,240	$2,496	60%	$1,800
3	$6,500	$2,596	60%	$1,800
4	$6,760	$2,700	60%	$1,800
5	$7,030	$2,808	60%	$1,800

As can be seen from this illustration, in just five years, this client would otherwise have a combined income (earnings plus residual benefit) of $4,398, but because of indexing of prior average earnings, the combined income is $4,608 — a difference of $210 per month.

The percentage minimums and maximums vary from one company to another, and older contracts may be more generous than newer contracts. Many contracts today provide a minimum of 2% to a maximum of 10% compound.

OTHER POLICY PROVISIONS

Insurers use various policy provisions to enhance and distinguish their offerings. Some provisions that started out as unique and exclusive to one insurer have become standard in all insurers' products over time. An example of this is the presumptive disability provision, discussed below. Sometimes, new provisions emerge as a result of the need to clarify conditions eligible for claiming a benefit. An example of this is the transplant donor and cosmetic surgery provision, also discussed below. The cycle of development is never-ending, and the risky business of one-upmanship has often caused insurers to go too far, resulting in increased claims. This is followed by a cycle of risk reduction, where changes in policy provisions predominantly take the form of more restrictive versions of the same benefit or, in some cases, withdrawal of the provision altogether. Occasionally, something quite new and different emerges. Two examples of new-to-market provisions are the catastrophic disability benefit provision and the disability insurance to long-term care (DI to LTC) conversion provision. Both are discussed below, along with other frequent standard provisions.

Presumptive Disability Provision

The policy may contain a provision called "presumptive disability", which states that certain losses will be assumed to be totally disabling regardless of whether, in fact, they are. These conditions include loss of speech, total loss of hearing or sight, and loss of use of both hands or both feet or one hand and one foot. Under these circumstances, the full benefit is payable regardless of whether the individual actually experiences a loss of earnings or not. The person could still be able to perform all regular duties, and still collect full benefits. Most presumptive provisions state that the loss must be irrecoverable. The provisional wording may also state that when payment is made under this clause, the normal elimination period will be waived and benefits will begin immediately. This feature is usually contained in non-cancellable policies.

Example

Jeffrey, a computer programmer, was in a serious car accident that rendered him a paraplegic. Over the course of the next year, he underwent several surgeries, and during this time he collected full benefits under his non-cancellable residual policy. Although he could no longer walk, he was eventually able to return to work full-time as a programmer, without a change in his earnings level. His benefits continued uninterrupted and without reduction under the presumptive disability provision.

While in one respect, this appears to be a case of overinsurance, in Jeffrey's case there were numerous medical expenses incurred. He needed an attendant for a period of time, and there were home modifications required to accommodate his wheelchair. Thankfully, the additional income has helped him deal with many of the ongoing costs associated with his permanent disability.

Recovery Benefit

The concept of the recovery benefit evolved from the problem facing clients upon first returning to work following a lengthy absence. The issue is that there is often a continued loss of income during the first few months. This may occur for different reasons: A person in sales must take time to build their clientele again, and a delay often occurs between the point of sale and the receipt of commissions. Some professionals experience a delay due to the nature of their billing cycles. For instance, physicians who perform services must bill the government health insurance plan (GHIP) and await payment. Accountants, dentists, and other service providers may have similar delays between performing the service, invoicing the client, and receiving payment.

As the client is no longer under the care of a physician (an essential requirement for all disability definitions), benefits cease under the policy, even though there may still be an earnings reduction. Fear of this initial gap caused many clients to delay their return, and insurers saw the solution in the form of a recovery benefit as a win-win.

Today, virtually all insurers provide a recovery benefit, but the provision itself varies among insurers. One version of this benefit provides continuation of some level of benefits for two months after return on a full-time basis to one's regular occupation. The disability must have lasted a minimum period, such as three months. The benefit paid is 50% for the first month and then 25% for the second month. There may be other criteria that also have to be satisfied.

Another version of this benefit provides for a continuation of benefits for four months, in proportion to the ongoing earnings loss, upon return to work following a period of total or residual disability (if there is at least a 20% loss). If the return to work follows a period of claiming for partial (instead of residual) benefits, a payment equal to the last partial disability payment will be made for two months.

Other variations also exist, but some of the notable features that vary are those that deal with the following:

- The number of months during which benefits continue (two, three, or four months)
- Whether a period of total disability must precede the return to work (and if so, how long it must have lasted)
- Whether the benefit is payable for a return to a different occupation or only to one's predisability occupation
- The method of calculating the amount of benefit.

Regardless of these variations, there are some features that are standard:

- The amount payable always reduces to ease the person off benefits.
- The benefit payment period is very limited.

Non-Consecutive Accumulation of Periods of Disability

The policy will state whether periods of disability must be continuous in order to satisfy the elimination period. The more comprehensive definition is one that provides for the accumulation of periods of disability that are due to a related cause. The provision will indicate the maximum time frame within which they can occur (such as 6, 12, or 24 months). As a rule, the time frame is measured from the last day of disability, not the original day of disability. This, however, may vary by company. Measurement from the last day of disability results in a longer time frame within which the accumulation can occur and is, consequently, a more liberal provision than one measuring from the original date of disability.

Accumulation may be for periods of total disability only, or it may include periods of both total and partial disability. The general rule is that if the policy covers only total disabilities, the accumulation provision similarly accumulates only for periods of total disability. If the policy contains a residual provision, the accumulation provision usually allows for periods of both total and partial disability to be accumulated to satisfy the elimination period, provided they are due to the same cause and occur within the stated time frame.

This is a valuable feature because some disabilities are gradually debilitating and the insured might otherwise not qualify for benefits.

Recurrent Disability Provision

This provision deals with the issue of a premature return to work, followed by a subsequent recurrence of the disability. Under the recurrent disability provision, a disability that recurs within a stated time frame, such as six months or a year, is considered to be a continuation of the original claim if it is due to the same cause, and it will not require a new elimination period to be satisfied. As it constitutes a continuation of the original claim, the benefit period ends in accordance with the original claim as well. For example, consider a situation where a client is insured under a policy that contains a five-year benefit period. If the client suffers a recurrence following a two-month return to work after receiving three years' worth of benefits, the maximum benefit entitlement would be two more years. However, if the benefit period were to age 65, the benefits would resume for up to the maximum age of 65, as long as disability continued.

The recurrent disability provision is important because it ensures that the client is not penalized for an unsuccessful attempt to return to work. Without this feature, the client may be reluctant to return to work unless absolutely certain that there is no chance of a relapse.

Concurrent Disability Provision

This is a standard provision in all DI contracts. It states that if a disability is caused by more than one injury or sickness, or by a combination thereof, the insurer will pay benefits as if it were one, and the benefits will be based on the greater of the periods of disability. This provision states that the client cannot claim for double benefits as a result of a disability that has multiple causes.

Transplant Donor and Cosmetic Surgery Provision

This provision, which sometimes takes the form of two separate provisions, deals with voluntary disabilities that may be covered under the policy. It provides that in the event the client has surgery for the purpose of donating an organ or undergoes voluntary cosmetic surgery, it will be deemed to be a sickness under the policy contract, and benefits will be payable. The provision covers such risks only after it has been in force for more than six months, to avoid anti-selection. Some policies cover the transplant donor provision and not voluntary cosmetic surgery. In this instance, cosmetic surgery will only be covered if it is required for medical reasons. Given the growing popularity of cosmetic surgery among the "forever young" boomer generation, it may not be long before all companies cease to offer the promise of benefits during voluntary cosmetic surgery.

Survivor Benefit

Under this benefit, if the insured dies while receiving disability benefits, a lump-sum benefit equal to three times the regular monthly benefit for total disability is paid to the insured's estate. Some insurers require the client to have been on total disability for a minimum of one year. This provision is not found in all insurers' policies.

Catastrophic Disability Benefit

Another provision not found in all insurers' policies is the catastrophic disability benefit. It deals with the loss of independent existence, either if a condition renders a person unable to perform two or more activities of daily living or if a person suffers a cognitive impairment. The benefit under the policy will be increased by 25% and paid out, along with the regular benefit, to the end of the benefit period. In addition, a lump-sum payment is payable equal to the lesser of three times the increased monthly benefit and $15,000.

The activities of daily living refer to the inability to do two or more of any of the following tasks:

- Bathe oneself in a tub or shower, or by sponge bath
- Dress oneself, including all appropriate clothing, braces, artificial limbs, or surgical appliances
- Perform hygiene associated with toileting and the ability to get to and from the toilet
- Transfer from a bed to a chair
- Eat food that has been prepared and made available.

A cognitive impairment, for this purpose, must be one that has an organic cause and that renders the person incapable of independent living and in need of daily supervision. Not included are any mental or nervous disorders without organic cause, such as anxiety disorders, mood disorders, sleep disorders, pain disorders, personality disorders, or psychotic disorders.

Disability Insurance Conversion to Long-Term Care Provision

As a client nears retirement, the need for DI begins to diminish and the need for long-term care coverage begins to increase.

This provision, occasionally found in a DI policy, gives clients the right to convert their policy to long-term care (LTC) insurance if they are between the ages of 55 and 65. The conversion may be full or partial, subject to the company's issue limits. The conversion offered is on a dollar-for-dollar basis. For example, $1,500 of a DI benefit can be converted to a $50 per day LTC benefit, with an upper maximum of $200 per day. The change can be made without medical underwriting. To be eligible, the DI policy must have been in force for at least 24 months, and the client must not have been disabled in the 12-month period prior to the conversion. The rates will be based on the client's attained age.

Rehabilitation Benefit Provision

Most DI policies contain a provision that allows the client to participate in a planned program of rehabilitation without the termination of benefits. This facilitates a return to work at an earlier date. Companies have found that the longer a person is on claim, the more likely that a "disability mindset" occurs, making a return to work less probable. The client benefits by being able to attempt a return to an active life without jeopardizing benefit payments. Given the choice, most people want to get back into the mainstream as soon as their condition permits.

Insurers vary their approach to this benefit in two areas:

- **Defining the Dollar Amount:** Some state a specific dollar maximum, while others have no defined amount.
- **Defining the Services Promised**: Some state a vague general promise to work with the client and develop a mutually agreed plan of rehabilitation, while others provide a detailed, defined list of various types of services that may be made available.

Regardless, the client must first secure the approval of the insurer before participating in the rehabilitation program, in order to be eligible for continuation of benefits. Generally, the rehabilitation plan is arranged by the insurance company, which works with medical and vocational rehabilitation specialists, and with the client's personal physician, to structure a planned program. Participation is purely voluntary. However, should the client refuse to participate in such a recommended plan, benefits will cease following the expiry of the own-occupation period.

The amount payable under this provision may provide for reimbursement of related costs in addition to the regular monthly benefit. The insurer may alternatively offer an advance of monthly benefits as a lump sum to facilitate a speedy recovery.

Some of the assistance made available may include costs associated with the following:

- Medical investigation and treatment.
- Physical, psychiatric, or psychological rehabilitation.
- Vocational evaluation.
- Education or occupational retraining.
- Job placement assistance.
- Financial or business planning that supports a return to work.

- Worksite modification, including the use of ergonomically designed furniture or equipment. Some insurers are moving away from the term "rehabilitation" and are instead emphasizing the assistance available to support the client's "return to work". These insurers feel that the term "rehabilitation" conjures up negative images more closely linked with "disability", "inability", and "forced change". This may have led to the adoption of more positive phrases that create a client-centred feeling, such as "return-to-work assistance", which is also suggestive of a broader approach that encompasses a look at the workplace environment itself for changes or devices that support the return.
- Mobility-enhancing equipment.
- Visual or audio equipment.

Waiver of Premium

Unlike with life insurance, where the waiver of premium provision must be selected and purchased by the client, DI policies provide it as a standard feature. There is no additional charge, as it is not an optional benefit. Premiums are usually waived through to age 65, regardless of the benefit period, although more recently developed products for non-traditional markets often limit the premium waiver to the end of the benefit period only. This distinction is important, because higher-risk occupations frequently have benefit periods that are less than age 65, such as two or five years. In this instance, the client must resume the payment of premiums when disability continues after the maximum benefit period has been paid. The contract will otherwise lapse for non-payment of premiums. Clients should maintain the protection, because they may return to work at some later point. It is likely that they would not qualify for the purchase of new protection, given how recently they were disabled. Resumption of premiums ensures that they can continue to have DI protection for possible future disabilities right through to age 65.

The client must continue to pay the premiums for the first 90 days of disability. If the disability continues after 90 days, future premiums are waived and those paid during the 90-day period are refunded.

Variations in the Waiver of Premium Provision

Five variations to the standard provision follow.

1. The provision may state that periods of disability do not need to be continuous. The client can collect non-consecutive periods to satisfy the 90-day provision if the periods of disability are due to the same cause and occur within a stated period of time, such as 180 days or 365 days.
2. The provision may state that premiums will be waived after "the lesser of 90 days or the elimination period". In this case, premiums

would be waived after 30 days on a contract that contains a 30-day elimination period.

3. The provision may limit waivers to periods of total disability only, or it may include periods of partial disability as well.

4. The provision may provide for waiver of premiums beyond age 65 where the client has included the optional rider of lifetime accident and sickness, which was available under older policies.

5. The wording may be such that premiums will be waived "during disability", as opposed to waiver of premiums "that fall due during disability". Under the first version, a policy in which the premium is payable annually will have premiums proportionally waived for the number of months that disability continues, even if the annual premium due date does not fall during the period of disability. The premium would not be waived, however, under the provisional wording in the second version, as it did not fall due. Conversely, if the annual premium did fall due during the disability, it would be waived in its entirety, rather than proportionally.

As there are many variations, the adviser should be cautious about making assumptions or providing advice without a thorough review of the actual wording.

Exclusions

This provision is also known as "exceptions" and defines the risks not covered by the policy contract. A series of policies for professionals will contain fewer exclusions than policy series developed for high-risk occupations. Two standard exclusions found in disability contracts follow.

Wars

Acts of war, whether declared or undeclared, are excluded.

Normal Pregnancy

Complications from pregnancy are generally covered by the policy contract unless specifically excluded during the underwriting of the client. For a short period of time, a small number of insurers removed the "normal pregnancy" exclusion from their policy, promising to pay benefits for a limited number of months following normal delivery. It was not long before women planning to start a family purchased policies in anticipation of claiming. Some sales representatives went so far as to illustrate the cost by reducing the premiums by an amount equal to the claimable pregnancy benefit. This feature was short-lived, for obvious reasons.

Exclusions in Policies for High-Risk Occupations

Exclusions that may be found in contracts for high-risk occupations include the following in addition to the above:

Pre-Existing Condition Limitation

Precludes any condition for which the client received treatment, was advised to have treatment, or for which symptoms were experienced that would cause a person normally to seek medical advice. This provision further protects the company concerning any medical conditions that might have been missed during the underwriting process, and essentially removes the restriction associated with the two-year incontestability provision.

Criminal Offence Exclusion

Precludes claiming for a disability that occurs while the client commits or attempts to commit a criminal offence. This may be extended to include accidents that occur when the client is driving in an intoxicated state, whether driving a car or a boat.

Travel Exclusion

Limits payment to a maximum of 12 months when the client is disabled outside of North America. This provision may be worded as a limitation rather than a full exclusion. As such, payment would resume after 12 months if the client returned to North America. The intent is to limit disability payments in circumstances where the claims adjudication process would be encumbered by distance. The requirement to return to North America additionally facilitates appropriate medical treatment, as health care may be more readily available.

Air Travel Exclusion

Precludes payment for a disability that occurs when flying as other than a fare-paying passenger, and may be extended to also exclude flying on a non-powered aircraft, such as a glider.

Recreational Activities Exclusion

Precludes payment if the client was disabled in activities such as mountain climbing, scuba diving, and racing.

Drug and Alcohol Exclusion

Precludes payment if the client was disabled while using any drug, poisonous substance, narcotics, or intoxicant.

Inhalation of Poisonous Gas or Fumes

This may be excluded.

Intentionally Self-Inflicted Injury

Intentional self-inflicted injury causing disability may be excluded.

Attempt To Commit Suicide

Suicide attempts that result in disability may be excluded.

Limitations

In addition to specific exclusions, some policies for high-risk occupations also include a list of limitations, restricting payment to a lesser time frame than other disabilities. This enables the insured to offer coverage to a certain risk class that would otherwise be ineligible for DI. It also is used as a cost containment feature to make the coverage more affordable. Limitations can take many forms. The insurer tries to identify those that their experience demonstrates to be the fastest rising or most frequent in occurrence. An example follows.

Soft-Tissue and/or Degenerative Disc Disease Limitation

This limitation restricts payment for soft-tissue injury or degenerative disc disease to a maximum per occurrence, such as 15 days. It may also state a specified cumulative maximum overall, such as four months during the life of the policy. The limitation usually applies to degenerative disc disease, carpal tunnel syndrome, and other repetitive strain injuries, such as bruises, strains, sprains, tendinitis, and whiplash.

Contestability

The insurance company can contest a policy for misrepresentation during the first two years. Thereafter, the insurer must prove fraudulent intent. The onus is on the insurer to prove that a misstatement was fraud and not oversight or lack of knowledge on the client's part.

Disability insurers will generally exercise their right to void, rather than amend, the contract in the event of a material misrepresentation. This can have unfortunate ramifications for the client who is claiming benefits. The adviser must exercise the utmost care to ensure that statements asked of the client during the application are not phrased in a leading manner and that all answers are completed thoroughly and forthrightly. This applies equally in the areas of medical and financial information recording. The greatest area of rescission is in respect of misstatement of earnings. Therefore, the adviser should request and submit the Canada Revenue Agency documentation, such as tax returns, at the time of underwriting, regardless of whether or not the insurer has made this a standard underwriting requirement. In the event of a claim, such safeguards help to protect the client from a rescission due to misrepresentation.

Chapter 5

Optional Benefits for Disability Insurance Policies

Optional benefits, or "riders", as they are also called, can perform three different functions. They can enhance the base contract through the addition of a new benefit. An example of this is the addition of a hospitalization indemnity benefit. They can also alter the base definition. An example of this is the addition of an own-occupation extension rider, which lengthens the own-occupation period of the base contract, or an HIV and hepatitis B and C rider, which broadens the base definition of disability. Finally, riders can occasionally serve to restrict the base definition, as may be the case when a rider is used to amend a basic provision to a more restrictive version, in return for a lesser premium ("cost-containment options"), or when the insured in some other way gives up privileges normally provided by the policy. An example of this is the addition of a second payer option.

Optional benefits are one way insurers can differentiate their disability insurance (DI) portfolio from other insurers. The more popular options are discussed below; however, other options exist beyond this list.

GUARANTEED INSURABILITY OPTION

One of the most popular options is the guaranteed insurability option (GIO), which provides the client with the right to increase monthly benefits at specified times, referred to as "option dates", without evidence of medical insurability. The client must still provide financial evidence that earnings are sufficient to financially qualify for the benefit amount. Option dates found in older products may be at two- or three-year intervals. Products available in today's market often provide the client with the right to exercise the option on any anniversary until the overall benefit maximum has been purchased or the maximum issue age has been reached.

The Insured's Rights and Guarantees

The GIO, while similar in concept to its counterpart in life insurance policies, contains many valuable promises that go beyond the right to buy more insurance regardless of changes in health. All of these promises are important rights to discuss with the client.

Right To Purchase Regardless of Health Changes

The client may have developed a medical condition since the date of purchase of the original policy that disqualifies him or her from purchasing coverage on a standard basis today. The condition may not be disabling today, but could deteriorate in the future, as is the case with carpal tunnel syndrome. The GIO ensures that the client can increase coverage to keep pace with his or her increasing income. If the base policy was issued on a standard basis, the additional coverage issued under the GIO will also be standard. In this respect it is similar to its life insurance counterpart. Its importance is further highlighted by the fact that while 7% or 8% of life insurance applications are rejected or issued on a substandard basis, disability insurers commonly modify as many as 25% of their cases. There are conditions that affect the disability application that would not affect a life insurance application, such as a strain or sprain. These are conditions that could later be the cause of a disability. This makes the GIO on disability insurance all the more valuable and essential.

Guarantee Regarding Changes in Occupation

There is also a guarantee that coverage purchased using the GIO will be issued at the same occupational classification as the base policy. The client may have changed occupations to one of greater risk, but, regardless of this, the coverage under this option will still match the base policy. The definitions of disability contained in products designed for high-risk occupations are less comprehensive than those found in products for low-risk occupations. This means that the client continues to be eligible for the more comprehensive definitions associated with the products for the client's original occupation.

As occupation class is not a determinant of life insurance rates (except in extreme-risk circumstances, where a rating may be applied), this is an additional promise in the DI guaranteed insurability option.

Guarantee Regarding Insurer's Changes to the Occupation Guide

A GIO that provides for coverage to be issued on the same terms as the base policy will also protect the client against changes made by the insurer to its occupation guide. For example, insurers have reclassified different occupations in the past based on their claims experience. While this did not affect rates for in-force policyholders, new applicants must pay a higher rate. This has occurred in the past with dentists and real estate agents, for example. They are subject to not only a higher rate, but also to the more restrictive product features of the riskier occupation class. However, if purchasing additional insurance by means of exercising the GIO, the client will still be able to purchase new coverage with the same product features and at the premium rates associated with the original occupation class. The client's current age would be used, however, in determining the rate. This is another advantage that goes beyond the life insurance equivalent.

Guarantee Regarding New Recreational Activities

The client also has protection against exclusions being added to new coverage with regard to new recreational activities pursued since the date of the original purchase. These include activities such as contact sports, racing, and mountain climbing. By using the GIO, the client can purchase additional insurance that is free of exclusions that would otherwise arise from lifestyle changes. Lifestyle underwriting is a more significant component of DI underwriting, and this makes this promise even more important.

Proof of Income

In order to exercise the GIO, the insured must provide evidence of income to support the financial need for the additional insurance. This, of course, is not a requirement under the life insurance version. Overinsurance is a greater concern with DI, and insurers must manage the risk by maintaining proper maximum ratios of earnings to benefits. Lacking this, the incentive to claim and to remain on claim following a disability increases.

Other Features and Guidelines

Companies set limits regarding how much can be exercised at any one time, the overall amount that can be purchased during the life of the policy, and the maximum age for exercising options. This is necessary to protect the company from anti-selection. A person whose health is beginning to fail is more likely to purchase greater amounts in anticipation of claiming for benefits. Similarly, the closer one gets to retirement, the more appealing it may be to purchase large sums and claim them, particularly under policies with benefits that extend beyond age 65.

There are many different formats that companies use in the design of their GIO offerings. For example, the overall maximum may be a multiple of the base benefit, such as two or two-and-a-half times the base amount. Some companies allow significantly higher limits for young professionals with high future earnings potential. In this instance, the overall maximum may be as high as five times the base amount. The overall maximum that can be purchased is $25,000, and the maximum age for exercising coverage is 55. However, some insurers will only issue up to $15,000 and age 50. If the total amount has been purchased before the maximum age is attained, no further options can be exercised.

The "per option" amount may be expressed either as a dollar amount, such as $1,500 per option, or as a percentage amount, such as 20% of the overall maximum. Some insurers protect against anti-selection in the later years by reducing the per option amount after a stipulated age, such as age 45.

While special features vary from company to company, some that may be found follow.

Higher Option Amount

The insurer may allow for the first option to be double the normal limit. A variation of this allows for election of a one-time double amount at any time prior to a cut-off age, such as age 55. Older policies were more generous, allowing for the first two or three options to be exercised for the entire overall maximum. The belief was that the company was still relatively protected against anti-selection during the years immediately following issue of the policy.

Exercise While on Claim

Insurers may allow the client to exercise an option that falls due while on claim for benefits. Approaches vary among insurers regarding whether the increase will apply to the current claim. Some companies honour the increased benefit in a future claim only, while others allow the client to exercise the option and collect it during the current claim with some restrictions. The amount that can be exercised may be less than the usual per option amount, and the commencement of benefits may be subject to a waiting period, such as 90 days. This helps to reduce the risk of anti-selection. Some older policies may contain a more generous provision, which again highlights the importance of reviewing all benefits prior to replacing older policies.

Exercise Following Loss of Group LTD

Sometimes, terminated employees respond to their loss of LTD benefits by purchasing DI to supplement group LTD. As the base of LTD is now gone, there may be a need for more DI. Consequently, insurers may offer a special GIO in this case. The option must be exercised within a specified window of time or is otherwise lost, and the privilege is usually a one-time event during the life of the GIO. The insured may be required to confirm that he or she is not covered under a new plan of group LTD. Normal financial evidence must be provided, as is always required when exercising a GIO option.

Premium-Related Features

The premium for this optional benefit ceases when the rider itself expires. The rate charged for coverage purchased is based on the client's current age. The new coverage is identical to the plan and design of the base policy, and will include any exclusions or riders contained in the original policy.

The GIO is one of the most important optional benefits available and should be discussed with every client when designing the DI plan.

COST-OF-LIVING RIDER

This optional benefit protects the client from the erosive effect of inflation during a long-term claim for benefits. It is perhaps the second most important optional benefit.

In 1975, a pound of butter cost $1.11, and by 2005, the price was $4.01. Eggs cost 92 cents and rose to $2.22 (2005). A quart of milk was 43 cents, then went up to $1.97 (2005). A loaf of bread could be purchased for 43 cents but, by 2005, cost $1.79.[1] Fortunately, wages rose as well. A secretary starting out made $8,500 a year in 1975, but similar work performed in 2005 paid about $25,000 to $30,000. Imagine if income did not increase and people had to pay for current expenses on 1975 wages.

Clients who are just beginning their career may purchase DI. They may have as many as 30 to 40 years ahead of them. The earnings they make at the beginning of their career will be modest when compared with the rise in income over the future, assuming they do not become disabled. Similarly, the cost of goods and services will rise in the future, as they have in the past. If clients experience an LTD, these costs must be paid for from their disability benefits. In the absence of a cost-of-living rider, this means paying for rising expenses from a fixed income.

The cost-of-living rider provides protection by annually increasing the monthly benefit amount according to the rate of inflation, as measured by the Consumer Price Index (CPI). The CPI is an indicator of the consumer prices encountered by Canadians. Through the monthly CPI, Statistics Canada tracks the retail price of a representative shopping basket of about 600 goods and services from an average household's expenditure (including food, housing, transportation, furniture, clothing, and recreation). It is widely used by governments and businesses as a measure of the changing purchasing power of money in Canada. The chart below shows the rate of inflation as measured by changes in the CPI for Canada, all items, not seasonally adjusted, between 1991 and 2010.

---

[1] Adapted from James Powell, "Appendix A: Purchasing Power of the Canadian Dollar" in *A History of the Canadian Dollar*, http://www.bankofcanada.ca/wp-content/uploads/2010/07/dollar_book.pdf (Bank of Canada, 2005).

Consumer Price Index, 1991 to 2010	
The Consumer Price Index for Canada, all items, not seasonally adjusted, historical data 2002 = 100	
As at January	**Annual Average Percent Change**
1991	5.6
1992	1.4
1993	1.9
1994	0.1
1995	2.2
1996	1.5
1997	1.7
1998	1.0
1999	1.8
2000	2.7
2001	2.5
2002	2.2
2003	2.8
2004	1.8
2005	2.2
2006	2.0
2007	2.2
2008	2.3
2009	0.3
2010	1.8
Extracted from the *Consumer Price Index*, December 2010, Statistics Canada, Table 5, Catalogue no. 62-001-X	

The cost-of-living rider provides increases on either an annual or semi-annual basis, beginning after the first full year of claim. Adjustments may be based on compound indexing or simple indexing.

Some of the areas to consider when reviewing a cost-of-living rider are:

- Whether the indexing occurs during periods of total disability only or also during periods of total, residual, and partial disability
- How the amount of increase will be determined
- Whether the compound adjustment is cumulative from the onset of disability
- Whether there is an overall maximum amount
- Whether there is a buy-back provision following return to work.

Features To Consider

Type of Disability Covered

Disability can be total, residual, or partial, and not all cost-of-living riders cover every type of disability. Some specify that indexing of benefits applies only during periods of total disability. Yet a client may be on residual or partial benefits for the long term. The cost-of-living rider is needed to protect against inflation during periods of long-term disability, and it is wise to ensure that the rider will fulfill this goal.

Amount of Increase

As previously indicated, the adjustment, which begins after the first full year of claim, may be calculated on either a compound basis or a simple basis. Compound-calculated options are tied to the CPI. Simple-indexing versions provide a flat-rate annual indexed benefit, such as 4% or 5%. The advantage of the simple method is that the client knows from the outset what the adjustment will be. Older policies issued in the 1990s sometimes included simple indexing as high as 8%.

CPI-linked riders may have an annual minimum adjustment, such as 2%. They also have a maximum to which the base benefit may increase in any given year, such as 5% or 10%. (There are older policies out there with maximums as high as 15%!) Benefits may be adjusted downward if the CPI falls below that of the previous year. However, benefits could never be adjusted below those provided in the base policy. The advantage of this version is that the adjustment more accurately reflects the change in the cost of living, as it is tied to the CPI.

Carryforward of Unused Annual Adjustment Limit

Some riders have a carryforward feature such that if the increases based on the CPI are lower than the maximum percentage stated in the policy, the unused difference can be applied to exceed the stated maximum in a year in which the CPI rises above it. In other words, there is a cumulative maximum increase compounded annually from the onset of disability.

Example of Carryforward

Based on $1,000 Monthly Benefit and a 5% Compound COLA

Completed Year of Claim	Change in CPI	Adjusted Benefit with Carryforward	Adjusted Benefit without Carryforward
0		$1,000	$1,000
1	1.5%	$1,015	$1,015
2	2.0%	$1,035	$1,035
3	3.5%	$1,071	$1,071
4	6.0%	$1,135*	$1,125
5	8.2%	$1,228*	$1,181
6	11.0%	$1,340**	$1,240
7	12.0%	$1,407***	$1,302

* In Years 4 and 5, CPI exceeds the annual maximum of 5%, while in Years 1 to 3, CPI fell below the annual maximum. The "unused" amount from Years 1 to 3 is carried forward for use in Years 4 and 5.

** Year 6 illustrates that there is still some carryforward applied.

*** Year 7 shows adjustment at the 5% maximum, as the carryforward has been used up.

The Overall Maximum Amount

Some cost-of-living riders stipulate that once the benefits have doubled or tripled from the original amount, no further indexing will occur. In this instance, the benefit would thereafter remain level through to age 65. Some companies do not impose a ceiling, but allow the benefit to continue to increase annually through to age 65 (subject to the company's overall maximum issue limits for the particular occupation class).

Buy-Back Provision

Once the client returns to work, the benefit amount reverts to the original base amount. The cost-of-living rider may contain a buy-back provision, whereby the client has the right to purchase the increased benefit without medical or financial evidence. The premium for this additional coverage is based upon the client's attained age. To qualify, the client must exercise the right within a stipulated period of time, such as 60 or 90 days. The client must be working full-time, and the in-force coverage together with the amount applied for cannot exceed the company's maximum issue and participation limits. Some companies may further stipulate a maximum age for exercising this provision, such as 55 or 60.

LIFETIME BENEFIT EXTENSIONS

The trend in benefits has been away from lifetime extensions because they result in greater exposure for insurers and it becomes much more appealing to claim for benefits during economic downturns as one nears retirement. However, as many policies were issued in the past and the adviser may have clients with older policies, these benefits are reviewed below.

Lifetime benefit extensions may take the form of either of the following:

- Lifetime accident
- Lifetime accident and sickness.

Companies have not offered a sickness extension independent of accident.

Lifetime Accident

This rider extends the benefit period on a policy for life when disability is the result of an accident. The accident must occur prior to a certain age, such as 60.

Lifetime Accident and Sickness

This rider was only offered to low-risk occupations. For a claim to qualify under the lifetime benefit, the disability must occur before a certain age, such as 55 or 60. Older versions of this benefit may still be found in policies purchased many years ago, where the sickness benefit contains a reduction schedule of 20% for each year that disability commenced after age 55. For instance, if the client's illness started at age 57, then 60% of the benefit would be payable for life. If no disability has occurred prior to age 60, the rider expires and the benefit period for sickness reverts to age 65. The premium correspondingly decreases.

In place of lifetime benefits, many companies have introduced a retirement savings rider, which fulfills the need for income during retirement following a long-term disability on a more cost-effective basis to the client and at a lower risk to the insurer.

RETIREMENT SAVINGS RIDER

This benefit is often available as either a rider to a base disability income policy or as a stand-alone contract. It assists the client in maintaining regular contributions towards retirement savings during periods of total disability. Contributions are made to a locked-in account for payment at age 65, although some riders provide for a partial withdrawal each year to pay the annual tax due on interest earnings. Some insurers make provisions for transfer to a designated RRSP. The client purchases a benefit amount, usually between $300 and $2,000 for low-risk occupations (maximum $1,500 for high-risk occupations). There is generally a percentage of the base monthly benefit that cannot be exceeded, such as 15% or 20%. The rider may include a qualification period that must be satisfied, such as three months. If the client is disabled for less than the qualification period, no contribution is made to the account, as the purpose is to maintain contributions to savings during long periods of total disability, not short interruptions in earnings. Older policies covered only periods of total disability but today's versions include total, residual, or partial disability.

The rider does not generate contributions when a client is covered under an "own occupation" definition and is earning an income in a new occupation.

Eligibility is usually open to all insurable occupations, and not restricted solely to low-risk occupations.

OWN-OCCUPATION EXTENSION RIDER

This provision extends the own-occupation period in the policy to a longer term.

PARTIAL DISABILITY RIDER

Short-Term Partial

This benefit provides for payment of 50% of the monthly benefit for a specified period of time, such as 6 or 12 months. Clients must be unable to perform their usual duties for at least half of the normal time, or be unable to perform one or more of their primary daily duties. Some, but not all, companies require that when the disability is due to a sickness, a period of partial disability must be preceded by a period of total disability for which benefits have been paid. When disability is the result of an accident, no period of total disability is required. However, the elimination period must be satisfied in either event.

Long-Term Partial

Some companies have adapted this concept to a long-term version for use where an earnings-based definition (i.e., residual) is less appropriate. A client who owns a small incorporated business may not show an earnings loss, as it is possible to control the nature and timing of earnings. Such a client may be better suited to a duties-based definition. A long-term partial rider may pay benefits on a fixed reduction scale through to the end of the benefit period. The reduction scale varies by company. An example of a reduction scale is 50% for the first 24 months, then 30% for the next 12 months, and then 20% for the balance of the benefit period. Alternatively, the long-term partial benefit may remain level for the benefit duration. Some level versions vary the duration based on the occupation class being covered.

The client must suffer a loss of either time or duties to qualify for payment. Earnings loss is not a determining factor for payment under a partial disability rider.

HOSPITALIZATION BENEFITS

First Day Hospitalization Benefit

This rider provides the client with immediate benefits when hospitalized. The normal elimination period is waived and benefits will be payable during hospital confinement. The normal monthly benefit is prorated to determine the amount payable. Once the client leaves the hospital, benefits cease until the remainder of the elimination period has been satisfied. If the client is hospitalized for the entire elimination period, benefits will continue uninterrupted. The minimum period of hospitalization required varies from one company to another, ranging from 18 hours to 72 hours of hospitalization.

Hospital Indemnity Rider

Unlike the first day hospitalization benefit, which is designed to fill the gap during the elimination period, the hospital indemnity rider is designed to pay a daily benefit to assist with the added expenses during the period of hospitalization. As it is not a reimbursement plan, the benefits can be used for any purpose that the client wishes. For example, a hospitalized spouse may need to hire child care assistance, and the funds can be used for this purpose.

The amount is purchased as a daily benefit. The minimum and maximum amounts vary by company but are generally between $50 and $250 per day. The amount does not usually require a relationship to base policy benefits. Benefits begin on the first day of a hospitalization that exceeds 24 hours and is payable to a maximum, such as three or four months per occurrence. When attached to a base policy containing an early elimination period, a benefit may be simultaneously payable under each portion.

Most riders contain a coordination of benefits provision, whereby the company will not exceed participation with other insurers beyond a stated amount, such as $350 in aggregate. As this is a rider, the exclusions contained in the base policy also apply to the rider, and no payment will be made for a specific condition or risk not covered by the base plan.

LIMITED FIRST DAY ACCIDENT BENEFIT

This option commences benefits starting with the first day of total disability caused by an injury that occurs off the job. This reduces overlap with workers' compensation benefits.

RETURN OF PREMIUM RIDER

This rider returns a portion or all of the premiums paid after a period of time under certain conditions. For example, the client may be entitled to a refund of all premiums paid, less all benefits received, at age 65, provided the total of claims paid does not exceed the total of premiums paid. If the client discontinues the policy prior to age 65, a smaller, prorated refund may be available. If, however, claims exceed the premiums paid, there is no refund.

Some return of premium riders feature a provision for an earlier return if the client has had a favourable claims history. An example may be that at the end of any 10-year period (or, in some policies, an 8-year period) during which the client had no claims or which such claims total less than 20% of premiums paid, the client receives a stipulated refund, such as 70% or 80% of all premiums paid during the period. Once the client has total claims exceeding 20% of premiums paid, the refund period starts over again after the client recovers. Versions vary slightly from company to company, but the concept is similar.

The premium for this rider is generally in the range of 40% to 60% extra. Some believe that it helps the client to overcome the concern that, unlike life insurance, where everyone will die at some point, disability is not a certainty. A return of premium rider addresses this concern by returning the premiums when the benefits are not required and paying a benefit when they are required. As the refund is a return of premiums, it is non-taxable, and this may offer certain tax advantages to the client. It may also cause a client to consider carefully any decision to terminate coverage before receiving the return, as a substantial portion or all of the refund may be forfeited. In this respect, it functions as a persistency tool by encouraging the client to keep the policy in force.

A counter-argument is that the client may fear claiming for short-term benefits, while the coverage was purchased to provide financial protection. Also, had the additional premium been invested in a true savings vehicle, both the disability benefit and the savings would be available to the client. The client has, in essence, prepaid a "substandard medical load". A claim that results in the client being ineligible for the refund would mean that the client paid more for the same amount of insurance than a similar claimant who did not purchase the rider.

PREDISABILITY INDEXING BENEFIT

This benefit provides the client with an automatic increase in the monthly benefit amount without medical or financial evidence before a disability occurs. Unlike the GIO, which must be applied for, the predisability indexing benefit is an automatic adjustment and helps the benefit to keep pace with small changes in the client's earnings. The increase is usually in the range of 4% to 5% of the principal amount and the premium rate is based upon the client's attained age. The client has the right to refuse the additional insurance, although no further indexing will apply. This helps to prevent anti-selection. The benefit must be renewed at a regular interval, such as three or five years. The renewal process requires submission of financial evidence to ensure that the new amount does not exceed overall issue and participation limits. It may also require periodic health evidence with some insurers.

HIV AND HEPATITIS B AND C RIDER

Health care professionals have greater exposure to HIV and hepatitis B and C viruses. They may even suffer a loss of income when they exhibit no loss of physical ability to perform their occupations. Some of the issues they face include:

- Revocation of their licence to practice
- Inability to obtain malpractice insurance
- Laws may compel health care professionals to disclose their condition to their patients, who may thereafter refuse to be treated by them.

Clients in this group include physicians, surgeons, dentists, dental hygienists, dental assistants, chiropodists, podiatrists, lab technicians, nurses, paramedics, respiratory therapists, and acupuncturists.

The rider pays a benefit when the client has tested positive for either HIV or hepatitis B or C, and suffers at least a 20% reduction in earnings. The income loss must be a direct result of the infection, as triggered by the revocation of the client's licence, the inability to obtain malpractice insurance, or the legal requirement to disclose the condition to their patients. The benefit is payable even though the client may not yet qualify for benefits under the base policy.

Clients may not be eligible to claim under this benefit if they had elected not to take a vaccine that became available prior to their becoming infected, such as the vaccine for the hepatitis B virus that exists today. As this vaccine currently exists, the applicant may be required to be vaccinated in order to be eligible to purchase the benefit.

A few insurers offer a rider that goes beyond the legal issues, and also covers the ethical or moral considerations that infected people may be faced with. In situations where there is a reasonable expectation that continuing to work would prove a health risk, whether real or perceived, to clients, they can choose to stop work or restrict their duties. Under the rider, there is no requirement for them to reveal their status to others in order to qualify for benefits, and they do not need to be subject to any type of official sanction, such as losing their licence.

The premium that is charged for this option can be changed at any time, although the insurer may guarantee not to make a further change for five more years if a rate change is initiated. Typically, premiums on optional benefits attached to a non-cancellable DI policy are guaranteed like the base contract. This is one of the few instances where an optional benefit's rate guarantee is different from that of its base policy.

CATCH-UP RIDER

This option is a unique rider that provides a lump sum equal to the monthly benefit for total disability multiplied by the number of months in the elimination period. The disability must be a total disability that lasts for a period of at least 180 consecutive days. Another way to consider this is that this feature provides retroactive payment from the first day of disability (effectively waiving the elimination period) so long as there has been a minimum of 180 days of total disability.

SECOND PAYER OPTION

The second payer option allows clients to purchase DI even though they have coverage at work through a mandatory group LTD plan. The reasons they might want to do so are many, but some follow:

- Individual DI is more comprehensive than group LTD.
- Non-cancellable DI has guaranteed rates; LTD does not.
- A departing employee leaves behind the LTD and may risk being uninsurable under another plan of insurance.
- The LTD may not provide enough coverage, leaving an uninsured gap.
- The LTD coverage may have only a two-year regular-occupation definition, and the insured may be fearful that the insurer could force him or her into lower-paying work or terminate benefits.
- The LTD may not cover reduced periods of disability, only total disability.
- The LTD may not provide inflation protection through cost-of-living adjustments during a long-term claim for benefits.

Insurers, on the other hand, must guard against overinsurance. Group LTD does not usually contain an offset to personally owned DI. Neither does individual DI normally contain an offset for group LTD. The second payer option takes care of this concern by amending the policy to pay in circumstances where the group LTD does not. In return for accepting this restriction, the DI insurer grants a discount, usually in the range of 10%. In the event the insured ceases to have group LTD, some insurers require notification, so that they can remove the rate discount. If not notified, the insurer would reduce benefits during a claim by 10%.

Companies take different approaches regarding how the offset works during a claim, but a typical example would involve a dollar-for-dollar offset on only the portion that exceeds the company's maximum limits.

Chapter 6

Disability Insurance Plans and Options for Contract Workers

THE RISE OF CONTRACT WORK

Traditional non-cancellable disability insurance first appeared in the United States as early as 1915. These products were designed to insure people in traditional white-collar occupations, and they evolved in an era when insurers viewed professionals as the most desirable clients. Product designs over the next few decades favoured own-occupation definitions, lifetime benefits, and large benefit amounts.

By the 1970s, insurers sought to expand their business beyond the narrow professional market by targeting the growing number of business owners. Features associated with the existing products were not well suited for business owners, and insurers responded with new products that addressed issues unique to business owners.

Throughout this time, there was a predictable order and timing of major life events — education, then career, marriage, children, grandchildren, and retirement. For most people, employment with large companies offered stability, upward mobility, benefits, and an adequate, predictable pension at age 65.

Traditional products served these markets quite well.

By the 1990s, job creation was no longer prevalent in the sectors that historically purchased disability insurance. Instead, the growth was occurring in temporary employment. For example, in the five-year period between 1989 and 1994, there was a 21% increase in the number of temporary workers, from 799,000 to 970,000.[1] Even these figures underestimate the actual extent of temporary employment, because they do not include those who are legally defined as self-employed, such as individuals who work primarily for one organization but are classified as contract freelancers or consultants. Between 1997 and 2003, temporary work accounted for almost one-fifth of overall growth in paid employment, even though this was a period of economic growth and favourable employment conditions.[2]

[1] Canadian Council on Social Development, "Temporary Employment in Canada", February 26, 1996. http://www.ccsd.ca/pubs/archive/tec/es.htm (accessed from the Internet on September 21, 2011).

[2] Statistics Canada, "Earnings of Temporary versus Permanent Employees", *Perspectives on Labour and Income* 6, no. 1 (January 2005), 75-001-XIE, http://www.statcan.gc.ca/daily-quotidien/050126/dq050126b-eng.htm (accessed from the Internet on September 21, 2011).

In 2009, there were 2.7 million self-employed workers, representing about 16% of all employed workers in Canada. In the past decade, the number of self-employed workers has increased by 11%, while the growth rate in the overall labour force was 17%. Roughly one-third of self-employed workers were female.

This growth was due in part to the inability of individuals to find a permanent job, but it was also due to changes in employers' hiring strategies. Businesses found that temporary work helped them achieve the flexibility required to face strong competition and to deal with rapidly changing technologies and volatile consumer demands. They could hire quickly during peak business periods and cut back just as rapidly when the economy slowed. Because of these workers' temporary status, companies did not have to deal with minimum notice periods and levels of compensation.

Another contributing factor to the growth in this type of job creation was the growing number of women in the labour force, which increased the number of pregnancy-related leaves from 134,000 in 1980 to 254,000 in 1994. This increased the need for hiring temporary workers.

Temporary workers are not a homogeneous group. They are found in almost all industries and occupations. There are almost an equal number of men as there are women. They are found in such fields as clerical work, education, health care, construction and the trades, transportation, and the services industry. They work on contract, as seasonal or casual workers, or through an employment agency. Their education level is also wide ranging, and temporary work is not a youth phenomenon. While some temporary workers earn fairly high wages, most earn lower incomes than those in traditional employment. Those who work as contract employees show the smallest gap in earnings between temporary workers and employees.

Statistics indicate that just under half of these temporary workers move on to their next assignment in less than a month.

Temporary workers can be thought of as predominantly falling into two groups — those who are often referred to as "temps" and those who are "independent contractors". The former are primarily workers who fill lower-paid jobs, and their rise in numbers has been caused largely by cost-reducing considerations on the part of employers. Although this category has been given much media attention, they do not make up the bulk of temporary workers. It is independent contractors who make up close to 75% of temporary workers.

THE CHANGING LABOUR FORCE

A collective look at the labour force as a whole prior to 2006 reveals that the occupation of truck driver was the most prevalent for men, and while this occupation group continued to grow substantially, by 17.4%, between 2001 and 2006, retail sales was the most prevalent occupation for men and women in 2006. One of the fastest growing occupations from 2001 to 2006 was the construction industry — specifically, the number of trade helpers and labourers, which increased by 57.2%. There were large losses in manufacturing occupations during this period, some of which included machine operators, metal fabricators, mechanical and electronics assemblers, and inspectors and testers.

The industry that grew the most quickly was mining and oil and gas extraction, where employment reached an annual average nationwide gain of 7.5% between 2001 and 2006, with Alberta accounting for 70% of this.

Occupations within the expanding spa industry, including aestheticians, electrologists, and other related occupations, experienced the sixth-fastest growth rate, up 57.4% from 2001.

Health care and social assistance, which is Canada's second-largest service industry, increased by just under 200,000 workers, or roughly a 2.6% yearly average increase, which was above the national average. The increases were largest in Ontario, Quebec, and Alberta.

All of these industries and occupations have many people working as independent contractors and temps, and the insurance industry has responded to their unique needs by creating new forms of disability coverage.

Fastest-Growing Occupations in Canada from 2001 to 2006

Occupation	2006 Employment	Percentage Employment Growth, 2001 to 2006
Oil and gas well drillers, servicers, testers, and related workers	11,500	77.8
Production clerks (such as those employed by construction businesses to prepare production schedules)	24,100	73.3
Post-secondary teaching and research assistants	61,500	65.7
Loan officers	35,400	64.5
Construction inspectors	13,700	61.8
Aestheticians, electrologists, and related occupations	36,500	57.4
Construction trades' helpers and labourers	143,900	57.2
Administrative clerks	101,700	53.9
Refrigeration and air conditioning mechanics	21,400	53.6
Petroleum engineers	9,000	53.5

Source: Statistics Canada, censuses of population, 2001 and 2006

Most Prevalent Occupations for Men and Women in Canada, 2006

Men	2006 Employment	2001 to 2006 Employment Change
Retail salespersons and sales clerks	285,800	63,600
Truck drivers	276,200	40,900
Retail trade managers	192,200	-8,100
Janitors, caretakers, and building superintendents	154,100	18,800
Farmers and farm managers	147,800	-21,200
Material handlers	147,000	13,900
Automotive service technicians, truck and bus mechanics, and mechanical repairers	143,000	20,400
Carpenters	142,400	32,900
Construction trades' helpers and labourers	133,600	47,500
Sales, marketing, and advertising managers	102,600	10,200
Women	**2006 Employment**	**2001 to 2006 Employment Change**
Retail salespersons and sales clerks	400,000	68,600
Cashiers	255,500	35,500
Registered nurses	249,400	33,800
General office clerks	244,200	23,100
Secretaries (except legal and medical)	237,300	-16,500
Elementary school and kindergarten teachers	214,600	19,900
Food-counter attendants, kitchen helpers, and related occupations	194,800	23,100
Early-childhood educators and assistants	157,700	31,700
Food and beverage servers	152,000	-2,900
Light-duty cleaners	147,400	24,400

Source: Statistics Canada, censuses of population, 2001 and 2006

Another notable change is the decline in middle-class jobs. There is also a trend towards multitasking and multiskilling in the workplace. The full-time, full-year job is rapidly disappearing. It is estimated that one-third or more of Canadians who remain employed can be found in non-standard work arrangements. In many cases workers voluntarily accept these arrangements; however, a growing segment are entering these arrangements because there are no better employment opportunities available. This affects many aspects of work beyond simply the number of hours worked, such as:

- Access to fringe benefits, including pensions and health, dental, and other insurance programs
- Responsibility and recognition within the workplace
- Promotional opportunities
- General job security
- Power, authority, and ability to directly participate in decision-making processes.

THE UNBUNDLING OF DISABILITY INSURANCE

One of the most notable ways in which products have evolved is the unbundling of disability insurance into its two fundamental components: injury and illness benefits. Now, a person whose primary need is for workplace injury protection can address this risk without concern about insurability for illness coverage. This unbundling also enables the adviser to implement immediate protection that starts the day the application is completed and the policy paid. Those who want to include illness protection can add it as an option, with coverage on this portion of benefits commencing after underwriting is completed. Unbundling of injury and illness also enables greater flexibility in choosing plan design features, such as different amounts, elimination periods, and benefit periods.

Another significant change is how disability is defined. Definitions that use occupation in defining disability create problems for workers during periods of work transition. With the rise in the number of temporary workers, some insurers have responded to this issue by developing alternative definitions based on "tasks" instead of "duties".

A third major difference deals with calculating earnings. Traditional disability income insurance protects "earned income". This definition considers earnings before tax but after business expenses. A problem arises for certain individuals, such as contract workers, who for tax purposes are able to show less annual income than the true value of their earnings, or what can be thought of as "lifestyle income". To recognize this, some insurers have developed special products that are based on gross business revenue instead of net earned income. This enables the insured to purchase coverage that corresponds more closely to the true cash flow that supports his or her cost of living.

Together, these three changes in the fundamental approach to disability insurance have opened up a wide range of coverage options to deal with the changing labour force.

Guarantees in Rates and Coverage

There are many policy formats available in the industry today, offering a range of guarantees. Although they are covered in more detail elsewhere in this book, a few points regarding this topic are worth revisiting at this time.

Insurers offer different formats of disability coverage, including the following:

- Cancellable policies
- Conditionally renewable policies
- Guaranteed renewable policies
- Non-cancellable policies.

Each one offers a different level of guarantees, with cancellable policies offering the least and non-cancellable policies offering the highest.

Cancellable policies allow the insurer to terminate coverage at any time for any reason, upon notification to the policy owner. Any advance premiums paid are refunded.

Conditionally renewable policies provide a limited right to the insurer to refuse renewal of the coverage at the end of a premium payment period for specific reasons listed in the policy. An example may be if the insured changes occupation or ceases to work full-time.

Guaranteed renewable policies must be renewed by the insurer as long as premium payments are made on time up to the age specified in the policy contract. The insurer can change the premium rate on any anniversary, but only if this is done for an entire group of insured individuals. An individual insured cannot be singled out due to a claim for benefits.

Non-cancellable policies prevent the insurer from making changes of any kind without the authorization of the policy owner. Rates cannot be increased and coverage cannot be cancelled. Neither can restrictive riders or exclusions be added to the policy after its purchase. Policies may be classified as both non-cancellable and guaranteed renewable (or non-cancellable and conditionally renewable). In this instance, there is a specified age to which the non-cancellable provision applies (such as age 65), after which it becomes guaranteed renewable (or conditionally renewable) to a certain age (such as age 75).

Early forms of accident coverage were cancellable policies often sold door-to-door in farming communities. Later, conditionally renewable plans emerged and were sold to a wider range of people. Today, injury income plans are available as guaranteed renewable coverage, meeting the needs of independent contractors, retailers, tradespeople, drivers, part-timers, and a host of other workers who may otherwise not qualify for disability income insurance.

Definitions of Disability

Most unbundled injury and illness plans follow the standard occupational approach in defining total disability. The variable from one company to another is in the duration of the "regular occupation" period after which the measure becomes "any occupation". The standard regular occupation periods are 24 months, 36 months, 60 months, and through to age 65. Some companies start with a basic duration, to which the insured can add a regular occupation extension rider, which lengthens the regular occupation period.

The regular occupation period may vary based on occupation class as well. Thus, a 4A category may qualify for a regular occupation period through to age 65, while a 3A receives a 60-month period, and 2A, A, and B receive a 24-month period.

The "regular occupation" refers to the occupation that the insured was performing at the time of disability.

Occupation During the "Any Occupation" Period

How companies define "any occupation" following the regular occupation period may differ from one company to another. Some simply look at the person's education, training, and experience level at the point in time when the definition changes from "regular occupation" to "any occupation". Others may also consider earnings or potential earnings. In this case, the insurer may look at what the insured can currently earn, but also at what the individual might be reasonably *expected* to earn within a reasonable period of time.

Non-Occupational Coverage

Some unbundled injury and illness plans offer people who are covered by WCB/WSIB a method by which they can round out protection by purchasing coverage that only insures against injuries that occur off the job. This provides a lower-cost method of insuring against injury by recognizing that the plan will otherwise offset these benefits received during a claim.

The risk, however, is that in the event of a dispute regarding whether an injury was work-related or not, the insured might receive no benefit from either source.

Partial Disability for Loss of Time or Duties

The policy usually covers insured individuals during periods when they cannot perform all the important duties of their regular occupation, or when they can perform all the duties but for only half the time. This is generally not an income-related measure, but a time and duties measure. The policy sometimes requires a prior period of total disability that precedes the partial disability. This period may match the plan's elimination period, or the policy might stipulate a different time frame, such as 30 days, regardless of the elimination period.

The amount of benefit payable may be fixed at 50% for a period of time, such as two or six months, or it may be reducing, as in the example below:

Sample Definition:

You are entitled to receive 50% of your regular monthly benefit for up to 24 months; then 25% thereafter to the end of your maximum benefit period. In no event can your benefit exceed the benefit period under your contract.

Periods of Unemployment

As periods of unemployment may occur, the policy often defines what will constitute total disability during a period of unemployment.

Sample Definition:

Total Disability means you are unable, due to an accident or due to an illness, to look for remunerative work for which you may be reasonably suited based on your education, training, or experience.

The policy may also include a provision limiting the duration during which the insured remains covered.

Sample Definition for Injury Income Benefits:

Extension of Coverage During Unemployment:

During a period of unemployment, you remain insured for the first 12 months of unemployment in case of total disability due to accident.

The definition for illness income benefits may differ during a period of unemployment, such as in the following example.

Sample Definition for Illness Income Benefits:

During a period of unemployment, you remain insured for 12 months for total disability due to any of the following chronic conditions: stroke, cancer, heart attack, kidney failure, or coronary artery bypass.

Classless Coverage

While most disability plans are based on occupational classification (4A, 3A, 2A, A, B) as the determinant of eligibility, plan design choices, provisions, and rates, some insurers offer unbundled injury and illness plans that do not specify occupational classes at all.

Such policies offer a lower monthly income benefit (such as a $2,000 maximum) and optional illness income benefits that focus on critical conditions only. These conditions include cancer, stroke, coronary artery bypass, heart attack, and kidney failure.

Insurers offer a wide variety of elimination periods, such as 0-day, 14-day, 30-day, and 120-day, and injury income benefits for up to one year, two years, or five years, or through to age 65.

This can be an excellent source of coverage for people whose occupations would otherwise prevent buying any disability coverage, such as people in uninsurable occupations, those lacking stability in work history, and those who are newly hired or are lacking job experience.

Coverage for People Without Remunerative Work

The need for income during injury or illness is not restricted solely to those who have earned income. Consider the following examples:

- Spouse who is home raising children
- Person recently laid off work with fixed debts, such as a mortgage
- New immigrant who is not yet in the workforce
- Volunteers
- Part-time workers with very low earnings.

Unbundled injury and illness plans are available for people who do not have remunerative work. These policies measure total disability as the inability due to injury or illness to perform usual "daily tasks" and any other tasks for which they are reasonably qualified by education or experience. The maximum benefit is $1,000 per month and can begin as early as the 14th day of disability, payable for up to five years. Integration provisions allow the full $1,000 benefit to be collected for the first 24 months without offset from other sources. Thereafter, offsets from other sources may occur.

OTHER PROVISIONS

Insurers have developed many new and innovative provisions to enhance coverage within unbundled injury and illness income plans. They are built into the contract without additional charge. Some increase the regular benefit under certain circumstances; others ease the return to work. There are also provisions that help with major adjustment expenses by paying a lump-sum benefit when it may be needed the most. Following are some examples of these innovative features.

Provisions That Increase Benefits

Increase for Loss of Two or More Activities of Daily Living

This benefit is designed to increase the regular monthly benefit by a fixed percentage, such as 25%, if a total disability prevents the insured from performing two or more activities of daily living ("ADLs") unassisted. These activities include eating, dressing, using the toilet, transferring, and bathing. ADLs are a common part of long-term care insurance plans.

Automatic Benefit Increase

This benefit is a form of predisability indexing. The insured can decide at the time of purchasing the original policy whether or not to "turn on" this feature. It provides for an automatic increase in the amount of coverage equal to the CPI index (up to a stipulated annual maximum, such as 3%). If the automatic increase feature is turned on, this adjustment takes place annually on the contract renewal date. There is a corresponding increase in the monthly premium for the additional coverage each year. If the increase is refused on the anniversary date, no further increases take place.

Accident Medical Reimbursement Benefit

This benefit reimburses medical expenses related to an injury, such as hospital and ambulance costs, and other practitioners' fees not covered by the provincial health insurance plan. The amount covered may vary, starting at $10,000.

Provisions That Ease Return to Work

Insurers recognize that medical expenses may continue initially following a return to work, and to encourage the insured through the adjustment, most offer some continuation of benefits. The following are examples of benefits offered.

Return-to-Work Bonus

This benefit provides a lump-sum bonus based upon how long the duration of the disability was prior to the return to work. For example, a disability that lasted two to five years may pay the equivalent of three times the regular monthly benefit in the month following return to full-time work, while a disability that lasted five years or more may pay six times the regular monthly benefit.

Rehabilitation Assistance Benefit

This benefit provides financial assistance to support an early return to work. Rather than a fixed and predetermined benefit, the insurer works together with the insured to offer rehabilitation assistance that supports a return to work.

Extension Benefit for Commissioned Workers

This benefit is a form of recovery benefit intended to recognize that upon return to work, commissioned workers require time to build up their earnings, either because they have lost customers and need to re-establish a client base or because there is a lapse between the occurrence of a sale and the payment of a commission. It provides for three months of continued benefits according to a reducing scale, which generally provides for 75% of the regular monthly benefit in the first month of return, 50% of the regular monthly benefit in the second month following return, and finally, 25% of the regular monthly benefit in the third month following return. There may also be a requirement that the total disability must have lasted at least six months or more in order for the insured to be entitled to the benefit.

Provisions That Provide Lump-Sum Payment

Lump-Sum Death Benefit

This benefit pays a lump sum equal to three times the regular monthly benefit in the event of the death of the insured, if total disability has lasted for 12 or more months and results in death.

Lump Sum Upon Permanent, Total Disability

This benefit pays a lump sum of 50 times the monthly benefit up to a stipulated maximum, such as $100,000, if the insured suffers a disability that is total and permanent. The additional dollars help to cover the additional expenses related to suffering a severe disability. This is not a buyout of the disability income benefit, but a payout that is in addition to the regular monthly benefit.

Provisions Related to Premium Payments

Waiver of Premium

As with other forms of disability insurance, unbundled injury and illness plans provide for premiums to be waived when the insured is disabled. There are two features to look at when reviewing this provision:

- How soon are premiums waived?
- For how long are premiums waived?

Some plans waive premiums sooner than others — some as early as 30 days following disability, others not until 120 days. Some plans only waive premiums while benefits are being paid; others waive premiums so long as the person is disabled. This could mean a longer period of waiver for someone whose disability extends beyond the maximum benefit period purchased.

Premium Reimbursement Benefit

To encourage the insured to maintain coverage in force, some policies include a provision for partial reimbursement of premiums less claims paid, after the insured reaches a certain age. This feature normally provides for 50% of the premiums to be reimbursed at age 65, less any claims paid during the life of the policy. The insured may still be entitled to a partial refund upon early cancellation of coverage, if coverage has been maintained to at least age 60. In this event, the refund is reduced by a stipulated factor for each month of early cancellation prior to age 65. This provision may apply only to an insured who has purchased coverage before a specified age (such as age 45), thereby ensuring that the company receives a minimum of 20 years of paid premiums.

This feature is similar, but not identical, to the premium refund option, described later in this section.

Provisions That Reduce Benefits

Integration of Benefits with Other Sources

Most policies protect against overinsurance by means of an integration provision, which reduces benefits by income from other sources. This provision defines the other sources that will be offset, and also describes how the calculation will be made. Some plans may offset only for income from government benefits, while others may also include other personal disability insurance plans. The adjustment may be a dollar-for-dollar reduction or only the amount in excess of a certain percentage, such as amounts above 80% of the insured's predisability earnings.

Some policies ignore other sources of income for an initial period of time, such as in the example below.

Sample Provision:

> For the first 24 months of disability benefit payments, the first $1,000 are guaranteed. Only the amount in excess of $1,000 is reduced by the amount of any benefits payable under other plans.

Such policies are very useful as a means of insuring loans, such as mortgages, car payments, or outstanding credit card balances. In the event of injury or illness, the insured will have $1,000 to put towards debt, and the regular disability benefits or government benefits can be used for other necessities.

Organ Donation

Some policies contain a provision to recognize organ donation as an "illness", which is therefore eligible for claiming a benefit. Without this provision, a person who voluntarily donates an organ, such as a kidney, to another person would not be considered disabled under the terms of the policy contract. In an unbundled injury and illness plan, this provision clearly defines organ donation as related to illness coverage, and consequently, no benefit would be paid to an individual who purchased injury-only coverage. This provision normally requires that the insured's policy has been in force for at least 12 months. This helps to protect the company from anti-selection, where people purchase the illness benefits knowing in advance that they will be donating an organ.

OPTIONAL RIDERS

Premium Refund Option

Some companies provide the option for the insured to receive a full or partial refund at age 65 or upon early termination. An additional premium is charged for this optional benefit. This feature helps clients to deal with the concern, "What if I purchase this plan and I don't need it?" The maximum refund entitlement may be based upon the age when the insured signed their application. For example, it may provide a 100% refund to an insured who purchased coverage before age 46, but only 50% refund to an insured who purchased coverage after age 45. This guarantees the company a certain minimum number of premium-paying years.

In the event of early termination after age 60 but before age 65, this maximum amount is then further reduced by a stipulated adjustment factor for the number of months of early termination.

A claim for benefits does not necessarily mean that the insured forfeits the right to a premium refund; however, as the sum of claims paid during the life of the policy are subtracted from the premium refund entitlement, a large claim could wipe out the balance otherwise refundable.

Indexation of Benefits During a Claim

This option is a cost-of-living increase to help the insured deal with inflation during a long-term claim. For an additional rate, the insured can have benefits adjusted after being on claim for 12 months. The increase is tied to the Consumer Price Index up to a stipulated maximum, such as 3%.

Health, Drug, and Dental Benefits

Some companies offer optional health, drug, and dental benefits, which can be added to an injury and illness benefit plan to create a comprehensive range of personal benefits. More about health, drug, and dental plans is covered in Chapter 15.

Critical Illness Benefits

Some companies offer critical illness coverage, which is used as an alternative to an illness income rider for various reasons. There are two types of riders: one that covers primary conditions only (stroke, cancer, heart attack, kidney failure, coronary artery bypass) and one that covers a much wider range of conditions (often 16 or more). Critical illness insurance is dealt with in more detail in Chapter 18.

Hospital Allowance Benefits

This coverage pays a benefit as a daily allowance when the individual is hospitalized due to illness or injury. Amounts can range from $25 per day to

$100 per day. This benefit helps the insured to deal with incidental expenses while hospitalized. For instance, a spouse who visits may incur parking expenses, child care costs, and other incidental costs.

Accidental Fracture Benefit

This benefit pays a lump sum in the case of fracture of a bone. The amount payable varies depending on the fracture incurred. For instance, a significant fracture, such as a fracture of the skull, spinal column, pelvis, femur, or hip, may pay the full principal amount of the benefit, such as $5,000 or $10,000. Fractures in other bones may pay one-quarter of the principal amount or less. This payment helps to deal with expenses that may be related to the injury. Payment of the benefit is not based upon whether or not time is lost from work.

Accidental Death and Loss of Use

This benefit pays a principal sum in the event of death due to an accident and a percentage of the principal sum in the event of a covered loss, as listed in the benefit. The principal sum purchased may be as high as $500,000, depending upon the limit set by the insurer. The benefit stipulates the maximum elapsed time between the accidental event and the date of death that will be considered as the related event causing death (such as 12 months). Some policies will also pay the principal sum if the insured becomes a quadriplegic or paraplegic.

Some companies distinguish their benefit from "plain vanilla" versions by adding additional payment features such as daycare, education, home alteration, and vehicle modification benefits.

Some companies unbundle the benefit into two separate options — accidental death benefit and loss of use benefit.

Post-Accident Adaptations Benefit

This benefit provides coverage for adaptations to a vehicle and the person's residence following a permanent motor impairment caused by an accident. The cost of such benefits is relatively small. For example, $15,000 of coverage can cost as little as $1 per month, making it a relatively low-cost benefit with high value.

Medical Expenses Due to Accident Benefit

This is another relatively low-cost benefit with high value. For less than $1 a month, this benefit provides for reimbursement of medical expenses that result from an accident. The coverage may provide for unlimited expenses related to the purchase or lease of equipment such as respirators, wheelchairs, oxygen systems, and crutches. Other expenses may be covered, up to specified limits in the policy, for prostheses and accessories, chiropractic X-rays, ambulance, lab tests, preferred hospital accommodation, paramedical services, nursing care, and accident-related dental care.

Travel Insurance

This benefit covers unexpected emergency medical expenses when the insured travels outside the province or country of residence. The plan will cover an unlimited number of trips per year, and it will specify the maximum number of days the person can be travelling at any one time. Examples include 15 days, 30 days, or 60 days per trip. Plans normally exclude pre-existing conditions that were present within a period prior to each departure, such as the past 90 or 180 days.

Some may include trip cancellation, early return, and lost baggage. The insured must be covered by the government health insurance plan, as this type of coverage is for unexpected expenses over and above the government's coverage. This benefit will contain other specific exclusions and limitations that apply outside of the limitations and exclusions that apply to the base policy to which this rider is added. More information about travel insurance as a stand-alone policy is covered in detail in Chapter 17.

LIMITATIONS AND EXCLUSIONS

There are limitations and exclusions in all policy contracts. These are situations or conditions for which the policy pays no benefit or only a limited benefit. The adviser should review all in detail at the point of sale, so there are no surprises at the time of a claim. Some standard examples follow.

Pre-Existing Conditions

To protect against anti-selection, insurers may exclude any disability that begins within the first 12 months of the effective date of coverage if it is related to a condition that existed prior to the purchase of the policy. This means that if the insured had a medical consultation, took a prescription medication, or incurred any health-related expenses on the advice of a physician, the condition is considered pre-existing and not covered in the first 12 months. It may also be excluded, even if no medical advice was sought, if it is proven that the insured had symptoms that would normally prompt a prudent person to seek medical advice.

Limited Payouts

Some policies have limited payouts for certain conditions, such as back, neck, and soft tissue problems. In the past, insurers have had difficulties with repeated claims in these areas. They have also had difficulties with pain-related claims based on self-reported symptoms rather than independent diagnostic tests. For instance, consider the following scenario. Jack, facing a layoff at work, suddenly reports soreness in the lower back. He visits his doctor and reports the pain, and the doctor prescribes a muscle relaxant and advises him to stay home and rest a while. Jack puts a claim in for his insurance. Tests do not substantiate that there is any physical condition or anatomic abnormality to explain Jack's symptoms; the individual simply reported pain to his physician. The presumption is that since the doctor fills in an attending physician's report confirming the visit, the symptoms are reported, and the medication is prescribed, it should qualify as a claim. Was the pain real? Perhaps, but when he was not faced with stress from the fear of layoff, Jack was coping well and able to work. In this respect, there is some interaction between workplace stress and claims for back, neck, and soft tissue conditions.

To deal with these issues, insurers use specific language in policies indicating that related claims must be substantiated by diagnostic medical tests; and the repetitive nature of claims for these conditions has led insurers to limit back, neck, and soft tissue claims.

The length of payment for these claims may differ based on the occupation classification, as incidence rates rise with heavier manual work, but not all companies differentiate by occupation classification. Following are some examples of policy wording that might be used by a company to limit claims in these areas:

Example 1:

> Benefits payable due to herniated disc, as cause or effect, are limited to a maximum of six months per event.

Example 2:

> Back and neck injuries must be substantiated by diagnostic medical tests in order to qualify for payment.

Example 3:

> Soft tissue injuries are limited to a maximum of 40 days for Class B and 60 days for Class A. Once you have received a total of 180 days of payments, no further claims can be made for soft tissue injuries.

Soft tissues are the muscles, nerves, ligaments, tendons, and joints. Soft tissue injuries may include sprains, strains, tendinitis, carpal tunnel syndrome, bursitis, and also plantar fasciitis. These are often referred to as "repetitive strain injuries" or "cumulative trauma disorders". The incidence rates for claims in this category are increasing. They can be gradually debilitating; that is to say, the passage of time from when the initial symptoms appear to when the person is no longer able to cope with work due to the problem can be quite long. According to the Manitoba Workers' Compensation Board, an average of eight months elapses between the initial symptoms and the filing of a claim.[3]

---

[3] http://www.qp.gov.bc.ca/rcwc/research/hogg-johnson-interventions.pdf (accessed September 21, 2011).

Lower-back pain, neck pain, and arm pain are among the most common causes of disability in industrialized countries. Evidence suggests that between 50% and 80% of the population will experience back pain during their lifetime. Cases of back pain constitute the largest single category of lost-time claims to workers' compensation boards in North America, representing about 30% of all lost-time claims, with the majority of these being for sprains and strains. The initial cause may be a traumatic incident, such as a fall or a blow, or repetitive or continuous exposure to physically heavy work, vibration, bending and twisting, or sedentary posture. There is evidence suggesting that psychosocial stressors at work also play a role in both the development of and the recovery from back pain.

Neck pain is also common in the working-age population, and it also results from a combination of work-related physical and psychosocial factors.

Statistics show that if it is possible to get these claimants back to work fast, the recovery rate improves; lacking that, they often turn into long-term claims. Offering coverage with limited payouts is a method of encouraging early return, and it is also a way to protect the insurer from the soaring costs related to rising claims in this area, which otherwise would necessitate one of the following:

- Eliminating certain occupations deemed to be at high risk
- Excluding coverage altogether for these types of claims
- Increasing rates to a point where the coverage would not be affordable.

The goal of unbundling injury and illness coverage is to enable a broader range of people to be able to purchase insurance protection. Use of limited payment provisions helps to support this goal of making some coverage available to people who might otherwise not be able to get any coverage.

Degenerative Disc Disease: Injury or Illness?

Some insurers consider this to be an illness and, therefore, subject to the terms of payout under the illness benefit if purchased in addition to injury coverage. As with other back limitations, it may be subject to a maximum payout per claim (such as 15 or 20 days) and a lifetime maximum for the life of the policy (such as 120 or 160 days).

Excluded Risks

There are many excluded risks considered standard; normally, they would not be of concern to the average buyer. Examples of these are:

- Flying in an aircraft that is not a certified passenger aircraft
- Participating in professional athletics

- Injury while committing a criminal offence
- Being a member of the armed forces
- Alcohol abuse
- Attempted suicide
- Intentionally self-inflicted injury
- Normal pregnancy or childbirth
- Cosmetic care or treatment
- Experimental care or new procedures not commonly used
- Participation in insurrection, riot, or war
- Operating a motor vehicle while intoxicated
- Participation in dangerous or risky sports such as hang-gliding, parachute jumping, rock climbing, bungee jumping, car racing, or scuba diving
- HIV/AIDS whose symptoms manifested themselves prior to the effective date of coverage
- Subjective conditions, such as chronic fatigue syndrome, chronic pain syndrome, fibromyalgia, and Epstein-Barr syndrome
- Mental and nervous disorders, such as depression, burnout, anxiety, or other psychotic, emotional, or behavioural disorders.

Perhaps most controversial in this list is the exclusion of claims due to subjective conditions and mental/nervous disorders.

Why Exclude Subjective Conditions?

Some conditions, such as chronic fatigue, chronic pain, fibromyalgia, and Epstein-Barr syndrome, have no "marker" that can prove definitely whether or not the person has a disabling condition. Further, it is fair to ask if it should even be considered for payment in an injury-only policy; perhaps, if anything, its rightful place is in the illness category. These "hidden conditions", like depression and back or neck pain, present a challenge for insurance companies because they are generally based on self-reported symptoms and not verifiable standard medical tests or procedures. It is difficult for the insurer to separate them from psychological illnesses or even outright fraud.

Subjective complaints alone are not considered conclusive evidence of a disability, and attending physicians must be able to provide objective medical evidence to support their opinion as to why the client is not able to perform the duties of their occupation (or any other occupation for which they may be qualified). Diagnosis alone does not equal disability. Disability occurs when an individual lacks the ability to perform the duties of an occupation.

In the absence of these safeguards, anyone could claim not to be able to work because the pain is too great. Pain is something that cannot be seen on an X-ray or other diagnostic imaging test, but the presence of an underlying condition causing pain may be.

Claims adjudication relies on objectively verifiable data, which is not present in these types of claims. The incidence of disability claims based on self-reported conditions has increased dramatically in the last two decades, and studies have shown that such claims are among the fastest growing causes of disability claims in North America.

While there surely are good-faith subjective disability claims, the area holds enormous potential for fraud and abuse. The claims are problematic because the complaint is easy to make but almost impossible to refute. In response to these difficulties, some carriers simply refuse to cover these risks under their policies.

Why Exclude Mental and Nervous Disorders?

Approximately 8% of adults will experience major depression at some time in their lives.[4] At any given time, approximately three million Canadians have serious depression, but only 6% of those people are diagnosed and treated effectively. Lost work time among those who suffer mood disorders is 60% greater than among other employees. According to the Public Health Agency of Canada, one episode of major depression is a strong predictor of future episodes. More than 50% of individuals who have an episode of major depression experience a recurrence.[5] Thirty per cent of all disability claims are related to a mental illness. Depression is the fastest-growing category of disability claims in North America.

Claims Submission

Companies require timely submission of claims, and the deadline for submission must be met if the claim is to be considered for payment. This is usually 90 days from the date of the incident that gave rise to the claim. Failure to submit a claim within the stipulated time limit does not invalidate the claim if it can be proved that it was physically impossible to submit the claim and that it was submitted in as timely a fashion as possible, and it was submitted not later than 12 months following the date the disabling incident occurred.

Companies are quite strict in enforcing this provision, and the adviser should stress the importance to the client of timely submission. Even a claim under a policy that has a 120-day elimination period should be reported immediately.

---

[4] Health Canada, *A Report on Mental Illness in Canada*, http://www.phac-aspc.gc.ca/publicat/miic-mmac/chap_2-eng.php (Ottawa 2002), accessed September 15, 2011.

[5] D. Spaner, R.C. Bland, and S.C. Newman, "Major depressive disorder", *Acta Psychiatrica Scandinavica* (1994) Suppl 376:7-15.

Companies use programs such as early intervention and stay-at-work programs as means of reducing or eliminating claims. It has been shown that a disability mindset can otherwise set in and delay the ultimate return to work. By breaking the disability cycle, insurers have success in reducing the incidence and duration of claims. Early notification that a claim may be forthcoming enables the insurer to initiate programs that help both the insured and the insurer.

INSURING INDEPENDENT OPERATORS

Unbundled disability insurance policies are a popular method of covering independent operators (sometimes referred to as independent contractors) who are not covered by workers' compensation in provinces where workers' compensation is optional for such individuals. An independent operator is a self-employed individual who does not have any other paid staff and operates independently.

Unbundled disability insurance policies can be tailored to closely replicate benefits provided through workers' compensation, as illustrated in the chart below.

	Workers' Compensation	**Unbundled DI**
Coverage Type	On-the-job injury	24-hour injury
Elimination Period	1st day	1st day
Benefit Period	To age 65	Age 65 to 70
Lump-Sum Benefits	For permanent impairments	Provided by adding AD&D benefit
Rehabilitation	Assistance with return to work	A combination of benefits under AD&D and the policy's rehabilitation benefit
Optional Enhancement		Can include sickness income benefits if desired

One of the most problematic areas of workers' compensation coverage involves independent operators. They are found in many high-risk occupations such as construction, landscaping, mechanical trades, and trucking. In Ontario, the Workplace Safety and Insurance Board (WSIB) uses a series of questionnaires by industry to determine whether the independent operator's status is considered "independent" for WSIB purposes. This series includes a questionnaire for each of the following industries: trucking, taxi, retail, courier, general independent operator, logging, and construction. To determine their status, the WSIB examines their relationship with employers in the following areas:

- The number of hours worked for each specific "employer".
- Who provides and pays for the equipment and tools necessary to perform the job.

- Whether the individual can set his or her own hours of operation, days of work, and location for work.
- Whether the individual hires staff or helpers.

The more control the business has over the independent operator, the less likely he or she will be viewed as an independent operator. If an employment relationship is deemed to exist then the employer must provide coverage through workers' compensation and the individual does not have the choice to buy private coverage in lieu of it.

Several provinces have concerns about the exposure facing independent operators and feel that in addition to the safety risk, those who opt out have an unfair competitive advantage by not having to pay workers' compensation premiums. Ontario has addressed this with new legislation (Bill 119) expected to be effective in 2012. It will be joining other provinces that have already done the same, including Alberta, Saskatchewan, Manitoba, and New Brunswick.

The changes will affect independent operators in the construction industry only, but this includes (but is not limited to) a variety of occupations such as electrical, mechanical, and sheet metal work, drywalling, painting, carpeting, and roofing. It does not extend to trucking.

The concern in the construction industry is that individuals often work as independent operators without paying workers' compensation premiums. In some situations this person may be injured and deemed to be actually working for an employer, thereby entitling him or her to benefits through workers' compensation even though no premiums have been paid on his or her behalf. This is seen as both unfair to companies who pay premiums and as undermining the basic principles of risk-sharing that workers' compensation is founded upon. The new legislation is seen as helping to "fight the underground economy in construction" while simultaneously improving workplace health and safety.

Under the new rules, if an independent operator does not comply with payment obligations, the hiring company must pay the premium and may then deduct the equivalent amount from payment owed to the independent operator. The hiring company could face a fine of up to $100,000 (individuals face a fine up to $25,000 and/or six months in prison) for hiring the independent operator without checking for a clearance certificate.

The new legislation is expected to affect roughly 150,000 individuals. In 2007, there were 3,500 independent operators covered by workers' compensation optional coverage, and 77 injuries were reported.

Chapter 7

Designing the Disability Insurance Plan

During the plan design stage, the adviser's primary objective is to tailor the plan to the client's priorities while working within the parameters of the product and underwriting guidelines. This stage, also known as "programming the coverage", occurs after the adviser has completed a detailed fact-finding session with the client. There are six steps to this phase:

1. Create a synopsis of relevant information.
2. Select the series.
3. Select the product and optional benefits.
4. Select the benefit amount.
5. Select the elimination period.
6. Select the benefit period.

The adviser must help the client strike the right balance between cost containment and provision/features enrichment. This is accomplished through discussions regarding financial priorities and risk tolerance during the fact-finding interviews that precede the plan design phase of the planning process.

Once the plan design has been drafted, the adviser is ready to prepare the quotation for presentation to the client. The adviser can prepare the quote using company-provided illustration software, or request its preparation through the insurer's sales and service office. The illustration should include an overview of the product's provisions and features.

CREATE SYNOPSIS OF RELEVANT INFORMATION

To begin the plan design process, the adviser must assemble the following client details from the fact-finding session previously conducted. This information will be used to generate a client quote.

Personal Information

- Birthdate and gender
- Current smoker status and length of time as such
- Current general health status and significant medical conditions
- Confirmation of permanent resident status if not a Canadian citizen.

Income Details

	Current Year	Last Year	Two Years Ago
Base Salary or Draw			
Bonus			
Commissions			
Unearned Income			
Net Worth			

- If the client uses spousal income splitting (sharing of the client's income between spouses for tax-planning purposes), the same information should be gathered concerning the spouse's earnings, along with an outline of exact hours worked and duties performed by the spouse within the client's business and outside the client's business.
- If the client is a sole proprietor, partner, or shareholder in a business, the adviser must also gather the business financial information for the past two full calendar years, including the statement of income and expenses and the balance sheet of all related businesses, for a consolidated view of the client as a whole.

Securing detailed financial information may seem like a daunting task. Some advisers are initially not comfortable requesting it from the client, fearing a request for a significant amount of personal information may jeopardize the sale. Clients are more likely to have a negative reaction if they have not been briefed early in the process regarding the overall steps that will take place, and how this process protects the client, not just the insurer.

Let us assume that the client is 35 years old and is purchasing a $3,000 monthly benefit to age 65. The value of this benefit is $1.26 million, not $3,500 (the full income stream generated if the client is disabled after purchasing the policy). A client who approaches a bank for a $1 million business loan must provide similar financial information plus a business plan to the financial officer, and the bank underwrites the loan prior to its approval. The bank wants to be sure that the business is financially sound and not likely to close. Insuring the client's earnings through disability insurance (DI) involves income verification in addition to medical information (income is being insured for medical reasons). By completing this process at the time of purchase, the client can be confident that overinsurance has not occurred. Overinsurance (purchasing more than the insured was entitled to) discovered during a claim results in reduced benefits or rescission. Banks do not defer underwriting loans until the business files for bankruptcy; and neither do insurance companies. The application is a legal document, like a loan application, and the client's signature attests to the amount of earned income (among other details). Insurers have a specific definition of what they consider insurable earned income. The adviser plays a significant role in terms of explaining the process, clarifying the definition, and securing the information.

Employment Information

- Length of time in current occupation, and if current length of time is less than three years, length of time in previous occupation
- Length of time with present employer
- If self-employed, length of time and number of employees
  - Determine whether business is located within the residence
  - Determine whether there are written contracts with business clients
- Job title
- Description of duties
  - Percentage of manual duties
  - Percentage of selling duties
  - Percentage of administration
  - Total number of days per year spent outside of Canada, average stay per trip, and countries visited
- Average number of hours worked per week.

Particulars Concerning Existing Benefits

- Whether Employment Insurance (EI) and/or Workers' Compensation Board (WCB)/Workplace Safety and Insurance Board (WSIB) are in place
- Total amount of existing DI benefits (taxable or non-taxable)
- Total amount of existing group long-term disability (LTD) insurance benefits (taxable or non-taxable)
- Indication of whether any existing benefits are being terminated upon acceptance of new plan
- Eligibility in the near future for group insurance benefits if not presently covered today.

SELECT THE SERIES

The adviser assists the client in selecting coverage from the appropriate contract series:

- Non-cancellable
- Guaranteed renewable
- Conditionally renewable.

The cost of the plan reduces with the degree of guarantee provided. While the premium savings may be attractive, consider the time frame for coverage and the effect of trends in claims from emerging illnesses and changes in economic cycles. Rates that are not guaranteed can increase in the future.

Lower-risk clients, such as professionals, executives, and office workers, will have more choice, while higher-risk occupations, part-time workers, newly self-employed people, and certain home-based workers will have less choice.

When presenting an illustration to a client, explain the potential for rate changes under the guaranteed renewable series as well as the insurer's right to terminate coverage (if the conditionally renewable series has been recommended).

Suggesting to the client that a rate change is unlikely simply based upon an insurer's previous history is not wise, because no one knows what the future holds. Explain both the benefits and the limitations of the product proposed. Insurers are shifting to non-guaranteed rates to enable themselves to take corrective action if necessary in future years. Advisers who promise otherwise may be faced with problems similar to past problems that faced the life insurance industry involving "vanishing premiums" that failed to vanish when interest rates did not meet expectations.

SELECT THE PRODUCT AND OPTIONAL BENEFITS

The client's occupation will narrow the range of options for products and riders. Most companies offer two or three product alternatives and a variety of riders to the lowest-risk occupations, while high-risk occupations may have only one product with a smaller range of optional riders available.

Shareholder-Employee Considerations

Shareholder-employees have the ability to control their income during a disability. They can leave income in the business simply by choosing not to take a salary or draw. For this reason, some argue that they are best advised to purchase an occupational contract with a "duties-based" partial disability rider instead of an "earnings-based" residual definition policy. (This may be a requirement, not an option with some insurers.) This enables them to measure disability at the time of a claim based solely upon whether the client is able to perform his or her regular duties or has a loss of time.

Some insurers simply use the earnings-based definitions and address this concern by defining "earned income" as including the insured's portion of net profits of any business in which the insured has an ownership interest. As a result, money left in the business will still be considered earnings to the insured. These insurers hold the view that the issue is not whether the insured can work; it is whether the insured is continuing to receive an income. Where the business is large enough to continue to generate revenue during the shareholder-employee's disability, a duties-based definition is of greater benefit to the client. However, when the business chiefly consists of the shareholder-employee and revenue to the business is directly affected by the disability, the earnings-based definition will provide the client with benefits closely linked to financial changes.

Optional Benefit Considerations

Some riders are available as stand-alone policies, such as the retirement savings rider and the critical illness rider. There may be minimal difference in cost as a stand-alone policy, but the client may achieve greater flexibility by purchasing two separate policies.

Value Addition Checklist

Some options add value, while some are merely window dressing. A fully loaded contract may cost the client a significant premium, and the dollars may be better utilized for maximizing RRSP contributions or investing in mutual funds. The following checklist may aid in the assessment.

- ❐ Does the rider directly and significantly increase the amount of monthly benefit? (e.g., cost-of-living protection, guaranteed insurability protection)
- ❐ Does the rider make the definition of disability more comprehensive for a broad range of disabilities, as opposed to only a limited range of conditions?
- ❐ How likely is the protected event to occur? (e.g., adding protection for voluntary cosmetic surgery versus allocating extra dollars to planned retirement)
- ❐ Is the event already covered under some other form of insurance that the client has? Duplication of benefits provisions may result in the payment of premiums for benefits that the client will not be able to collect.

SELECT THE BENEFIT AMOUNT

During the needs evaluation process, advisers work with the client to determine the ideal income requirement by deducting existing monthly sources from monthly expenses. But how reliable are existing sources? (Some will be more reliable than others during a disability.) The adviser should work with the client to arrive at a "weighting" (reliability factor) as to how well each existing source eliminates exposure during a disability. Some risk is always present; the goal is to minimize it by reviewing definitions of disability, exclusions, and potential situations not covered, and arrive at individual weightings — "highly reliable", "somewhat reliable", "reliable", "somewhat unreliable" (unlikely to pay), or "very unreliable" (high risk of continued exposure). The client can then decide how comfortable he or she is with the degree of risk exposure for each income source, and whether or not to address it. A review might include looking at each source regarding how well it addresses areas such as total or reduced disability (in the client's own occupation or another occupation), injury at work or at home, illness, short- and long-term disability, periods of high inflation, and fluctuation in interest rates or capital values (for non-insured sources). Income adequacy should always be measured on a net after-tax basis, given that some sources may generate taxable income while others may not.

Example of Evaluating Risk Exposure for Each Existing Source

EXISTING SOURCE:	HIGHLY RELIABLE	SOMEWHAT RELIABLE	RELIABLE	SOMEWHAT UNRELIABLE	VERY UNRELIABLE
Can't work at all (own occ or another)					
Can't work in own occ; able to work in new occ (but does not)					
Can't work in own occ; able to work in new occ (and does)					
Can work in own occ, but on reduced basis only					
Injury at work					
Injury at home					
Sickness					
Short-term needs					
Long-term needs					
Periods of high inflation					
Periods of fluctuating interest/capital values					

The ultimate goal is to avoid overreliance on benefit sources that could be limited, ultimately cease, or never pay a benefit. For example, workers' compensation never pays a benefit for injury at home, leaving high exposure in this area. Similarly, group LTD may not pay a partial benefit for periods of reduced disability in one's occupation. This helps the client to better appreciate the many different faces of "disability" and his or her personal areas of vulnerability.

Each insurer has its own maximum limits set forth based upon the lesser of the amount stated in the Income Ratio Guide and the company's maximum issue and participation limits. The former is an earnings-based scale, and the latter is an occupation- and age-based scale. Regardless of the client's "ideal income requirement", it will not be possible to purchase more than the lesser of these two scales.

In most circumstances, clients will require the maximum amount allowed, as this will still fall short of their normal earnings level. Insurers have designed the Income Ratio Guide to maintain an incentive gap, thereby encouraging a return to work, and this shortfall is usually in the range of 20% to 25%.

The evaluation of existing sources may reveal client concerns about the reliability of existing mandatory group LTD benefits. Second payer provisions provide a method of protecting against limited payment or no payment under some disability scenarios where group LTD does not pay but individual DI will pay.

Health care expenses often increase during a disability, so there may also be a need for other health coverage, such as extended health benefits and critical illness insurance. The client should also address the area of long-term care planning, as a permanent injury or illness can cause inability to perform activities of daily living or a permanent cognitive impairment. (Advisers can review the sections dealing with these topics for more information.)

Some advisers might consider underinsuring the disability income need and adding the guaranteed insurability option, given that some insurers allow it to be exercised during a disability.

There are several potential flaws with this strategy:

1. Only one or two companies allow the benefit being exercised under the option to be collected during the current claim. Most insurers stipulate that the additional benefit can only be collected during a future claim. Those that do allow it limit the benefit amount and impose a waiting period.

2. The client's income may have decreased during the immediate years prior to disability, so the client is now unable to support the exercise of the option with financial evidence. Had the benefit been purchased at the time the client originally qualified, the benefit during the claim would be based upon the full amount purchased.

3. The option cannot be exercised until the next policy anniversary. If the disability occurs just after the anniversary has passed, the next opportunity for increase could be as long as 11 months away.
4. Several optional benefits are based upon the policy amount of the basic plan. Lowering the base policy amount also limits the optional benefit amount that can be purchased. The guaranteed insurability option may allow an increase of the base policy only, and not of the riders. This could affect features such as the increase under a cost-of-living rider and the amount of coverage that can be purchased as a retirement savings rider.

SELECT THE ELIMINATION PERIOD

The "elimination period" refers to the number of days of disability that must pass from when the disability occurred to the time the benefit is payable. It is a self-insuring period and is similar to a deductible found in other types of insurance. Besides allowing the plan to be tailored to fit the financial ability and priorities of the client, the wide range of elimination periods can also be used to program coverage around other existing sources of income. Examples include 30, 60, 90, 120, 365, and 722 days.

Consider the sources of income that the client will have available during disability, such as accounts receivable, and financial commitments, such as mortgages or loans.

Keep in mind that benefits, like paycheques, are received in arrears. Therefore, a client who has a 60-day elimination period will not receive the first benefit payment until the 90th day. When a client is off for a period of less than one month but has satisfied the elimination period, the insurer will prorate benefits. For instance, under a policy containing a 60-day elimination period, a client who returns to work 15 days following the elimination period will be entitled to receive 15/30 of the benefit.

Insurers prefer longer elimination periods, because they reduce the cost of administering short-term claims. This is reflected in the premium. The savings to the insured on a 60-day elimination period versus a 30-day one is greater than the savings on a 120-day versus a 90-day elimination period. The client may be better advised to select a somewhat longer elimination period and to apply the savings to the addition of a cost-of-living rider, which will ultimately lead to more benefits in the long term. Consider the example below.

Value Analysis of Short and Long Elimination Periods

Assumptions

- 46-year-old client
- Benefit amount of $2,450

- Executive occupation class
- A five-year claim occurs under a policy containing an age 65 benefit period
- Plan A: 30-day elimination period with no riders
- Plan B: 90-day elimination period with 4% cost-of-living and guaranteed-insurability rider

Year of Disability	Annualization of Benefit on Plan A	Yearly Payout on Plan A	Annualization of Benefit on Plan B	Yearly Payout on Plan B
1	$2,450 × 11	$26,950	$2,450 × 9	$22,050
2	$2,450 × 12	$29,400	$2,548 × 12	$30,576
3	$2,450 × 12	$29,400	$2,646 × 12	$31,752
4	$2,450 × 12	$29,400	$2,744 × 12	$32,928
5	$2,450 × 12	$29,400	$2,842 × 12	$34,104
Total Paid Five Years		$144,550		$151,410

Value Analysis

- Cost is less for Plan B by roughly 16%.
- Plan B delivers 5% more benefit over five years.
- Plan B will continue to increase its benefit if the claim continues — the focus is on the long term.
- Plan A pays more if the claim lasts less than three years — the focus is on the short term.

SELECT THE BENEFIT PERIOD

Introduction

The benefit period is the amount of time that benefits are payable for any one disability. The most popular benefit period is "to age 65", because it covers clients throughout their earning years to retirement. Shorter benefit periods are also available, such as two-year and five-year plans. Even though clients may be disabled beyond the maximum benefit period for which they can collect benefits, it is beneficial to retain the policy in force so that a future claim can be covered. Premium payment may or may not be required following the end of the benefit period to keep the policy in force, depending upon the provisional wording contained in the waiver of premium clause.

The cost of the plan is affected by the benefit period chosen. It was once thought that blue-collar occupations were adequately protected with a short-term benefit period for illness if it was coupled with a long-term benefit period for injury. The premise was that the average illness claim lasts about five years, after which most clients are either "dead or better". The thought was that disabilities of a more permanent nature were those caused by accident. In reality, this planning philosophy evolved from the lack of availability of longer benefit periods for high-risk occupations.

Today, there is broader access to longer benefit periods for everyone and a trend towards coterminous benefit periods for accident and sickness. Premium dollars are generally better allocated to a full working-term benefit period than they are to plan designs that combine short-term elimination periods with short-term benefit periods. Some people choose early elimination periods because they believe that they are more likely to make several short-term claims than a long-term claim. They see value in exchanging "premiums" for "claim benefits" and have a high expectation of utilizing the plan. This strategy results in increased costs for all policyholders and has helped to fuel the movement by insurers away from locked-in rates. Clients should be advised of the greater risk and the risk of catastrophic loss, and while a one- or two-month claim may be a serious financial inconvenience, a long-term claim would be financially devastating.

Integration with Government Benefits

Certain provincial and federal programs provide benefits to disabled Canadians. Those of concern are the various provincial workers' compensation programs, EI, and the CPP/QPP.

Workers' Compensation Programs

Known by different names in different provinces, these provisional programs provide benefits for workplace injuries. This benefit generally has no effect on programming individual DI for policies issued to low-risk occupation classes (e.g., Classes 4A and 3A), because there is very low risk of an executive having a work-related injury. Therefore, many insurers do not include offset provisions for these professions.

Medium- and high-risk occupations (Classes 2A, A, and B) are more susceptible to on-the-job injury.

There are two methods used to control overinsurance:

1. Offset clause
2. Issuance of non-occupational benefits.

Offset Clause Approach

With this method, benefits under the disability contract are offset dollar for dollar by benefits received from the provincial workers' compensation plan to the extent that the combination exceeds some stated maximum, such as 75% of prior average earnings. This method relieves the client of any concern regarding disputes about whether the disability was work-related or not.

Non-Occupational Benefits Approach

With this method, the policy covers accidents that occur off the job only. As an option, the client may also have the right to purchase 24-hour sickness protection.

The Canada/Quebec Pension Plan

This government benefit provides a disability income to contributing participants. As the definition for qualification is quite strict, many clients who qualify for payment under their individual disability contract will not qualify for disability benefits under the government plan. For this reason, few insurers require any integration or offset clause in the individual disability contracts that they offer to low-risk occupations. However, most insurers do include dollar-for-dollar offset provisions for policies offered to medium- and high-risk occupations. The integration wording is generally included in the same offset clause as is the workers' compensation benefit offset provision, which provides that the offset will be dollar for dollar for benefits above a stated percentage, such as 75% of prior average earnings.

Employment Insurance Benefit

Benefits from EI are integrated by the use of elimination period selection. The time during which the EI benefit is payable is "carved out". The insurer's Income Ratio Guide generally shows a breakdown of the amount of benefit available following EI and the amount of benefit overall. The difference is the amount that can be included with an earlier elimination period.

Illustrative Diagram

Example Using $36,000 earnings
Assumes benefits on a non-taxable basis

	90 EP	$1,075
Plus	120 EP	$ 950
Total Benefit to Age 65		$2,025

Income Ratio Guide

Applicant's Annual Earned Income	Total Monthly Benefit (All Sources) Non-Taxable	Amount Available With 120-Day EP if Covered by EI Non-Taxable
30,000	1,775	950
36,000	2,025	950
50,000	2,675	1,150

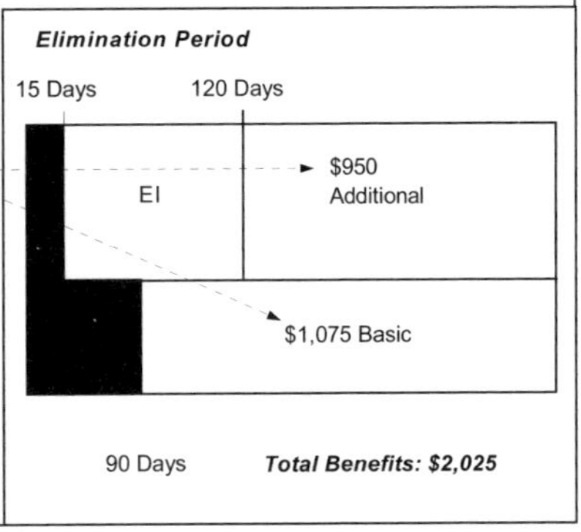

The above graph illustrates that during the initial four months, the client receives an EI benefit in addition to the basic benefit of $1,075. Once the EI benefit ceases, the individual disability plan is programmed to increase benefits by an additional $950, which is an approximate after-tax equivalent to the EI benefit entitlement. Benefits continue to the end of the benefit period, which, in this example, is age 65.

There is no integration required, however, for corporate-owned individual DI that is part of a wage-loss replacement plan, because EI benefits are the second payer to an employer-paid benefit package. Consequently, the employee would not be entitled to collect disability benefits from the EI plan, and overinsurance issues would not arise.

Integration with Group Insurance Benefits

As the Income Ratio Guide maximum amounts are based on benefits from all sources, the adviser must program around any existing group weekly income benefits or long-term disability benefits.

Programming with Weekly Income Benefits

Weekly income (WI) benefits, as the name suggests, are calculated as a weekly amount. Many WI plans commence payment with the first day of accident and the eighth day of sickness (referred to as a "1/8 plan"). However, other alternatives also exist, such as an "8/8 plan" and a "15/15 plan". The standard benefit periods are 17 weeks, 26 weeks, or, occasionally, 52 weeks. Most plans are followed by an LTD that commences following the end of the WI. The formula for calculating the amount of benefit payable under the WI may be different from the formula for calculating the LTD, with the former generally paying a greater benefit.

Some companies self-insure the short-term period and simply continue salary without reduction for an initial period of time until the LTD benefit begins.

The following illustration demonstrates integration of personal coverage for a client who has a WI benefit only.

Illustrative Diagram

Example Using $42,000 earnings

Assumes benefits are non-taxable, WI benefit period is 26 weeks, and plan provides 60% to a maximum of $333 per week.

The elimination period of 180 days is selected because it matches the WI benefit period of 26 weeks.

	90 EP	$ 832
Plus	120 EP	$1,443
Total Benefit to Age 65		$2,275

Income Ratio Guide

Applicant's Annual Earned Income	Total Monthly Benefit (All Sources) Non-Taxable	Amount Available With 120-Day EP if Covered by EI Non-Taxable
36,000	2,025	950
42,000	2,275	1,200
50,000	2,675	1,150

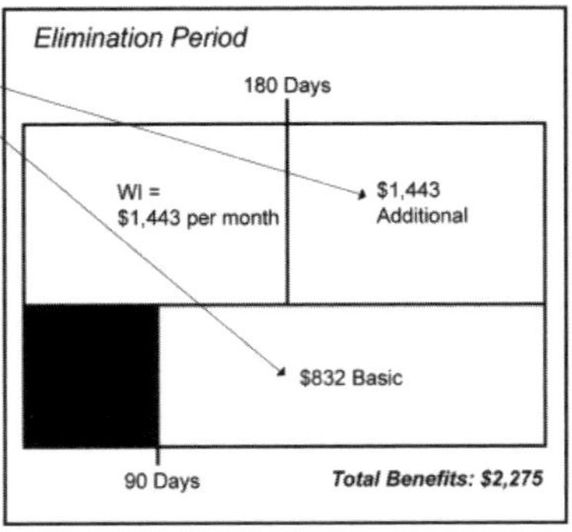

The adviser must first calculate the client's eligibility under the WI benefit:

$$\$42{,}000/52 \text{ weeks} = \$807.69 \times 60\% = \$484.61 \text{ per week}$$

However, the plan maximum provides for a benefit of up to $333 per week only and, therefore, this plan maximum is used instead of the benefit percentage. As individual DI is calculated as a monthly benefit, the WI benefit is converted to an equivalent:

$$\$333 \times 52/12 = \$1{,}443$$

The Income Ratio Guide states that the maximum benefit available from all sources is $2,275. As a result, the basic benefit amount is the difference:

$$\$2{,}275 - \$1{,}443 = \$832$$

The client receives the basic coverage of $832 while collecting the WI benefit, and when the WI benefit ends, the individual plan increases by an equal amount to maintain a level overall monthly benefit of $2,275 through the duration of the claim.

Programming with LTD

LTD is treated as though it were another individual insurance plan. Some companies may have a special Income Ratio Guide with a higher limit available for individual disability that is purchased as a "top up" to a base of LTD — known as "combo limits". Applicants in high-income brackets (above $110,000) may qualify for slightly higher amounts. When the client has both WI and LTD, the greater of the two benefits is the amount subtracted from the Income Ratio Guide limit to determine the eligible benefit amount.

Illustrative Diagram

Example Using $42,000 earnings

Assumes benefits are non-taxable and LTD plan provides 60% to a maximum of $1,000 per month.

The LTD benefit amount is $1,000 because 60% of (42,000/12) would exceed the plan maximum of $1,000.

90 EP	$ 832
Total Benefit to Age 65 (including LTD)	$1,832

Income Ratio Guide

Applicant's Annual Earned Income	Total Monthly Benefit (All Sources) Non-Taxable	Amount Available With 120-Day EP if Covered by EI Non-Taxable
36,000	2,025	950
42,000	2,275	1,200
50,000	2,675	1,150

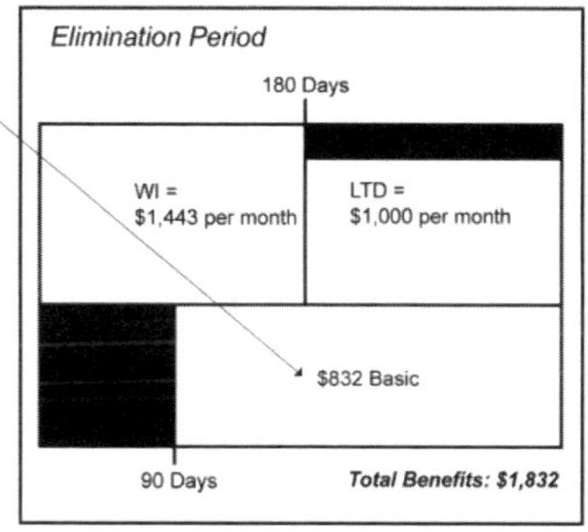

TAX CONSIDERATIONS

The adviser may encounter a situation where the client has a base of taxable group LTD and wishes to supplement it with the purchase of a personal-owned non-taxable individual disability plan. Each insurer has its own formula for adjusting the amount to take into consideration the difference in tax status. One method used is to calculate the percentage "used up" of the Income Ratio Guide taxable limit. The inverse percentage is applied against the non-taxable limit to determine the eligible amount. The same method would be used if the base group LTD was non-taxable and the individual plan was being purchased on a taxable basis. The adviser should check with the insurer to determine the method used by the insuring company. This also highlights the importance, during the fact-finding stage with the client, of collecting information regarding the taxability of existing benefits, as it can otherwise result in either an under- or overinsurance situation at the time of a claim. While underinsurance would leave the client short, overinsurance resulting from a material misstatement could result in a policy rescission, leaving the client with no benefits during a claim.

PREMIUM REDUCTIONS

A number of premium reduction programs exist that a client may be eligible for and that can lessen the premium otherwise payable. Some of these are discussed below. Insurers also set guidelines concerning "stacking" of discounts.

Quality Risk Upgrade

Many insurers establish quality risk factors that enable the client to upgrade to a lower-risk occupation class. Stability factors that may be part of the eligibility criteria include:

- Number of years with existing employer
- Number of years with earnings above a stipulated level
- Location of client's office is not in the home, or the job requires work outside the home over a certain percentage.

The discount may be in the range of 5%.

Preferred Risk Upgrade

Some insurers offer an upgrade to certain top occupations, thereby creating a further "preferred risk" group. This may be restricted to a handful of occupations, such as actuaries, architects, computer consultants, optometrists, pharmacists, professional engineers, and physician specialists. Other criteria must be satisfied, such as employment stability and earnings levels. The discount may be in the range of 5%.

Small Group Discount

Some insurers offer a discount when several clients in the same company purchase coverage at the same time. The minimum is usually set at three participants, and the discount ranges from 10% to 15%, depending on the product and occupation class.

Large Case Discount

Some insurers offer a discount when the volume and number of lives being insured through the same employer exceeds certain limits. Other criteria may also apply. The discount may depend upon the number of lives and the total volume of premium.

Dual Purchase Discount

Some insurers offer a discount when a client buys more than one product at the same time (such as buying both DI and critical illness insurance simultaneously). The discount is in the range of 5%.

Wage Loss Replacement Plan Discount

Some insurers offer a discount for coverage purchased as part of a wage loss replacement plan that includes at least two insured individuals buying coverage simultaneously. The discount is in the range of 5%.

Second Payer Provision Discount

Some insurers offer a discount when coverage has been purchased to complement a group. In this instance, a second payer endorsement is added to the individual policy, making the group first payer. In return for this, a discount is given, usually in the range of 10%, for as long as the second payer provision remains in effect.

Policy Change Discount

Some insurers offer a small discount, in the range of 5%, to clients who wish to make changes to their existing coverage but can only obtain what they want by cancelling their old coverage in favour of a new policy. The discount is intended to give some recognition to the fact that they are giving up coverage issued at a younger age for new coverage being issued on their attained age.

Student Professionals Discount

Some insurers offer special discounts to attract graduating professionals. These discounts may be in the range of 15% and include other special incentives.

GRADUATING PROFESSIONALS

Graduating professionals have high-income potential, but upon first graduating, their incomes may be relatively low. Added to this, many have the burden of setting up a new office while still repaying student and educational loans. Insurers offer special incentive programs to attract young professionals. Some of the features include:

- Higher issue limits than normally available for their current earnings and without income verification
- Waiving certain guidelines, such as minimum number of years in business to qualify for overhead expense coverage
- Special limits for future purchase option addition
- Discount programs.

Some of the professionals who may be eligible for special programs include:

- Accountants
- Actuaries
- Chiropodists
- Chiropractors
- Orthodontists
- Dentists

- Lawyers
- MBA graduates
- Medical doctors
- Computer industry professionals
- Occupational therapists
- Optometrists
- Osteopaths
- Pharmacists
- Physiotherapists
- Podiatrists
- Professional engineers
- Psychologists
- Speech pathologists
- Veterinarians.

Special automatic issue limits can range from $1,000 to as high as $9,000 (medical specialists), based on the specific field and whether the professional is a final-year student or whether the professional has newly commenced his or her career.

Some insurers also offer step-rated plans, whereby there is a lower rate for the initial period (such as the first five years), after which there is a one-time rate increase and rates remain level thereafter. Sometimes, this one-time adjustment occurs at a specific age, the usual being age 35, after which the rate remains level for the duration. This helps young, not-yet-established professionals get the coverage and options they need, but at a more affordable rate.

Chapter 8

Disability Insurance Underwriting and Claims

FUNDAMENTAL PRINCIPLES OF THE DISABILITY INSURANCE RISK

Disability insurance (DI) is a unique risk in many ways. Nowhere does this become more obvious than in the underwriting and claims management of this product. There are three areas of risk exposure that the underwriting process must manage:

- The moral hazard
- The physical hazard
- The legal hazard.

These areas are directly affected by the applicant's stability and motivation, and by our society's social environment, which has nurtured what we refer to as the age of entitlement.

The underwriter collects and analyzes various pieces of information to determine the applicant's level of risk in these areas. This procedure is often complex and demanding, requiring strong analytical skills, attention to detail, and responsible judgment. The underwriting department is the fulcrum between the sales and marketing function and the claims function. An excessively conservative approach will protect the claims department from heavy claims, but it is likely to result in the sales and marketing function falling short of its goals. Conversely, when underwriting guidelines are overly relaxed, sales may soar, but eventually so will claims. Striking the right balance is the challenge facing underwriters on a daily basis. The ultimate goal is to produce a profitable book of business for the insurer, and clients will benefit as they can be confident that the company will be in business for many years to honour claims as they arise.

The Moral Hazard

In economic theory, a *moral hazard* is a situation in which a party insulated from risk behaves differently from how he or she would behave if he or she were fully exposed to the risk. For example, a person with homeowner's insurance may be less concerned with locking his or her door given the knowledge that the insurance company will replace anything that is stolen. With life insurance, the client does not directly benefit from a claim, whereas with disability insurance, the client has a direct financial gain. The risk or hazard arises because of information asymmetry: the individual has more knowledge about his or her personal situation and daily behaviours than the insurer, who is reliant upon the individual to provide information pertinent to making a risk decision. This can increase the chance of loss.

The underwriter must ensure that the applicant has entered into the contract in good faith, that the applicant has not provided misleading information, and that the amount of coverage approved will not act as an incentive to claim for benefits. The Income Ratio Guide helps to ensure that the applicant shares in the risk of loss by not allowing 100% of earnings to be insured.

The Physical Hazard

A physical hazard is a physical condition that increases the chance of loss, such as a health condition, a former injury, or a family history of a hereditary disease. Life insurance and disability insurance are the same in terms of the need to evaluate the insured's health to determine his or her risk of becoming a claimant. However, with disability insurance, the physical hazard and the moral hazard interact to some extent. For example, when a client is faced with being laid off work, the client may decide he or she is no longer able to cope with depression and claim for benefits. This is sometimes referred to as an "elective disability".

The Legal Hazard

Both life insurance and disability insurance are based on promises that are defined in the policy contract. In the case of life insurance, the triggering event is understood. But the term "disability" is subjective, and it must be defined in the policy contract. Insurers make different definitions available in various disability products based on the risks associated with the product's target market. The underwriter must consider the overall risk in connection with the product's definitions. Sometimes it is necessary to reduce the company's risk by offering the applicant a different product from the one applied for.

Motivation and Stability

Motivation is the internal force that causes an individual to behave in a specific way. A highly motivated person tends to work hard at the task at hand, while an unmotivated person does not. It is an internal process that results from a person's needs, the ability to make choices about these needs, and the environment that allows the needs to be met and the choices to be made.

Motivation has a significant impact on how soon an individual returns to work following a claim for benefits. It is affected by many factors, including the state of the economy at the time of the claim, the individual's work environment, and stress.

Stability has a direct impact on motivation. For example, an individual with a long-term employment relationship in a particular company or industry is less likely to claim than a person with a history of changing jobs frequently. A successful business owner is more likely to return to his or her business quickly following a claim than the owner of a failing business. Statistics have shown motivation to work is greater as earnings rise, and greater amongst professionals than amongst labourers.

The underwriting guidelines set by the insurer take all of these factors into consideration.

The Age of Entitlement

It has been said that we are living in the age of entitlement, and that our level of social benefits has contributed significantly to this mentality. Many people believe that social benefits are a right. Their mentality is, "If I paid for the benefit, I am entitled to use it". This entitlement mentality contributes to claims incidence and duration.

THE OCCUPATION CLASSIFICATION SYSTEM

Introduction

Occupation is a primary factor affecting several aspects of disability insurance (DI), including whether the client can purchase disability insurance protection, the products the client can purchase (and therefore the provisions that will apply), the cost of coverage, and the flexibility in designing the plan.

Not all occupations are insurable. For example, even though an air traffic controller works in an office, has a high level of academic achievement, and has high earnings capacity, insurers do not offer traditional DI to this occupation. The reason is that air traffic controllers have an extremely high degree of job-related stress. The extreme pressure results in a high level of career burnout, as demonstrated by the fact that the average career lifespan for an air traffic controller is approximately five years. Regulations prohibit air traffic controllers from working when they are taking medication, or if their vision falls below a certain level. These are risks not associated with most occupations, and they place the occupation of air traffic controller outside the list of insurable occupations for traditional DI.

Occupation affects price. The exposure to physical risk on the job varies by occupation, as does the length of time before an individual can return to work following a period of disability. Motivation plays a significant role in claims experience, which in turn affects pricing. Within every occupation there are individuals who exhibit high levels of motivation and individuals who exhibit low levels of motivation. Studies of statistically significant groups with common incomes and academic achievement reveal that motivation, on average, rises in correlation with higher levels of earnings and academic achievement.

Insurers also determine risk categories by looking at internal experience, the industry's collective experience, and changes in the external environment, which can impact various occupations. This includes monitoring government regulatory changes, economic conditions, the competitive environment, changes in health care, and any rising incidence of illnesses. All are reviewed to determine impact on various occupational segments. Those that show the emergence of a new trend may be adjusted by changing the occupation classification to one that more accurately reflects the new level of risk.

For instance, in the early 1990s, the medical profession in the United States was undergoing a major restructuring. Physicians' net incomes were flat or decreasing, because of reductions in Medicare reimbursements and higher malpractice premiums. The introduction of managed care reduced patients' access to specialists, and this caused their incomes to decrease. In addition, proposed changes to the American health care system during the Clinton administration of the mid-1990s threatened to reduce the incomes of American physicians. Many physicians saw their DI as an attractive solution to their decreasing incomes. Although the Clinton changes never came to pass, the threat of these changes, together with the introduction of managed care, resulted in an increase in U.S. claims in this occupational segment, and American insurers corrected pricing by downgrading the occupation classification to reflect the new trend in claims experience. Similarly, in the 1980s, the Canadian real estate market was very volatile, and this in turn caused significant swings in year-to-year earnings of real estate agents. Insurers corrected negative claims experience in this occupational segment by downgrading the occupation class from low-risk to mid-high-risk classifications. Adjustments are not always negative, as demonstrated by the rise in demand for computer programmers and consultants. The computer industry is a growth industry, and a supportive external trend toward outsourcing gives insurers confidence that the favourable experience achieved to date will continue for the foreseeable future. This has resulted in improvements in classifications for many occupations within the computer industry.

Other factors also influence the determination of occupation classification, such as:

1. Moral hazards associated with the occupation

2. Instability within the industry

3. Seasonal nature of the work performed.

Classifying Occupations

Most companies use a five-tiered system to classify occupations into common risk groups. These are:

Class 4A. Primarily composed of professionals, consultants, and executives. A few professions, such as dentistry, have been downgraded based on claims experience. Executives must generally meet extended criteria, such as earnings and management duties. Consultants must generally meet extended criteria in the areas of travel, office location, contract commitments, and earnings.

Class 3A. Composed of office, clerical, and administrative personnel, some sales representatives, and a few professionals who do not meet the Class 4A criteria.

Class 2A. Consists of supervisory positions overseeing light trades, some sales representatives, and certain skilled and technical personnel.

Class A. Includes light trades, light delivery, and skilled manual workers with no hazardous activities.

Class B. Includes heavy manual workers, work requiring physical exertion, unskilled workers, and workers in jobs where there is considerable risk of accident or where absenteeism is unusually high. Also included are workers who use heavy hand tools, machinery, or moving equipment, or who are exposed to extreme heat or temperature changes.

Insurers provide detailed alphabetical listings of all occupations. While the majority of classifications are consistent from company to company, there are a few occupations that may vary based upon an insurer's own claims experience. Advisers should also check with the specific insurer regarding the company's use of modifiers that may upgrade or downgrade a particular occupation.

Upgrade of Occupation Class

Clients may qualify for an upgrade to a lower-risk occupation class based upon their earnings and years of experience. The actual income bands and number of years required vary from company to company. Some companies restrict the upgrading of occupations to self-employed clients, while other companies have also developed upgrading criteria for employees. Upgrading is generally limited to one level of increase, such as from Class 3A to 4A.

Determining the Correct Occupation Class for the Client

The client's duties determine the correct class, not the client's job title. Advisers should ask the client for an exact list of duties performed on a daily basis, the degree to which they vary over a month or throughout the year, and the percentage of time spent performing the various tasks. This may include data collection concerning the industry, the client's area or department within the company, the type of materials, tools, and equipment handled, and the process engaged in. Also of importance is whether the client is an employee, a manager, or self-employed.

Adviser's Checklist

Fact Finder — Client Data Required To Assess Occupation Class

❒ Current earnings level and number of years at this income

❒ Employee versus self-employed status

❒ Length of time self-employed or with current employer, and length of time in current occupation

❒ Managerial responsibilities, including number of employees supervised and type of work performed by subordinates

❒ Exact description of duties, including percentage breakdown of manual, selling, administrative, and supervisory duties, and travel

❒ Description of the industry itself

❒ Description of the company for which the client works, including number of employees, whether or not the company operates internationally, and years in business

❒ Description of the specific area or department within the company

❒ Type of materials handled, tools and equipment used, and process engaged in.

Clients Who Have Dual Occupations

There is a trend toward individuals having more than one occupation. Part-time, home-based businesses are on the rise and are often pursued in combination with other work. Job-sharing in the workplace has led to clients having more than one job. The seasonal nature of certain businesses, such as landscaping, also results in some clients having more than one occupation.

If the second occupation is performed less than 10% of the time, then the duties performed within it will generally not affect the classification. However, if more than 10% of the client's time is spent in the second occupation, the class will be based upon the riskier of the two. The client's earnings are treated as a whole to determine the eligible benefit amount.

Most insurers will not allow a client to insure just one occupation. Duties, earnings, and group benefits cannot be ignored simply because the client wishes to focus on a single portion of what they do. In the event of a claim, if the client can perform the duties of one occupation but not the other, they will be deemed partially disabled instead of totally disabled. Benefits would then be based upon the type of coverage purchased.

FIELD UNDERWRITING

The Application

Proper completion of the DI application is of equal importance to the analysis and design of the plan itself. Insufficient focus at this juncture can lead to the client not being approved for coverage, or even finding during a claim that benefits have been denied and the contract rescinded.

The application is the primary tool from which the underwriter obtains information. The adviser plays a significant role and must use probing skills to generate complete and accurate responses to all questions. There is a duty of care that must be met in fulfilling responsibilities to both the client and the insurer.

The Basics

1. The adviser must personally ask the questions and complete the application. An adviser who signs an application for another adviser, regardless of whether that adviser is licensed or not, is at risk of losing his or her licence, according to the Financial Services Commission of Ontario. This practice, known as "fronting", was one of the focal points in a bulletin released by the Financial Services Commission of Ontario, which stated, "Not only is fronting improper from a consumer standpoint, but if something goes wrong, it is the agent who will be held accountable. Agents who have participated in such arrangements in the past have not only lost their licences, but have also frequently been left with substantial chargebacks."[1]
2. The application is part of the legal contract. All questions must be completed in front of the client, and changes must be initialled by both the client and the adviser. Chemical erasers cannot be used.
3. The application must bear proper signatures of the insured, and where the owner is to be a corporation, it must be signed by one of the corporate signing officers and accompanied by the corporate seal.

Lack of Candour

Insurers must concern themselves with non-disclosure of material information at the time coverage is being applied for. The underwriting process involves a lot of time and resources, and this outlay of expense is intended to ensure that all relevant information is developed prior to making the final underwriting decision. When information is discovered that is contrary to what has been revealed on the application itself, it can present an increased risk, as any significant omission at the time of underwriting calls into question the legitimacy of all of the information in the application. Failure

---

[1] Bulletin No. LH-1/99 Life & Health. Financial Services Commission of Ontario, *Update on Regulatory and Administrative Matters Affecting Ontario's Life Agents,* p. 8.

to disclose significant information normally results in the application being declined for lack of candour.

Some people may feel that this is an unfair approach and that the insurer should simply proceed to issue the coverage, taking into consideration any additional information discovered from other sources. The problem is that a client who tries to hide information in the hopes of getting a better underwriting offer is very likely the client who will try to hide information during a claim, either to get a claim approved or to stay on payment longer than necessary. This costs the insurer, and ultimately all clients pay for it through increased premium rates.

Advisers play a vital role in stressing to clients the need to be forthright, and they need to ask questions in a manner that will uncover all relevant background details.

The Conditional Insurance Receipt

Most DI companies provide that the conditional insurance receipt will be valid, provided the following conditions are met:

1. The client passes a pre-screening contained in the application, usually pertaining to whether the client has had recent time off work due to illness, or has experienced back, heart, or circulatory ailments;
2. The client has paid the minimum required deposit; and
3. The client is found to be insurable on some basis and accepts the policy.

As a significant percentage of DI is approved with either exclusions, ratings, or plan design changes, the third criterion above is an important distinction from other forms of insurance, which require the client to ultimately be found insurable on a standard basis.

High-risk occupations may be limited to the amount of insurance provided under the conditional receipt, while most companies do not limit the conditional insurance benefit amount for low-risk occupations.

The receipt takes effect from the later of the application date and the date of submission of medical exams or tests. It is valid for 60 days.

If, during this time, the client becomes disabled, the insurer will complete the underwriting process to determine on what basis it would otherwise have issued coverage. When the policy is issued and accepted by the client, and placed in force, the claim may then be processed. The client, however, must notify the company immediately of the disability.

Policy Delivery

Insurers provide a time limit for delivery of the policy, after which, if it remains undelivered, it is treated as not accepted and any money paid is refunded directly to the client. This highlights the importance of making arrangements to deliver the policy promptly in person and to review any changes. In preparation for the delivery appointment, advisers should review the documents enclosed for the client's signature, and also review the policy face page to ensure that an issue error has not been made.

In the event that either a health or occupational change has occurred prior to delivery of the policy, or the client has seen a doctor since the date of submission of the application and prior to delivery of the policy, the contract must not be delivered. It should be returned to the company for re-evaluation. This is true regardless of whether or not the conditional insurance receipt was issued.

Requests for Information Disclosure

Information developed during the underwriting process is confidential and cannot be disclosed either to the adviser or to the company directly. It is not unusual, however, for the client to request further information when a decision has resulted in an unexpected exclusion or possibly even a decline. As the information is confidential, the company must have a written authorization from the client requesting release of the findings to his or her personal physician. The insurer will respond by sending the findings directly to the physician. The client can then arrange an appointment to meet with the physician to discuss the feedback. In the event that medical tests were conducted in regard to the insurance, and such tests were found to have abnormalities, most companies will notify the client's physician immediately so the client's health can be addressed.

Misunderstandings do arise occasionally, and underwriters are generally willing to review any additional information that they may not have originally been aware of, with a view towards improving the offer.

HEAD OFFICE DATA COLLECTION

Introduction

The risk is evaluated from three perspectives:

- Medical
- Financial
- Occupation and lifestyle.

The application is the primary source of data. Inclusion of a cover memo is the adviser's opportunity to position the case with the underwriter.

Independent verification is also required, and this is secured using secondary sources. This thorough approach is a form of protection — for the client as well as the company — because it lessens the potential for later rescissions during the claims process. The underwriter must weigh the expense to the company of securing the information opposite the risk of potential future expense associated with litigation, if essential information is not secured up front. Deciding what constitutes frivolous versus significant information is a continual point of discussion between the adviser and the disability underwriter. However, the adviser must keep in mind that persuading the underwriter to waive a request only increases the risk to the client of a later rescission if the missing details would have resulted in the underwriter arriving at a different decision. The adviser may have won the expediency of the case, but he or she may have done so at the cost of the client, whose future benefits were put at risk in return for a quick turnaround in underwriting.

Once the data is collected, the underwriter evaluates the risk. While each component is reviewed for "micro" implications, the final decision is based upon an evaluation of the "macro", or the interrelationship, of all three areas: medical, financial, and occupational/lifestyle.

Medical Data

The Attending Physician Statement

The underwriter may request an attending physician statement — either in response to a specific condition listed in the application or as a standard underwriting procedure — based upon the amount of coverage applied for. Other medical tools used by the underwriter include paramedical tests; supplementary tests, such as a blood chemistry profile, urinalysis, and electrocardiogram; or other specific tests that may be based upon the client's personal or family history.

Each insurer establishes non-medical underwriting limits. A "non-medical" refers to the medical questionnaire contained in the application form and is completed by the adviser asking the questions of the client. When the amount exceeds the company's limit, a paramedical is required. The paramedical questionnaire is completed by a registered nurse at the client's home, and usually requires accompanying tests, such as a urinalysis test and, for certain coverage amounts, a blood chemistry profile. Due to the higher risk of HIV and hepatitis B and C among health care workers, clients in these occupations are usually required to complete a blood chemistry profile test regardless of the amount of coverage purchased.

Sharing Papers Between Two Insurers

A client who has recently completed a paramedical, or another medical test for life insurance, may wish to have the disability insurer contact the life insurance company for the purpose of "sharing papers". Some disability insurers are reluctant to do this, because of the difference in the underwriting of disability and life insurance. A physician who has completed a report for life insurance may not have indicated a non-life threatening injury, and this would be highly relevant information to the disability underwriter. This omission can often be attributed to the difference between company forms, as the phrasing of questions posed is directed for life underwriting, not for disability underwriting. Similarly, the use of blood testing may vary between insurers. Nevertheless, if the tests for life insurance have been completed within the past two or three months, it is advisable to inquire of the insurer whether, for the client's convenience, the recent tests are acceptable. The underwriting department generally knows which companies have compatible forms, and the insurer has the opportunity to benefit from expense reduction through cost-sharing medical expenses.

Medical Information Bureau

The Medical Information Bureau (MIB) is a non-profit membership organization of insurers whose purpose is to create an information exchange on behalf of its members. Member companies are required to code information into the MIB during the underwriting process. This information acts solely as a red flag, and cannot be used to decline or rate a policy. The underwriter begins by accessing the database to check for existing red flags, and then uses other sources, such as the physician statement, to develop the information first-hand. Finally, any new information that has been collected during the underwriting process is coded into the MIB for access by other member companies.

Financial Data

Background

Historically, independent verification of data in the application focused only on health history and career/lifestyle. During the early 1990s, though, insurers discovered that a rising incidence in claims was largely caused by overinsurance on business written in the 1980s. For example, misinterpretation of what constitutes "earned income" resulted in clients and advisers stating gross earnings on the application form instead of net earnings after business expenses. This came to light during the claims process when the examiner would ask for copies of the Canada Revenue Agency tax forms. The true net earnings of the client were discovered to be considerably less than the income stated on the application, and rescissions occurred.

Automatic Requirements

Today, the underwriter verifies the income stated in the application by using Canada Revenue Agency tax forms. The automatic requirements usually include submission of the past one or two years of T1 General tax forms, including all attachments, such as T4, T4A, or T5 statements. Business owners must also provide their company business statements and corporate tax returns covering the previous two years. Alternatively, a non-incorporated business client may be required to submit the appropriate Canada Revenue Agency form, such as a T2124 Statement of Business Activities or a T2032 Statement of Professional Activities, or an income and expense statement plus balance sheet, including notes to financial statements. When business statements are used in lieu of Canada Revenue Agency forms, they must have been produced by an independent accountant, and not generated from the client's personal records. The statements may be either audited or unaudited statements.

Income Splitting Documentation

The underwriter may ask for additional information, based upon the specific client's circumstances. For instance, if a client is using spousal income splitting for tax purposes and wishes to include this income as part of his or her earnings, the underwriter will request tax information on the spouse as well as a memo outlining the duties performed by the spouse. Both the T1 General and all T4 statements will be required to give a consolidated picture to the underwriter concerning the spouse's overall activities.

Bonus Inclusion

A client who wishes to include bonuses or commissions as part of earnings will be required to provide evidence of the consistency of these earnings over a longer period of time, such as three years. The insurer will use an average to avoid basing the insurance amount on an unusual peak income period.

Here again, the insurable earnings are calculated by taking the gross earnings less deductible business expenses. The stated earnings on the application must match those declared to the Canada Revenue Agency.

Consolidation of Shareholders' Related Businesses

A client who is a shareholder in a corporation that consists of several affiliated companies will be required to provide business statements and tax returns of all the affiliated companies. This enables the underwriter to consolidate the statements and evaluate the bottom-line earnings. Lacking this, an operating company may show a profit only by virtue of carrying a loss in a related business. The shareholder's financial status is based on the whole.

Occupation and Lifestyle Data

Investigative Reports

The insurer uses either an investigative consumer report or a customer interview service provider, who calls the client to review information contained in the application. This enables the company to ask questions for both verification and clarification. In addition to reviewing the lifestyle questions concerning participation in recreational sports, hobbies, etc., the interview also confirms information concerning occupational, financial, and occasionally, medical data. Some insurers use their own trained employees for this purpose, but most subscribe to an outside service vendor who works on a fee-for-service basis.

The adviser should prepare the client for receiving a contact of this nature. Lacking this, the client may be reluctant to openly respond to the interviewer's questions, and the sale itself could be jeopardized.

Internal Company Records

The underwriter also checks the company's records to determine if the applicant is a current or previous client of the company. Information on the application will be compared with that currently on the company's files from previous applications. Discrepancies will be further investigated by the underwriter to determine whether they are willful distortions or innocent misstatements. The underwriter will generally decline any cases that appear to be intentional misrepresentations.

HEAD OFFICE RISK EVALUATION

Medical Evaluation

Although only 7% or 8% of life insurance applications are rejected or issued on a substandard basis, disability insurers commonly modify or reject as many as 25% of the applications submitted. While these numbers have been reduced slightly in recent years with the introduction of new products for non-traditional markets, there still remains a greater need for disability underwriters to standardize the risk through the use of various tools at their disposal.

While life expectancy has lengthened as a result of advanced medical and surgical knowledge, new medications, improved standards of living, and reduced occupational hazards, a whole new set of disorders now plagues modern society. The frenetic pace, fear of layoffs, and overall increased levels of expectation in the workplace have collectively contributed to the dramatic increase in stress-related illnesses. There has been a significant increase in soft tissue injuries, such as carpal tunnel syndrome, as well as in the area of subjective disabilities. This latter category includes illnesses that are diagnosed by the process of elimination and are based upon self-reported symptoms, as opposed to independent medical tests. While musculoskeletal injuries, and heart and circulatory conditions, remain among the leading causes of disabilities, mental/nervous claims and soft tissue injuries are among the fastest growing.

A declared history of back problems will likely not be a cause for concern in a life insurance application; conversely, in a DI application it will necessitate an investigation for full details of symptoms, diagnosis, and treatment.

Nervous problems are extremely difficult to quantify. Yet they affect motivation in a major way, and this in turn has a significant impact on claims incidence and duration.

Most insurers have established an internal panel for review of borderline risks. It consists of underwriters working in concert with medical specialists to review and determine the best underwriting decision that can be offered to the client.

Methods of Standardizing the Impaired Risk

The underwriter may use one or more methods to standardize the impaired risk. Each client's personal and family medical history is considered, and frequently, a combination of methods is required. The medical information cannot be evaluated independently of the other risk dynamics. For instance, a person's occupation must also be considered, as, depending on the occupation, there can be an interrelationship between health conditions and their direct impact on a person's ability to perform work. Stress in a person's life can also affect the risk. Consider a person who, within the span of the past 12 months, has gone through a divorce, experienced the death of a loved one, and also changed employers. A consultation with a physician for a mild stomach disorder would be of greater concern than for a client who was not currently experiencing numerous stressors. The stomach condition could be an indication that the client is no longer coping well. Thus, the underwriter not only looks at the client's medical history, but also checks for early warning signals of where the client's health condition may be headed.

An underwriter would be more conservative in the medical underwriting of a client who is borderline insurable in other risk areas, because when evaluated overall, the collective risk is greater than it is for a client who is marginal in only one risk area.

The descriptions below of methods used by the underwriter should not be interpreted as underwriting decisions for the condition referenced, but simply as an illustration of how the different methods of standardization may be applied to a client's policy.

Exclusion

Where the health impairment has symptoms of a specific and confined nature, it is excluded from being covered by the policy. For example, a client who has experienced repeated lower-back discomfort will be likely to have an exclusion for the lower spine included in the policy. The underwriter will often advise whether the exclusion is one that is permanent or one that may be reconsidered at a later date. Generally, those that can be reconsidered require the client to be symptom-free for three to five years. Chronic conditions, or those where the prognosis is deterioration or recurrence with the aging process, are unlikely to be reconsidered at a later date.

The adviser should try to work with the underwriter to determine that the exclusion is the most specific that the current condition permits. For instance, if back pain is confined to the lower back area and has shown no history of upward radiation, the exclusion should be similarly confined, and not exclude the upper-back and neck areas.

It may be necessary for the underwriter to apply both an exclusion and a premium rating to the policy. The exclusion is intended to address the primary condition, and the rating is used to offset increased morbidity from secondary causes. For example, a client's medical file may reveal a stress-induced ulcer, making it necessary for the underwriter to additionally apply a stress exclusion and an increased premium for conditions not directly protected by the exclusion itself. Stress could manifest itself later as a heart condition, and neither the ulcer exclusion nor the stress exclusion would protect the company from this risk. The premium rating is used to offset the additional substandard risk.

Limited Period Exclusion

Some impairments, if disabling, are likely to be short term only. In such instances, it may be possible for the underwriter to offer a policy that provides standard coverage for all disabilities, including the impairment, but with the impairment covered from a later elimination period. This provides the client with protection against unrelated, long-term injuries that might occur. The adviser should work with the underwriter to determine if a particular exclusion can be issued as a limited period exclusion.

Altered Plan Design

The underwriter may feel that it is necessary to limit the company's overall risk by reducing the coverage amount, lengthening the elimination period, reducing the benefit period, or removing optional riders requested. A change in the plan design may eliminate the need for excluding a condition.

Extra Premium Rating

An extra premium charge is used to compensate for the increased morbidity factor where it may be difficult to isolate the specific condition. For example, a condition such as hypertension does not lend itself to being excluded, because it can manifest itself as a heart attack or a stroke. Consequently, when blood pressure readings are slightly elevated and other factors, such as family history, are good, the underwriter may be able to offer coverage by adjusting the risk through a premium rating.

This method is often used in conjunction with a reduced benefit period, such as in the case of mild diabetes with late onset. Again, the condition is one that cannot be handled by an exclusion, because the disabling condition is actually secondary. The diabetes causes something else, which in turn becomes the actual cause of the disability. The problem the underwriter faces is that there is no way to know in advance what that secondary cause will be.

Financial Evaluation

Home-Based Employment

The rise in the number of people who work from home has prompted insurers to examine their guidelines in this area. The underwriter must consider the degree to which a claims supervisor would be able to monitor the claim for someone who does not have an office outside the home.

Some of the factors that impact the insurability of a client who works from home are:

- The nature of the work performed and whether it can be continued during periods of disability
- Whether the work requires the client to go out of the home to perform the duties, and what percentage of the time is split between performing the work inside and outside the home
- The length of time the client has been operating on this basis and the degree of success of the business
- Whether the occupation is in a low-risk or high-risk category
- Whether clients come and go from the business
- Whether there is a separate entrance to the office from outside, and whether there is a connecting internal door to the family living quarters
- The degree of commercialization, as evidenced by indicators such as external signage, separate parking facilities, a formal reception area, separate business telephone lines, and employees other than family members.

Most professionals who have established their practice within the home will be considered insurable. The fact that they have a clientele that comes and goes from their business provides a basis for monitoring a claim to determine whether they are still performing work during a disability. Similarly, clients in occupations that require them to leave the house on a regular basis to perform their tasks, such as sales, are more likely to be considered for insurance. Clients less likely to be considered are those whose tasks are performed totally within the home and whose roles do not require physical contact with customers outside the home to continue the work. An example of this is someone who is a writer or translator. These occupations can be performed even during a disability through the use of fax machines and the Internet, and this makes the process of monitoring the claim extremely difficult.

When a client has an office in the home but performs contract work at the business location of the customer, the insurer will be likely to approve the insurance, provided they meet the company's "self-employed occupation guidelines".

Many insurers have also developed special products for clients who work from home. These products usually provide benefits only during a period of total disability. The removal of residual benefits allows the insurer to focus primarily on the physical capability to perform related duties during a disability, as determined by independent medical evaluation.

The insurer may identify percentage categories linked to risk class and in-home duties within which a client may be considered insurable. The higher the risk class, the more the emphasis will be placed on the percentage of duties being performed outside the home. For example, an insurer may allow accountants to perform their duties 100% from home and sales representatives to perform 50% of their duties from within the home, but require carpenters to perform their duties completely outside the home. Where the client has a separate building located on the residential property, it is usually treated as "home-based" and the above guidelines would be applied.

Bankruptcy

If a client has previously declared bankruptcy, the underwriter must determine whether recurrence is likely. There are several indicators that the underwriter may use as a benchmark, such as:

- The reason for the bankruptcy
- How much time has passed
- Whether the client entered self-employment following bankruptcy and, if so, how recently
- Current earnings level and degree of job stability.

To be considered, the client must have been discharged. A client who is an employee will be considered with a shorter elapsed period, such as 12 months following the discharge, than one who has gone into self-employment. The latter would generally be required to wait two or three years until the business can provide complete statements as evidence of its financial stability.

Seasonal Employment

A client who performs work on a seasonal basis will generally still be considered for insurance. The insurer will normally require a longer elimination period to match the period of the off-season. If, however, the off-season is greater than three months, the client is unlikely to be considered for insurance unless he or she has a stable insurable second occupation that is performed during the off-season of the primary business.

Graduating Professionals

For various categories of professionals, insurers generally provide a guaranteed minimum amount of DI that can be purchased without financial evidence. This recognizes the high earnings potential of young people. As their earnings rise and justify increased amounts, they can obtain insurance through normal underwriting.

To qualify, the professional must apply for coverage within 12 months of graduation. This reduces the risk of anti-selection to the insurer. Eligible categories usually include doctors, lawyers, optometrists, dentists, accountants, pharmacists, chiropractors, veterinarians, and engineers.

New Canadians

As stability of earnings and occupation are two fundamental principles of traditional disability income insurance, clients who have recently moved to Canada are not eligible for traditional DI products until they have resided in Canada for a minimum of two years and have a minimum of one year of work experience. This time provides the opportunity for the client to become established and to build a track record of earnings stability. It also provides time for the client to establish a medical record in Canada, which will enable the insurer to complete the health verification. Furthermore, as financial verification is a major component of the underwriting process, the client must be able to provide the required Canada Revenue Agency tax forms and/or business financial statements; consequently, coverage will usually be postponed until the client has completed his or her first filing with the Canada Revenue Agency.

The insurer will generally require the client to have permanent resident status, which provides some evidence of intent to stay in the country. This is important to the insurer for several reasons:

- The contract is generally not cancellable by the insurer if the client moves back to his or her homeland.
- The insurer would be challenged to administer a claim in another country.
- The risk dynamics vary from one country to another, and the policy is priced and provisions scripted for Canadian morbidity experience.

The client must also be able to speak, read, and write either English or French to be eligible for insurance. It is a legal requirement that the contract be fully understood to be valid, and so it is essential that the applicant fully comprehends the implications of the questions and terms of the policy. When a disability claim occurs, the insurer must be able to deal directly with the client and not require the use of an interpreter to administer the claim.

As a further safeguard against clients deciding at a later date to resume permanent residence in their homeland, the company may include a travel exclusion that limits protection while outside continental North America.

Occupation and Lifestyle

Occupation

The underwriter reviews the client's employment history to determine job stability. If there is a history of frequent change in employers or occupations after short periods, an application for non-cancellable DI is likely to be postponed until a more favourable track record is established. Employees who have been with their employers for less than one year may have their applications postponed until a year has passed, especially if the client is within a high-risk occupation or has changed fields of employment. The adviser should contact the insurance company and submit an inquiry to the underwriting department before proceeding to present the plan and complete the application. Most insurers have stringent guidelines for clients who have recently become self-employed.

Eligibility Factors for Recently Self-Employed Clients

The underwriter takes the following into consideration when insuring clients who have become self-employed within the past year:

- Whether the client has changed either industries or fields within the industry
- Degree of relatedness of new employment to prior employment
- Volatility of the industry and whether it is in the growth phase or has reached maturity
- Whether the client has written contracts for work and, if so, their duration, and the spread in number of contracts
- Whether the client has an exclusive contract with the prior employer
- Earnings level provided by the contracts
- Level of business expenses
- Whether the client works from home or has established an office outside of the home
- Whether the client has a previous history of bankruptcy.

The underwriter will consider a client as a better risk if the business was purchased and has an established profitable track record. The underwriter will be unlikely to approve a client who has commenced self-employment following the expiry of unemployment benefits, or if the client has been in business less than six months with no contracts to show a committed revenue stream. The underwriter will also consider the number of other positive or negative risk factors present, such as current medical condition and lifestyle factors. Overall, the underwriter must weigh the probability of financial success in the new business venture against the probability of failure. The adviser can assist in this evaluation by asking probing questions of the client and submitting third-party evidence, such as business statements, accountant's memos, or perhaps a business plan summary, including cash flow projections. The adviser's goal should be to provide insight and concrete, independent evidence that supports a high probability of the business venture's financial success and a profile of the client's successful track record with prior initiatives.

Lifestyle Considerations

Disability insurers consider the following lifestyle considerations in evaluating the risk.

Smoker Status

Many DI products are offered on the basis of regular rates for smokers and discounted rates for non-smokers. The definition of what constitutes a non-smoker and the number of months of abstinence required to qualify for the non-smoker rate vary from company to company. Some companies include use of all nicotine products, including nicotine gum, in the definition, while others restrict the definition to those that are smoked. The more restrictive definitions usually have a 12-month stipulation, while the broader definition usually requires 24 months of non-smoking to qualify.

Recreational Activities

A client who participates in certain recreational activities may be issued DI that contains an exclusion for that activity. Examples of these activities include racing, hang-gliding, private flying, motorcycle riding, heli-skiing, rodeo participation, snowmobile racing, and bungee jumping. The adviser should provide the underwriter with details concerning frequency of participation and plans for future participation.

Also excluded from coverage is any amateur sport that the client may participate in, such as hockey, football, or wrestling.

Driving Record

A client who has too many moving traffic violations or impaired driving charges is usually declined for coverage. When a client reports on the application that he or she has been involved in a car accident, the underwriter will generally cross-reference the information with the non-medical to determine whether injuries were sustained that impact the risk, such as whiplash.

Alcohol and Drug Use

Alcohol that is used in moderation presents no concern to the risk evaluation. However, when used in excess, the result is increased morbidity. There is not only an increased risk of accidental injury, but also a debilitating effect on the person's health overall. It may also result in reduced motivation and increased absenteeism from work. Each company establishes a limit that is considered within the acceptable range. Many companies include a questionnaire for completion by the client if alcoholic beverages are used above a certain limit.

When a client has been recommended to undergo treatment that has not been completed, the insurance will be postponed. However, a client who has undergone a treatment program and abstained for an extended period, such as five or six years, will generally be insurable for disability coverage.

Drug addiction or abuse results in a higher rate of morbidity and it is not restricted to certain socioeconomic classes or geographic regions. A client who uses any chemical substance that alters mood, perception, or consciousness is not insurable for disability coverage.

THE CLAIMS PROCESS

Introduction

Companies have evolved their management methodologies from the 1980s model that emphasized claims processing to a new-millennium model that emphasizes benefits management. The insurer's objective is to pay all claims fairly and as promptly as possible. At the same time, the insurer has an obligation to protect policyholders from unjust claims, as this results in increased costs.

This philosophy emphasizes early intervention and prevention. Insurers have found that breaking the cycle of disability that sets in as a person develops a disability mindset requires getting involved as early as possible following the disability occurrence. Insurers accomplish this by getting directly in touch with the client as soon as notification of a claim is received, and staying in touch by telephone throughout the process.

Programs offered by insurers today focus on partnering to help the client to an early return to work, and may even involve a willingness to look at the worksite environment for possible changes that may help the client get back to work sooner.

Clients should be advised to call the company as soon as the disability occurs, even if they are not certain whether the disability will last beyond the elimination period. This enables the insurer to begin the process of benefits management, which results in faster claims payment to the client.

Once the client has notified the insurer, the company will send a claim form for completion by the claimant and the attending physician. The insurer will generally also request copies of the most current Canada Revenue Agency tax forms to establish the predisability earnings. This may be required even when the policy does not contain residual benefits. When the claim occurs within the first two years, the insurer will check for discrepancies between statements made in the original application and information provided at the time of claim. A material misrepresentation will most likely result in the immediate rescission of the policy, and no benefit will be paid. When the policy has been in force for more than two years, the insurer will check for any appearances of fraud. As fraudulent claims affect insurance costs for everyone, insurers are taking significant legal action to deal with situations that arise.

When the client makes the initial call to the insurer to advise of the disability, a benefits adjudicator will be assigned to the case. The adjudicator's role is to manage the claim through the process of evaluation to ultimate payment and close. A claim form is mailed to the client, and upon its return, the benefits adjudicator will assemble an internal review panel that usually consists of a physician working in conjunction with medical and vocational rehabilitation specialists.

Field Visits

The benefits adjudicator may arrange for a field specialist to investigate the claim by contacting the insured. When fraud is suspected, the adjudicator may arrange for a special field investigator to complete a detailed check, which may include the use of surveillance. Only a very small percentage of cases will require this extensive search, and this method is only used in situations where the adjudicator has strong evidence that fraud may be involved.

Optional Payment Programs

Some insurers make optional payment programs available to claimants when circumstances suggest that it would be beneficial to the client's recovery. For instance, the insurer may offer a lump-sum payment as an advance of benefits on an out-of-contract basis to help the client get re-established in a new line of work. Not all insurers, however, agree that this is a beneficial strategy; many prefer to make benefit payments within the contract terms. If the client is offered an alternative method of payment, he or she should seek professional advice concerning whether this would be of benefit. There is a risk with some clients that they may not appropriately manage the funds, and necessary income during a period disability may no longer be available.

Rehabilitation

Rehabilitation is an important component of the claims process. A claimant who is receiving benefits under the own-occupation definition will not be offered rehabilitation assistance, as the policy continues to pay full benefits when the client is working in a new occupation. In this respect, the benefit itself is a form of rehabilitation payment. However, when the client may be able to work in a reduced capacity within the client's own occupation, the insurer will work with the client to assist in his or her efforts towards an early return to work.

A client who is covered under a contract that has a limited own-occupation period must commence the rehabilitation process before the expiry date. If the claimant waits until the own-occupation coverage has expired, the benefits will cease, and the opportunity for medical and vocational assistance will no longer be available.

Time Limitations for Claim Submission

At the time of sale, the adviser should explain the general process associated with a claim. This includes advising the client to immediately contact the insurer upon the occurrence of a disability. The policy contract contains a time limitation within which a claim must be reported. Insurers do not generally waive this limitation when the claimant is delinquent. Most policies provide that the disability must be reported within 90 days where possible, and that it should never be reported later than one year.

The Adviser's Role

The adviser's role is to encourage the client to promptly contact the insurer when a disability has occurred. The adviser should explain the general process involved:

- Contact the insurer to advise that a disability has occurred.
- Receive claim forms that the insurer will forward for completion by the client and the physician.
- Include copies of recent Canada Revenue Agency tax forms.
- Be available to speak or meet with the benefits adjudicator.
- Keep the company informed of changes in status.

The adviser should not get involved in counselling or in completing the claim form itself, or make interpretive statements as to whether the claim will be covered under the definition of disability. There have been situations where incorrect advice has been given by an adviser, and the result has been a lawsuit by the claimant against both the insurer and the adviser when the claimant was denied payment. The insurer will not deal through the adviser during the claim, as information is confidential and the insurer can manage the claim process more effectively by dealing directly with the client. Some insurers will keep the adviser abreast of the progress of the claim by providing copies of correspondence that are not confidential in nature.

Chapter 9

Individual Disability Insurance in the Workplace

WAGE LOSS REPLACEMENT PLANS

Wage loss replacement plans are usually funded by group long-term disability (LTD) contracts within a broader group plan containing other benefits, such as extended health care and dental benefits. This method poses a problem for smaller companies, who may not be able to obtain adequate benefit levels, either due to the nature of their business, the size of their organization, or a high level of family content within the group. The solution can be to use individual disability contracts banded together by means of a board resolution. While the premiums may be higher as a result of funding benefits with individual contracts, the desire to provide certain employees with enhanced benefit provisions and the increased plan flexibility derived may be appealing to the employer.

When a wage loss replacement plan is funded by individual disability contracts, it is commonly referred to as a "grouped sickness and accident plan".

The Concept

Two or more employees can be "grouped" together, and if properly structured, this results in favourable tax treatment for both the employer and the employee. The employer generally owns the policy and pays the premiums, but benefits during a claim are paid directly to the disabled employee. When the employee leaves the company, it is up to the employer (as owner of the policy) to decide whether the ownership will be transferred over to the departing employee. Assuming ownership is transferred, the premium payments then become the responsibility of the employee and tax treatment under the plan changes. The employee has protection against changes in insurability that might otherwise prevent replacing the coverage personally. Insurers also set requirements regarding transfer of ownership, in order to protect the insurer from overinsurance.

Advantages for the Employees and the Employer

The employees benefit in many ways:

- They receive coverage paid for by the employer.
- There is no "add-back" into their salary related to the premiums — in essence, the person has a tax-free raise.
- While the benefits are taxable at the time of claim, the benefit is normally increased to offset the tax.
- Their insurability is protected if they leave the employer, assuming the employer agrees to transfer coverage.
- The benefits are much more comprehensive than those under traditional group insurance.
- The benefits during a claim represent "earned income" and can be counted for RRSP calculations.

The employer benefits as well:

- Enhanced benefits associated with individual disability plans can be an attractive feature for enticing highly qualified candidates for key positions.
- The employer can deduct the premiums as a business expense.

- A claim for benefits does not impact future rates charged to the employer, as can happen with group LTD.
- The premiums are level and guaranteed not to change, providing the employer with stable, predictable costs.
- The employer can select the group or class of employees that will participate in the plan and the benefits offered.
- Discounted rates normally apply when coverage is purchased for several employees in an employer setting.
- The group might also qualify for a guaranteed-issue plan, as described later in this section.

The programs discussed later in this chapter may make use of the "grouping" concept and receive the favourable tax treatment herein. The following section describes how to establish a qualified program.

Grouped Sickness and Accident Plans

Individual disability plans may be "grouped" and, as a result, qualify for the same tax implications as group LTD insurance. The conditions to qualify are:

1. There must be at least two people insured through the plan. This prerequisite is outlined in the CRA's Interpretation Bulletin IT-85R2. One person alone cannot constitute a "group". There must be a resolution outlining that the company has officially established the plan. This is commonly accomplished by a board resolution that is duly entered into the corporate minutes book. Without this resolution to group the policies into one common plan, there is simply a string of individual policies, and paragraph 6(1)(*a*) of the *Income Tax Act* will not apply.
2. The benefits at the time of claim must flow directly to the disabled person. If the benefits pass through the company first, then the proceeds are treated as key person insurance, for which tax implications differ.
3. The plan must define the eligible class. The class must be a logical group, not one that appears to have been formed for the purpose of offering coverage to a select group of people at the exclusion of others. This is particularly important where shareholder-employees are included.
4. Similar benefits must be offered to all members of the class (unless some are found to be uninsurable or subject to a premium rating by the insurer).

Eligibility of Benefits as Earned Income for RRSP

As benefits under a grouped sickness and accident plan are taxable as earned income during a disability, the client has the advantage of inclusion in calculating earned income for the year for determining RRSP limits.

Shareholder-Only Plans

When a plan consists solely of shareholders as its participants, the Canada Revenue Agency will disallow the plan. When a benefit is conferred on an individual in his or her capacity as a shareholder, those benefits are taxed in the individual's hands, pursuant to subsection 15(1) of the *Income Tax Act*, and the exception under subparagraph 6(1)(*a*)(i) will not apply. The premium will not be deductible by the corporation, since the payment is not incurred by the corporation for the purposes of gaining or producing income, as required under paragraph 18(1)(*a*). The result is that the shareholder will be charged with a taxable benefit equal to the amount of the premium paid by the corporation on his or her behalf, and additionally, the corporation will not be entitled to a deduction. Therefore, the remedy is for the corporation to include non-shareholders in the plan or, alternatively, insure shareholders on a personally owned and personally paid-for basis outside the corporation.

When the above criteria are satisfied, the tax implications of both paragraphs 6(1)(*a*) and 6(1)(*f*) will apply.

Provisions of Paragraph 6(1)(*a*) of the *Income Tax Act*

Paragraph 6(1)(*a*) provides that the premiums paid by the company are fully deductible as a business expense and do not constitute a taxable benefit to the covered employees. Had the equivalent amount been paid as a salary increase and the employees left to purchase the coverage on their own, they would have been subject to income tax on the money received, and the method would have a higher resulting cost overall.

While paragraph 6(1)(*a*) subjects the value of all benefits received in respect of employment to be included as income to the employee, it excludes the value of a group sickness and accident plan from being subject to such taxation as an employee perquisite. Note that it is the *premium* that is not attracting tax, not the monthly income benefit.

Provisions of Paragraph 6(1)(*f*) of the *Income Tax Act*

Paragraph 6(1)(*f*) provides that the monthly income payments received during a claim are subject to income tax. The exception is where a plan existed prior to June 18, 1971, and payment arises as a consequence of an event that occurred prior to 1974. In this respect, it is the event causing the disability and not the disability itself that must have occurred prior to 1974. In this instance, benefits are tax-free. When paragraph 6(1)(*f*) does apply, however, the taxation may be reduced by a credit equal to any and all contributions made personally by the employee to the plan. This is referred to as a "contributory plan".

Insurable Income and Shareholders

A shareholder-employee is being covered by virtue of employee status, not shareholder status. As such, the income included should be income received as an employee, and not income received by virtue of being a shareholder. This includes the following:

- Annual salary (T4 income)
- Bonuses received
- Contributions to a retirement plan or deferred profit sharing plan made on the employee's behalf by the employer.

Sources that should be insured outside of a grouped plan include:

- Salary paid to a spouse for income splitting purposes
- The shareholder's share of net before-tax operating income.

Employment Insurance Considerations

EI is the second payer to an employer-paid plan; consequently, the benefit design should ignore EI integration.

Larger Benefit Amounts for Taxable Plans

Most insurers offer higher issue limits when policies are purchased as part of a grouped sickness and accident plan to recognize the taxability of the benefits during a claim. This lessens the difference between the net benefit payable under a taxable plan and the amount payable under a non-taxable plan. Marginal tax rates of the insured should be considered to determine the true difference for any particular client.

Ownership of Policies and Provision for a Later Change in Tax Status

The Canada Revenue Agency does not require that the corporation actually own the policy contracts. However, most insurers make corporate ownership a condition for eligibility of the higher insurance amounts available on taxable plans. This is because they want to reserve the right to reduce the amount of insurance in the event that the policy ceases to be part of the grouped accident and sickness plan. There is a risk of overinsurance when policies have been issued with larger benefit amounts to cover the tax, if the plan later becomes non-taxable upon the covered employee's leaving the company and maintaining the contract.

Furthermore, as EI becomes the second payer to an employer-paid benefit, the elimination period selected for the plan may be one that overlaps with the usual time frame for EI benefits, since the employee would be ineligible to claim them. Upon leaving the company, the employee may once again be eligible to claim EI benefits while simultaneously collecting full benefits under the individual disability policy contract. No offset of EI benefits occurs for personal plans; hence the risk of overinsurance. The insurer will consequently modify the elimination period on some or all of the benefits to eliminate the overinsurance factor.

To accomplish this, the insurer includes a provision in the policy contract that authorizes the company to re-evaluate the amount of coverage in the event the ownership changes from corporate-owned to personal-owned insurance. The change of ownership acts as a trigger to the company advising them that the tax status may have changed. In the absence of this, the insurer would have no way of knowing that the insured employee has left the company and, therefore, caused the policy to no longer be taxable. The insurer's objective is to restore the plan to what would have been issued originally had it not been part of a grouped disability program. This usually means the issue limits considered would be those that were in effect at the time the policy was purchased, not current limits in effect at the time the change is made.

Sample Board Resolution

The following shows a standard board resolution commonly used to group together individual disability policies under a wage loss replacement plan. This is a sample resolution only. Clients should consult their legal adviser for completion of a resolution for their company.

Resolution to Establish a Grouped Sickness and Accident Plan

Whereas, in the common interest of ___________ (hereinafter referred to as the "Corporation"), and certain of its employees (hereinafter referred to as the "Eligible Employee Class"), it is deemed desirable to establish a Grouped Sickness and Accident Plan to provide an income during disability to the Eligible Employee Class;

Now therefore be it resolved, that individual disability insurance policies will be purchased for each of the employees within the Eligible Employee Class from ___________ (hereinafter referred to as the "Insurer"). Benefits are to be payable as outlined in the policies during disability.

The "Eligible Employee Class" is defined as ___________.

The Corporation will own and pay premiums on the policies involved in the plan.

Benefits will be payable directly from the Insurer to the covered employee in accordance with the terms of the policy contracts.

Certified a true and correct copy of a Resolution passed on the day of ___________, ________.

____

____

(one signing officer and corporate seal or two signing officers without corporate seal)

Non-Grouped Sickness and Accident Plans

Introduction

A plan is "non-grouped" when one or more of the criteria for grouping is not satisfied. Most typically, these include:

- Absence of a board resolution
- Fewer than two qualified participants.

When the employer pays premiums on behalf of an employee under a non-grouped plan, the premium must be included in the taxable earnings of the employee. However, Interpretation Bulletin IT-428 provides that the monthly income benefit received at the time of a claim will be tax-free. This is the case regardless of who is the actual owner of the policy.

Salary Increase Versus Payment of Premiums by the Corporation

The question arises as to whether it may be advantageous to have the corporation give the employees raises and allow them to pay the premium directly to the insurer. The tax treatment of premiums and benefits will still be the same as with a non-grouped plan. The salary will be a deductible business expense just as the premium payment is allowable as a deductible business expense, provided the insured is not a shareholder. The insured employee is subject to income tax regardless of whether the money is "salary" or "premium". In both instances, the benefit during a claim is tax-free.

Combining Group LTD as a "Second Life"

The adviser may be faced with a situation where there is only one person whom the corporation wishes to cover under individual disability insurance (DI). The temptation may be to view the individual disability contract as part of an overall existing wage loss replacement plan within which other employees are covered through a traditional group LTD plan. This does not enable the individual policy to be treated as though it were part of a grouped sickness and accident plan.

Interpretation Bulletin IT-428 provides that an employer may have two benefits included as one plan, but only if the same class of employees is entitled to participate in both plans and the premiums or other cost of each plan is shared in the same ratio by the employer and employees. Otherwise, each will be recognized as a separate plan and, hence, require a minimum of two participants in each plan. In other words, the one-person addition is treated as a non-grouped plan.

Contributory Plans

Employee Pay-All Plans

When the employer makes no contribution to the plan whatsoever, the premiums paid by the employee are not deductible, and the monthly income benefits received during a claim are tax-free. This may occur when an employer establishes a benefit plan whereby the employees can voluntarily purchase benefits through payroll deduction.

Interpretation Bulletin IT-428 specifies that the onus is on the employer to clearly establish that a plan is an employee pay-all plan. Consequently, to avoid any potential taxation of benefits under paragraph 6(1)(*f*), the plan should be documented at the time it is established as being an employee pay-all plan.

An employee pay-all plan is attractive for companies that cannot afford to install a company-funded benefit plan. Many insurers offer discounts ranging from 10% to 20% as an incentive to the employee to enroll in the program, provided a certain minimum participation rate is achieved.

Shared Contribution Plans

The adviser should caution the employer against establishing a shared contribution plan, whereby the employer and employees jointly contribute to the cost of the disability benefits. Interpretation Bulletin IT-428 provides that regardless of the premium split ratio and regardless of whether the plan is grouped or non-grouped, the benefits received at the time of a claim are taxable to the extent they exceed the total premiums paid by the employee. Often, the employer simply assumes that the benefits will be taxed in the same proportion that the premium contribution has been shared, and this is not always the case. Consider the example below:

Illustration of Shared Contribution Plan

Michael has an $8,500 monthly disability benefit provided through the employer, and the premium is shared 50/50. The annual cost of the plan is $5,000, so Michael's portion is $2,500 each year.

Assume that after five years, Michael becomes disabled. The sum of premiums paid by Michael to the date of claim is $2,500 × 5 years = $12,500. Therefore, the first 1½ months of benefits are tax-free, with all remaining benefits being fully taxable ($12,500/$8,500).

Calculation of Employee's Contributions

For an employee's initial claim under a shared premium arrangement, the calculation includes all of the employee's contributions to that plan after 1967. For a subsequent claim, the deduction of personal contributions by the employee is restricted to contributions made since the last taxation year in which a benefit was received. If, at the time of the previous claim, the employee's contributions exceeded the benefits received, the excess contributions cannot be carried forward as a deduction against the benefits of a future claim.

To determine the taxable portion of benefits, the Canada Revenue Agency requires inclusion in the tax return of some form of evidence of the premium paid. This may take the form of receipts or statements from the employer or the insurer.

Contributions by the Employer on Behalf of Only Certain Employees

If an employer establishes a plan covering a group of employees and contributes towards the cost of the plan on behalf of only some of its participants, the tax treatment for all employees will be as though the contributions had been made on behalf of all employees. That is, the plan will be taxed as a shared contribution plan, regardless of the fact that the employer's contributions may be on account of specific employees only.

To avoid this, a separate plan should be established for the class of employees for whom the employer wishes to fund 100% of the cost. This is achieved by implementation of separate board resolutions for each plan.

Unincorporated Businesses

A sole proprietor or partners under a limited partnership may establish a grouped sickness and accident plan for the benefit of their employees with the same tax implications as incorporated businesses. However, the sole proprietor or partners may not include themselves in the plan. The adviser should structure the coverage for the business owners on a personally owned and personally paid-for basis.

To establish a grouped sickness and accident plan for the employees, the business owners should consult their lawyer for establishing appropriate documentation to validate the intention of the plan to be a grouped sickness and accident plan.

DEALING WITH EXISTING GROUP LTD

Trends in Benefit Plans

Our population is aging, and within the next 10 years, most organizations will see an increase in the proportion of employees in the 50-plus age category. This aging in employee groups is exacerbated by a change that took place in the 1980s in pension benefits. Companies began the move away from defined benefit plans to defined contribution plans. This trend, together with the elimination of mandatory retirement, will mean delayed retirement by many baby boomers. As the average age of the employee population rises, so does the cost of employer-sponsored benefits. This is due to greater utilization, the increased cost of drugs, diagnostic tests, and technology. Like the shift two decades ago in pensions, which placed greater accountability on employees, employers are continuing a similar evolution in health plans using programs such as flex benefits and health spending accounts.

Two trends have altered the cost of group LTD: the increase in the average age of the employee population and the shift in the nature of disability. Employees who are over age 50 account for 40% to 50% of all disability claims. Claims for musculoskeletal injuries; soft tissue injuries, such as carpal tunnel syndrome; and mental/nervous disorders have grown at alarming rates and represent about 45% of disability claims. During economic downturns, employees sometimes see disability benefits as an attractive alternative to being laid off. This further fuels claims costs. Added to this is the fact that when the economic environment triggers interest rate reductions, claims reserves must be bolstered to make up the difference — a further expense to insurers, who must account for it in the rates charged to employers. Employers have, consequently, been open-minded to cost-containment methods, which is one reason for the attractiveness of flex benefit plans and the tendency towards shorter own-occupation periods, longer pre-existing condition limitations, and other cost-containment options. This creates a gap that the adviser must fill by using individual DI.

Obtain Details of Existing Benefits

Most clients think of their LTD as adequate, with their focus being on the percentage of income promised during a disability. They are unaware of salary limits, offset provisions, graded formulas, and the fact that the benefit even has a definition of what will be considered as a qualifying disability. Advisers, in order to become completely familiar with the details of the existing benefit plan, must ask the client for a copy of the employee benefit booklet, or an authorization letter to secure information directly from the plan administrator. The information to be determined is:

- Whether the client has a sufficient amount of protection
- Whether the plan provisions are comprehensive enough to meet the needs and risk-tolerance level of the client
- Whether the benefits provide portability through the exercising of a conversion provision and the type of coverage provided under any terms of conversion.

There are several ways that an adviser may design personal DI to deal with any deficiencies found in the group LTD plan. These include the use of:

- An executive carve-out plan
- A supplemental DI plan
- An overlapping DI plan
- A guaranteed-issue program.

Analysis of LTD Insurance

An analysis of the group LTD should include an assessment and personal review regarding the sufficiency of current coverage opposite the client's goals and risk tolerance. The areas to be examined are listed below. It is also wise to revisit the following chapters that cover these provisions in detail:

- The section on group LTD contained in Chapter 2, "Sources of Income During a Disability"
- The subsections on definitions of disability, exclusions, and limitations in Chapter 4, "Disability Insurance Policies and Provisions"
- The subsection on integration with group insurance benefits in Chapter 7, "Designing the Disability Insurance Plan".

Group LTD Review

❒ What is the waiting period for eligibility (not to be confused with the "elimination period"), and has the client satisfied it?

❒ What is the maximum coverage available?

❒ What is the non-evidence maximum?

❒ What is the formula for determining benefit entitlement?

❒ What is the definition of "earnings"? Are bonuses, profit-sharing, commissions, etc., covered?

❒ Is the benefit taxable or non-taxable?

❒ What is the elimination period for LTD, and is it preceded by short-term disability?

❒ What is the maximum benefit period for any one claim?

❒ What is the all-source maximum percentage? Does it include primary sources only, or both primary and secondary sources of income? Does it include personally owned disability income?

❒ What is the pre-existing condition limitation, and is the client currently affected by it?

❒ What happens if the client leaves the employer? Is there an extension of coverage for a specified time? Is there a conversion option? Within what time frame must it be exercised? What are the terms and provisions of the converted policy?

❒ What risks are excluded by the policy? (e.g., travel, criminal offences)

❒ What is the definition of total disability and how long is the own-occupation period?

❒ Is the client covered for partial disability? (Loss of duties? or loss of earnings?)

- ❒ When do partial benefits cease?
- ❒ In order to be covered, must a period of partial disability be preceded by a period of total disability?
- ❒ How does the plan cover a recurrent disability? Does it cover both total and partial?
- ❒ Are benefits indexed for inflation during a claim? If so, what is the maximum?
- ❒ Can the elimination period be satisfied through the accumulation of nonconsecutive but related periods of disability? If so, over what time frame?
- ❒ Will employee contributions be waived during periods of disability?
- ❒ Is there a recovery benefit that provides for some transitional assistance upon return to work?
- ❒ Is there a presumptive disability provision?
- ❒ Does the plan include a rehabilitation provision? Is participation mandatory?
- ❒ What is the process for reporting claims? Will the client be contacted directly by the insurer?
- ❒ What is the ratio of open files per claims examiner? Will the client receive prompt benefit payment?

ADDITIONS AND ALTERNATIVES TO GROUP LTD

The Executive Carve-Out Plan

This method of programming involves having the executive opt out of the group LTD plan altogether. In its place, the executive purchases individual DI. This is intended to accomplish the following objectives:

(a) Increase the overall benefit amount provided during disability by

- insuring the total earnings, not just the base salary, as many group plans do not include bonuses or other profit-sharing income
- dealing with the cap contained in the group LTD formula, which may be limiting the executive from receiving the full percentage amount.

(b) Provide portability within the area of disability benefits, so that the client is covered regardless of changes in employment at a later date.

(c) Enhance the protection through more comprehensive provisions and a broader range of benefits.

This solution is not always an option, however, as many group LTD plans require 100% participation. Alternatively, some group carriers will accommodate this but add a surcharge to the rate if the participation level is lower than a certain percentage, such as 70% or 75%. This surcharge is intended to account for the increased risk of anti-selection that can occur, and the tendency for plan usage rates to increase when participation becomes voluntary.

The Supplement Plan

This method refers to the purchase of individual DI as an addition to the existing group LTD plan. It is sometimes referred to as "topping up" coverage. No change is made to the base LTD plan.

As some insurers have a higher Income Ratio Guide for DI that is purchased as a supplement to an existing base of group LTD, this method may provide an overall higher level of benefits than the carve-out method. However, in the event that the client leaves the current employer, the base group LTD is no longer available, and the DI policy that the client carries thereafter is for a much smaller benefit than would have been retained under the carve-out method. This limitation may be minimized for clients whose group LTD plans contain a conversion option upon termination. As this is not an automatic provision in all LTD plans, the adviser may wish to determine its applicability by reviewing the client's benefits booklet or by contacting the plan administrator. Another alternative is to add a guaranteed insurability option to the individual DI plan. Many insurers include a special one-time right to exercise this option upon leaving a group plan, although, of course, it is subject to financial underwriting at the time of exercising the special option.

The supplement plan is a popular method used by advisers to deal with the "reverse discrimination" that occurs in group LTD due to the plan maximum contained in the group LTD benefit formula. This refers to the tendency for lower-paid employees to receive a higher percentage of earnings during a disability than higher-paid executives. It occurs because the executives are generally limited by the plan maximum, either because their base salary is much higher or because the formula itself covers base salary and not bonuses. Some clients may receive as much as half of their income in the form of profit-sharing, leaving them grossly underinsured. The following example illustrates the concept of reverse discrimination.

Illustration of Reverse Discrimination

Formula for LTD: 60% of salary to plan maximum of $5,000.

An employee earning $50,000 per year is entitled to group LTD benefits of $2,500 (60% of salary).

An employee earning $150,000 per year is capped at a group LTD benefit of $5,000 (40% of salary).

The adviser can rectify this inequity by implementing a supplemental DI plan. When there are a number of executives within the same company, this may be accomplished through the establishment of a corporate-owned grouped sickness and accident plan, provided it does not result in a shareholder-only plan. When there is a single executive or when the underinsured executives are all shareholders of the company, the supplemental protection should be established as personally owned insurance.

An important objective of the group LTD plan is to deliver to the owners of the company a method to attract and retain key people. A second objective is to deal with the issue of the moral obligation that a business owner may feel towards employees for their financial well-being during a disability. A supplemental DI plan provided by the employer removes the reverse discrimination that otherwise impedes achievement of these two objectives. In addition, it ensures that bonuses and profit-sharing paid to executives are accounted for.

The Overlapping DI Plan

This method deals with the existing group LTD by means of purchasing an overlapping DI policy that contains an amendment, whereby an adjustment will be made to the DI benefits at the time of a claim to account for the receipt of group LTD. This amendment is referred to as a "second payer" amendment, and hence the method is often referred to simply as a "second payer plan". The rate may be discounted by a nominal percentage (usually 10%) to reflect the fact that the benefit amount under the DI policy may be less or may not pay at all.

DI policies that contain second payer provisions have been referred to as "insurance that insures the group LTD benefit". As long as it remains available, it offers the primary advantage of enabling advisers to deal with a situation where a client wishes to obtain fully portable, comprehensive individual disability protection but is unable to opt out of the group LTD. It addresses the concern that the group LTD benefits might terminate at the end of a limited own-occupation period. Some advisers use longer elimination periods on the second payer plan as a means of programming the coverage to commence following the end of the own-occupation period under the group LTD. An example of this is the use of a 720-day elimination period on the DI policy to match a two-year own-occupation period on the group LTD. In the event that the LTD stops payment because the client is deemed to be able to perform a new occupation, the DI policy will begin payment, provided it contains a longer own-occupation period, such as to age 65.

This method also ensures that the client is protected regardless of future career changes, periods of layoff or waiting periods, and pre-existing condition limitations imposed upon joining a new group plan. It also enables an adviser to provide protection for partial disabilities when the client is not covered by the LTD plan. Furthermore, an adviser may be able to program an overall higher benefit amount than can be achieved under any other method.

Adjustment at Time of Claim

When a claim occurs, the insurer considers the maximum amount of monthly benefit currently available under its issue and participation limits and its Income Ratio Guide. From this amount, the insurer deducts 100% of the monthly group LTD. The client receives the lesser of the net maximum and the amount purchased.

Example:

DI Benefit Purchased:	$5,000
Existing Group LTD:	$2,000
Insurer's Current Issue Limit:	$6,000

Calculation: $6,000 less $2,000 = $4,000 net maximum.
Therefore, DI payment received is $4,000.

In the above example, it is assumed that both the DI and the LTD plans are taxed similarly (i.e., both are non-taxable or both are taxable). When one is taxable and the other is not, an adjustment factor is applied to first equalize the benefits. The adjustment factor varies, giving consideration to different tax brackets.

Second payer provisions differ from one company to another, and even within the same company over time. The provision forms a part of the policy contract, so that only new policies are affected by new practices. As the client may have an older policy, two other methods that have been used are reviewed below.

Adjustments on Older Policies

- Dollar-for-dollar offset
- Devaluation of group LTD by a fixed percentage

Dollar-for-Dollar Offset

The emphasis of this approach is to provide more comprehensive provisions than those contained in the LTD contract and, thus, ensure that the client will receive an income if the LTD pays either a lower amount or no benefit at all.

When the client's policy provides for this type of integration, the benefits under the DI policy are reduced by all benefits received from the group LTD plan. This method completely eliminates duplication of insurance. For instance, under a $5,000 DI policy purchased as an overlap to a group LTD plan of $5,000, no benefit would be paid unless the LTD benefit paid either no benefit or paid less benefit due to other integration provisions, such as the offset provision. In this method, there is no consideration given to the fact that the insured might have purchased less DI than entitled to under the company's issue and participation limits and the Income Ratio Guide.

Devaluation of Group LTD

This method of integration adjusts the value of the group LTD to a lesser amount, such as 75%. The adjusted amount is then subtracted from the insurer's current Income Ratio Guide to determine the maximum payable. The actual amount payable will be the lesser of this calculated amount and the actual DI policy amount purchased.

Illustration of Calculation

DI Policy Benefit Purchased:	$ 6,000
Client's Predisability Earnings:	$120,000
Income Ratio Guide Maximum:	$ 6,500
Group LTD:	$ 5,000

Assume that a claim occurs and the group LTD pays the full $5,000.

DI Payout

Step 1 **Group LTD is devalued to equal 75% of its actual payment**

$5,000 × 75% = $3,750

Step 2 **Subtract this amount from the current Income Ratio Guide limit based on predisability earnings**

$6,500 - $3,750 = $2,750

Step 3 **Amount payable is the lesser of Step 2 or the DI policy amount purchased**

$6,000 > $2,750; therefore, the benefit payable is $2,750

Comparison to Dollar-for-Dollar Offset Method:

$6,000 DI - $5,000 LTD = $1,000 payable under dollar-for-dollar method

The devaluation of group LTD method pays a higher benefit, because it uses the Income Ratio Guide maximum and because it deducts only 75% of the LTD. However, the Income Ratio Guide used is the one that the company currently has in effect at the time of claim. Therefore, the benefit paid may be more or less than projected when the program was implemented, due to changes in the published Income Ratio Guide itself. Furthermore, variances in the client's earnings over the years could also affect the amount payable under this method. This underscores the need to conduct regular annual reviews to check with the insurer concerning changes to these variables.

As this method is more generous than the dollar-for-dollar offset method, the discount given by the insurer is often lower.

GUARANTEED ISSUE PLANS

Some insurers offer guaranteed-issue programs that enable the adviser to use individual disability protection to insure groups or classes within a group, provided certain conditions are met. These conditions include criteria such as the size of the group, the occupation classification, the average age, the aggregate premium minimum, and whether the coverage will be a mandatory requirement of all employees within the eligible class.

Guaranteed-issue plans may be one of two types:

- Guaranteed standard risk plan
- Guaranteed-to-issue plan.

Guaranteed Standard Risk Plan

A guaranteed standard risk plan means that the insurer promises to issue the policy without ratings or exclusions for medical conditions. There are stricter guidelines for guaranteed standard risk plans than for guaranteed-to-issue plans. For instance, an insurer may require the arrangement to be employer-paid, or to have 100% participation of the defined group. A short-form application is used, and the underwriting is generally restricted to existing presumptive disability conditions, such as loss of hearing or sight. To qualify, the client must work a certain number of minimum hours (e.g., 30) and not currently be on disability.

Guaranteed-to-Issue Plan

A guaranteed-to-issue plan means that the insurer promises to issue coverage but does full medical underwriting and may add necessary ratings and/or exclusions. The insurer may also alter the plan design to conform to the risk being insured. The commitment is to issue some type of coverage, but not specifically on the same basis as applied for. The insurer may be more liberal regarding the nature of insurable groups and may offer higher amounts of coverage than under the guaranteed standard risk plan. To qualify, the client must still meet a minimum number of hours of work, such as 30 hours per week; must not currently be on disability; and must complete the medical underwriting process.

Pros and Cons of Guaranteed-Issue Plans

Guaranteed-issue plans are an attractive alternative to group LTD coverage for less cost-sensitive groups, such as executives and professionals. While coverage costs more than group LTD does, these clients may place a greater value on gaining more comprehensive provisions and securing full portability.

One challenge with this type of program, however, is that the amounts available may be insufficient unless combined with a base of group LTD. A second issue is that the insurer has the right to terminate the guaranteed-issue program at any time. Under the termination provision, it is not the current in-force coverage that terminates, but the offer to insure new plan entrants or to further increase coverage for existing plan members. A third issue is that as individual DI continues to evolve and become provisionally more like group LTD, the value derived becomes less.

Guaranteed-issue programs remain a controversial topic among industry insurers. Many feel that the programs have led to claims problems and driven up the cost for all those insured, and that these programs should be withdrawn from the market. While they remain available, though, advisers should not overlook this tool for professional and executive markets.

Chapter 10

Business Needs and Products

DISABILITY BUY-SELL INSURANCE

The Need

Introduction

Disability buy-sell insurance is designed for partnerships and private companies to provide funds that facilitate a transfer of ownership in the event of a partner or shareholder's disability. The provision of liquidity during disability avoids the risk of liquidation or sale to a competitor, among other things. There is a greater probability that a client will be disabled in any given year than that the client will die. Therefore, it is important to discuss this need with your client when reviewing business insurance requirements.

Risks and Benefits

The following concerns should be discussed:

- Although no longer active, the disabled party continues to have the right to make decisions that affect the growth and profitability of the business.
- The disabled party's family may feel the need to become involved in the running of the business to protect its interest.
- The disabled party may become more risk averse regarding business investment and operational decisions.
- Both parties may want to complete a purchase and sale of the shares but lack capital funding to do so.

A structured buy-sell (also known as "buyout") agreement should include provisions for the sale of the business in the event of the permanent disability of one of the parties, and the agreement should be funded by disability insurance (DI). A properly structured agreement will provide advantages to both the disabled and the healthy members. Benefits include:

- Assurance that the business interest will not be sold to an outsider or left in the control of the disabled party, who could be unable to make business decisions due to the impairment.
- A guarantee that only active members participate in the growth of the business.
- Funding to reduce or eliminate the need to borrow from the bank with interest charges, preserving the company's normal cash flow.
- The disabled party being assured of a buyer and the ability to convert the business investment into cash at full market value.
- Relief for the disabled party's family from the need to get involved in running the business to protect its interest.
- Protection from the risk of future business losses, and the ability to reinvest the funds into other income-generating or capital appreciation assets that they control.

Agreement Structure and Tax Considerations

Introduction

Professional advisers should be involved in determining the best structure for the agreement, as not only tax advantages should be considered, but also legal implications. Each situation is different, and the personal circumstances of the clients and their relationship with their partners and/or their spouses may affect the choice of what constitutes the best method for them.

The temptation may be to simply insert a disability provision into an existing buy-sell agreement that was designed to cover transfer of business ownership upon death. However, the adviser must consider the differences. For instance, corporate ownership of life insurance policies enables the client to take advantage of tax-free distribution of proceeds through the capital dividend account. However, there is no similar option for electing a tax-free distribution of disability buy-sell proceeds. Non-tax issues must also be reviewed. The wishes of a client who is still alive, though disabled, may be quite different from that same client's wishes with death imminent.

The agreement must also address how soon the buyout should be triggered following a disability, how disability will be defined, and how the business will be valued. In addition, it must take into account the availability and design of funding vehicles. This ensures that the wishes of the owners can be fulfilled in the event of a long-term total disability of one of the partners. Insurers must protect against the risk of anti-selection; product designs and limits are an important part of accomplishing this. The agreement and the funding vehicle must be in alignment; otherwise, the agreement may be triggered while the funding may not.

Cross-Purchase Agreements

Each shareholder or partner purchases a policy insuring the other in an amount equal to their value of the business. During a claim, the benefit recipient is the policy owner. Unlike life insurance, the amount of DI cannot be greater than the current business value based upon a valuation method that is approved by the insurer. This principle is consistent with the concept of avoiding overinsurance, as this can otherwise create an incentive for a benefit claim. Each policy owner pays the premiums on the contract he or she owns and cannot deduct this as a business expense. Therefore, the adviser must consider the marginal tax rate of the owners as a means of determining the true cost of this method. Cross-purchase agreements are effective when the insured individuals are relatively close in age and when the number of owners is not greater than three.

Example of Three-Party Cross-Purchase

⊕
6 Policies in Total

		Owner		
		A	B	C
	A	■	⊕	⊕
Insured	B		■	⊕
	C	⊕	⊕	■

When a disability occurs, the benefits are payable on a non-taxable basis to the owner of the policy, who then exchanges the funds for the shares. A shareholder disposing of a business interest triggers a taxable capital gain or loss, and a partner is taxed as he or she would be on a sale of partnership interest. If the business is a qualified small business corporation, as defined in the *Income Tax Act*, the gain may be sheltered by the capital gains exemption available on disposition of shares from a qualified small business corporation. If a monthly funding method has been used, rather than a lump-sum purchase, the disabled owner can claim a reserve for the payments not yet received, and this results in spreading out the capital gain over several years.

Considerations — Cross-Purchase Method

- There is an increase in the adjusted cost base to each of the remaining shareholders/partners, thereby reducing the taxation to the healthy members when their shares or partnership interest is ultimately surrendered.

- It is a complex method when there are more than three, as the number of policies required grows considerably.
- A significant difference in age results in the youngest paying a much higher cost to insure the oldest member.
- The oldest member may have a larger ownership interest in the business, and this further contributes to an inequity in the funding of the agreement.

Corporate Share Redemption

The corporation owns and pays for the policies. Premiums are not a deductible business expense, but the true cost may be lower than under the cross-purchase method for shareholders if the corporate tax rate is lower than the personal marginal rate of the shareholders. This method may be preferable when dealing with disparities in age or percentage ownership of the shareholders.

During a disability, the proceeds of the disability buy-sell policy are paid to the corporation. The corporation then buys back the shares of the disabled shareholder.

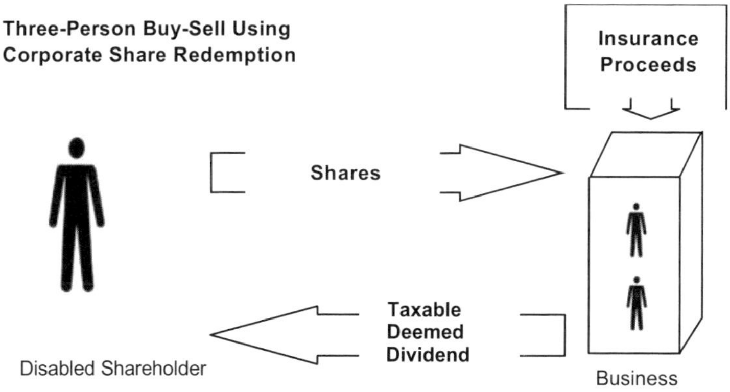

Under this method, there is no increase in the adjusted cost base of the remaining shareholders' shares. The benefits have been paid tax-free to the corporation. However, unlike with life insurance, the DI proceeds do not qualify for credit to the capital dividend account. The disabled shareholder receives a taxable deemed dividend when the corporation buys back the shares. The disabled shareholder is required to pay tax on the excess of the dividend received over the paid-up capital amount of the shares, and is not able to use the capital gains exemption, as a capital gain is not realized.

Considerations — Corporate Share Redemption Method

- When the corporate tax rate is lower than the shareholders' personal marginal tax rate, the cost of the insurance may be less.
- It may be a more effective way of dealing with age and share percentage disparities.
- Although the proceeds are paid to the company tax-free, the corporation cannot use the capital dividend account as a means of dispensing the proceeds.

Entity Purchase Agreement

This method is similar to a corporate share redemption, except that the ownership of the business is a partnership format, not a corporation. There is no adjustment to the cost base upon the termination of the disabled partner's interest, premiums are not deductible, and the benefit is received tax-free. The liquidating partner is taxed as he or she would be on a liquidation of partnership interest.

Use of a Trust

A trust arrangement is sometimes used as a means of guaranteeing that the buy-sell agreement be executed in accordance with its terms. As under a cross-purchase agreement, each party pays the premiums directly to the insurance company. The owner of the policies is the trustee. During a disability, the trustee receives the tax-free policy proceeds from the insurance company and arranges for the transfer of the business interest in accordance with the provisions.

Advantages

- A third party holds the funds for release upon completion of the terms of the agreement.
- Both the healthy and the disabled partner are assured that the funds will be available and used for the intended purpose, and that the terms of the agreement will be fulfilled.

Each method has both advantages and limitations, and the adviser should work with the client's team of professionals to consider not only the financial considerations but also the client's legal requirements, as these may be more compelling than the tax savings associated with a particular method.

Payment Considerations

Elimination Period

Unlike with individual DI, an early elimination period is not desirable, because it means that the owner must now dispose of his or her ownership interest in the business. Conversely, waiting too long can mean that the disabled partner and his or her family are involved in running the business when active partners would prefer that they were not. Most insurers make a variety of elimination periods available, such as 12, 18, and 24 months, usually stated in days (365, 540, and 730 days). As the elimination period lengthens, the maximum allowable benefit indicated on the company's issue and participation limits chart increases. Therefore, a client may need to decide between a 12-month elimination period that only partially insures the business value and a 24-month elimination period that fully insures the value but requires the trigger date to be two years instead of one.

The adviser must find a reasonable balance between triggering benefits too soon and waiting too long. This is a plan-design decision that should be discussed with all the partners in a group meeting, weighing the risks and benefits associated with each option.

Payment Stream

There are three types of payment streams: lump sum, fixed monthly payment, and combined. Some insurers offer more than one format, while others may not. Each offers advantages and limitations.

Lump-Sum Payment Policies

The lump-sum payment is most similar to life insurance, insofar as the payment is immediate and the transfer of shares is complete. There are no lingering obligations. However, insurers offer lower maximum issue and participation limits for this type of payment option.

Fixed Monthly Payment Policies

The monthly plan is a monthly payment over a stated period of time, usually five years. Payments are made on a non-interest-bearing basis. In the event the insured recovers after monthly payments have commenced, the remaining payments continue. In other words, the insured is presumed to be totally disabled once payments have commenced. However, if the insured dies, payments will cease. It is critical, therefore, for the adviser to stress to the client the importance of maintaining the life insurance funding in place throughout the disability payment period. Most insurers provide a partial refund in this situation. For instance, the refund may be based on the last 12 months and relate to the premiums paid in excess of what would have been payable for the insurance benefits during that time.

Combined Payment Policies

Some insurers allow the insured to wait until the time of claim to decide how payments will be structured. This policy format offers greater flexibility, enabling the owner to elect full lump-sum benefits, a combination of a lump sum and instalments for the balance, or an instalment with no down payment. Insurers sometimes refer to instalments of this nature as "settlement options" or "flexible funding". There are several ways in which these instalment options are different from those payable under fixed monthly payment policies. First of all, the duration can be much longer, stretching out as long as 10 years, instead of only five years. In the event of the insured's death during the monthly instalment payments, payments continue, unlike the fixed monthly payment policy, in which they cease. Another difference is that monthly instalments under the flexible funding method earn interest, while fixed monthly payments are non-interest bearing. As with the fixed monthly payment policies, this method spreads out the tax consequences of the buyout. The owner does not have to decide on the income stream until the time of disability and can consider the current tax situation, among other things, as to the structure that will be most advantageous. Of course, this depends, as well, upon the terms that have been included in the buyout agreement itself.

Renewability

The Non-Cancellable Provision

Most buy-sell contracts are non-cancellable and conditionally renewable to a specified age (such as age 62, 63, or 64). Although the policy may say "non-cancellable", the guarantees the company is making include the following promises:

- The company relinquishes the right to change premiums, thereby providing a promise that rates will never change after the policy is in force.
- The company relinquishes the right to make changes to the policy, thereby providing a promise that no restrictive riders or changes in policy provisions will be made after the policy is in force.

The company reserves the right to terminate coverage in the event of changes in certain circumstances. These conditions are listed in the policy. In this respect, it differs from non-cancellable personal disability income insurance and is better described as "conditionally renewable with guaranteed rates". The renewal conditions are intended to protect the insurer from the risk of anti-selection. A large sum of money is at stake, and if the intended purpose of the coverage no longer exists, the likelihood that the insured will seek a "windfall" benefit rises. The following are standard renewal conditions listed in buy-sell policies:

- The insured's age is less than the maximum specified age (the closer to retirement, the more appealing it becomes to trigger a buyout).
- The buy-sell agreement is still in effect (some insurers only require evidence of this at the time of claim).
- Payment has not been triggered.
- The insured's share of ownership of the business is not more than 90%.

- The insured is with the same company (the policy is based on the specific business but may contain a transfer provision, as described elsewhere in this chapter).
- The insured continues to work full-time.

Maximum Renewal Age

Prudent business continuity planning includes provision for transfer of the business ownership upon retirement of one of the owners. In this respect, the need for buyout funding in the event of a long-term disability lessens as the partner nears the final years just before retirement. Insurers regard the final five years prior to age 65 as presenting a higher risk of anti-selection. For instance, let us say a client developed a heart condition that he or she was able to cope with over the past several years. But the person now finds retirement more desirable and, consequently, finds it more difficult to cope with the condition, primarily due to a changed frame of mind. There is medical evidence supporting the heart condition, and the insurer would have difficulty proving that the client was not experiencing increased symptoms of difficulty.

Insurers deal with this by using a declining benefit schedule. The reduction scale acts as a form of co-insurance. The following example illustrates a declining benefit schedule:

Example:

Schedule of Reduction in Benefits	
Age at Onset	Benefit Is Reduced To:
60	80%
61	60%
62	40%
63	20%

In the above example, the insurer promises renewal through to age 64 (age 64 is the expiry). Some insurers terminate coverage at age 63, and in that case the cut-off point is 40%. At least one insurer terminates coverage at the anniversary nearest age 62, with the cut-off point being the value at age 61, 60%.

Policies differ not only in their chosen cut-off age, but also in their approach to defining the expiry age. Some expire on the policy anniversary "nearest the specified age"; others, on the policy anniversary when the insured "is the specified age"; and a third, on the "monthly anniversary following the specified age".

For instance, let us assume the policy states an expiry of the anniversary *nearest* age 62, the insured's birth date is in July, and the policy anniversary is in February. In such a case, the policy will actually terminate five months short of the insured's 62nd birthday, as it is the nearest policy anniversary. Conversely, if the policy anniversary is December, then the insured will have coverage almost five months after his or her 62nd birthday. Under the "is the specified age" method, coverage could continue up to 11 months beyond if the policy anniversary was one month before the birthdate. Under the "monthly anniversary following" method, the termination date most closely matches the actual age, as it does not wait for the policy's annual anniversary date.

Buy-Sell Agreement in Effect

Disability buy-sell insurance has been available for many years but has not been offered through many insurers. First-generation policies required the insured to produce a copy of the actual buy-sell agreement as an underwriting requirement. Not only did this give the insurer the ability to review valuation methods matched, but it also acted as a safeguard for the insured, since the policy stipulated that the agreement must be in force at the time of claim for payment to be made. It was felt that it was not in the insured's interest for the insurer to issue coverage that would not pay a benefit, and the insurer had a duty of care to minimize this by taking appropriate steps to ensure that the agreement was in place before release of the policy. The problem that arose was that it often took considerable time for partners and lawyers to agree on wording and to get the final document produced. The delay was not always related to the disability provisions, but rather sometimes to other clauses. A delay by the lawyer resulted in delaying the underwriting process, and this meant continued exposure for partners in the meantime. This led to the practice of allowing insurance to be underwritten and placed in force, with the safeguard moved to a later point.

Insurers use one of two approaches regarding when the actual buy-sell agreement must be in place. One method is to state that the buyout agreement must be in force at the time of claim, but not necessarily at the time coverage is purchased or issued. Another method is to state a time frame following purchase of coverage within which the agreement must be in place. Examples of these two methods follow:

Version 1

The existence of a formal disability buy-sell agreement is not required at time of issue but will be required at time of claim.

Version 2

A formal disability buy-sell agreement must be in effect within one year from the purchase of policies or the coverage is voidable at the insurer's option.

Some policies are silent regarding the need for a formal disability buy-sell agreement and, instead, outline the conditions that must be satisfied, such as that the elimination period has been fulfilled, the person is found to be totally disabled and was still actively at work on a full-time basis in the same business, and the insured's interest is sold to the other owners of the business or to the business itself. If the sale itself does not take place, no benefit is payable (a standard requirement of all disability buyout policies).

Some insurers stipulate that the agreement must be provided at the time of claim and that the agreement itself must be in place prior to the onset of total disability. If total disability occurs within one year of the policy date and the agreement is not yet in place, then one company will accept an agreement that is signed during the elimination period. The policy is silent regarding what happens if disability occurs after one year and the agreement is still not in place. It may be assumed that the policy is then voidable at the insurer's option.

Changes in Ownership

Most policies restrict changes in ownership or assignment without the insurer's authorization. Consequently, if a company changes the structure of the buy-sell agreement and this affects policy ownership, the insurer must be notified and underwriting may be involved.

Conversion Privilege

Over time, businesses may change and a partner may leave the business for various reasons. Some policies contain a "conversion privilege", which enables the individual to convert the buyout insurance to a personal disability policy without evidence of insurability. The coverage amount and plan design are limited, and may provide for a maximum benefit period of two years, with an elimination period of 90 days. The amount of coverage is usually related to the insured's occupation class, ranging from $1,000 to $2,500. It helps to provide some level of coverage while the insured applies for a higher level of benefits on a medically underwritten basis. In the event that the person is no longer insurable, at least he or she will have some level of benefits in force.

Transfer Privilege

A partner who leaves the business to join or start another business may continue to need buyout insurance in the new business. The transfer privilege contained in some policies provides the right under certain conditions to transfer the buy-sell coverage to the new business without evidence of good health. The application for the new coverage must be made within a stipulated time after leaving the business (usually 90 days), and if coverage is approved, the insured's original age will be used. The coverage will not exceed the amount under the prior policy, nor can the elimination period be less than the one contained in the original coverage.

Documentation

As indicated, most disability insurers will issue the buy-sell insurance policies before the client actually implements a legal buy-sell agreement, as this facilitates getting the funding in place while simultaneously getting the legal agreement completed. As there is a possibility that one of the insured partners may become totally disabled prior to the finalization of the legal agreement and after the policy is in force, advisers should investigate the company's practices regarding payment in this situation.

The section above described how the industry practice varies concerning whether payment will be made should a claim arise before the agreement is put in place. When the insurer makes the agreement itself a condition of payment, an otherwise valid disability will not trigger payment under the policy if it occurs prior to the implementation of the agreement. Another approach is for the insurer merely to require evidence at the time of a claim that the sale of the business ownership is taking place. This method relieves any concern of a disability occurring prior to the completion of the agreement itself and, therefore, is a better method.

Regardless of whether the insurer requires an agreement as a condition of payment, it is nevertheless important to advise the client company that one should be implemented. The client's lawyer should prepare this.

The following checklist indicates some of the provisions that should be considered.

Checklist of Provisions

- ❐ A method of valuation used to determine the purchase price should be selected from one of the insurer's listed valuation methods, so business value and insurance benefit will match.
- ❐ The definition of what constitutes disability should be the same as the definition contained in the policy contract, to avoid triggering the sale of the shares without the funds to complete the transaction.
- ❐ The number of months of continuous total disability required to trigger the buy-sell ("trigger date") and the elimination period should be the same.
- ❐ Determine who controls the business during the elimination period.
- ❐ Determine entitlement to fringe benefits and salary during the elimination period.
- ❐ Specify the method of payment — lump sum, monthly instalment, or a combination thereof.

Defining Disability

The definition of "disability" is the trigger under the buyout agreement and the payment under the funding vehicle. It only makes good sense that the definition in these two contracts be synchronized. In individual disability income plans, a "good" policy protects against short-term and long-term disability as well as partial and total disability. Conversely, in buy-sell insurance, this would mean that the partner might be forced to sell under circumstances that are only temporary or partial. For this reason, the focus is on both "total" and "long-term" disability.

There are two schools of thought regarding the best way to define disability in a buyout agreement. Some people believe that the "own occupation" definition is best, because if the partner cannot function in his or her own occupation, the buyout should be triggered regardless of whether or not the partner can do other work in the organization. The belief is that his or her value to the organization is the talent exhibited in the usual occupation. Others believe, however, that a partner should not be forced out of his or her own business as long as there is other work within the company that the partner can perform. This latter view often gets to the emotional issue that a partner, who has invested years of hard work building the business, is unlikely to want to sell shares as long as it is possible to be a viable part of the business — even if it is in a different capacity. Proponents of this reasoning suggest an alternative definition: "regular occupation and not working elsewhere".

Definition of Disability

Buy-sell contracts contain duties-based definitions and cover total disability only. Disability may be defined using one of two occupational definitions:

1. Own occupation
2. Regular occupation and not working.

For clients to collect under the own-occupation definition, they must be unable to perform the primary duties of their regular occupation, and they must show evidence that the sale of the business interest has taken or is taking place. If the client can continue to work at the business, but in a much diminished role, the benefit may still be payable, as long as the own-occupation definition is satisfied and the sale of the shares has taken place. This protects the healthy partner in circumstances where the disabled partner can no longer run the business and can only work to a lesser capacity in a different role. The adviser should keep in mind, however, that the term "own occupation" does not refer to a person's job, but to the broader aspect of the nature of the duties and how the role is performed in the general economy.

A "regular occupation and not working" definition within a buy-sell contract generally refers to the inability of the person insured to perform his or her regular occupation, and provides that the person is not working elsewhere (in the business or outside the business). Some older policies, which are not sold anymore, provided that the person is not working elsewhere within the business. Here, the emphasis is on whether the client is making a contribution to the business, regardless of the nature of the work. In this instance, the buy-sell agreement would not be triggered.

Accumulation of Non-Consecutive Periods of Disability

The policy will generally provide that the client can accumulate periods of total disability, but not periods of partial disability, provided such periods occur within a stated time frame of each other, such as six months.

Other Features and Benefits

Legal and Accounting Benefit

This provision, when included, provides for reimbursement of legal and accounting expenses incurred in relation to implementation of the buy-sell agreement. The benefit is usually included in the policy without an additional premium charge. The amount varies from company to company, but is generally in the range of $1,000 to $5,000.

Lump-Sum Death Benefit

Some policies include a lump-sum death benefit in monthly benefit policies equal to a multiple of the monthly benefit, such as three times. (Monthly benefits otherwise cease upon death.)

Waiver of Premium Benefit

All disability buy-sell policies include a waiver of premium provision, in which premiums are waived during periods of total disability. A 90-day waiting period applies. Periods of related disability due to the same cause separated by up to six months are usually counted as one for satisfying the waiver of premium waiting period. Once the 90-day waiting period is satisfied, premiums are waived through the remainder of the elimination period and while benefits are being paid.

Exclusions

Coverage offered by insurers is very comprehensive. There are usually only two risks that are not covered: losses caused by war or insurrection and those caused by normal pregnancy.

Underwriting Considerations

Eligible Occupations

Buy-sell plans are normally made available to low-risk occupations only, such as occupation classes 4A, 3A, and 2A.

Eligible Businesses

Buy-sell insurance is intended for private-owned establishments with a limited number of partners or shareholders. While this range is normally two to five principals, there may be consideration given to insuring larger businesses having up to 10 partners or shareholders if the business itself does not have more than a stipulated number of employees (such as 40 or 50) and provided the annual sales of the business fall below a certain level (such as $8 million or $10 million). The business must also be in a stable industry. Buy-sell insurance is not generally offered to large corporations.

Businesses are classified as either commercial establishments or service establishments. Each category will have separate eligibility criteria concerning the maximum number of owners, percentage of ownership, and years in business. A business whose nature of work is service-oriented may be classified as a commercial operation for the purpose of buy-sell insurance underwriting guidelines if the size of the business and the number of partners is over a certain limit.

Some examples of businesses considered desirable include:

- Accounting
- Advertising
- Architectural
- High-tech and computer
- Medical practices
- Clinics
- Engineering
- Law practices
- Employment agencies
- Small manufacturers.

Among those not eligible are public corporations and non-arm's length relationships.

The business must be stable (usually defined as in operation for at least three years) and have a minimum net worth of at least $45,000 to $50,000.

Eligible Owners

Most insurers will not insure a one-way buy-sell. There are guidelines for the percentage of ownership, as well as for minimum earnings levels and years with the firm. All eligible owners must be purchasing insurance — if they are insurable. This requirement avoids anti-selection, where the firm seeks to cover only the higher-risk owners, such as those with the greatest amount of share ownership or existing health conditions. Insurers want to balance their risk exposure; to accomplish this, they need to insure the lower risks along with the higher risks in a group.

Coverage is usually available between ages 18 to 60. An owner cannot hold more than 90% of the shares in the business. Some insurers may also stipulate a minimum ownership level, such as 10% or a minimum dollar amount.

Family Members

Buy-sell insurance is not available for family-owned businesses where the relationship is parent–child or husband–wife. This is intended to avoid the potential for 100% ownership remaining within the family unit, or the potential risk of collusion. Some insurers, however, may consider covering brothers, sisters, and cousins.

Standardizing the Impaired Risk

It is in the client's best interest that, where possible, existing medical impairments are standardized by means of a premium rating instead of an exclusion. It is better for the client to pay a higher premium for insurance than to find that the buy-sell has been triggered as a result of an excluded condition and that no funds are available to fulfill the contract.

Therefore, whenever possible, the adviser should ask the insurer to consider a rating over issuance of the contract with a medical exclusion.

Determining the Benefit Amount

Issue and Participation Limits

The insurer has an established issue and participation limit that is based on three variables:

- Occupation class
- Elimination period
- Payout structure.

Occupations within the lowest-risk class will be eligible for higher amounts. The maximum issue limit increases as the elimination period lengthens. Fixed monthly payment plans offer higher amounts than lump-sum payment plans.

Most insurers will not share in the risk with another insurer and thereby offer a larger amount to a client whose business value exceeds the company's own issue and participation limits. Insurers generally do not allow the use of two different elimination periods as a means of securing the maximum allowable.

Example

Ineligible EP Selection	
Elimination Period	Monthly Benefit
360 days	$1,000
720 days	$ 500
Total Benefit	$1,500

This is due to the fact that the elimination period is tied to the trigger date. Benefits cannot be programmed to begin after the buy-sell has already taken place. Insurers also require each partner to have the same elimination period.

The minimum policy size with most insurers is in the range of $25,000 to $50,000. The maximum policy size is in the range of $1 million to $2 million, and this varies within the industry. One insurer offers more generous limits when the partners also have personal disability income insurance in place with the same insurer that conforms with certain guidelines.

Business Valuation

The eligible amount of coverage is tied to the valuation method used to determine the business value. Although the adviser and the client may wish to add extra insurance to cover business value fluctuations or future growth, insurers will not issue disability buy-sell for more than the current value of the business. However, most insurers do offer an optional benefit that can be purchased to protect insurability so that as the business value grows, the owners can increase their coverage without medical evidence.

Each insurer has its own list of acceptable formulas for determining the business value. These formulas vary based on occupation class and on whether the business is a personal service or commercial establishment. The insurer may be willing to consider a different method of valuation based on generally accepted business valuation practices if it is documented in the buy-sell agreement and would not create an overinsurance situation.

The valuation of a business for DI purposes may vary somewhat from valuation methods used for other purposes. For instance, some insurers do not include a goodwill factor or accounts receivable in the value of a service business.

For claims purposes, insurers generally use the valuation at the time disability occurs; however, some companies allow the valuation to be done at either the date of disability or the end of the elimination period. The amount payable is the actual value of the business using the valuation method agreed to at the time of underwriting, up to the maximum benefit amount purchased. The adviser should make the client aware that if the business value has declined, the lesser amount is payable. Therefore, if the client has sold a division of the business, the adviser should adjust the amount of insurance in place. However, if the value of the business has reduced due to minor fluctuations, it may be best to maintain the insurance to provide protection as the business value returns to its previous level.

Below are a couple of examples of business valuation methods that may be used.

Business Valuation Examples	
Business	**Valuation Method**
Medical Professionals	Business Value = Net Book Value + (Average Gross Billings × 0.75)
Legal, Accounting, Insurance Firms	Business Value = Net Book Value + (Average Gross Billings × 1.2)

Optional Benefits

Guaranteed Insurability Option

The client may purchase a guaranteed insurability option (GIO), which guarantees the right to purchase more coverage as the business value grows. This functions similarly to a GIO on individual DI. The client is able to purchase the insurance without medical evidence at defined option dates. Financial evidence for the change in business valuation must be provided. This is an important provision for a client whose business is growing.

KEY PERSON INSURANCE

The Need

Some employees contribute directly to the profitability and growth of the business and can be described as key people. They head departments or perform certain specialized services for the business. Their knowledge, skill, or talent is rare, so few others can duplicate or replace the value they bring to the business. The industry they work in is often highly specialized, and given the uniqueness of the person's skills, there are few others within the industry that have similar abilities. Many of their occupations involve design or research. Their skills are often associated with their own creativity and are not just education-related, which makes it more difficult to find a suitable replacement. Their absence due to a disability would cause financial hardship to the company in many ways:

- The business would suffer a loss of management skill and experience.
- There may be a decline in sales or production.
- The business may suffer a loss of available credit or be downgraded in its credit rating.
- The need to recruit and train a replacement will generate expenses for the business.

This represents an insurable business need for disability coverage. A special product is available for covering this need that is independent of insuring income to the disabled executive. It is called "key person disability insurance". Given its specialized nature, few insurers offer it. Nevertheless, it is an important component of an adviser's business portfolio.

Occupations that may be suitable include the following:

- Advertising executives
- Architects
- Research scientists
- Motion picture scriptwriters and directors
- Computer designers
- Museum curators
- Industrial designers
- Jewellery designers
- Engineers and physicists
- Publicity agents
- Executives who generate high sales
- Consultants with unique skills.

Structure

The business purchases a policy covering each key person in the company. The business is designated as both the owner and the beneficiary. Proceeds during a claim are paid to the company on a non-taxable basis. This helps to offset the loss to the business in profits and expenses associated with finding a replacement. The policy covers total disability, not partial disability. Key person insurance focuses on the company's needs, not the insured's needs, and therefore does not affect the individual's ability to also insure income for wage loss replacement during a disability. The two are separate policies with different purposes and issue limits.

Sometimes the term "key person insurance" is misused to refer to a formal executive wage loss program. The latter is actually a series of individual disability income plans purchased by the business as a means of providing salary continuation, or "wage loss replacement", to the insured executive. Benefits in this scenario flow directly to the disabled person during a claim. More information about insuring executives for wage loss is covered in Chapter 9, "Individual Disability Insurance in the Workplace". This chapter deals with true key person disability policies only.

Eligibility

The key person must provide a service that is unique or that clearly affects the company's profits. For instance, a design engineer who develops products plays a significant role in the company. The business cannot insure family members as key people.

The insurer will have requirements regarding minimum length of service and maximum share holdings. As a general rule, shareholder-employees can be considered if they do not own more than 50% of the shares. Insurable occupations are low-risk occupations, including Classes 4A and 3A. Some insurers may include Class 2A. Coverage is generally available between the ages of 18 to 55.

Renewability

The key person policy is a conditionally renewable plan with non-cancellable rates. Like the buy-sell policy, the insurer guarantees not to change the policy by adding restrictive riders or by otherwise reducing benefits. The conditions for renewal ensure that the individual will continue to fit the profile of a key person in the business. The standard conditions include:

- Continues to be a full-time employee; and
- Continues to be with the same business (it is the business being protected against loss of profits, not the insured against loss of earnings).

The policy will not be renewed beyond the maximum renewal age of 62. Some insurers define this as "age nearest", while others specify "the insured's 62nd birthday". Once total disability benefits have been paid for 12 months, the policy terminates.

Provisions and Plan Design

Elimination Periods

Standard elimination periods include 30, 60, and 90 days. Benefit periods are normally short, such as 12 months.

Benefit Amount

The risk of overinsurance has caused insurers to adopt a more conservative approach to the design of key person insurance than the approach that was taken in plans available a decade ago. Older policies offered longer benefit periods and higher multiples of earnings. Today, insurers generally cover no more than the monthly salary. The maximum benefit available is in the range of $15,000.

The benefit does not reduce the key person's insurable limit under personal DI, because the benefit is paid to the business, and the benefits are not for the personal use of the insured.

Companies also establish minimum issue limits, such as $2,500. The minimum policy size reflects the cost to the insurer of underwriting the risk, and also reflects the fact that the purpose is to protect financial loss that would have an impact on the business.

Definition of Total Disability

A key person disability policy covers total disability only. The definition of total disability may take one of two forms:

- Unable to do the important duties of the regular occupation and not engaged in another occupation.
- Unable to perform the important duties of the regular occupation.

The latter, the "pure own occupation" definition, is in keeping with the philosophy that the measure for a key person policy should be the loss to the company, which occurs when the key person cannot do the job that he or she was hired to do. Under a "regular occupation and not working" definition, if the key person can no longer do the job that he or she was hired to do but can (and does) pursue alternate work in a different occupation elsewhere, the business that lost the key person suffers financially. The insurance does not do the job for which it was intended and a financial loss occurs to the business.

Other Standard Provisions

Most key person policies contain the following standard provisions found in personal individual disability policies.

- Accumulation of non-consecutive periods of disability (usually six months, but may vary by insurer);
- Recurrent disability provision (usually six months, but may vary by insurer);
- Waiver of premium (during periods of total disability); and
- Standard exclusions (war, insurrection, normal pregnancy).

Special Provisions and Optional Benefits

Proof of Loss Benefit

Some policies require the business to remit written monthly confirmation as proof of loss during a claim. This provision acknowledges that there may be an expense associated with this requirement and compensates the business for a nominal amount, generally in the range of $50 each month.

Replacement Expense Benefit

When a key person has to be replaced, there are costs incurred associated with finding and hiring the replacement. Expenses may take the form of the agency fees associated with finding a suitable candidate and the replacement's salary and relocation costs. The replacement expense benefit may be a mandatory benefit in some policies, and it requires an additional premium. The business can select the maximum benefit amount as a multiple of the base coverage (usually up to four times the basic benefit). The coverage is reimbursement-based, for up to 80% of eligible expenses. A waiting period may be required (such as six months), and expenses are usually covered on a retroactive basis back to the date of disability, payable for a period of up to 18 months (or until the maximum replacement expense benefit has been reached).

The following are examples of expenses normally covered by a replacement expense benefit:

- The replacement's salary for up to three months
- Agency fees and executive search fees
- Charges for advertisements in classified ads
- Travel-related expenses for the candidates being interviewed
- Relocation expenses for the replacement.

It is a valuable feature of the key person policy.

HIV and Hepatitis Benefit

Some key people may be health care professionals who could be exposed through their work to the risk of HIV or hepatitis B and C. This optional benefit broadens the definition of disability. Under some conditions, individuals are not required to be under the care of a physician in order to qualify for the benefits to be paid. This would apply if they are HIV-impaired or hepatitis-impaired and, due to this, are restricted or prohibited from performing important duties, or if their patients refuse treatment after being told of the impairment as required by their licensing body.

Some insurers do not offer non-cancellable rates for this benefit (even though the base policy has non-cancellable rates), as the future impact of related claims is not fully known. A rate guarantee may be offered such that if premiums for this benefit increase, the new rate will be guaranteed for a further five-year period.

Taxation

The premium paid by the company is not deductible as a business expense. The premium paid is not added back into the earnings of the key employee. Benefits received during a claim are tax-free and are payable directly to the business. There is no capital dividend account election available for the proceeds. However, to the extent that funds are used to pay a replacement for the disabled employee or used for some other deductible business expense, the taxable disbursement will be offset by a tax deduction.

OVERHEAD EXPENSE INSURANCE

The Need

One problem facing small businesses is how to continue operating the business during the owner's disability so that he or she will have an active business after recovering. While some expenses may be reduced, many expenses, such as rent and taxes, are fixed. Even if it were possible for the owner to close the doors during his or her absence and somehow maintain relationships with clients, these overhead expenses would have to be paid, during a time when the revenue has reduced. Overhead expense insurance addresses this need by covering fixed expenses that continue for the business.

Structure

Overhead expense (OE) insurance can be defined as reimbursement insurance for owners of small, closely held businesses or professionals to help offset certain ongoing business expenses if the owner or professional becomes disabled. This is not the same as personal DI, which usually pays a benefit through to age 65 and can be purchased in addition. OE has a shorter benefit period and is usually between one and two years' duration after satisfying the elimination period. It is generally believed that a business is unlikely to stay open more than two years if the owner is disabled longer than this. OE helps to keep the business afloat until the owner's return or, if a return is unlikely, until arrangements can be made to dispose of the owner's interest.

The business or partnership can have more than one owner or professional. Each would take a policy out for his or her share of expenses. By having coverage in place, customers, creditors, and employees can be assured that the business will continue. Creditors are less likely to recall outstanding loans, and employees are less likely to quit to work elsewhere. Customers are retained because the business continues to operate.

Eligibility

The Business

OE coverage is designed for businesses where the applicants are key to the business, insofar as its income would cease or drastically be reduced in the event of the insured's absence. Generally, businesses with more than five employees and retail outlets are not eligible for coverage. The ideal businesses include professional and personal services. The business must be one that is stable and satisfies the insurer's minimum time in business (such as 18 months).

While home-based businesses may be able to purchase coverage, insurers generally limit benefits and/or plan design to those that meet additional eligibility criteria. Similarly, retail businesses may have additional eligibility criteria that must be met in order to qualify.

The Individual

In the past, OE was available only to the lowest-risk occupations (such as 4A and 3A). Today, coverage is broadly available to 4A, 3A, 2A, A, and B occupations in qualifying businesses covering ages 18 through to 60 (and on a more restricted basis up to age 63).

Issue and participation limits vary by occupation class, but maximum coverage ranges from about $3,500 for higher-risk occupations up to $60,000 for lower-risk occupations.

The individual must not only work full-time in the business, but must provide specialized personal or technical skills considered necessary to the ongoing operation of the business. Insurers may also establish a minimum ownership percentage that the person must hold to be considered insurable for OE, such as 40% of the business.

Eligible Expenses

Expenses that are eligible for reimbursement are those normally incurred in operating the business or practice. Many of these are listed below.

- Rent
- Property insurance premium
- Hydro
- Telephone and communications
- Postage
- Heat
- Water
- Gas

- Laundry
- Janitorial and maintenance services
- Employees' salaries
- Interest on business loans
- Depreciation
- Accounting and legal services
- Union or professional dues
- Business liability insurance
- Business taxes
- Leasing costs for furniture, equipment, and automobiles used in the operation of the business
- Other normal, fixed, customary expenses.

The OE policy will not cover salaries of employees with technical or specialized skills who can continue to generate revenue to the business. Also excluded are salaries paid to any person related to the insured by blood or marriage and who was hired during (or immediately prior to) a period of disability. Similarly, it will not cover increases given to a relative during a period of disability or "inflated" salaries. Also excluded are salaries to any member of the insured's profession or occupation who performs these duties for the insured during their absence. Any salaries or cash draws from the business by the insured during the disability are not considered eligible expenses.

An owner who owns the premises instead of renting may also be able to claim the greater of scheduled depreciation or scheduled repayment of principal for the portion of the premises used for the operation of the business. This is in addition to mortgage interest and taxes.

Overhead expense policies do not cover the cost of goods or merchandise purchased for sale (inventory), the cost of operating vehicles or equipment, the cost of entertainment or travel, or personal taxes.

Taxation

The tax status of OE insurance is covered in Interpretation Bulletin IT-223. To qualify as an OE plan for tax purposes, the plan must provide for reimbursement of the overhead expenses in the amount actually incurred or paid by the insured during disability. The amount cannot be a fixed benefit amount nor can it exceed the actual covered expenses.

The premiums paid for OE insurance are tax deductible as a business expense regardless of whether the business is incorporated or not. Benefits are treated as taxable income as received. The expenses covered by the insurance are, of course, tax deductible to the business and will offset the tax.

Renewability

OE plans are usually non-cancellable and guaranteed renewable through to age 65. Some may also be conditionally renewable after age 65 on a modified basis if the insured continues to work full-time and has ownership in the business. No medical evidence is required. Renewal after age 65 usually provides for a shorter benefit period without optional benefits. The maximum renewal is age 75.

Provisions and Plan Design

Most insurers offer a variety of elimination periods, including 15, 30, 60, and 90 days. Benefit periods are generally 12, 15, and 24 months. As the coverage is reimbursement for actual expenses incurred, there may be some months where expenses fall below the amount of monthly coverage purchased. Therefore, many policies extend the benefit period so coverage is not "lost". For example, assume the plan provides for $3,000 per month for 12 months. The overall maximum benefit is $36,000, from which the insured can draw monthly to reimburse incurred eligible expenses of up to $3,000 per month. Any unused benefit during a month remains in the "fund", so it will last more than 12 months. Some OE policies also allow the unused benefit in one month to be applied during a month where incurred expenses exceed the maximum purchased. If the owner in any way disposes of his or her interest in the business, payments would cease.

Some clients may find it advantageous to purchase two separate policies: one with a 12-month benefit period and one with a 24-month benefit period. This recognizes that higher expenses are incurred initially, and a business owner who does not return for an extended period of time is likely to cut back on certain areas, such as salaries. Some companies may allow the combination of two benefit periods under one policy for this purpose.

Definition of Disability

OE plans may contain any of the following types of definitions for disability:

- Pure own occupation
- Regular occupation and not working
- Unable to work in a regular occupation or another for which qualified.

These definitions are discussed in detail in Chapter 4, "Disability Insurance Policies and Provisions", and therefore are not elaborated on in this section. The more comprehensive definitions are found in benefits for low-risk occupations. Some insurers provide the option to "buy up" to a more comprehensive definition by adding an optional own occupation extension rider. Some policies also include benefits for partial disability and/or residual disability.

The partial disability provision, when included, provides for payment of 50% of the regular maximum benefit for up to three months (some provide six months as an optional benefit). A period of total disability does not have to precede a claim for partial benefits, so an owner who is never totally disabled may still qualify for partial payment. Benefits are always subject to reimbursement, and any payment is based upon the actual eligible expenses incurred.

Standard Provisions

There are a number of provisions that are standard in all insurers' OE policies. Some of these are listed below. Some of these features have been discussed in other sections and are, therefore, not elaborated on here.

- Waiver of premium
- Accumulation of days to satisfy the waiting period
- Recurrent disability
- Transplant surgery benefit
- Rehabilitation
- Benefit accumulation — This refers to the feature whereby benefits not used in one month can be carried forward for use in another month when actual eligible expenses incurred exceed the maximum monthly benefit.
- Benefit extension — This refers to the feature whereby the benefit period "extends" if less than the overall total maximum entitlement has been paid out. This can be calculated by multiplying the maximum monthly benefit by the total maximum months in the benefit period.
- Conversion — This feature is sometimes referred to as an "exchange privilege". It allows the insured to convert the OE policy to an individual disability policy prior to a certain age (such as age 60) without medical evidence. The policy will be of a similar elimination period and benefit period to the OE coverage, and is subject to the company's maximum issue and participation limits for individual policies.

Special Provisions

There are a number of provisions or special features that vary from insurer to insurer. They are often designed to differentiate one insurer's product from its competitors. A few of these features are outlined below.

Presumptive Disability

If the insured suffers the loss of eyesight, hearing, speech, or the use of two limbs, total disability will be presumed and benefits will be paid, regardless of whether the insured is able to work and regardless of whether or not the insured is under the care of a physician. The entire monthly benefit purchased will be paid throughout the full benefit period. The elimination period is waived and benefits are payable, even if the insured continues working full-time in his or her own or another occupation.

Survivor Benefit

This benefit provides the insured's survivors with a lump-sum death benefit equal to a multiple of the monthly benefit. This benefit in older policies was as much as four times the monthly benefit. Today, it ranges anywhere from one-and-a-half to three times the benefit.

Recovery Benefit

This benefit provides a continuation of benefits for a period, such as two months, following the return of the insured to full-time work. The insured must first have satisfied the elimination period and suffered a disability that lasted at least three months. In this event, the benefit paid is 50% of the regular maximum benefit in the first month of return, then 25% in the second month. This benefit encourages return to work and financially eases the transition off benefits and back to full-time work.

Optional Benefits

While optional benefits can vary from insurer to insurer, some of the more popular options are discussed below.

Partial Disability

The partial disability rider provides for continuation of benefits when the insured can work only up to half the time or is unable to perform all the important duties normally associated with the occupation. This option may serve to extend the basic partial disability provision, if one is contained as a standard feature in the policy, or to add this feature where it otherwise is not provided. It may be extended for the same term as the maximum benefit period or for a lesser period (depending upon the insurer).

Residual Disability

The residual disability provision, where available, covers the insured during periods of reduced ability to work in their regular occupation. A benefit is payable when eligible overhead expenses exceed gross business earnings by at least $200 (some companies state $100). Some policies apply this measure against 75% (instead of 100%) of gross earnings. The provision may require that a period of total disability precede a claim for residual benefits. In any event, the residual feature supports the business owner in a gradual return to work.

Some residual provisions give the insured the right to make a one-time election during a period of partial disability, whether the claim will be administered under a partial disability provision or a residual disability provision. This enables the insured to have the claim measured by a loss of time or duties (partial benefits) or based on reduced earnings (residual).

Another variation in this rider provides that during the first six months of residual disability, the benefit will not be less than 50% of the maximum monthly benefit.

Other Optional Benefits

Other options that may be offered include:

- Guaranteed insurability option
- Accidental death and dismemberment
- Return of premium
- HIV and hepatitis B or C rider (health care profession rider)
- Catch-up rider.

The catch-up rider provides a lump-sum payment equal to the amount not paid during the elimination period if the insured is totally disabled for more than 180 days. As OE policies do not necessarily pay the full benefit amount (in situations where actual incurred expenses are lower), the amount for this rider is based on the amount of the first reimbursement cheque issued after the elimination period has been satisfied.

Exclusions

The standard exclusions found in OE policies include the following:

- War
- Normal pregnancy
- Active duty in the armed forces
- Surgery to transplant an organ or other part of one's body to another, except as provided under the transplant surgery benefit.

Special Considerations for Students

Some companies make available special limits for students in professional occupations. Normally, OE insurance cannot be purchased until the business is established, but this special option allows for business overhead expense coverage to be purchased before the insured begins a practice or business. Initially, it helps to protect repayment of debt incurred, such as student loans. Once the insured becomes established in an office or business, the policy automatically converts to traditional OE coverage. Insurers offering this feature provide special issue limits and special conditions for eligibility.

BUSINESS LOAN PROTECTION POLICIES

The Need

Many businesses fund the operation of the business to some extent through business loans. In the event the owner is disabled, the business owner needs to ensure that outstanding loans and interest can continue to be paid. The business loan protection (BLP) policy is designed for this purpose.

Eligibility Requirements

Some of the types of loans that are eligible include:

- Loans for equipment
- Property and building loans (used in the operation of the business)
- Mortgages on premises
- Term business loans
- Small business loans from a government incentive program.

Loans that may only be eligible under a lump-sum plan include:

- Lines of credit
- Account overdrafts.

The BLP is intended for companies that have a stable history, usually described as businesses that have been in existence for three or more years, and that meet the insurer's minimum net worth requirements (usually about $50,000). The person insured must also meet certain underwriting requirements such as minimum ownership rules.

Insurable occupation classes normally include 4A, 3A, 2A, and A. Restrictions may apply to higher-risk occupations, such as those in Class A.

Renewability

The policy usually provides non-cancellable rates for the duration of the policy (up to age 65). It is conditionally renewable to age 65, subject to the following conditions:

- The insured continues to be with the business.
- The insured continues to be responsible for the loan.
- The insured continues to work full-time.

The Benefit

The benefit covers loans of up to $10,000 per month or up to a $250,000 lump sum. Lesser amounts may apply depending upon the occupation class.

The loan must meet certain criteria, such as:

- It is necessary in the operation of the business.
- The loan's interest qualifies as a deduction for income tax purposes.
- It is secured from a bank, trust company, or finance company.

A loan from a private investor would not qualify. There are two versions of benefits available: lump-sum and periodic (monthly) payments.

Lump-Sum Benefits

The insured must satisfy an elimination period during a period of total disability and, thereafter, is entitled to a lump-sum benefit equal to his or her portion of the business loan expense, up to the maximum amount purchased. The policy expires when the full benefit has been paid. Typically, the elimination period that must be satisfied is of one year's duration.

The amount is paid in three instalments (at 365, 540, and 730 days) and represents 75% of the actual business loan outstanding (up to the maximum amount purchased).

Periodic (Monthly) Benefits

An alternative version of this policy is one that provides for periodic payments instead of a lump sum. A monthly benefit is paid equal to the insured's portion of the monthly scheduled payment. Under this version, the insured can select a shorter elimination period, such as 30, 60, or 90 days, and the benefit is payable for 24 months.

The insurer usually requires a letter at the time of claim from the lending institution confirming that the business loan exists under the monthly payment method.

Features, Provisions, and Options

The definition of disability provides that insured individuals are unable to perform the essential duties of their regular occupation and that they are not engaged in another occupation. Many of the features, provisions, and options associated with other forms of DI are included in the BLP policy, such as:

- Waiver of premium
- Accumulation of days of disability
- Recurrent disability

- Presumptive disability
- HIV and hepatitis B or C rider (health care profession rider) as an optional benefit at an additional cost.

Exclusions

Standard exclusions apply to BLP policies, including the following:

- War
- Normal pregnancy.

Chapter 11

Special-Risk Disability Insurance

INTRODUCTION

Insurers have done a good job over the years of developing solutions for the disability insurance (DI) needs of most income earners. Products have evolved over time to recognize the changing demographics of the workforce, the changing nature of employment relationships, and the emergence of new occupations. However, traditional insurers (i.e., insurers in the "regular market") want to direct their focus to standardized products that can be sold in significant volumes because they have large potential markets. The result is that many consumers and businesses that have significant insurance needs, and the ability to pay, cannot obtain insurance in the regular market because they do not fit the risk parameters for which traditional products are designed and priced.

Although there are some individuals who are simply not suitable candidates for DI of any kind, there are alternative ("special risk") markets that offer at least partial solutions to most of those who have been unable to obtain satisfactory coverage through traditional insurers.

There are two broad categories into which these special-risk DI needs fall:

- Individuals who are unable to qualify for any DI at all.
- Individuals who can qualify for DI but whose needs are not fully addressed by traditional insurance.

Some of the common issues in each of these categories are outlined below.

THE NEED

Clients Unable To Qualify for Traditional Disability Insurance

There are a number of reasons why a client may not be able to qualify for traditional DI that can be addressed with special-risk DI products:

- They may have health issues.
- They may have foreign travel or residence issues.
- Their needs for coverage may be short term in nature.
- They may fall within an age range not covered in the regular market.
- Their occupation may entail high risk or they may have very significant income fluctuations.

Health Issues

The majority of declinations of individual DI applications are the result of a history of serious illness or a medical condition that has a significant probability of resulting in disability. Examples of medical conditions that typically preclude someone from obtaining regular DI coverage include the following:

Diabetes (type I or type II). Individuals diagnosed under age 30, or whose disease is of long-standing duration or not well controlled, will generally be declined. Exclusions are not viewed as a suitable tool through which to offer coverage to these individuals, since the disease can manifest itself in so many different ways.

Coronary artery disease. Those with coronary artery disease diagnosed under age 40 will generally be refused coverage permanently, as will those with later onset of more serious disease (e.g., multiple vessels). This is also an area where exclusions are not considered to be appropriate.

Obesity. Insurers will offer coverage with extra premiums and/or limited benefits to many overweight individuals, but there are weight limits above which no coverage is available.

Mental disorders. Although in some cases insurers will allow coverage with an exclusion and/or extra premium, those with more serious histories are usually declined.

Alcohol/drug abuse. Insurers will generally not offer coverage if the last use was within the past five years or if there is a history of cross-addiction (multiple drugs, or drug use and alcoholism) at any time in the past.

Cancer survivors. Depending on the type and severity of the disease, insurers will decline coverage for a number of years after successful treatment. Subsequently, they may consider coverage, often with an exclusion either for a specific type of cancer or for all types.

Multiple medical impairments. Sometimes there is no single impairment that would warrant a declination, but there are a number of different impairments that, taken together, present a risk that is too great for an insurer to consider.

When an insurer declines a non-cancellable disability income application due to medical or lifestyle history, they may offer accident-only coverage as an alternative. Most of the non-cancellable DI insurers have plans featuring accident-only coverage. These plans were developed for non-traditional employment situations, not for medically impaired risks, but they have been successfully used here, too. It is important to note, however, that many cases declined for full accident and sickness coverage are also not considered suitable risks for accident-only coverage. Also, from the perspective of the purchaser, accident-only coverage may not be satisfactory — in white-collar occupations, less than 20% of disability claims are a result of accidents, so this leaves a huge gap in their coverage.

Special-risk insurers may consider many individuals with such histories as suitable risks for DI, provided they meet the following criteria:

- They are actively at work full-time for at least the past year and not chronically ill.
- They are receiving appropriate medical care and follow-up for the medical condition, and making appropriate lifestyle choices (e.g., controlling diet, not smoking, etc.).
- They have a track record of consistent earnings over a period of a few years in their current occupation.

Foreign Travel or Residence

Individuals whose jobs require extensive foreign travel or temporary foreign residence, or any travel to high-risk locations such as zones of active military conflict or insurrection, are often declined for regular DI.

From an underwriting perspective, there are a number of concerns that lead to this underwriting stance. They include the following:

- war, civil unrest, or terrorism
- aviation and motor vehicle accidents
- disease or reduced access to medical care
- concerns over the security of the blood supply

- crime, corruption, and fraud
- environmental factors.

There is little or no statistical data on morbidity related to these foreign travel or residence exposures, and in the absence of credible data on which to base their underwriting and pricing, insurers necessarily take a conservative stance in underwriting these risks. Even if such data were available, insurers offering the long-term guarantees of non-cancellable coverage have to be concerned about the potential for increased claims as a result of deteriorating conditions in regions of the world that are prone to instability.

On the demand side, in an increasingly global world, we have more and more Canadian executives, consultants, business owners, and others who earn all or part of their living doing business outside Canada. These individuals may turn to special-risk DI insurers to satisfy their needs.

Transitional Employment Situations

Many employees who have employer-sponsored long-term disability (LTD) coverage rely solely on this coverage for their disability income replacement needs. Historically, full-time employees have not been a fertile market for those selling individual DI, despite the many advantages of individual, compared to group, coverage (including portability and superior benefit provisions).

Unlike health and dental benefits, however, group LTD coverage is usually not extended to employees who are terminated. In some cases, LTD coverage may be extended for the duration of the minimum statutory notice period, but this is typically much shorter than the period for which salary is continued or paid as a lump sum (the severance period), and certainly much shorter than the period of time it takes for most individuals to find another job.

The reason employers do not normally extend LTD coverage to terminated employees is that group insurers believe the risk of claims increases substantially with unemployed workers, who may look to their disability coverage as a source of income. Also, when claims do occur, it is difficult to assess the claimant's ability to work and to successfully facilitate a return to work. Even where group insurers are willing to extend this coverage, an employer who does so increases the risk of adverse claims experience and a resulting rate increase to the entire group LTD plan.

Similarly, individual disability coverage is generally not available to terminated employees during their career transition period. Individual insurers have the same concerns as group insurers, and in addition, they do not want to issue a policy that is likely to be in force only for a short time and may be cancelled if and when the insured once again receives group LTD coverage through a new employer. Even if the individual establishes a new full-time or part-time business, insurers want to see the individual well established with a track record of earnings in the new business before they will consider coverage.

On the other hand, the need for DI coverage for terminated employees is just as great as when they were working. Even though they may not have a current income, they still have very substantial income needs and expectations over the balance of their working lives.

From the employer's perspective, there have been legal precedents which suggest that employers may have a legal obligation to continue all benefits, including disability coverage, during the severance period.

There are a variety of options for temporarily unemployed workers to consider if they wish to replace the group LTD coverage they had through their former employer. In some cases, these plans provide very limited benefit amounts and restrictive benefit provisions. There is at least one special-risk insurer, however, that will essentially replicate the level of benefits that was provided under the group LTD, and with similar benefit provisions.

Short-Term Needs

There are a number of situations in which individuals find themselves with short-term exposure to uncovered disability. These include:

- The waiting period for group LTD at the start of a new job. It is common for an employer to provide that new employees are not eligible for group LTD benefits until they have been employed for a certain period of time, typically 90 days. Sometimes this can be waived during the negotiation of the employment offer, particularly for more senior positions, but this is not always the case.

- A break between the end of an old job and the start of a new one.

- Sabbaticals. Many employers are supportive of employees who want to take a period of time off, whether for personal reasons, to further their education, or to do volunteer work. Certain benefits may be continued during this period of time, but LTD is usually not provided.

Regular-market insurers are generally not prepared to provide coverage in any of these situations. Virtually all traditional products (both life insurance and living benefits) are designed for medium- to long-term needs. Their cost structure is characterized by high acquisition costs, including the cost of underwriting, policy issue, and compensation to their distributors. They cannot profitably manufacture and distribute short-term products.

There are special-risk insurers, however, that will offer coverage for as short a period as required, even as little as a week or less, although there is not much demand for such extremely short coverage periods. Certain minimum premiums may be required, though, in order to make offering this coverage financially viable for the special-risk insurer.

Older Ages

There are several situations in which older individuals may find that they need disability coverage. These include the following:

- Increasingly, corporations are retaining key employees and executives after the "normal" retirement age of 65 and want to provide continuing benefits to these employees, but the group LTD coverage almost always ends at age 65.
- Mandatory retirement at a specific age is no longer permitted in most Canadian jurisdictions. Many individuals will choose to work past their normal retirement age, in some cases because they enjoy their work, and in other cases because they cannot afford to retire. And if they cannot afford to retire, they cannot afford to lose their income as a result of disability. Here, again, their group LTD coverage will end when they reach age 65.
- Some individuals may take early retirement or otherwise leave their employer to pursue a second career, often in a self-employed capacity. The maximum issue age for individual disability coverage is typically 60.
- Some older self-employed individuals have a continually increasing income and are not fully covered by DI plans, which may have been purchased at a younger age. Quality individual plans can typically be renewed after age 65 as long as the insured continues to work. But again, new coverage is generally not available to those over age 60.

There are special-risk insurers that will offer disability coverage to those age 65 and older, as long as they are engaged in full-time employment or self-employment. Available benefit periods are likely to be relatively short, such as a maximum of two years after age 65, unless there is a longer-term employment contract, in which case benefits may be available to match the term of the contract.

Occupations That Entail High Risk or Income Fluctuations

Insurers in the regular market prefer individuals in stable occupations and in the standard career path characterized by positions of gradually increasing responsibility and increasing income. Some occupations do not fit this model, among them:

- Professional athletes — Athletes often earn very large incomes but for a limited period of time, typically while young. Incomes may fluctuate dramatically based on job performance. In some sports, the risks of injury are substantial, and career-ending injuries are not uncommon.
- Entertainers (actors, musicians, comedians, artists) — Entertainers can also earn very large incomes, but may experience dramatic fluctuations from year to year. Lifestyle issues are also often an underwriting concern in this class of employment.

- Pilots — Pilots must meet stringent medical requirements in order to retain their licences and must undergo regular physical examinations to ensure they meet these requirements. Insurers are justifiably concerned that a relatively minor condition that would not be disabling for most types of employment could result in loss of a pilot's licence and a claim for disability benefits.

There are special-risk insurers that cater to each of these occupational areas.

Clients Whose Needs Cannot Be Fully Met by Traditional Disability Insurance

High-Income Earners

There is a well-known phenomenon known as "reverse discrimination", under which those earning very high incomes cannot purchase as much DI, as a percentage of their income, as those at lower income levels. This table illustrates this phenomenon:

Annual Income	Monthly After-Tax Income*	Largest Non-Cancellable Disability Income Monthly Benefit			
		Non-Taxable	% of After-Tax Income	Taxable	% of Income
$50,000	$ 3,347	$3,050	91%	$3,800	91%
100,000	5,938	5,100	86%	6,950	83%
250,000	12,695	9,500	75%	14,950	72%
500,000	23,859	14,675	62%	24,550	59%
750,000	35,024	20,400	58%	35,275	56%
1,000,000	46,188	25,400	55%	44,650	54%
2,000,000	90,847	35,000	39%	50,000	30%

* 2008 Ontario tax rates; basic personal exemption only

There are a couple of assumptions underlying the relatively low limits for higher-income earners:

1. Earnings may not continue at such a high level. Since the insurer is offering a long-term guaranteed contract, the individual could end up being overinsured in the event of a substantial decrease in income, resulting in an increased incentive to claim.
2. High-income earners do not "need" this level of income. This is really a myth, since there is a near universal tendency to "live up" to one's income level. Even if this assumption were true, from a personal risk management standpoint the ability of individuals to generate this income is their greatest asset, and they should want to insure it to the greatest extent possible. People who own several apartment buildings will insure them all. If they buy another one, they will not fail to insure it based on the argument that they could afford to have it burn down, since it was only one of their many real estate holdings. The same logic applies with respect to income.

There are special-risk insurers that will offer at least 75% replacement of income, regardless of income level. For the $1 million earner, this would represent potential additional coverage of over $9,000 per month non-taxable, or about $18,000 per month taxable.

It is important to realize that the traditional insurers' limits are both issue and participation limits; that is to say, they will not issue more than this amount, nor will they issue an amount that, together with other in-force or pending coverage, exceeds their limit. This creates a challenge for the individuals who want to insure a greater percentage of their income than is available through regular markets. They cannot apply for a top-up at the same time as they apply for regular-market coverage. This leaves them two options. They can:

1. Purchase the full amount in the special-risk market. The problem with this is that specialty market products lack the guarantees available in non-cancellable products, and they also typically have less liberal benefit provisions.
2. Purchase the maximum available in the regular market and obtain additional coverage at a later time in the special-risk market. This is a viable approach, because the regular market products do not integrate with additional coverage that is purchased at a later date.

High Net Worth

Regular insurers are concerned about offering too much coverage on individuals with substantial net worth. A net worth of up to $3 million does not normally cause a problem, but amounts in excess of $5 million can result in insurance being denied altogether, particularly if a large proportion of the assets are relatively liquid. Insurers feel that these individuals can meet their income needs by liquidating assets. For intermediate amounts, insurers may offer limited coverage, reducing either the amount of benefit offered or the benefit period.

However, the same options that exist for high-income earners may be open to some high-net-worth individuals looking to insure their income. Although their ability to generate income may not necessarily be their greatest asset, it is still an asset, and their planning must take into account what happens in the event of income loss as a result of disability. Some of these individuals may want to fully insure their income, regardless of their level of net worth.

There are special-risk markets that will offer coverage based only on earned income, with no regard to the individual's net worth.

High Unearned Income

Unearned income is income that does not depend on the individual's ability to work and which would, therefore, not be affected by disability. Examples are investment and rental income, pension income, and spousal support payments.

Regular insurers are typically not concerned about unearned income if it is less than 15% to 20% of earned income. In fact, they may even allow significantly larger amounts if the source is of a non-recurring nature. Generally, however, for amounts in excess of this, insurers will begin to reduce the available monthly benefit amount. Typically, if unearned income exceeds 50% of earned income, insurers in the regular market will be reluctant to offer any coverage at all. The philosophy behind this is that since the individual would still have a substantial continuing income in the event of disability, they really don't need additional disability coverage.

Here again, however, many individuals who have very substantial amounts of unearned income may have valid reasons for wanting to insure their earned income to the greatest possible extent.

There are special-risk insurers that will offer coverage based only on earned income, with no regard for the level of unearned income.

High-Limit Disability Buy-Sell

Most privately held businesses with multiple owners have (or should have) shareholder or partnership agreements stipulating what happens in the event of the death or disability of a partner/shareholder ("owner"). Usually, in such an event, the remaining owners want to buy out the shares of the disabled or deceased owner. The funding of this share purchase may be problematic unless appropriate insurance is in place. Consequently, life and disability insurance are often purchased to provide at least partial funding.

Unfortunately, the maximum amount of buy-sell coverage available in traditional markets is $2 million, and has been so for a long time. In some cases the need is substantially greater than this.

Special-risk insurers can provide coverage up to at least $20 million. It is important to note, however, that the regular-market limits are both issue and participation limits. Consequently, the same caveats apply as those outlined for high-income earners.

Key Person Disability

There are many situations where businesses need to protect themselves against the adverse financial impact of the long-term disability of a key employee. In many cases, this is a requirement of a lender or investor as a precondition of providing capital to a business.

Unfortunately, the amounts offered for key person disability insurance in regular markets are very limited and not suitable for most key person needs.

Special-risk insurers can provide coverage up to at least $20 million.

Limited Benefit Periods

Insurers in the regular market will sometimes offer reduced benefit periods, such as two or five years, for a variety of reasons. This is most often due to a medical issue, but it could be the result of an occupational issue, an unearned income or net worth issue, or some other concern that makes the underwriter uncomfortable with a long-term benefit period.

Special-risk insurers may be able to offer coverage that commences after the benefit period of the regular-market policy expires, either as a lump sum or as a continuing monthly benefit. The elimination period for the specialty product is the benefit period of the regular-market product.

War Exclusions

War is normally excluded in both individual and association disability coverage. For most individuals who live and work in first world countries, this is not a particular concern. However, for those who must, as part of their job or for personal reasons, travel to or work in regions of active conflict, or regions that are unstable and possibly prone to emerging conflict, this exclusion can be a big concern.

There are special-risk insurers that will offer coverage for war only, to match the exclusion in the individual or association policy.

Avocation Exclusions

Certain hazardous hobbies may be excluded from coverage under a traditional non-cancellable policy. Typical exclusions would include flying (as a private pilot), mountain climbing, heli-skiing, or similar activities.

It is possible to purchase disability coverage from a special-risk insurer for only the activity that is excluded in the traditional policy.

Foreign Travel Exclusions

In an earlier section, we referred to cases that would be declined by regular insurers as a result of foreign travel or residence. In between the standard risk and the declined risk, there are a variety of travel exposures that might be handled with the use of an exclusion instead of an outright declination. There are two versions of travel exclusion generally used:

Version 1

> No benefits will be paid for any period in excess of a designated period (usually 90 days) of disability during which the insured is outside Canada or the United States.

This exclusion does not pose a particular problem for most individuals, since they can continue to collect benefits as long as they return home within the designated period.

Version 2

> No benefits will be paid for any disability that occurs in a designated country or countries, or that occurs elsewhere as a result of an injury sustained or an illness contracted while in the excluded country.

This exclusion may be a great concern for some individuals, particularly if they spend a substantial amount of time in the excluded country. A special-risk insurer could provide coverage only for disability that occurs in the designated country.

RISK MANAGEMENT TOOLS

How Do They Do It?

There are a number of tools that regular-market underwriters can use to structure a coverage offer to someone with a risk profile that is not acceptable for unrestricted coverage. These tools are discussed in detail in Chapter 8, "Disability Insurance Underwriting and Claims", but they are briefly repeated here:

- extended elimination period (sometimes for a specific impairment only)
- reduced benefit period
- exclusion for a medical impairment or hobby
- extra premium
- reduced monthly benefit.

In the end, however, even with these tools, there are many situations in which the underwriter will not be comfortable offering any coverage or the coverage offered is not sufficient to meet the applicant's needs. These have been discussed at length in the earlier parts of this chapter.

What are the tools and techniques that special-risk insurers use in order to be able to offer coverage where the regular market does not, or to supplement the coverage offered by the regular market?

Tools and Techniques

Pricing

Special-risk DI products typically come with a higher price tag than their regular-market counterparts, for a few reasons:

1. These niche markets are not as large as the mainstream markets, so there is not as much premium to spread the expenses over.
2. Special risks frequently involve greater underwriting effort and costs.
3. The risks are greater, and there are often no credible statistics on which to base the price, so there is an element of educated guesswork.

Guarantees

Non-cancellable products are guaranteed to be renewed to age 65, with guaranteed premiums and policy provisions. While this structure provides maximum accountability to the purchaser, it also forces a more conservative underwriting approach.

Special risk products usually do not come with long-term renewal guarantees or guaranteed premium rates. The insurer can be much more aggressive when they have the opportunity to reprice a risk or class of risks in the event of unfavourable experience, or to cancel a policy or class of policies. Having said this, special-risk insurers do not want to be in the position where these actions are necessary, as any such actions could have a long-term impact on their credibility in the marketplace. So these levers are generally used sparingly and with great care.

Policy Terms

Many special-risk disability products are characterized by shorter terms, sometimes as short as a year or less. This is an ideal approach to deal with certain kinds of risks. For example:

1. **The very high-income earner.** One of the concerns outlined earlier with respect to these individuals is that they are susceptible to sudden and dramatic decreases in income, potentially resulting in overinsurance. If the insurer has the opportunity to financially re-underwrite periodically, its exposure to a long-term overinsurance situation is reduced or eliminated.
2. **The terminated employee.** The terminated employee is in a period of career transition that typically will conclude within a couple of years at the most, either with a new full-time job or a successful transition to self-employment, or possibly to retirement. A special-risk plan to cover these individuals needs to be short term.

Regular-market products are all designed to be mid- to long-term solutions. Their cost structure requires an average duration of at least several years in order to be profitable.

The shorter policy terms are often seen by advisers and their clients as a severe limitation of the effectiveness of special-risk solutions. On the other hand, it is this very feature that allows the special-risk insurer to provide quality coverage where it would not be prudent risk management to offer long-term coverage.

Graded Benefits

This feature would entail a reduced benefit payment in the event of disability occurring within the first two or three years of a policy. This is particularly useful for medically impaired risks, where the anti-selection is particularly significant. These policies may provide for full benefits from the time of issue in the event that disability is the result of an accident.

Restrictive Policy Provisions

Special-risk products generally have definitions and benefit provisions that are not as liberal as those typically seen in a traditional non-cancellable contract. For example, the definition of disability may be more stringent, and the benefits for partial or residual disability may be more limited. Also, the special-risk contract usually contains more embedded exclusions than the regular-market policy. Typical exclusions that might be found in a special-risk contract (but not in a typical non-cancellable contract) include the following:

- attempted suicide or self-inflicted injury
- commission of a criminal act
- participation in hazardous activities such as bungee jumping, parachuting, or hang-gliding
- private flying as a pilot or passenger
- excessive use of alcohol, or use of non-prescription drugs
- mental disorders (psychological or psychiatric disorders)
- subjective pain (pain that is not verifiable by objective medical findings).

It is important to note that these exclusions may sometimes be negotiated or bought out.

Underwriting

Regular-market insurers have outstanding underwriting expertise that they have developed over the years, but it is focused on risks that fall within the parameters that they are comfortable insuring. They have very little experience with cases that fall outside these parameters.

Special-risk insurers, on the other hand, may access specialty underwriting expertise related to certain types of special risks. For example, if a product is "imported" from another jurisdiction where it has been successfully and profitably underwritten for a long period of time, this underwriting expertise may be brought to bear, which ensures a high probability of similarly successful results in Canada.

This may be the most important tool at the special-risk insurer's disposal. They can develop appropriate pricing and design the plan to appropriately manage the risk, but if they don't get the underwriting right, the results can be catastrophic.

THE ADVISER'S PERSPECTIVE

Insurance is one of the few businesses in which the adviser can work very hard to convince the client to purchase the product, only to be told by the insurer that they won't sell it to them! This can be a particularly frustrating aspect of the business for advisers. In the disability field in particular, the rate of modified issues and declines is much higher (25%) than it is in life insurance (7% or 8%). Part of this can be attributed to a lack of understanding on the part of some advisers of the underwriting philosophy behind the product and the resultant poor field underwriting. A large part of the reason, however, is the relative complexity of the product, and the greater anti-selection that occurs when the product purchaser is also the person who will benefit directly from the claim.

When advisers encounter clients who cannot be insured adequately in the regular market, they can walk away and move on to the next prospect ... or they can look at potential alternative solutions in the special-risk market. There are a number of compelling reasons for advisers to take the latter approach:

- **Satisfying client needs.** This should, of course, be the primary motivation in any client relationship. If the client cannot qualify for the desired coverage, then the question becomes, what can they qualify for? The alternative solution may not be as comprehensive, but it may be perfectly adequate for the client's needs. It is human nature to prefer to be told what you can have rather than what you can't have.
- **Repeat sales and referrals.** Although some clients will react poorly to a regular-market declination or substandard offer, many will have expected this, particularly where the adviser did a good job of managing expectations. Many of these clients will be grateful for the extra effort undertaken by the adviser to find an alternative solution that met at least a part of their need. This solidifies the adviser–client relationship and increases the opportunities for future business and referrals from a satisfied client.
- **Harvesting the rewards for their hard work.** The adviser may have invested a significant amount of time, effort, and cost in obtaining the client. A special-risk solution may result in the adviser earning a commission for a sale that would otherwise have earned nothing (if the client was declined in the regular market), or, perhaps, result in additional commissions, where a partial solution was found in the regular market but successfully supplemented with a special-risk solution.
- **Avoiding liability.** Advisers can be held legally accountable as much for what they fail to do ("omissions") as what they do incorrectly ("errors"). There is a strong argument to be made that a DI adviser has an obligation to look for and recommend alternative solutions wherever possible, or suffer the consequences in the event the client incurs a disability that could have been covered by a special-risk product that the adviser was not aware of or, worse still, was aware of but decided not to present to the client.

How To Find a Special-Risk Insurer

Special-risk DI is a highly specialized area. The best way to find special-risk products is through an agency with expertise in the product and established relationships with insurer and reinsurer partners, such as Lloyd's of London. One example of such a company is Hunter McCorquodale Inc. in Toronto. This organization has assembled a unique and exclusive portfolio of disability insurance solutions for clients whose needs cannot be fully met in the regular market. This can be a valuable resource for advisers who wish to broaden their access to the tools outlined in this chapter. More information is available on their Web site at www.hunter-mccorquodale.com.

Chapter 12

Mortgage Disability Insurance

INTRODUCTION

When buying a home, most of us take out a mortgage to pay for the purchase over an extended period of time. This financial commitment is often the largest investment we make, stretching 20 to 30 years into the future.

Lending institutions make insurance available to cover this debt in the form of life and disability insurance, known as "creditor insurance" or "mortgage loan insurance". In more recent years, critical illness insurance has been added to the list of insurance options. In the event of death (or critical illness), mortgage loan insurance can pay off the mortgage balance, up to the amount purchased. In the case of disability, it can pay the regular mortgage payments, often to a maximum of two years. In this way, it guarantees the insured person and their loved ones that the loan will not become a financial burden in the event of death, disability, or critical illness.

"Mortgage insurance", which is required by lenders for a high-ratio mortgage, is different from mortgage *loan* insurance. It protects the lending institution against mortgage default while enabling purchasers to buy a home with only a small down payment. The insurance industry often uses the same term to describe mortgage loan insurance. The remainder of this chapter will use the term "mortgage insurance" to refer to mortgage *loan* insurance.

PROTECTING HOME OWNERSHIP

Mortgage insurance helps protect homeowners against the risk of foreclosure, and it preserves personal life and disability insurance for other needs. It also safeguards savings, retirement funds, and other investments from erosion.

A number of insurers offer private mortgage insurance as an alternative to creditor insurance. Licensed intermediaries sell these products directly to the public. Perhaps the greatest difference between private mortgage insurance and bank mortgage insurance (creditor insurance) lies in who owns the policy and who receives the benefits at the time of a claim. In the case of creditor insurance, the lending institution is always both the owner and benefit recipient, whereas with private insurance, the insured always owns the policy, but depending on the insurer, the benefit recipient during a claim may be either the insured or the financial institution.

Private mortgage insurance is an excellent supplement to disability income insurance. The latter often covers only about two-thirds of a person's earnings. Mortgage insurance can be purchased in addition to disability income insurance, provided the loan meets certain eligibility requirements, which may vary from one insurer to another.

TERMS ASSOCIATED WITH MORTGAGE INSURANCE

Amortization Period

The amortization period is the total length of time it will take to pay off the mortgage. It is often a long period, such as 20, 25, or 30 years.

Term

Each mortgage has a start date and an end date. The end date is referred to as the "renewal date" or "maturity date". The duration between the start and end is referred to as the "term". It is commonly not more than five years. At the end of the term, one can either pay off the mortgage or agree to renew the mortgage for a further term based on the interest rate and other conditions set by the lending institution.

Loan Balance

The "loan balance" refers to the outstanding indebtedness at any given point.

Creditor

"Creditor" refers to the financial institution that makes the loan.

CREDITOR INSURANCE

Applying for Coverage

Creditor insurance is sold by bank staff, not by licensed advisers, and since staff are not licensed, the training they receive is usually focused on reasons why to buy the coverage rather than details about product provisions. Having bank staff sell creditor insurance makes purchasing coverage more convenient. Staff often receive bonuses based on sales.

At the time of securing the loan, the staff member asks the borrower if he or she wants mortgage insurance. The applicant is asked to read a statement and sign it, and that's it; coverage is easy to obtain.

Medical Questions

Perhaps the most important difference between creditor insurance and private mortgage disability insurance is the difference in the medical underwriting of coverage.

Creditor insurance is designed and priced on a group basis. Unlike with individual insurance, there is only limited medical underwriting. The initial application asks only a few health questions. If higher coverage amounts are applied for, a more detailed health questionnaire may occasionally be required. Failure to volunteer full information on the health questionnaire can result in coverage being voided during a claim.

Most of the process of underwriting the coverage usually takes place at the time of claim, not at the time of purchase, so underwriting costs are incurred only in relation to claims. The problem is that it gives a false sense of security to the buyer. The buyer's assumption is that once the application form has been filled out and accepted, it has been approved and benefits are guaranteed, but in reality, it means only that the individual has been accepted to pay premiums.

The claim can later be denied if the individual did not reveal tests or other medical information, regardless of whether or not it is related to the reason for the claim, if it was deemed to be pertinent to the underwriting of the insurance.

By contrast, insurers offering private mortgage insurance perform a more thorough underwriting process up front, at the time of purchase. A trained, licensed adviser asks the questions. The medical forms are generally more detailed and can better identify health history. The insurance can provide better guarantees, greater choice, and more flexibility.

Premiums

With creditor insurance, the premiums are added to the monthly loan payment, and the process of applying for coverage is streamlined. There is a perception that creditor insurance coverage offered through a financial lending institution costs less than a private individual plan. In reality, there is very little difference in cost. Private plans offer an affordable method of covering a mortgage, with better safeguards and the services of a licensed adviser.

PRIVATE MORTGAGE INSURANCE

Concept Versus Product

The term "mortgage insurance" is sometimes used in the insurance industry as a concept, rather than a product. In other words, people who have a mortgage might be encouraged to buy a renewable term insurance policy, such as 5-year or 10-year renewable term insurance, in an amount equal to or somewhat greater than their mortgage principal. Similarly, it might be used as a reason to buy a traditional disability income plan or critical illness insurance.

In the case of life insurance and critical illness insurance, this logic may be sound. When it comes to disability insurance, however, it is better to purchase a separate disability mortgage plan, because this will allow individuals to protect their mortgage payments in *addition* to protecting their earnings. People can purchase an individual disability plan to cover earnings, plus a mortgage disability insurance policy to cover the loan. During a disability, both will pay benefits. The insured individuals can use the regular disability income proceeds to meet their daily living costs, and the mortgage payments can be paid using the proceeds from the supplementary mortgage insurance policy.

How It Works

Some insurers offer disability mortgage insurance as a stand-alone policy, while others offer it as a rider to a mortgage life or mortgage critical illness policy.

The insured (or co-insureds) purchase a monthly benefit equal to the mortgage payment, which can include principal, interest, municipal taxes, and school taxes. Benefits are payable during a period of total disability, as defined in the policy. Insurers vary regarding their approach to the payment of benefits. Some insurers pay the benefit directly to the financial institution. This ensures that the benefit paid is used for the purpose of covering the mortgage payment and that it does not exceed the loan payment. This method protects the insurer from overinsurance, which could occur if the benefit were paid directly to the insured.

Some insurers pay the benefit directly to the insured, who then uses the proceeds to cover the mortgage payments. If the interest rate rises, resulting in an increase in the monthly mortgage payment, the insured has the right to purchase more insurance without medical evidence. Financial underwriting still applies to ensure that the amount of coverage does not exceed the monthly loan payments. If the loan interest rate decreases, the insured must contact the insurer to adjust the coverage amount. If the insured fails to do so, the insurer will pay the amount purchased without reduction only if it is not more than 25% above the loan's actual monthly payment amount.

Total Disability Defined

"Total disability" is defined as being unable to perform one's regular duties and not working in another occupation. After 24 months, it is defined as the inability to perform any occupation for which the person is reasonably qualified. If the person is not working at the time of disability, it may be based on the inability to perform normal daily tasks.

Eligibility and Benefits

Mortgage disability insurance can be purchased by individuals who are at least 18 years old and under age 60. Both spouses may purchase coverage up to the full amount of the mortgage loan payment. The coverage amount is sold in monthly benefit units of $100, with the maximum being in the range of $6,000. The insurer has established criteria that must be met in order for an applicant to be eligible to purchase coverage. These criteria may include the following:

- The money borrowed must be a mortgage loan for a building such as a principal residence or a second residence. If it is rental property, there may be limits to the size of the establishment (such as a maximum of eight units). The coverage is not intended for owners of large apartment buildings.

- It must be a formal mortgage through a lending institution, such as a bank.

- The insured must have regular gainful employment and work at least 20 hours per week.

- The insured may be required to occupy the residence or, if it is a multiple residential unit, live in the building.

Some insurers will allow the plan to be used for covering any formal long-term debts, such as the purchase of a recreational or motor vehicle, but coverage cannot exceed the loan amortization period.

There is a waiting period and an elimination period that must be satisfied at the time of claim. The insured must be disabled for at least the waiting period (usually set at 90 days), and after this has been satisfied, benefits will be paid retroactively back to the end of the elimination period (usually set at 30 days).

The insured can select the benefit period for coverage. The usual options are a 24-month plan or a plan that pays through to age 65. If the insurance is covering a mortgage on property that is not the insured's principal residence, some insurers may restrict the duration to 24 months, recognizing that there will be ongoing income from rental property to cover mortgage payments. This helps to protect against the risk of overinsurance and the risk of malingering during a claim for benefits.

In any event, the benefits cease on the earliest of the following occurrences:

- The end of the benefit period selected

- The end of the amortization period of the loan

- The contract anniversary coinciding with or following the insured's 65th birthday.

Premium Rates

Some insurers guarantee rates for the duration of coverage. Other insurers set the premium at the start of each loan term, and the rate then reflects the outstanding loan balance and the attained age. It then stays level for the remainder of the term, which may be stated as not greater than five years.

Change of Lending Institutions

Most plans provide a guarantee that if the insured changes lending institutions, the mortgage disability policy can be carried over to cover the new mortgage, without evidence of good health, for an amount up to the outstanding loan balance. This also applies if the residence is sold and a new property is purchased, provided the new loan is obtained within 60 days following the sale.

Other Policy Provisions

Waiver of Premium

The waiver of premium feature may be built into the contract, as it is with regular disability income plans, or, when the disability mortgage benefit is itself a rider, the waiver of premium is an optional feature available at an additional cost.

Exclusions

The common exclusions contained in a mortgage loan disability insurance plan include the following:

- Participation in a sport for remuneration or competition
- Participation in a race or speed contest
- Attempted suicide or intentionally self-inflicted injury
- Cosmetic treatment
- Experimental treatments or new procedures not commonly used
- Participation in a riot, insurrection, or war
- Operating a motor vehicle while intoxicated or taking drugs
- Flying other than as a fare-paying passenger on a regularly scheduled airline.

Comparison of Private Mortgage Disability and Creditor Insurance

Comparison Chart		
	Private Insurance	**Creditor Insurance**
Rates vary by smoker status	Usually	No
Owner of the policy	The insured	The lender
Who receives the benefits	Depends on plan — the insured or the lending institution, depending on the insurer's requirements	The lender
Rate calculation when both spouses apply	Separate rates based on age of each insured	Rate based on age of the oldest insured
Premium guarantees	Depends on plan — may be for the term, or may be for the amortization period	Not guaranteed
Can policy be cancelled	Only by the insured	By the lender at any time
Can policy be transferred for a change of lending institutions without evidence of insurability	Yes. Usually requires financial underwriting only	No
Detailed product information at time of purchase	Yes	No. Normally only provided in the form of the certificate after purchase
Services of a licensed, trained adviser	Yes	No
Thoroughness of medical underwriting	Thorough at the time of application. Questions on application form tend to be more detailed and broken down, requiring a response for each question. Advisers are trained on how to ask and explain. Doctors' reports are ordered at the time of application	Rigorous at time of claim. Interpretation is left up to the applicant. Questions are formatted for faster completion, usually bundled and asked in a summarized fashion as one or two broad questions. Staff members are not trained on medical forms completion. Doctors' reports are ordered at time of claim, not time of issue, to reduce time and underwriting costs
Premiums	Are paid by the insured directly to the insurer	Are bundled with the mortgage payment
Taxability of premiums	No GST or RST	RST payable in some provinces (Ontario and Quebec)
Cost	Is about the same, sometimes slightly less than creditor insurance	Is about the same, sometimes slightly more than private insurance

Mortgage Disability Versus Disability Income

While mortgage disability insurance is not as comprehensive as individual disability income plans, it still offers an affordable method of purchasing supplementary protection for covering a loan. Rates do not vary by occupation class, so some individuals who do not qualify for disability income insurance based on occupation can still qualify for mortgage disability insurance. Some of the ways in which it is less comprehensive than disability insurance are listed below:

- Definition of "disability" for first 24 months is regular occupation and not working.
- Covers total disability, but not partial or residual disability.
- A 90-day waiting period must be satisfied, even though the elimination period is 30 days.
- Rates on some plans are guaranteed only for the term, not for the full amortization period.

Regardless, it offers a viable alternative to creditor insurance.

Chapter 13

Taxation of Disability Insurance and Business Products

INTRODUCTION

The taxability of benefits received during a claim can significantly impact the client's cash flow during a disability. The tax status of benefits can be affected by ownership, and by premium payer and benefit recipient designations. These issues must be considered when structuring a client's disability insurance program. The taxation of various products is dealt with throughout this book in each chapter that deals with a specific product. A high-level summary is provided in this chapter. This is general information only. Advisers and clients should obtain specific financial and tax advice from their own independent accountant, or legal, financial, or tax consultant for their own specific circumstances.

PERSONAL DISABILITY INCOME

Owner:	Insured
Premium Payer:	Insured
Benefit Recipient:	Insured
Premiums Tax Deductible:	No — personal expense
Benefits During a Claim:	Tax-free
Premium Refund to Owner:	Tax-free

Owner:	Insured or employer
Premium Payer:	Employer — not grouped sickness and accident
Benefit Recipient:	Insured
Premiums Tax Deductible:	Yes — by employer, and taxable benefit to insured
Benefits During a Claim:	Tax-free
Premium Refund to Owner:	If insured: tax-free If employer: taxable

Owner:	Employer — under grouped sickness and accident
Premium Payer:	Employer
Benefit Recipient:	Insured
Premiums Tax Deductible:	Yes — by employer, not taxable benefit to insured
Benefits During a Claim:	Taxable
Premium Refund to Owner:	Taxable

RETIREMENT PROTECTOR DISABILITY INCOME

Owner:	Insured
Premium Payer:	Insured
Benefit Recipient:	Non-registered trust account
Premiums Tax Deductible:	No — personal expense
Benefits During a Claim:	Tax-free
Premium Refund to Owner:	Tax-free

Interest earned on proceeds in the non-registered trust account is taxed annually as interest income to the insured.

Owner:	Insured or employer
Premium Payer:	Employer — not grouped sickness and accident
Benefit Recipient:	Non-registered trust account
Premiums Tax Deductible:	Yes — by employer, and taxable benefit to insured
Benefits During a Claim:	Tax-free
Premium Refund to Owner:	If insured: tax-free If employer: taxable

Interest earned on proceeds in the non-registered trust account is taxed annually as interest income to the insured.

Owner:	Employer — under grouped sickness and accident
Premium Payer:	Employer
Benefit Recipient:	Non-registered trust account
Premiums Tax Deductible:	Yes — by employer, not taxable benefit to insured
Benefits During a Claim:	Taxable as earned income
Premium Refund to Owner:	Taxable

Interest earned on proceeds in the non-registered trust account is taxed annually as interest income to the insured.

DISABILITY BUY-SELL INSURANCE

Cross-Purchase Method

Owner:	Individual
Premium Payer:	Individual
Benefit Recipient:	Individual
Premiums Tax Deductible:	No — capital outlay
Benefits During a Claim:	Tax-free
Premium Refund to Owner:	Tax-free

It is the disposition of the business interest that creates the taxable transaction. The insurance proceeds are tax-free capital.

When a disability occurs, the benefits are payable on a non-taxable basis to the owner of the policy, who then exchanges the funds for the shares. A shareholder disposing of a business interest triggers a taxable capital gain or loss, and a partner is taxed as he or she would be on a sale of a partnership interest. If the business is a qualified small business corporation, as defined in the *Income Tax Act*, the gain may be sheltered by the capital gains exemption available on disposition of shares from a qualified small business corporation. If a monthly funding method has been used rather than a lump-sum purchase, the disabled owner can claim a reserve for the payments not yet received, and this results in spreading out the capital gain over several years.

Corporate Share Redemption or Entity Purchase

Owner:	Business
Premium Payer:	Business
Benefit Recipient:	Business
Premiums Tax Deductible:	No — capital outlay
Benefits During a Claim:	Tax-free
Premium Refund to Owner:	Tax-free

Corporate Share Redemption: During a disability, the proceeds of the disability buy-sell policy are paid to the corporation. The corporation then buys back the shares of the disabled shareholder. Under this method, there is no increase in the adjusted cost base of the remaining shareholders' shares. The benefits have been paid tax-free to the corporation. However, unlike with life insurance, the disability insurance proceeds do not qualify for credit to the capital dividend account. The disabled shareholder receives a taxable deemed dividend when the corporation buys back the shares. The disabled shareholder is required to pay tax on the excess of the dividend received over the paid-up capital amount of the shares, and cannot use the capital gains exemption because a capital gain is not realized.

Entity Purchase: This method is similar to a corporate share redemption, except that the ownership of the business is a partnership format, not a corporation. There is no adjustment to the cost base upon the termination of the disabled partner's interest, premiums are not deductible, and the benefit is received tax-free. The liquidating partner is taxed as he or she would be on a liquidation of a partnership interest.

DISABILITY KEY PERSON INSURANCE

Owner:	Business
Premium Payer:	Business
Benefit Recipient:	Business
Premiums Tax Deductible:	No — capital outlay, not taxable benefit to insured
Benefits During a Claim:	Tax-free
Premium Refund to Owner:	Tax-free

OVERHEAD EXPENSE INSURANCE

Owner:	Business
Premium Payer:	Business
Benefit Recipient:	Business
Premiums Tax Deductible:	Yes — business expense
Benefits During a Claim:	Taxable
Premium Refund to Owner:	Taxable

The expenses covered by the insurance are tax deductible to the business and will offset the tax.

BUSINESS LOAN PROTECTION INSURANCE

Owner:	Business
Premium Payer:	Business
Benefit Recipient:	Business
Premiums Tax Deductible:	No — capital outlay, not taxable benefit to insured
Benefits During a Claim:	Tax-free
Premium Refund to Owner:	Tax-free

PERSONAL HEALTH AND DENTAL PLAN

Owner:	Individual
Premium Payer:	Individual
Benefit Recipient:	Individual
Premiums Tax Deductible:	No — but may be claimed under medical expense tax credit
Benefits During a Claim:	Tax-free
Premium Refund to Owner:	Tax-free

Owner:	Business
Premium Payer:	Business
Benefit Recipient:	Individual
Premiums Tax Deductible:	Yes, by business — not taxable benefit to individual
Benefits During a Claim:	Tax-free
Premium Refund to Owner:	Taxable

Chapter 14

Public Health Insurance

HEALTH INSURANCE DEFINED

Health insurance is a means by which people can protect themselves from the potentially devastating financial costs of medical treatment if they become critically ill or injured, and by which they can ensure that they have access to regular health care when they need it. The cost of even the most basic health care is increasing, and in the absence of insurance, many people would not be able to afford proper care.

PUBLIC AND PRIVATE HEALTH INSURANCE

Canada's health insurance system is composed of a combination of public and private health insurance. Public programs include provincial government health insurance plans (GHIPs), veterans benefits, workers' compensation programs, and other publicly funded social security plans. Private insurance plans include group, union, association, and individual benefit plans through private insurers.

Private Insurance and Pooling of Risk

Private health insurance pools the risk of health care costs across a large number of people, so that each person can pay a rate that represents the average cost of medical care for the group as a whole, making the cost affordable. The concept dates back to the Roman Empire, but it was not until the 18th century that it became more formalized. For health insurance to work well, expected costs in the risk pool should be reasonably predictable and relatively stable over time. While costs will rise over time as a result of increases in price and utilization, the average level of health risk should remain roughly the same as in the general population. Insurers use various methods to avoid "adverse selection", that is, attracting a disproportionate share of unhealthy people. It is no surprise that people who know or suspect that their health is deteriorating are more likely to seek out and purchase health insurance. When this happens, in the absence of safeguards implemented by the insurer, the average cost to everyone in the pool will rise, and healthier people will leave the pool to seek out lower-cost alternative coverage, which further exacerbates the problem for the remaining insured individuals. This is known as a "death spiral". In practice, insurers establish several different risk pools, based on industry, geographic location, or other criteria. "Underwriting" is the process used to evaluate an applicant's suitability for the coverage applied for and to determine on what basis, if any, the coverage will be made available. As the expected health costs for people over age 50 are more than twice as much as for those under age 20, premiums take this increased utilization into consideration.

Public Versus Private: Covering the Risk

Collectively, the provincial GHIPs are unofficially referred to as "medicare". Private health insurance plans can provide coverage only for services that the public health plans do not cover, such as preferred accommodations in hospitals, prescription drugs, and dental care, to name a few. In 2005, the Supreme Court of Canada ruled that the prohibition on private insurers from duplicating coverage already funded by the provincial plan could constitute an infringement of the right to life and security if long wait times prevented prompt access to medical care.[1] While this has not changed the overall direction of private health insurance in Canada, it has increased the focus on reducing wait times. It is estimated that roughly 65% of Canadians have some form of supplementary private health insurance, with most individuals being covered by group insurance through their place of employment. With the increase in the number of contract workers, an increasing number of insurers have begun offering individual health and dental plans.

MEDICARE

History of Medicare

Globally, Canada is held in high esteem for its approach to health care, which was founded on the principles of universality and accessibility. The goal was for Canadians to have access to health care based on need, not ability to pay. Canadians, who fund medicare through taxes, not only cherish it as their single-most valued social program, but have come to expect it as a right of being Canadian. Since its introduction a little more than half a century ago, there has been ongoing friction and conflict over funding and delivery. Despite this, medicare's core values have prevailed.

In 1947, the Saskatchewan government, headed by Tommy Douglas, introduced Canada's first hospital insurance program. A decade later, despite some opposition, the federal government introduced the *Hospital Insurance Diagnostic Services Act* (1957), a national hospital insurance program that brought funding to the various provincial programs. In 1962, when medicare was introduced in Saskatchewan, physicians went on a three-week strike to show their opposition but eventually relented due to lack of public support for their cause. Several provinces followed Saskatchewan's lead and introduced programs of their own. Tommy Douglas is commonly credited as the father of Canadian medicare; however, Tommy Douglas and others have referred to Justice Emmett Hall as the father of Canadian medicare, as it was Hall's *Royal Commission on Health Services* (1964) that led to the introduction of medicare. His report called for a universal and comprehensive national health insurance program, and on July 1, 1968, the federal government launched its national medicare program, financed 50% by the federal government and 50% by the provinces.

---

[1] *Chaoulli v. Quebec*, 2005 SCC 35.

By 1977, this funding arrangement began to change. With the federal government feeling that it had no say in how money was spent, it reduced funding to the provinces. Eventually, a new system of block funding was put in place that was tied to the rate of growth in gross national product (GNP). As health care expenses were growing faster than GNP, this resulted in reduced federal support. Reduced funding in the system eventually led to the practice of "extra-billing" by physicians in an attempt to increase their incomes. In response to mounting pressure to resolve this issue, the *Canada Health Act* was passed in 1984, and extra-billing was banned.

Many felt that the national medicare system did not go far enough, and the 1997 National Forum on Health called for it to be expanded to include a national home care program and national pharmacare, and to phase out fee-for-service for doctors. In 2002, Commissioner Roy Romanow presented a report, the *Royal Commission on the Future of Health Care in Canada*, containing 47 recommendations for change.

All observers agree that the system will need updating to serve the needs of Canadians into the 21st century. What that change will be, however, is to be a topic of ongoing debate. The fear is that health costs will continue to increase faster than the growth in the economy. The problem is that both the federal and provincial governments suffer from insufficient revenue because of the pressure to cut taxes, and they are challenged with having sufficient revenues to meet the demands of health care as well as other essential services such as education, roads, and the environment. Some believe the solution is a two-tiered health system involving parallel private and public systems. Those that oppose this idea point to England and New Zealand as examples of the failure of this method, citing significantly longer wait times in their public system when compared with their private system. Others believe we need to stay true to the underlying values and focus on making the system work better. Still others believe that overhauling the current system will not be enough to resolve the issue and that a combination is needed of system changes and the introduction of user fees. The system has come a long way from its initial introduction and will continue to evolve in the future.

The *Canada Health Act*

Our medicare system is a publicly financed, privately delivered system involving three primary groups: the federal government, the provincial and territorial governments, and private physicians. The system is based on the philosophy of universal prepaid coverage for medically necessary hospital and physician services, regardless of the ability to pay. The chief role of the federal government is to oversee its delivery through legislation, such as the *Canada Health Act*, and to monitor compliance. The federal government also assists with funding through transfer payments. The provinces and territories set their own priorities within the overarching federal guidelines, and private physicians deliver the services. Their fees are paid by the respective provincial health insurance plan, as negotiated by their provincial association.

The system is actually a series of 13 interlocking provincial and territorial plans — all similar, but not identical. There are some groups to which the federal government provides direct health services. These include the Canadian Forces, veterans, the Royal Canadian Mounted Police, inmates in federal penitentiaries, First Nations people, and the Inuit. The federal government is also accountable, outside of the *Canada Health Act*, for disease protection and health promotion.

The provinces are responsible for managing their own public insurance plans, and for their pharmacare programs, which provide prescription medication to seniors and other low-income groups. Pharmacare programs are not covered in the *Canada Health Act.*

Five Governing Principles

There are five principles the provinces must adhere to in order to qualify for transfer payments. They are:

1. **Public Administration.** A public non-profit authority must carry out administration of the program.
2. **Universality.** Universal benefits must be available for all insured people.
3. **Comprehensiveness.** There must be coverage for all medically necessary services provided by doctors and hospitals.
4. **Portability.** Coverage must be maintained if the insured moves or travels within Canada or outside the country.
5. **Accessibility.** There must be access to services regardless of income, age, health status, or gender.

In addition to meeting the five governing principles, provinces must also satisfy two conditions related to health services and extended health care services, and criteria related to extra-billing and user charges. The practices of extra-billing and user fees were seen as limiting access to health care services based on financial status. Consequently, a dollar-for-dollar penalty was initiated to stop this practice.

There was growing concern by late 1994 regarding emerging two-tiered health care, which saw private clinics charging facility fees for medically necessary services. The private clinics offered services for surgery, ophthalmology, and abortion. And as recently as 2005-2006, private surgical clinics were a concern in Quebec and British Columbia. Lack of accessibility and long wait times are often blamed for their emergence, as well as a practice known as "queue jumping" by those able and willing to pay for medically necessary services. Diagnostic clinics have emerged for the same reasons not only in British Columbia and Quebec but also in Alberta, Manitoba, and

Nova Scotia. The federal government responds to these issues by reducing transfer payments to the provinces.

Covered Individuals

The Canada Health Act provides that all residents of Canada are eligible, and defines a "resident of Canada" as follows:

> ... a person lawfully entitled to be or to remain in Canada who makes his home and is ordinarily present in the province, but ... not ... a tourist, a transient or a visitor to the province.

Each province determines its own minimum residence requirements, but the maximum waiting period is three months. In addition, provinces establish a maximum period during which the insured can be out of the country in a 12-month period and still be covered, such as 212 days. Some provinces will grant exceptions for temporary absences beyond this, such as for students who study or work abroad.

Insured and Non-Insured Services

Provincial programs must cover all medically necessary hospital, physician, and surgical-dental services on a prepaid basis. While hospitalized, insured persons are covered for medically necessary services as either in-patients or outpatients. Accommodation fees are covered at standard (ward) level or, if deemed necessary, at the preferred accommodation level. Medical services include the following:

- Nursing care
- Physiotherapy
- Physician fees
- Diagnostic procedures
- Medication while hospitalized
- Operating room fees
- Anaesthetics
- Other related medical or surgical supplies during hospitalization
- Surgical-dental procedures performed by a dental surgeon in a hospital.

"Insured health services" are described in the *Canada Health Act* as "hospital services, physician services and surgical-dental services provided to insured persons, but ... not includ[ing] any health services that a person is entitled to and eligible for under any other Act of Parliament or under any Act of the legislature of a province that relates to workers' or workmen's compensation".[2]

[2] R.S.C. 1985, c. C-6, *Canada Health Act*, section 2, "insured health services".

Other health care expenses that a person may incur must be paid for personally or through a plan of private insurance. Some examples of these are dental expenses; prescription drugs; preferred hospital accommodation fees; paraprofessional services, such as those administered by chiropractors, chiropodists, and massage therapists; and durable medical equipment.

Physicians can charge the provincial health care plan only for services that are medically necessary. Consequently, most physicians charge the patient for non-necessary services, such as the following:

- Paperwork or exams related to insurance claims
- Applications requiring a physician-completed health statement
- School or camp enrolment forms
- Health forms for drivers' tests
- Transfers of records to another physician
- Paperwork related to an application for supplemental government funding on catastrophic drugs not covered by the pharmacare program
- Telephone consults
- Prescription renewals by telephone.

Physicians usually charge a rate as recommended by their provincial medical association for non-insured services.

Insured Services While Travelling

One of the guiding principles of the *Canada Health Act* is that an insured person must be covered when travelling throughout Canada. This is accomplished by a series of bilateral reciprocal billing agreements signed by all provinces except Quebec. The goal is that the insured person need only present a health card, regardless of the province, and should not incur any out-of-pocket expenses. The physician or hospital will directly bill the home province and will be paid for the services at the rate normally charged in the visited province. Quebec has not agreed to this and, instead, pays at the rate that applies within Quebec. Consequently, residents of Quebec obtaining services while visiting other provinces are often asked to pay out-of-pocket and apply for reimbursement once they return home.

A person who travels outside the country has limited coverage. Most, but not all, services are reimbursed up to the amount that would have been paid if the treatment had occurred within Canada. Some services are capped and a lesser amount is paid. Medical charges in many countries, particularly in the United States, are significantly more expensive than in Canada. Recognizing this, the various provincial governments post recommendations on their Web sites advising their residents to purchase private travel insurance before leaving Canada. A person with a known condition who may be expected to need treatment while out of the country may find his or her provincial coverage limited or even excluded.

If a resident of Canada requires a treatment not available in Canada, he or she can apply to the government and request that it be covered outside Canada.

PHARMACARE

Provincial Pharmacare Programs

Each province provides a drug benefit plan for certain eligible groups, primarily seniors and other low-income groups. There is also a "catastrophic drug program" for individuals who may need access to higher-cost drugs that they would not otherwise be able to afford, such as treatment for cancer and palliative care. To be eligible, in addition to meeting income criteria, the individual must be covered by the provincial health plan. The user must pay a deductible, which varies based on the province, but it is usually a nominal fee based on income.

Each province maintains a list of over 3,000 eligible drugs, known as a "formulary", which is reviewed periodically. The formulary lists drugs using a "drug identification number" (DIN), which is assigned by the Health Protection Branch of Health Canada. Before a new drug is added to the formulary, it is assessed by the Common Drug Review (CDR) Process, which all provinces except Quebec use to provide impartial advice and evidence-based information about drug effectiveness, rather than relying solely on clinical trials conducted by the drug manufacturer. The Canadian Expert Drug Advisory Committee (CEDAC) is the independent advisory body that makes recommendations based on its findings to all participating bodies (i.e., the federal, provincial, and territorial drug plans) regarding whether new drugs should or should not be added to the formulary. The participating body makes the final decision regarding whether or not it will be added. Drugs not listed in the formulary may be considered on a case-by-case basis through an "exception" process, called the Exceptional Access Program. A drug that is not yet approved by Health Canada for marketing in Canada can be considered by a province for addition to its formulary or for its Exceptional Access Program through a special review process. Some drugs are designated as "conditional" or "limited use" and are subject to specific conditions for their eligibility under the program. Codes in the formulary listings provide information to pharmacists and physicians regarding details such as the maximum allowable cost and interchangeable groups of medicines.

Drugs are often covered only up to the "least cost alternative" (LCA) price. This is the lowest unit cost established for a drug product within a set of interchangeable drug products. The user must pay any cost above this. In circumstances where a higher-priced product is required, the physician may seek to obtain special approval for it to be covered.

National Pharmaceuticals Strategy

With the exception of hospital care, Canada spends more on drugs than on any other major category of care. The total of public and private expenditures on prescription drugs has grown by roughly 12% annually since 2000, and this significantly impacts the sustainability of government pharmacare programs.

Dialogue between governments, patients, and health care providers has led to an acknowledgement by all parties involved that there is a need to improve access to timely and quality care. Part of this involves ensuring that Canadians do not suffer undue financial hardship in obtaining essential drug therapies. This underlying principle is based on the premise that affordable access to drugs is fundamental to optimal health outcomes for all Canadians. A ministerial task force was established in 2004 (Quebec chose not to participate) to develop and implement a national pharmaceuticals strategy. Their strategy report, presented in 2006, contained nine elements for achieving better pharmaceutical access:

- Focus on developing catastrophic pharmaceutical coverage.
- Create a common National Drug Formulary based on safety and cost effectiveness.
- Improve the drug approval process for faster access to breakthrough drugs for health needs for which there are no other alternative therapies.
- Improve the evaluation of real-world drug safety and effectiveness.
- Pursue purchasing strategies for obtaining the best price on drugs and vaccines.
- Influence professionals to prescribe drugs only when needed and to prescribe the "right drug for the right problem".
- Broaden the practice of "e-prescriptions", and accelerate deployment of the Electronic Health Record.
- Improve access to non-patented drugs and achieve international parity on their prices.
- Analyze cost drivers and cost effectiveness in pharmacare policies and identify best practices.

These nine elements can be summed up into these fundamental themes: improve access, safety, effectiveness, appropriateness of use, and system sustainability.

HEALTH CARE DELIVERY SYSTEM

Primary Health Care

Our system of health care is based on primary health care, which involves the provision of services through teams of health professionals, where the first point of contact is the family physician, a hospital, or another health care professional. Following the initial point of contact, referrals may be made to other specialists for further evaluation, including diagnostic testing. Most hospitals deal with acute conditions, are publicly funded, and operate with a board of trustees. Persons requiring long-term care are cared for in nursing homes equipped to deal with ongoing maintenance care. Long-term care institutions may be either publicly or privately owned. Some privately owned institutions receive their funding from public sources (the provincial government) and must meet certain criteria to maintain their funding, such as occupancy levels, budget adherence, and compliance with stipulated charges for accommodation fees.

Some health care services are provided in the community or at home. These services require a referral from a family physician, and they help patients recover following release from the hospital or provide people with the light assistance they need to remain living in the community.

Some special groups, such as seniors, children, and social assistance recipients, are eligible for additional services not offered to the general public under medicare. Some of these services include medication, dental care, vision care, medical equipment, and appliances, such as wheelchairs. The general public is required to pay for these services personally or through a private plan of insurance.

VETERANS BENEFITS

Veterans Affairs Canada offers a wide range of benefits to qualified veterans, members of the Canadian Forces, and members of the RCMP. These services recognize the contribution such people have made to their country and help them to live with dignity and independence.

The *New Veterans Charter*, which was enacted on April 1, 2006 (*Canadian Forces Members and Veterans Re-establishment and Compensation Act*), provides for:

- personal case management
- rehabilitation services
- financial benefits
- group health insurance
- job placement assistance

- a lump-sum disability award and other allowances
- support to their families.

Veterans may be eligible for a disability pension if they have a medical disability related to service in the armed forces or civilian service in close support during wartime, or if they are a serving or discharged RCMP member.

Compensation is also available to a veteran or qualified civilian who was a prisoner of war. A veteran of the Allied Forces may also qualify for a disability pension if the person lived in Canada prior to serving in the First or Second World War.

Special awards may be provided in addition to disability pensions, such as an "attendance allowance" to help a totally disabled person perform activities of daily living (such as bathing), or an "exceptional incapacity allowance", which is payable to a qualifying person who has exceptional incapacity caused by a pensionable condition. In addition to these special awards, qualifying individuals may also be eligible for a "clothing allowance" if they require adaptive clothing to suit special devices they wear.

Surviving spouses and dependants may also qualify for benefits upon the death of the qualifying disability pensioner. Dependent children's benefits include provision for education assistance.

Qualifying low-income persons may also be entitled to a special allowance if they meet certain income and residency requirements. These individuals may additionally qualify for financial help through the Assistance Fund if they have an emergency situation and no other way to pay for the expenses involved.

Health care assistance is also available in the form of health benefits, the Veterans Independence Program (VIP), and long-term care. Health benefits include medical, surgical, and dental care; prescription drugs; and hearing and vision aids. This assistance may also include travel assistance to obtain medical treatment. Through the VIP, eligible persons can receive funds to help pay for grass cutting, snow shovelling, housekeeping, personal care, adjustments to the home, and personal support by health professionals. Long-term care is provided through contracted facilities across Canada and at Ste. Anne's Hospital, which is owned and administered by the Veterans Affairs Department.

Funeral and burial assistance is also available for qualifying persons whose death resulted from a pensioned or awarded disability, or when there are not sufficient funds in the person's estate.

Information on services and benefits can be obtained by calling 1-866-522-2122 or by visiting the Veterans Affairs Web site.

WORKERS' COMPENSATION INSURANCE

History

Before the development of workers' compensation insurance, injured workers had to rely on the courts and the legal system to force employers to provide financial support. Most could not afford legal fees, and those who could found that employers were not held responsible if in any way the employee contributed to the accident. Even those who were successful sometimes found that the employer was unable to pay, ultimately declaring bankruptcy.

The concept of workers' compensation insurance did not originate in Canada. It dates back to the late 1800s, when it appeared in Germany, Great Britain, and the United States. Around 1885, Chancellor Otto von Bismarck introduced a mandatory state-run accident plan in Germany. Workers and employers jointly financed the benefits. In 1897, Great Britain passed the first *Workers' Compensation Act*, based on no-fault principles. It was different from earlier schemes in that it made employers responsible for compensating injured workers, without the employee having to prove employer fault. While the employer was held responsible, there was no requirement for employers to insure this risk, and many employers found themselves unable to pay. The concept came to North America between 1908 and 1915, when several states in the United States passed compensation laws. As states have jurisdiction over these programs, they vary from mandatory insurance to self-insurance, and combinations thereof.

The first province in Canada to develop a workers' compensation program was Ontario. In 1910, the Province of Ontario appointed William Meredith to head a Royal Commission to review workers' compensation legislation, and this led to the five Meredith Principles.

Meredith Principles

Meredith envisioned a system in which workers would give up the right to sue their employers in return for guaranteed protection from loss of wages, regardless of fault. He also believed that the amount of compensation should have some relationship to the worker's earning power (i.e., a wage loss system).

On January 1, 1915, the Ontario *Workers' Compensation Act* was proclaimed, based on the five Meredith Principles:

1. **No-fault compensation.** Fault becomes irrelevant, and providing compensation to the insured worker becomes the focus. In return, the worker forfeits his or her right to sue the employer for damages. Neither can the employer sue the worker. Responsibility and liability are not issues.

2. **Collective liability.** Financial liability becomes a collective issue, because all employers contribute to a common fund from which money is drawn to pay injured workers.
3. **Security of payment.** Insured workers are assured of prompt and future compensation, because a guaranteed fund exists from which the money is drawn.
4. **Exclusive jurisdiction.** A compensation board exists with sole decision-making authority on payment of claims. The board is not bound by legal precedent and has the power and the authority to judge each case on its own individual merits.
5. **Independent board.** The governing board is both autonomous and non-political. There is no financial relationship to government or any other special interest group. The administration of the system is focused on the needs of the worker and the employer, creating impartiality and efficiency.

These principles are the fundamentals that all provinces have used to develop their respective workers' compensation plans. Thus, unlike the United States, where underlying principles of programs vary widely from one state to another, the plans across Canada are similar, though not identical.

Prior to the Meredith Principles, the "assumption of risk" rule provided that workers were essentially free to work or not to work and were responsible for ensuring that their wages were adequate to cover the risk of injury or death. In addition to challenging this common-law principle, Meredith also challenged the concept of "joint negligence", which suggested that workers should be blamed for their own injuries and illnesses. His proposed trade-off of a worker's right to sue in return for guaranteed compensation regardless of fault became known as the "historic compromise".

Workers' Compensation Today

Based on the Meredith Principles, each province has a workers' compensation board, which administers the workers' compensation insurance. Boards are completely funded by employers' premiums and have full authority to assess claims for compensation and reimburse doctors and hospitals for providing medically necessary services to claimants. Medical expenses related to a workplace injury for a covered worker are the sole responsibility of the board, and not of the provincial health insurance plan. The board negotiates with local health care service providers, who are then paid by the board.

Premiums and Employer Assessments

Employers' premiums fund the benefits payable to injured workers. The government does not contribute to the fund, nor can premiums be charged to employees. The employers' premium (also known as the "assessment rate") is based on a rate per $100 of payroll, up to the maximum-covered payroll set annually by the province's board. The assessment rate varies by industry, with higher-risk industries paying a higher rate than those considered to be lower in risk. Rates are further refined within an industry by class, with consideration for the types of occupations found within. Generally, rates do not vary within a company by occupation; consequently, the employer's rate for its trade workers will typically be the same as it is for its supervisors. An employer who has a separate building for administration might be granted a lower assessment rate for those employees.

Each province starts with an average provisional assessment rate. This is further refined by industry, and by class within each industry, using Statistics Canada's Standard Industrial Classification (SIC) Guide. The experience rating further determines what an individual employer will be charged. The experience rating takes into consideration how many work injuries and work-related diseases have occurred at the employer's business.

Each province's board has its own guidelines regarding which industries are subject to compulsory participation and which are considered to be individually liable. For instance, there may be Schedule 1 and Schedule 2 businesses, whereby those that fall under Schedule 1 are required to participate, while those in Schedule 2 are individually liable for compensation and health care costs. The latter are still required to contribute financially to the board for administrative costs, as the board is still responsible for evaluating their injured workers' claims and determining the benefits payable to the injured worker directly by their employer, not through the fund. A few examples (although they vary by province) of Schedule 2 employers include municipalities, school boards, libraries, airlines, railways, and Crown corporations or agencies. Some industries whose participation is not compulsory may choose to participate voluntarily (known as "voluntary industries"), and still others are completely excluded from the province's legislation or regulations.

The board in most provinces posts its annual Rate Guide for download from its Web site, and this is available to advisers who want to learn more about their local industries' rates.

Benefits for Injured Workers and Dependants

The benefits provided by most boards fall under the following categories:

Weekly Benefits for Temporary Disability. Benefits for loss of wages are payable in the form of income. Older formulas often provided for 75% of gross earnings to a stated maximum. More recent benefits provide for 80% to 90% of net earnings, up to the stated maximum earnings. Currently, only Manitoba does not have a maximum annual amount. The maximum covered earnings figure in other provinces ranges from $47,800 in Prince Edward Island to $82,800 in Alberta (2011 figures).

Permanent Disability. Benefits for permanent disability are based on two components: a payment for non-economic loss to recognize permanent clinical impairment, plus a payment for economic loss to recognize the impact the injury or disease may have on one's capacity to earn wages.

Fatality Benefits. Provision is also made for death and survivor benefits to dependants following a fatal injury or disease. They consist of the following:

- An immediate, lump-sum payment
- An additional payment to cover funeral costs
- An additional payment to cover expenses related to transportation of the body
- An additional monthly payment to the deceased's spouse plus a monthly payment for dependent children.

In most cases, the amount of monthly payments varies based on the age of the spouse and both the age and number of children. CPP/QPP benefits may or may not be deducted from the spouse and children's benefits, depending on the province. Most provinces also provide rehabilitation assistance to the spouse to become employable or to increase his or her earnings capacity.

Rehabilitation Benefits. Rehabilitation services and programs are covered to restore the worker to pre-injury health. Some of the vocational rehabilitation assistance provided includes work assessment, training, tuition, placement assistance, workplace modification, and ergonomic services. Other services may include relocation assistance, home modifications, vehicle adaptations, counselling, child care, legal services, home maintenance, and a personal care allowance.

Medical Aid. Health care expenses related to the worker's injury are also covered. Some of these include fees for acupuncture, audiologists, chiropractors, optometry, physicians, physiotherapy, prosthetics, orthotics, psychologists, speech pathologists, other specialists, dental work, dietician or nutritionist services, hospital fees, and occupational therapy.

Responsibility to Mitigate Injury

An injured worker has a responsibility to take reasonable steps to mitigate injury. If they fail to do so, they risk loss of entitlement to benefits. The following are actions that may cause benefits to cease:

- Failing to take all reasonable steps to reduce or eliminate a permanent impairment
- Failing to pursue medical treatment that would promote return to work
- Failing to provide full information or to report changes in circumstances

- Failing to report for an examination
- Failing to cooperate with a plan of rehabilitation.

Increasing Focus on Safety and Prevention

Many provinces are moving beyond workers' claims management by increasing their focus on safety and prevention. In New Brunswick and in Newfoundland and Labrador, the governance board responsible is known as the Workplace Health, Safety and Compensation Commission (WHSCC). In Ontario, it is known as the Workplace Safety and Insurance Board (WSIB).

In Ontario, for example, the Ministry of Labour determined in 2004 that 2% of all firms (6,000 businesses in total) accounted for 10% of all lost-time injury claims and 21% of the claim costs.[3] This led the Ministry of Labour to set a target to reduce injuries by 20% from 2004 to 2008 through a targeted enforcement strategy referred to as the "Road to Zero Tolerance". This would translate into a savings of $300 million to the Board. The program developed was called the "High-Risk Initiative". An additional 200 inspectors were hired to target high-risk businesses.

Inspectors were given greater power to shut down businesses, and offending employers would be automatically prosecuted with fines and/or imprisonment. In addition, inspectors were given authority to issue fines on the spot. The Ministry wanted to make a philosophical shift to the belief that there really are no accidents, just injuries, and that someone is always to blame. Victims could now be found to be at fault (or to have contributed) and could now be fined up to 25%.

In March 2005, the Ministry of Labour announced a second strategy to deal with another group, the next 8% worst offenders. This was referred to as the "Last Chance" initiative. Roughly 5,000 businesses were given the opportunity to voluntarily improve their health and safety record by working collaboratively with the Ontario Service Safety Alliance, which would assist them to develop an action plan for safety improvement. The Minister of Labour suggested that if this attempt did not bring about improvements, these businesses could attract the attention of the Minister of Labour enforcement.

Several other initiatives were also undertaken to target groups with higher-than-average injury rates. With an increased number of inspectors now available, more audits were being undertaken, fines issued, and penalties imposed.

The success achieved with these programs has resulted in further goals and initiatives, including the use of more inspectors, audits, and penalties for offending companies.

---

[3] *Thinking Differently About Health and Safety: Successful Partnerships That Make a Difference*, presentation by M. Shaw, Industrial Accident Prevention Association (Toronto), and H. Tosine, Ministry of Labour (Toronto), IALI Conference Toronto (April 18, 2007).

National Focus, Bill C-45, and the *Criminal Code*

On March 31, 2004, the *Criminal Code* of Canada was changed. Bill C-45, which amended the Code, came into law and provided that employers could now be sued with criminal negligence and face prosecution for the actions (or lack of action) of a supervisor or representative who oversees the day-to-day operation of the organization. It created a new duty for workplace safety: everyone who undertakes or has the authority to direct how another person performs work has a legal duty to take reasonable steps to prevent harm to that person caused by that work or task.

An employer's only defence is to prove "due diligence" — in other words, that all reasonable steps were taken to prevent the incident from happening in the first place. Employees similarly have a responsibility to take care of themselves, such as following safety practices and adhering to regulations.

Due Diligence

The concept of "due diligence" applies to officers, directors, supervisors, and workers, as any or all can be charged under the *Occupational Health and Safety Act*. The concept of due diligence was first discussed by the Supreme Court of Canada, which stated that an accused can avoid liability by proving that all "reasonable care" was taken to avoid the particular event. Demonstrating reasonable care requires giving evidence to prove that the steps were taken *before the injury occurred.*

Due diligence refers to the level of care, prudence, judgment, and activity that a person could reasonably be expected to ensure in a given set of circumstances. In the case of occupational health and safety, it means that an employer must take all reasonable precautions to prevent injuries and occupational disease in the workplace.

To prove due diligence, the officers, directors, and supervisors must have appropriate policies in place, a training and education program, and a method to ensure that supervisors are competent as defined by the *Occupational Health and Safety Act*. They must also have a method to ensure that policies are being followed and disciplinary action taken for violations. Furthermore, they must show they have an accident investigation and reporting system and that policies are regularly reviewed and updated. All of these actions must be documented to be able to show that these steps had been taken before an injury occurred, in the event that they are required to prove due diligence.

Collective Liability Model and Unfunded Liabilities

When he was establishing the workers' compensation system, William Meredith heard debate about using pay-as-you-go funding versus using a pre-funded model, like that used by the private insurance industry. He believed that the concerns that led to a full-funding model among private insurers do not apply to a collective liability model, where all employers in a class of industry contribute to the cost of injuries in that class.

In recent years, there has been an increasing focus on the unfunded liability existing in most of the provinces' Workers' Compensation schemes. The unfunded liability represents the difference between the lump sum that would be needed to pay all future costs of claims currently on the books as compared with the reserves available today. Boards are required only to ensure that current costs are funded and that there is an adequate reserve for contingencies. In other words, it is a pay-as-you-go system that relies on current employers' assessments to pay for current workers' claims. On the other hand, private insurers offering disability insurance must currently fund the future cost of claims by establishing a reserve at the time of the claim approval sufficient to pay the claim for its full duration. The rationale is that a private insurer could go out of business and the claimant would be abandoned. Meredith believed that, because the workers' compensation system is perpetual and ongoing, the notion of having to pay all its obligations at one time is not relevant.

The assessment system differs from that of a private insurance system in terms of how rates are charged. Instead of charging a premium per $100 of coverage, the system uses an assessment against total payroll. Thus, as a business grows and its payroll gets larger, its annual contribution to workers' compensation increases, too.

If a business owner were given a choice of prepaying for future claims today, as opposed to paying today's claims with today's dollars, some believe that most would opt for the pay-as-you-go option, as this would enable them to retain more money in the business for other purposes. Consequently, while some believe that the goal of boards should be to pay off the unfunded liability that exists, others believe that the more appropriate question should be regarding the proper funding ratio — how much reserve funds are appropriate to cover potential changes in accident rates and claims duration?

Proponents of eliminating the unfunded liability believe there are intergenerational considerations that should not be ignored. The fact that an unfunded liability exists is evidence that the cost of past injuries is being passed on to current employers. Given the fact that manufacturing industries have been in decline relative to service and high-tech industries, this means that costs of past accidents are being transferred to current and future generations of employers. This could place them at a disadvantage in an era of global competition. Therefore, they believe, boards should focus on eliminating unfunded liabilities.

Chapter 15

Individual Health Insurance Plans

Individual health and dental plans are sometimes referred to as "supplementary health plans", because they focus on services that are not fully covered by government plans. Since government benefits vary by province, insurers also vary their offerings for individual health and dental plans by province. This is necessary to avoid duplication and to conform to provincial legislation. People who purchase coverage in one province and then move to another should, consequently, check with their insurer regarding the impact on their personal plan.

Individual health and dental plans are most often purchased by people who are self-employed or who, for other reasons, may not be covered by a plan of group insurance. Occasionally, some people purchase it to "top up" their group insurance and thereby provide a higher level of reimbursement. When coverage is being purchased for this purpose, the buyer needs to be aware that the coordination of benefits provisions contained in the contract will reduce the amount otherwise payable. This ensures that a person will not be able to collect more than 100% of the cost incurred. Some examples of this can be found later in this section, under "Coordination of Benefits".

DEDUCTIBLE, COINSURANCE, AND MAXIMUMS

A "deductible" is the amount of eligible expenses that the insurance requires the insured to pay each year before coverage begins for medical (or dental) expenses. In addition to a deductible, the plan may also have a "coinsurance" factor. Coinsurance is a cost-sharing requirement requiring the insured to pay a portion of each eligible expense once the deductible, if any, has been satisfied. The term generally refers to the percentage of eligible expenses paid by the insurance company, and the remaining percentage, known as the "copayment", represents the portion that must be paid by the insured.

For instance, a plan that has a $25 deductible and an 80% coinsurance requires the insured to pay the first $25 of medical expenses each year, after which the insurer will then pay 80% of the eligible expenses incurred. In other words, the insured pays a 20% copayment on each $1 of expenses incurred in addition to the deductible of $25. The use of a deductible helps to eliminate minor claims that would otherwise drive up the cost of administration, while coinsurance acts as a form of risk-sharing that encourages reduction in utilization. The use of deductibles and coinsurance reduces the monthly premium and makes coverage more affordable to the insured.

Some insurers use only the term "coinsurance", as in the following example:

> Drug and dental benefits are subject to an 80% coinsurance factor.

In this example, it is understood that the insured's copayment is the remaining 20%. Conversely, some plans may make reference only to "copayment", as in the following example:

> The insured's copayment is 20% on routine dental expenses.

In this example, it is understood that the plan provides 80% coinsurance. This is sometimes abbreviated simply to "80/20" (meaning 80% coinsurance and 20% copayment).

The deductible and coinsurance factors vary within a policy by the line of benefits. For instance, the dental coverage may have a 20% copayment, while the same policy may provide drug coverage with a 30% copayment. Most individual health plans do not make use of a deductible and, instead, use coinsurance to keep the premium rate affordable. This also encourages appropriate usage of the plan and reminds the insured to shop wisely for medical purchases.

In addition to the deductible and coinsurance factors, each line of coverage also has a maximum annual reimbursement. The higher the maximum, the more expensive the premium will be.

The maximum time period may be stated as a calendar year, a benefit year, or an anniversary year. A "calendar year" is the period of 12 consecutive months beginning January 1 each year. Where maximums are based on a calendar year, they may be prorated in a start-up year to reflect the fact that it is a partial year.

A "benefit year" means the period of 12 consecutive months following the date a claim for a specific benefit is first incurred. When this method is used, the maximum acts as a "rolling 12", measured from the date a particular category of claim is first incurred. An "anniversary year" means the consecutive 12-month period following the effective date that coverage commences, and annually thereafter.

A plan may use any or all of these definitions. For example, it may stipulate that the maximums for drug and dental benefits are measured on an anniversary year basis, while vision care and hearing aid benefits are measured on a benefit year basis. Rates for the plan may be adjusted on a calendar year basis (so all insured individuals of the same age and plan have the same rates), or on an anniversary year basis (in which case the rate adjustment gets applied on the plan's anniversary).

BENEFITS AVAILABLE

The benefits payable under most individual health and dental plans include the following lines of coverage:

- Accidental death and dismemberment
- Extended health care
- Prescription drug benefits
- Dental benefits
- Vision care benefits
- Emergency travel medical care benefits.

Occasionally, but less typically, some individual health plans will also include the following lines of coverage:

- Life insurance
- Dependant life
- Critical illness
- Catastrophic coverage.

Accidental Death and Dismemberment

This benefit, commonly referred to as "AD&D", provides a lump-sum payment in the event of death due to accident, and a lesser lump sum in the event of loss of limbs (or lesser losses, as listed in the benefit). Historically, the loss schedule for payment due to something other than death was limited to dismemberment, but today, definitions describe the loss as "loss of use", where such loss is permanent and total. For this reason, this benefit is also known as accidental death and loss of use (AD&L).

The benefit is not intended to cover high-risk scenarios and, consequently, will specifically list situations that are excluded, such as intentionally self-inflicted injury or attempted suicide, participation in dangerous sports, operation of a motor vehicle while intoxicated or impaired by drugs, flying other than as a fare-paying passenger on a regularly scheduled airline, war or civil disorder, and injury incurred while participating in a criminal offence.

The policy will also stipulate a maximum time within which the loss must occur following the accident that caused the injury, and this is normally 365 days.

Extended Health Care

This benefit, known as "EHC", covers the insured for medical expenses not covered by the provincial health plan that are incurred due to illness, injury, or pregnancy in the province of residence. Expenses incurred outside the province of residence, if covered, will be described under a different line of coverage, called "emergency travel medical care benefits". Not all individual plans automatically cover travel outside the province, so the contract provisions should be reviewed carefully to determine if this coverage must be added as an extra option or through an upgrade to a higher "package" of benefits.

EHC comprises several categories of expenses, each with its own deductible (normally nil), coinsurance, and annual maximum. In addition to annual maximums by expense category, EHC may be subject to a lifetime maximum, such as $100,000 or $300,000, although many plans offer an unlimited lifetime maximum.

Following are the categories of benefits most typically found under EHC.

Hospitalization

Some, but not all, plans include hospitalization benefits as part of EHC. This feature provides for the additional cost of preferred over basic accommodation to be covered up to a stated maximum charge per day and a limited number of days per year. The preferred accommodation may include both private and semi-private rooms, or only the latter. This has traditionally been a valued feature but more recently has been seen as an area for cost reduction. The reality today is that hospitals have room shortages, and this means that patients must accept standard accommodation even if they have insurance for preferred accommodation. Consequently, the insured could be paying for a benefit that will not be available during an illness. Some plans will provide a daily allowance to compensate for this, such as $50 or $100, for a limited number of days while preferred accommodation is unavailable. This may apply only after passage of a minimum number of days, such as four, of being without preferred accommodation.

Specialists' Services

Benefits are payable for the services of various specialists (sometimes referred to as paraprofessional or paramedical services) after the yearly maximum allowed under the provincial health plan has been reached. These specialists usually include the following:

- Chiropractor
- Acupuncturist
- Osteopath
- Physiotherapist
- Podiatrist
- Psychologist
- Speech therapist

- Chiropodist
- Naturopath
- Ophthalmologist or optometrist
- Registered massage therapist.

The annual maximum coverage for specialists may be a flat amount per visit, such as $12 or $20, up to a specified number of visits, such as 20 or 25 visits. Another variation is a fixed maximum "pot", such as $600 total, combined for all specialists annually. This latter method provides for full payment per visit until the pot is depleted for the current year.

Equipment Purchase/Rental and Medical Supplies

This benefit covers charges for the purchase or lease of devices such as wheelchairs, crutches, walkers, canes, splints, braces, trusses, cervical collars, ostomy supplies, oxygen, respirators, and non-motorized hospital beds. Also included is the cost of some supplies, such as syringes, hypodermic needles, and reactive strips for diabetics, and equipment and accessories for ostomates.

The contract provides a maximum for annual reimbursement, such as $2,500 per year.

Prostheses and Accessories

This benefit covers the initial cost of various prostheses, artificial eyes or limbs, and a wig if required as a result of chemotherapy. It may also include custom-made orthotic shoes and surgical stockings, or these may be included as separate benefits with separate annual maximums. This category is usually reimbursed up to an annual maximum of $2,500 per year.

Nursing and Home Care

This benefit covers the cost of a registered nurse, registered practical nurse, or certified home support worker (personal care worker) who is not related to the insured and is recommended by the insured's personal physician. Some contracts may stipulate that this service is only available following a period of hospitalization and may require the insured to be unable to perform two or more activities of daily living, as defined by the contract. Some contracts may simply say that the benefit is payable if certified by the insured's physician as a "medically necessary service" and if it is "approved in advance by the insurer". Services are not intended as an alternative to those available through government sources. Other services that may fall into this category include those of an occupational therapist or registered dietician.

The contract provides for a maximum for annual reimbursement under this category, such as $2,500 per year, and within that, reimbursement at a rate that is reasonable and customary.

Accidental Dental Benefits

This benefit covers the cost of dental treatment due to an accident that causes injury to natural teeth, and it may also cover expenses for the reduction of a fractured or dislocated jaw. It would not cover an injury caused by an object placed into the mouth. There is normally a requirement that the insurer must be notified within 90 days from when the accident occurred and that the treatment must commence within a stipulated time from the date of injury, or the plan may require that the work be completed within a stipulated amount of time from the date of the injury. The insurer may require a written estimate in advance for predetermination of benefits payable. The reimbursement will not exceed the recommended rate according to the dental association fee schedule.

The maximum reimbursement per year under this benefit is usually in the range of $2,000, but it may be subject to coinsurance.

Benefits payable under this provision do not reduce the amount payable under the regular dental benefit provision, which is a separate line of coverage.

Hearing Aids

This benefit covers the purchase of and repairs to hearing aids, and it may include the initial batteries, but not ongoing replacement batteries. The maximum is usually in the range of $300 to $500. This benefit can only be claimed at fixed intervals, such as three, four, or five years. To deal with the risk of anti-selection, some insurers set a waiting period, such as three months following the effective date of the plan, to deter people from buying coverage solely for the purpose of purchasing hearing aids and then cancelling coverage immediately thereafter.

Ambulance Services

This benefit covers charges incurred for transportation by ambulance, up to the difference between the coverage provided by the provincial health insurance plan and the customary charges in the province of residence.

Exclusions

In addition to the regular exclusions that apply to all lines of coverage, this line of coverage may also contain additional exclusions. A common exclusion relates to pregnancy and hospitalization. In order to prevent anti-selection, which could occur if someone suspects they are pregnant and therefore purchases the benefit, the plan will exclude hospitalization or other costs related to a pregnancy during the first eight months following the effective date of coverage. Other common exclusions under this benefit include cosmetic treatment, experimental treatments, family planning services, and voluntary or involuntary inhalation of gas or ingestion of poison.

Prescription Drug Benefits

Pharmaceuticals are a primary component of health care. They play a vital role in terms of preventing, treating, and curing diseases and other health conditions. According to the Canadian Pharmacists Association, there are about 22,000 drug products on the market today.

There are two categories of pharmaceuticals: prescription medication and non-prescription medication, the latter more commonly referred to as "over-the-counter" (OTC) medication. A physician usually prescribes prescription medication, although other professionals, such as a dentist, may prescribe it, and pharmacists dispense it. OTC medicines are purchased directly by consumers through retail pharmacies and include cold remedies, pain relievers, and various other health remedies. Each year, more and more medications become available to treat disease.

Drug benefits in individual health plans cover drugs that require a prescription, and not OTC medicines, even if a physician prescribes them. The insurer establishes a formulary (list of eligible drugs) that is usually broader than the provincial formulary. It may provide for the amount payable on drugs that have a generic equivalent to be limited to the lower of the actual cost or the lowest cost generic equivalent. This is known as a "generic plan". Some insurers offer "brand name" drugs on their higher-level plans. In this instance, the higher-cost medication will be covered.

Generic and Brand Name Drugs

Generic and brand name drugs are similar in many ways. Both generic and brand name drugs have the same active ingredients in the same amount. The generic must match its brand equivalent in dosage and the way it is administered (e.g., orally). Both contain the same cautions, warnings, and labelling. The generic must have an absorption rate that closely matches the brand (the time it takes for the body to absorb it). The generic must meet the requirements for consistency in strength, purity, and quality.

Where generic and brand name drugs differ is in the inactive ingredients, as well as in the colour or shape. So it is possible for someone to experience a reaction if he or she has sensitivities to the inactive ingredients or dyes used in colouring the drugs.

The most notable difference between generic and brand name drugs is the cost, which reflects the high level of development expenses incurred by brand name drug manufacturers. The research and development of a new drug can cost over $250 million and take 10 or more years to complete. Because there are no price controls, the maker of the brand name drug can establish any price, and generally sets it at a level high enough to try and recoup the high cost of research before the patent protection has expired (after 20 years). Generic manufacturers do not incur these high costs and are able to offer their versions at a significantly lower cost — as much as 80% lower — than the brand name equivalent. It takes a generic manufacturer about two or three years to develop the generic equivalent, at a cost of about $1 million.

Most people do not have a problem with a generic substitution. However, for the minority that do, some insurers will allow coverage of a brand name drug under a generic plan if the physician writes "no substitutes" on the prescription or if there is no generic equivalent.

Following are a few examples of brand name drugs with their generic equivalents:

- Amoxicillin (generic) and Amoxil (brand), an antibiotic medication
- Amitriptyline (generic) and Elavil (brand), an anti-depressant
- Hydrochlorothiazide (generic) and Hydrodiuril (brand), for controlling blood pressure.

Expenditures on prescription and non-prescription drugs reached $31.1 billion in 2010.[1] Given that the private sector is responsible for almost 84% of all drug expenditures, insurers use various tools, such as generic substitution and managed formularies, to control the escalating costs on private sector health plans.

Managed Therapeutic Formulary

A managed therapeutic formulary encourages the use of cost-effective drugs by using a two-tiered formulary, whereby the preferred drugs are reimbursed at a higher level (i.e., the insured pays a lower copayment). It helps to reduce the cost per prescription by encouraging individuals to request the lower-cost alternative from their physician. It targets medications that are not interchangeable and that, therefore, cannot be substituted by the pharmacist. This is not a widely used method for controlling costs in individual health plans. Instead, insurers make greater use of generics.

Drugs Not Covered

Some, but not all, plans cover birth control pills, and those that do usually do not cover other forms of contraception. A few insurers also cover fertility drugs on higher-level plans, but generally individual health plans do not cover vitamins, fertility drugs, or smoking cessation medication. Diabetic supplies, such as testing strips, are normally covered under the "medical supplies" section of EHC and are subject to the coinsurance and annual maximum for the medical supplies category.

Copayments and Annual Maximums

The proportion of drug costs that the insured is responsible for paying can range from 20% to 30%. Some plans offer a tiered copayment, whereby the insured pays an initial copayment rate, such as 10%, 20%, or 30%, and

---

[1] Canadian Institute for Health Information, *Drug Expenditure in Canada, 1985 to 2010* (Ottawa, Ontario: CIHI, 2011).

then the copayment rate "steps down" to a lesser amount — even zero — once the annual drug costs incurred reach a certain threshold level.

As expenses related to prescription medication are increasing, insurers control their exposure by establishing an annual maximum that can be claimed. Despite this, for clients who are willing to pay, very high levels are available to those who qualify based on their current health status. Some examples of annual drug maximums currently offered are:

- $245 (a basic guaranteed plan)
- $280 for Years 1 and 2, and $400 thereafter (a tiered maximum in a basic guaranteed plan)
- $500 for Year 1, and then $750 thereafter (a tiered maximum in a guaranteed plan)
- $2,500 (a medically underwritten plan)
- $5,000 (a medically underwritten plan)
- $10,000 (a medically underwritten plan)
- Unlimited (a medically underwritten plan with a catastrophic benefit).

As can be seen from these examples, individual health plans offer a wide range of options, from an annual maximum of $245 up to unlimited annual protection, thereby catering to a wide range of clients' concerns.

Shared Dispensing Fee

Some plans limit the amount that will be covered for the pharmacist's dispensing fee. Fees charged by pharmacies can vary widely, from $4 per prescription to $15 per prescription. Pharmacies that offer additional services can charge twice as much for dispensing the same medication as others, so some insurers encourage users to "shop wisely" by capping the amount that they will cover for the dispensing fee. Any charge above this cap must be paid for by the insured at the time the medication is purchased, in addition to the regular copayment.

Drug Card

The insured is provided with a drug card, which is presented to the pharmacist when purchasing a prescription. By scanning the card, the pharmacist can immediately inform the insured what is allowable under the plan and, consequently, the out-of-pocket cost the insured must pay. Electronic submission eliminates the need for filling out claim forms and waiting for reimbursement.

Exclusions

In addition to the standard exclusions, the contract will also list exclusions specific to this line of coverage. This will include medications not covered, such as those for weight control and smoking cessation, growth hormones, anabolic steroids, sexual stimulants, hair growth stimulants, vaccines, dietary supplements, experimental drugs, infant food preparations, over-the-counter medications, and soaps.

Dental Benefits

Dental benefits continue to be one of the more popular features of an individual health plan, as not everyone purchases a prescription each year, but virtually everyone who has dental coverage will utilize this benefit every year. For this reason, insurers build cost controls into the design of the plan to help protect against anti-selection and excess utilization.

While some companies advertise "dental only" plans, the reality is that all such plans have a base of EHC.

Coinsurance and Annual Maximums

The structure of copayments required on dental benefits falls into three categories:

- Flat percentage
- Reducing tiered schedule
- Increasing tiered schedule.

Under the flat percentage method, the copayment does not change. An example is 20% payable by the insured.

Under the reducing tiered schedule, the insured has a lower copayment on some initial level of expenses, and then the copayment increases on amounts above it. An example is 20% on the first $500 of routine expenses, and then 40% on further amounts. This method encourages the insured to keep the costs lower by encouraging wiser plan utilization.

Under the increasing tiered schedule, the insured has a higher copayment amount in the first year, which reduces each year until it eventually becomes level. This method helps to discourage someone from purchasing the plan as a short-term solution, knowing that extensive dental work is needed, and then cancelling the plan. An example is 30% in Year 1, 25% in Year 2, and then 20% in Year 3 and thereafter.

The annual maximum tends to be substantially lower than those found under the drug benefit, with the exception of basic plans, where annual maximums are relatively modest. Several examples of annual maximums found in plans regarding covered dental expenses are $245, $500, $1,000, and $1,500.

The annual maximum may also increase each year over a specified period, such as three years, as in the following example: Year 1: maximum $750; Year 2: maximum $1,200; Year 3+: maximum $1,500.

Routine and Major Services Covered

The dental benefit will identify the services that can be claimed under the benefit. "Routine" expenses include preventative care (examinations, diagnostic services, tests) and basic maintenance care (fillings, cleanings, simple extractions). Another category of expenses is "major restorative" services, which encompasses more extensive work, such as extensive restorative procedures, crowns, inlays, and bridges. Some plans additionally include orthodontics as part of major restorative services. Endodontics (root canal treatment) and periodontics (treatment of gum disease) are usually included as part of routine services.

Major restorative services are covered at a lower coinsurance rate, requiring the insured to pay 50% of the cost. There is often a lower annual maximum that applies to major restorative services, such as $500, which falls within the overall annual maximum for dental benefits. As a further precaution against anti-selection, major restorative services are normally not covered until the third plan year.

Recalls

The term "recalls" refers to the number of checkups that will be covered in a year. The normal variations are 6-month, 9-month, and 12-month recalls. A plan that provides for recalls at 9-month intervals, for instance, will not cover an interim checkup that occurs less than nine months from the last appointment for which the code for a checkup was entered on the claim form. However, if the insured needs treatment between recalls, the required services will be covered in accordance with the annual reimbursement maximums stated in the plan. In addition, the insured may be able to go for additional hygiene appointments between checkups.

Scaling Units

Each insurer has a maximum allowable number of "scaling units" allowed annually for dental hygiene. Most plans provide around 10 units. A unit is equal to 15 minutes of service. Consequently, the insured can usually go for several interim hygiene appointments between checkups.

Provincial Dental Association Fee Schedule

Each provincial dental association sets an annual recommended fee schedule listing the recommended charge for each procedure, and the dental benefit covers procedures up to the recommended maximum only. While most insurers adjust their plan to cover the new annual fee schedule, there can be a lapse between the release of the new fee schedule and the update to the individual health plan. In other words, the insurer may still be applying the previous year's maximum fee schedule, and not the current fee schedule. This could result in the insured having to pay for service charges in excess of it.

Predetermination of Benefits

When dental services involve extensive work, the insurer requires submission of an estimate in advance of work being performed. The contract will specify the amount above which an estimate must be submitted in advance (usually about $500). The insurer will respond with an outline showing what they will pay and the amount that the insured will be required to cover. This gives the insured an opportunity to further discuss the recommended procedures with the dentist. Occasionally, dental offices miscode services, and when this happens, the insurer may deny an expense that would actually be covered. While it does not happen often, it is worth reviewing with the dental office, as it could make a significant difference regarding how much the insured must pay out of pocket.

A person who fails to obtain an estimate in advance for predetermination of benefits will not be refused reimbursement. However, the amount covered may not be the full expense if the claims adjudicator assesses the rate to be more than normally charged or if the procedure employed is seen to be more extensive than normal. Insurers make use of professional consultants in reviewing claims to determine whether a lower-cost alternative treatment may have been of equal therapeutic value.

Electronic Claims Submission

Claims are submitted electronically, eliminating the need for paper submission. However, procedures vary by dentist as to whether the insured must pay at point of service and wait for reimbursement from the insurer. Some dentists allow the insured to merely pay the difference between the amount reimbursable and the charges incurred. They then receive payment from the insurer. This is referred to as "assignment of benefits". It is up to the dentist to decide which method they follow.

Exclusions

In addition to the standard exclusions for health benefits, there are additional exclusions that may be found under the dental benefit:

- Treatment for cosmetic purposes only
- Treatment by a dental hygienist not working under the supervision of a dentist
- Services covered by a government plan or by workers' compensation
- Any services related to dysfunction of the temporomandibular joint (TMJ).

Vision Care

The "vision care benefit" is often included under EHC. It provides for reimbursement towards the cost of prescription lenses and frames, or contact lenses, but does not include safety glasses and may also exclude prescription sunglasses. The amount ranges from $100 every two years to $250 every two years. The measure is often based on a benefit year (i.e., from the last date glasses were purchased). One specialty insurer offers an enhanced optional benefit that provides up to $500 every three years. This benefit may also provide for reimbursement towards the cost of optometrist fees, usually in the range of $30 to $50.

Emergency Travel Medical Care Benefits

The emergency travel medical care benefit provides the insured with protection against the cost of emergency hospital and medical care when travelling outside the province of residence or out of the country. The benefit covers an unlimited number of trips of up to a specified number of days each, such as 30 days. If individuals will be travelling longer than the maximum covered period, they can purchase "top-up insurance" from a private insurer for the additional days of coverage required. When purchasing the additional insurance, people should indicate that they want top-up insurance coverage.

To be covered by this benefit, the insured (and his or her spouse or dependants) must be covered by the provincial health insurance plan.

Standard Benefits

The benefits usually covered include the following:

- Overall maximum of $1 million (some maximums are as high as $5 million)
- Hospital accommodation charges at basic rate
- Physicians' fees, diagnostic tests
- Ambulance services, including air ambulance
- Paramedical services
- Prescription drugs
- Medical appliances
- Accidental dental for accidental injury to natural teeth of up to $2,000
- Air transportation costs for emergency return to residence
- Flight costs for family member if the insured is confined to hospital
- Return of deceased's body up to a stated maximum, such as $3,000
- Return of vehicle
- Return of family pet

- Meals and accommodation up to a stated maximum, such as $1,500, if insured is unable to return due to the illness or injury of a travelling companion
- Automatic extension of coverage beyond the expiry date for a period (such as 72 hours) if return is delayed due to hospitalization of the insured or a travel companion (or advice by the physician not to travel), due to mechanical failure of the aircraft, or due to weather conditions that prohibit return.

Pre-Existing Condition Limitations

The contract will outline what constitutes a pre-existing condition and is, therefore, not covered under the travel benefit. Generally, a pre-existing condition includes any condition for which the insured had symptoms, visited a doctor or was advised to do so, sought medical treatment, or took medication, whether the condition is diagnosed or not, if the activity in question occurred within a specified period of time prior to departure. The time frame varies from one company to another, with the usual variations being 90 days and 180 days.

The pre-existing condition period is measured from each departure date from the home province, and is not measured only from the plan's inception.

Exclusions

In addition to the general exclusions, the following additional exclusions specific to this benefit are often included:

- Travel for the purpose of seeking medical treatment
- Travelling against doctor's orders
- Travel to a location where the Canadian government has issued a travel advisory warning
- War, invasion, hostilities, and any act of terrorism
- Operating a motor vehicle while under the influence of alcohol or drugs
- Participation in risky sports, such as racing or mountain climbing
- Treatment required for a mental and nervous disorder
- Failing to notify the insurer upon admission to a hospital or in advance of surgery.

Some contracts provide that failure to notify the insurer upon admission to a hospital or in advance of surgery will result in no payment, while others limit payment to a percentage, such as 75%, or even to a maximum amount, such as $25,000. Consequently, it is an important feature to discuss with clients.

Claiming for Benefits

At the time of claim, the insurer requires proof of the departure and return dates. It is important to review this feature with the insured and recommend that the insured retain the boarding pass or some other evidence that would establish the departure and return dates from the home province.

Other Assistance

The insured can also call the provider's assistance line to access a range of additional support services. Some of these services include the following:

- Help locating a physician, hospital, or medical facility
- Arrangement with payment of medical expenses
- Assistance contacting family to keep them informed
- Translation services
- Coordinating return home following a medical incident
- Assistance with replacing a lost or stolen passport or airline ticket
- Legal assistance in the event of a serious accident
- Assistance contacting the local embassy or consulate.

Life and Dependant Life Benefits

Most individual health plans do not provide life insurance. However, a few offer it as an optional benefit. This benefit, when available, is in the form of term insurance.

Critical Illness Benefit

Some insurers make available a critical illness benefit covering major critical illness events, including the following:

- Heart attack
- Stroke
- Cancer
- Coronary artery bypass.

Catastrophic Coverage

A few insurers make available enhanced coverage to protect against catastrophic loss for people who want protection in case of a serious accident or major illness. A deductible must first be satisfied, usually in the range of $2,500 (although some plans' deductibles are as high as $4,500), after which the insured is protected against drug expenses. Some plans may limit the amount of coverage per incident. The maximum that can be claimed in total is generally in the range of $10,000 to $25,000, but some plans provide for unlimited coverage. This unlimited coverage must be checked against any overall lifetime maximum that may be stated for the plan as a whole, such as $300,000. The catastrophic benefit may be used to enhance drug coverage under a basic plan and pay costs once the basic plan's maximum has been reached, or for the person who is only concerned with the risk of catastrophic loss and wants to reduce premiums by having a high deductible.

Some plans provide for enhanced coverage under other benefits besides drugs, and may include additional costs related to home care, and nursing and medical equipment, once the maximums have been reached for each category under the basic plan.

UNDERWRITTEN AND GUARANTEED PLANS

Individual health plans are available on both a medically underwritten basis and a guaranteed-issue basis. A medically underwritten plan offers higher annual maximums for reimbursement and lower premium rates, because the insurer has the opportunity to review the applicant's health in advance and determine the basis on which coverage will be offered. The underwriter will look for existing conditions and recent history of medication and use exclusions and/or ratings to adjust the risk. The underwriter will also request a report from the attending physician and may also obtain records from the provincial health insurance program to substantiate doctors' visits and medical treatment received. Paramedicals, urine specimens, and blood chemistry profiles are not a normal requirement associated with underwriting individual health plans.

If more than three exclusions are required, the coverage is likely to be declined. When an applicant is taking existing medication, some insurers will exclude only the medication from the drug benefit, while others will exclude the underlying condition and the medication from both the drug and the extended health care benefits. The adviser should, therefore, be sure to determine how extensively the exclusion is being applied and explain this to the client in detail. Insurers will generally reconsider removal of an exclusion once the insured has been off medication and symptom-free for two full years, unless the condition is one that has a high probability of recurrence in the future. Some insurers measure the passage of time from when the insurance was purchased, while others measure it from the date of the last symptoms, the last treatment, or the last medication taken. This could make a significant difference in how long the exclusion remains in place.

Some plans do not require applicants to complete a health questionnaire, but provide a standard exclusion for pre-existing conditions. These plans should not be mistaken as guaranteed issue plans, which do cover a pre-existing condition.

Several insurers offer coverage on a guaranteed-issue basis to people who had recently been covered by a group plan that they have now left behind. Eligibility is contingent upon applying for coverage within 60 days of the expiry of the group plan. Benefits offered have lower annual reimbursement levels and higher premium rates than medically underwritten plans but are ideal for someone who has a pre-existing condition. They cover existing medication and conditions. In planning coverage, the best approach is to determine which members of the family have a pre-existing condition (perhaps only one member). Coverage can be applied for through two separate policies — one that is guaranteed issue and one that is medically underwritten. The children can be added to the appropriate plan (single-parent coverage) based on whether or not one of the dependants has a pre-existing condition. This combination will provide the best coverage at the best rates for the family as a whole.

For families or individuals who have a pre-existing condition and who have not been a member of a group plan in the past 60 days, there are still coverage options available. Insurers make available basic plans that provide either a basic level of drug coverage (such as $250, $500, or $750) or dental benefits with basic EHC and no drug coverage. Some insurers limit such plans to those who can pass a few qualifying questions, to ensure that they are not currently disabled or hospitalized, and were not previously declined by another insurer. This helps them to maintain a reasonable level of risk in the pool, and it stabilizes future rates.

DESIGN CONSIDERATIONS

With the variety of plans available, how does one determine the right mix of benefits? The first consideration is to determine the client's objective. Is he or she more concerned with routine expenses, such as the cost of dental care, the purchase of eyeglasses, and the occasional prescription? Or is the client more concerned with catastrophic expenses and what could happen if a major illness or accident occurred? While most people find it a nuisance to pay routine medical expenses, they are likely to agree that it would be far more serious to deal with the very substantial costs of a major illness or accident.

Some basic fact-finding is also needed to explore whether anyone in the family currently takes (or recently took) medication or has a chronic (i.e., an ongoing) condition. This will often lead to a discussion about the current related costs, and whether this is the chief driver behind investigating plans today or whether the real concern is what could happen in the future. Explaining the difference between medically underwritten plans and guaranteed issue plans at this stage helps prepare the client for probable exclusions, and it underscores that there is still value in protecting against the unknown that could happen in the future, unrelated to today's problems.

If the client has just ceased to be covered by a group plan, a guaranteed "conversion" plan is likely the best option if the chief concern is covering the costs of existing medications or medical conditions.

Some clients may feel that their area of concern is dealing with the cost of dental care and have little interest in drug coverage, because they have rarely needed prescription medication in the past. Others are suddenly spurred into action because the cost of their monthly medication has escalated to the point that they now want to compare whether it is cheaper to pay a premium than it is to continue buying the medication personally. If only these two groups could talk to each other! Although it is too late for the second group, they could at least sound the wake-up call for the first group. No one plans to get sick or have an accident. But sicknesses and accidents happen nonetheless.

Consider, for example, the rate of occurrence of prostate cancer in men. In Canada, one in eight men will get it. The hormone injections that some will require quarterly for three years cost over $1,000 per shot. This is just one example of a client who will be thankful to have health insurance in place. Focus on the catastrophic and on the need to have coverage, before signs of deteriorating health begin to appear. Where possible, choose coverage with a higher copayment (20% or 30%), to keep the premium affordable, and a higher annual reimbursement on drug coverage ($5,000 or $10,000), to protect against severe economic loss. Also consider adding a catastrophic rider rather than a vision care enhancement. Finally, look for options that allow specialist limits to be "pooled", so that there will be higher reimbursement for the one or two specialists most likely to be used.

Annual travel insurance plans are available at a reasonable cost to supplement coverage under a plan that does not provide this benefit. It is often a more cost-effective way to obtain coverage for the traveller who goes away three or more times per year. Conversely, a client who seldom goes out of the province should look for unbundled plans that do not contain a travel benefit, as the individual is otherwise paying for coverage that will definitely not be needed. This individual is better off purchasing travel coverage as needed.

GENERAL PROVISIONS

There are a number of general provisions contained in the individual health plan contract that pertain to benefits as a whole. Some of the more significant provisions are outlined below.

Payment of Benefits

This provision explains that benefits are payable only for expenses that are usual, reasonable, customary, and necessary. The insurer determines this, and may refer to other points of reference by line of coverage, such as the provincial dental association fee schedule under the dental benefits section. It also explains that coverage is supplementary and does not cover charges insured under the provincial health insurance plan or where otherwise prohibited by law. Cosmetic procedures are considered unnecessary and are, consequently, not covered unless proven to be necessary due to an injury or illness. Charges that are incurred for experimental treatments are not covered.

The coverage insures only expenses incurred in the province of residence. If the policy contains a travel benefit, any out-of-province expenses incurred are covered in accordance with that benefit.

Lifetime Maximum

Some plans stipulate an overall lifetime maximum that can be claimed through the plan. This lifetime maximum usually applies only to EHC. Lifetime maximums can range from $100,000 to $350,000, although some plans are unlimited.

Claiming for Benefits

This provision outlines the claims procedures and time frames within which a claim for benefits must be submitted. In general, the insurer accepts only claims where evidence is submitted within 12 months from the date the expense is incurred. However, individual lines of coverage may have further requirements and shorter timelines that must be met. EHC requires completion of a paper-based claim form that is submitted for reimbursement. Drug benefits are claimed at the point of purchase using a drug card that is electronically swiped and provides immediate determination of payment. Dental benefits may or may not require out-of-pocket payment, depending on the individual dentist's procedures. Regardless, the dental claim is electronically submitted and does not normally require completion of a paper claim form for submission by the insured.

Most insurers provide claim forms for download from their Web sites.

Claims are reviewed on medically underwritten plans for non-disclosure and misrepresentation during the first two years that the plan is in force. The result can be that the contract is voided or the claim is denied. After two years, the insurer must be able to prove fraud.

Dependants' Maximum Age

Insurers' practices differ from one company to another regarding the maximum age up to which offspring can be covered as dependants. Some provide for a maximum age of 21 if they remain financially dependent upon the insured. Other companies will extend coverage to age 25 so long as the dependant continues to be registered and attending school full-time.

Adding Dependants After Issue

Additional insured individuals are not automatically covered and must apply for coverage providing medical evidence as if they had applied at the time the contract was originally issued. If the coverage already includes dependants' benefits, the insurer may specify a limited time following the birth of a child during which the child can be added without medical evidence, provided the forms are completed and submitted to the insurer within the stipulated period (usually 30 days).

Increasing or Reducing Coverage

The contract will provide details regarding rights and procedures for making changes to coverage after issue. Normally, changes that result in a decrease cannot be made in the first year. This is necessary because the insured may have claimed a higher amount as eligible under the existing plan that would be in excess of the maximum set under the lesser plan that the insured now wants. For similar reasons, reductions may be restricted after the first year to either the anniversary of the plan or the beginning of a calendar year (depending on how the insurer measures years for calculating benefits).

Increases in coverage can usually be made at any time, subject to medical underwriting. However, this is an administrative issue and can vary from one company to another.

Repurchase of Coverage at a Later Date

Individual plans have greater exposure to anti-selection caused by insured individuals "opting in" and "opting out" so as to match premium payments to the timing of expenses incurred. ("Why pay premiums if you don't need to claim on the coverage?") To protect against this, the insurer restricts the repurchase of coverage if the insured cancels the plan. Some insurers allow repurchase after a specified period has elapsed, such as two years. Other insurers prohibit later repurchase altogether. Given the limited number of insurers offering individual health benefit plans, the adviser has an obligation to ensure that the client understands this provision. Otherwise, the client may, at a later date, be unable to obtain coverage despite having good health.

Most insurers will make an exception if the insured cancelled because he or she became eligible for group insurance. Therefore, if that is the reason for the termination, the termination letter sent to the insured should always state this fact.

Subrogation

Subrogation is the substitution of one person in the place of another with respect to a lawful claim against a third party. The substituted party "stands in the shoes of" the other to claim that person's rights. Insurance companies have used the doctrine of subrogation for many years. In situations where injuries resulting in claims for benefits appear to have been caused by the negligence or fault of a third party, the insurance company exercises its right of subrogation to pursue claims against the third party by "standing in the shoes of" the claimant. In the meantime, the insurer pays the benefit under the contract, and then recovers from the third party.

Misrepresentation and Set-Off

If the insured has misrepresented, concealed, or failed to disclose a material fact, either in the application form or in a claim form, the insurer has the right to void the policy and return the premiums paid. The right to "set off" refers to the insurer's right to withhold from the return of premiums any amounts that have been paid in claims. "Voiding" a policy is different from simply "cancelling" it; voiding a policy means "it never was", so the insured was not entitled to any benefits, and the insurer has the right to retrieve them by deducting them first from any refund of premiums.

Indemnification of Insurer

This provision makes the insured financially responsible for all costs incurred by the insurer related to investigating and processing a fraudulent claim.

COORDINATION OF BENEFITS

Individual plans are considered to be supplementary to other coverage. As such, after benefits payable by government plans have been determined, excess benefits available are coordinated with benefits under other policies. How the insurer calculates the benefit payable under the individual plan when coordinated with coverage from another insurer's plan (such as an employer's plan) may differ from one company to another. The goal is always to ensure that the combined payment never exceeds 100% of the expense being claimed. Below are examples of some of the methods used.

Individual Plan as Second Payer

The claim is first submitted to the primary carrier (such as the group plan). Following payment, the claim, including the primary carrier's payment breakdown, is submitted to the individual insurer. The individual insurer calculates its payment as if there were no other insurance in place, then subtracts the amount already paid by the primary carrier and pays the balance up to the plan's maximum. The total cannot exceed 100%.

Example:

Expense Amount $1,000

Group carrier covers 80%; individual insurer covers 70%

(a) Submit to group carrier, who reimburses as follows: $1,000 × 80% = $800 (balance not covered is $200)

(b) Submit to individual carrier, who reimburses as follows: $1,000 × 70% = $700 entitlement. Amount not covered by group carrier is $200, which falls within the individual carrier's entitlement of $700. Therefore, the full remaining amount of $200 is reimbursed. If it had exceeded the maximum entitlement, the payment would have been cut back to the maximum entitlement

(c) Total combined reimbursement is 100%

Proportional Allotment

If both plans provide for coordination, the insurers prorate the amount between the two carriers in proportion to the amounts that would have been paid under each plan had there been coverage by only that plan.

Example:

Expense Amount $1,000

Second carrier covers 80%; individual insurer covers 70%

(a) Determine the prorated percentage for splitting the benefit by first adding the coinsurance factors together in decimal format: 0.80 + 0.70 = 1.50

(b) Divide the expense amount by this combined factor: $1,000 / 1.50 = $666.67

(c)	Second carrier's portion: $666.67 × 80% =	$ 533.34
(d)	Individual insurer's portion: $666.67 × 70% =	$ 466.67
(e)	Total combined reimbursement = 100%	$1,000.01

GENERAL EXCLUSIONS

In addition to specific exclusions by line of coverage, the contract outlines some general exclusions that apply to all lines of coverage. Most of the normal exclusions are listed below:

- Expenses incurred for services while confined to a chronic-care hospital, long-term care centre, or psychiatric hospital or institution
- Injuries sustained as a result of war, insurrection, riot, or civil disorder
- Drugs, medicine, supplies, or services that have been self-prescribed or prescribed by a family member

- Limitations related to an existing pregnancy or one that occurs shortly after the effective date of coverage (this protects against anti-selection)
- Charges that the government has ceased to cover after the effective date of the contract.

One particular exclusion noted above points out that the plan will not pay for a charge previously covered by the government that ceases to be covered after the contract has gone into force. This protects the insurer from changes the government makes to the provincial health insurance plan. Consider, for example, past changes made in Ontario to physiotherapy. When the government cut back coverage in this area, claims to insurers' plans increased, and rates had not been calculated based on the private benefits plan being the first payer. Thus, the provision protects the insurer from charges that were not actuarially factored in and could not be anticipated in advance. There is concern among insurers that the government will make further cutbacks, which result in "downloading" to private insurers, causing their claims to rise significantly.

GROUP PLANS VERSUS INDIVIDUAL PLANS

While individual health plans provide similar benefits to those found in group insurance, there are ways in which they differ. Some of these are highlighted below.

Group Plans	Individual Plans
• Group insurance provides a life insurance benefit	• Individual plans usually do not
• Group insurance provides health and dental benefits without evidence of insurability (with some exceptions)	• Most individual plans require medical underwriting
• Group plans often have a deductible for drug and dental benefits	• Individual plans rarely have a deductible for drug and dental benefits
• Group plans allow employers to select higher annual maximums for dental coverage than individual plans do	• Individual plans have lower annual maximums for dental coverage
• Group plans offer higher formulas for major dental benefits	• Individual plans have lower formulas for major dental benefits

Group Plans	Individual Plans
• Group plans offer higher amounts for covering specialists and paramedical services	• Individual plans have lower amounts for covering specialists and paramedical services
• Group insurance rates can be lower than those for similar coverage under an individual plan	• Individual insurance rates are rarely lower than those for similar coverage under a group plan
• Group plans will cover a pre-existing condition for a new employee who is taking prescription medication on an ongoing basis	• Individual plans will exclude the pre-existing condition during the underwriting process
• Group plans are not portable	• Individual plans are fully portable when the insured moves around within the province or from job to job
• Group plans cannot be paid by credit card and earn "loyalty award points" for the insured	• Individual plans can be
• Group plans have "one size fits all"	• Individual plans allow customizing of benefits "by person" when used in an employer setting
• Group plans require an employer contribution	• Individual plans have no stipulation requiring employer contribution — an employer can contribute something or nothing at all towards the cost of individual plans
• Under a group plan, the insured is a certificate holder only and has no control over the benefits	• Individual plans are two-party contracts between the insured and the insurer
• With group insurance, the employer's claims experience directly impacts renewal rates	• Individual plans have rates that are relatively stable
• Group plans may be available only to groups consisting of two or more unrelated employees	• Individual plans have no minimum participation requirement

Group Plans	Individual Plans
• Group plans are underwritten by the employer's industry classification and occupation of the employees, and are not available in situations where individual insurance may be available	• Individual plans are not underwritten by the industry or occupation of the insured and are available in situations where group insurance may not be available
• Group plans consider "family content". Therefore, they may not be offered to a business that has a large number of related owners or employees	• Individual plans do not consider "family content". Therefore, they may be offered to a business that has a large number of related owners or employees

While many other differences exist, suffice it to say that both have their strengths and weaknesses and that individual plans can provide the adviser with access to additional markets beyond those served by traditional group insurance.

Chapter 16

Health Spending Accounts and Private Health Services Plans

INTRODUCTION

There are different opinions among plan administrators regarding the subject of health and welfare trusts, health spending accounts, and private health services plans. Therefore, the approaches used by some plan administrators may vary somewhat from the information in this chapter. Advisers should consult with their own accountants and subject matter experts when deciding what methodology they will use with their clients. This chapter should not be construed as tax advice.

Health benefits are sometimes provided for employees of corporations through a vehicle commonly referred to as a health spending account (HSA) within a health and welfare trust (HWT). For self-employed individuals or unincorporated businesses, there is the "private health services plan" (PHSP). The rules for each type of plan are different but the premise is the same. The plans can be used as the sole health benefit plan, or they can be used in conjunction with an existing traditional insured group benefit plan ("defined benefit plan").

Defined Contribution Versus Defined Benefit

HSAs and PHSPs enable the employer to define how much it will contribute, rather than what benefit the employee will receive, and for this reason, they are referred to as "defined contribution plans".

A defined contribution plan has many advantages for the employer. It creates budget certainty, since the employer knows precisely how much the plan will cost each year. The cost will change only to the extent that the census data of the employee group changes during the year due to organic growth and terminations. This ability to control cost is extremely attractive to the employer or plan sponsor in the current environment, where defined benefit plan costs have been growing annually, and the plan sponsors have limited ability to influence the pricing of the plan. In utilizing a defined contribution plan, the employer delegates the decisions about the allocation of scarce resource dollars to the employee. In essence, once the eligibility is determined and the contribution levels have been set, the employer funds the plan and its obligation is complete. A third party administers the plan to maintain eligibility. This makes the plan very simple to set up and administer.

How Funds Can Be Used

Once eligibility for the plan is determined and funding levels are set, the contributions begin. Most plans allow for annual, quarterly, or monthly contributions. Once the funds are in the account, the employees are solely responsible for deciding how to spend the contribution. They can decide to buy a level of protection against unpredictable risk and use pre-tax dollars within the plan to fund the premium. They can save the funds for a large expenditure, such as laser eye surgery or orthodontics, items not generally covered by a traditional benefits plan. Or they can use the plan to fund everyday expenses, such as drug or dental needs. They can also use the plan for copayments and expenses in excess of maximums for their traditional plan. The list of eligible expenses is determined by the Canada Revenue Agency (not by an insurer) and is much more comprehensive than most traditional insured benefit plans.

The amount of control that employees have can generate more appreciation for the plan. For example, the employee may spend on a fertility treatment or laser hair removal, expenditures that are not typically covered by traditional group insurance. Similarly, with a traditional defined benefits plan, the plan sponsor may be paying for benefits that the employee neither needs nor wants, such as prescription eyeglasses or orthotics. But with a defined contribution plan, since the employee wants to maximize the utility in the plan, he or she will try to maximize spending. The onus is on the employee to maximize the value received with the dollars available. As a result, the employee most effectively allocates the scarce funds among his or her needs and wants by controlling the plan spending.

HEALTH SPENDING ACCOUNTS

Employee Eligibility

To be eligible for an HSA, the employee must earn employment income from the corporation. The contribution cannot be made on the basis of ownership or it will be deemed a "shareholder benefit". The benefit levels should be defined by class of employee — union, clerical, manager, executive — or by seniority. The employer can decide if employees with families should have the same or different levels of contribution, thus levelling the playing field for singles relative to families.

When enrolling, the employee must designate dependants. The guidelines are based on CRA rules and are different from a traditional insurance plan. Dependants are "related by blood, marriage or adoption". If the employee lives in a common-law relationship, he or she must have cohabited for a minimum of 12 months for the spouse to be eligible for a traditional plan. Parents and grandchildren may be included, provided that they are financially dependent on the employee. A dependant must be a Canadian resident, having resided in Canada for a minimum of six months of the year.

If the employee leaves the company, the funds do not revert back to the employer. They remain available for the employee to spend on medical expenses until depleted in accordance with the administrator's guidelines.

Plan Administration

As with all other benefit plans, the HWT must be administered by a third party. This maintains the tax-free status for the employee. The plan administrator charges a fee for services performed. This may be an annual administration fee, a fee for processing each claim, or both.

What To Expect from an Administrator

When setting up an HSA, it is wise to ensure that the administrator does the following:

- Maintains all contributed funds separately from the administrator's own operating funds.
- Provides billing for contributions.

- Has their accounting reviewed or audited by a third party.
- Maintains the privacy of the employees according to the *Personal Information Protection and Electronic Documents Act.*
- Adjudicates claims based on qualified medical expenses and reimburses employees in a timely fashion.

The employer is not entitled to know how the contributions are spent or what the balance is in each employee account. The administrator may provide information only on a summary, privacy-protected basis on types of spending.

The Health and Welfare Trust

In 1986, the federal government created the health and welfare trust, as described in Interpretation Bulletin IT-85R2, to allow businesses to put funds aside for their employees' health benefit needs. The HSA can be thought of as an "RRSP for health care expenses", with a couple of major differences. The employer makes the contribution to the HSA, and the employer receives a business expense deduction in the year the contribution is made. The employee receives the contribution amount on a tax-free basis in an account specifically set up for qualified health care expenses. If structured properly, there is no "add-back" into the employee's salary, either at the time the funds are deposited to his or her credit or at the time the employee uses them (except in Quebec, where reimbursements are considered taxable for provincial income tax purposes only). The funds may be withdrawn only for qualified expenses as defined by the Canada Revenue Agency or the Quebec *Taxation Act.* Once deposited, the funds may never revert to the employer.

There are no contribution limits on the plan; however, "the employer's contributions to the fund must not exceed the amounts required to provide these benefits". This has been interpreted to mean that the plan should not be overfunded, but rather contributions should be reasonable relative to the expectation of the provision of benefits to satisfy the health and welfare of employees.

Forfeiture or Carryforward

The interpretation bulletin is silent on the issue of time limitations for using the contributions. Some administrators use the two-year rule that applies to a PHSP, as described below. Others allow indefinite carryforward, to enable the employee to save for larger-cost items, such as laser eye surgery or orthodontics.

PRIVATE HEALTH SERVICES PLANS

A private health services plan, or PHSP, is governed by the Canada Revenue Agency's Interpretation Bulletin IT-339R2. The PHSP was created to provide many of the same benefits as an HWT and is applicable for self-employed individuals or unincorporated businesses. Today, it is one of the most popular ways for sole proprietors and unincorporated partners to pay for health expenses.

Limits

Premiums to a PHSP are tax deductible if net income from self-employment is greater than 50% of total income, or income from sources other than self-employment is $10,000 or less for the current or previous year. The individual must be actively engaged in the business on a regular basis. The premium cannot be claimed if another person deducted the amount or if someone else claimed the premium as a medical expense on an income tax return.

There are contribution limits per employee based on the number of members in the family. For each eligible employee, the contribution can be a maximum of $1,500 per adult family member and $750 per child under age 18. If the child continues to be financially dependent after age 18, the contribution can increase to a maximum of $1,500. Unlike with traditional plans, there is no requirement for the dependent child to be enrolled in a post-secondary school. Contributions are prorated based on the calendar year.

If the sole proprietor has employees, an HWT must be offered to the employees, and a PHSP must be available to them as owners. Additional limitations regarding contribution maximums exist if the sole proprietor has employees, so it is recommended that advisers work through a firm that specializes in this area, to ensure that the plan conforms to CRA guidelines.

Forfeiture Rule

Other than contribution limits, the other major distinction between an HWT and a PHSP is the forfeiture rule. If the funds remain unspent in the employee account after two years, the funds are forfeited.

Advantage to the Sole Proprietor

If the tax savings are greater than the cost to the business of operating the PHSP, then having a PHSP is beneficial. The fee charged by the administrator must be taken into account. In most cases, particularly with one-person consulting firms, the benefit is generally significant and immediate. The PHSP does not replace the need to have some form of catastrophic medical coverage in place in the event a major illness or injury occurs. It can, however, reduce the cost of the insurance by enabling the individual to purchase extended health and drug coverage with a high deductible, such as $1,500. Insurers who offer individual health plans make catastrophic coverage available for this purpose.

ELIGIBLE SERVICES AND EXPENSES

Eligible expenses for HSAs and PHSPs are determined by the Canada Revenue Agency's Interpretation Bulletin IT-519R2, "Medical Expense and Disability Tax Credits and Attendant Care Expense Deduction". It provides that a licensed medical practitioner must perform the service and a licensed medical practitioner must prescribe items. Licensed practitioners will vary by province. Excluded are expenses covered by the provincial health plan.

Professional Services

In order for the medical expenses to be eligible, the service provider must be licensed to practice under the laws of the provincial jurisdiction where the service is rendered. Therefore, this should not be considered a complete list.

- ❒ Audiologist
- ❒ Chiropodist
- ❒ Chiropractor
- ❒ Christian Science practitioner
- ❒ Dentist
- ❒ Dental hygienist
- ❒ Dental technician
- ❒ Denturist
- ❒ Massage therapist
- ❒ Naturopath
- ❒ Neurologist
- ❒ Occupational therapist
- ❒ Optician
- ❒ Osteopath
- ❒ Pharmacist
- ❒ Physician
- ❒ Physiotherapist
- ❒ Podiatrist
- ❒ Psychiatrist
- ❒ Psychoanalyst
- ❒ Psychologist
- ❒ Radiologist
- ❒ Registered nurse
- ❒ Respiratory therapist
- ❒ Speech therapist
- ❒ Surgeon

Eligible Expenses

Essentially, the expenses eligible for reimbursement are the same as for the medical expense tax credit (METC), and the expenses encompass a broader range than expenses covered under regular insured health benefit plans. In addition, they are 100% deductible and have no percentage threshold of 3% of taxable income, as is the case with the METC (subject to the limits as outlined under PHSPs). The following are examples of eligible expenses.

- ❒ Anti-aging treatments[1]
- ❒ Assistive devices[1]
- ❒ Audiology
- ❒ Botox
- ❒ Chiropody
- ❒ Chiropractic services
- ❒ Christian Science practitioner services
- ❒ Contact lenses
- ❒ Cosmetic dentistry
- ❒ Cosmetic surgery
- ❒ CPAP machines (sleep apnea)
- ❒ Crowns and bridges
- ❒ Dental cleaning
- ❒ Dental repairs
- ❒ Dentures
- ❒ Dermatology
- ❒ Diabetic pumps
- ❒ Dietician services[1]
- ❒ Elderly parent & dependant care
- ❒ Eye exams
- ❒ Fertility drugs and treatment services
- ❒ Hair replacement surgery[1]
- ❒ Hearing aids
- ❒ Hospital coverage
- ❒ Individual health care premiums
- ❒ Laser eye surgery
- ❒ Laser hair removal[1]
- ❒ Medical laboratory services
- ❒ Naturopathy
- ❒ Nursing services
- ❒ Orthodontics
- ❒ Orthopaedic shoes
- ❒ Orthotics
- ❒ Osteopathy
- ❒ Overseas specialty medical services
- ❒ Physiotherapy
- ❒ Podiatry
- ❒ Prescription eyeglasses
- ❒ Prescription medicines, drugs, and vitamins
- ❒ Prescription sunglasses
- ❒ Psychology
- ❒ Radiology
- ❒ Registered Massage Therapy (RMT)
- ❒ Special needs schooling (tuition)
- ❒ Special surgery
- ❒ Speech-language pathologists
- ❒ Teeth whitening
- ❒ Transportation costs
- ❒ Wigs (for cancer patients)
- ❒ Wisdom teeth removal

---

[1] Prescribed, dispensed, or supervised by a registered medical practitioner.

Facilities

- Payments to a licensed private hospital
- Semi-private, preferred, or private accommodation expenses in the hospital
- Meals and lodging in an alcoholism or drug rehabilitation centre
- Nursing home care
- Institutional care
- Care of a blind person
- Full-time attendants or care in a nursing home (if confined to a bed or wheelchair).

Recommending and Presenting Plans

HSAs and PHSPs are a specialized area of benefits planning, and advisers should work through a firm that concentrates specifically in this area, in order to be fully compliant with all requirements when recommending and setting up a plan for a client. An example of a company that administers these programs is Benecaid, located in Toronto. It is the fastest growing provider of benefits administration for small to medium-sized employers in Canada. More information about HSAs and PHSPs is available on the company's Web site, at www.benecaid.com. As always, it is important to apply the test of "reasonableness" to plan designs and their utilization. Many "creative" plans have not stood up to audits when the boundaries of what is reasonable have been crossed.

Chapter 17

Travel Insurance Plans

INDIVIDUAL EMERGENCY MEDICAL INSURANCE

Outbound Canadians

When it comes to planning a trip, it is a good idea to look at travel insurance if a person is not otherwise covered as part of a health benefits plan. While many people consider this need when travelling outside Canada, some have not considered its advantages when travelling within Canada to another province. Provincial health plans focus on medical needs, but non-medical expenses also arise as a consequence of illness or injury. A traveller may need to fly home and, therefore, have his or her vehicle returned at a substantial cost. A traveller may need family to fly to a different province where the traveller is hospitalized. Children may be with the traveller and need an escort to return home. Or if the injury or illness is fatal, there can be substantial costs associated with repatriation to the residence.

When travelling outside Canada, the cost of medical care can be substantially greater than the cost of care in Canada. This is particularly true when travelling to the United States. The provincial Ministry of Health Web sites advocate the purchase of insurance prior to leaving Canada. For example, the Ontario Ministry of Health states the following:

> **When I travel outside of Canada will OHIP pay the same medical expenses that are covered in Ontario?**
>
> No. If you are a resident of Ontario and you are insured under OHIP, you are entitled to very limited funding for a limited range of medical services when you are travelling outside of Canada. For this reason, you are strongly advised to purchase additional health insurance every time you leave Canada.[1]

While this excerpt was taken from the Ontario Web site, most other provinces have similar warnings. The Foreign Affairs and International Trade Canada Web site for travel reports and warnings contains a similar message advising all Canadians to purchase travel insurance due to the limited protection under provincial plans when travelling outside of Canada. The following information is from the Ontario provincial Web site, but it is representative of the limitations that can exist in provincial plans when travelling outside of Canada.

The Ontario Health Insurance Plan (OHIP) will pay only for emergency out-of-country health services. To be considered an "emergency", the treatment must meet the following conditions:

- It must be medically necessary.
- It must be performed at a licensed hospital or licensed health facility.

---

[1] Ontario Ministry of Health and Long-Term Care Web site, http://www.health.gov.on.ca/english/public/pub/ohip/travel.html, accessed September 21, 2011.

- It must be in relation to an illness, disease, condition, or injury that:
  - Is acute and *unexpected*
  - Arose outside of Canada
  - Requires immediate treatment.

If the emergency was related to something that was likely to occur (a pre-existing condition with a predictable history of occurrence, for example), it is unlikely that it will meet the definition of "unexpected". The Ministry Web site states, "If the illness, disease, condition or injury arises before you leave Canada, or if it is not acute or unexpected, no payment can be made".

The amount payable is described by the Ministry as "very limited". Ambulance services or transportation costs are not covered, nor is out-of-hospital food, accommodations, or prescription drugs. Physicians' services are payable only up to the level payable in Canada, and Canadian costs are substantially lower than those charged in many places outside of Canada. The maximum payable for health facility services is C$50 per day. The maximum payable for in-patient services is C$200 per day. The maximum for an operating room, coronary care unit, intensive care unit, or neonatal or pediatric special care unit is C$400 per day. These limits include accommodation, meals, prescription drugs, surgically implanted devices, and nursing services.

Daily room charges can exceed $5,000 in some American hospitals. *USA Today* reported that the average cost in California for an appendectomy, which requires about two days in the hospital, is $18,000, and the national median charge for treating a heart attack is more than $20,000.[2]

As with travel to other provinces, non-medical expenses can occur as a result of illness or injury. These can add up quite quickly.

When To Purchase Coverage

While a few insurers will allow travellers to purchase coverage after departure, many insurers make it available for purchase only prior to departure from the person's province of residence. When it is available after departure, insurers usually impose a waiting period on illness benefits. This protects the insurer from anti-selection that can occur when a person waits until symptoms appear to purchase insurance. The waiting period is usually in the range of 48 to 72 hours. Any illness whose onset can be traced back to this initial period will not be covered regardless of when the expense is incurred. This applies not only if the insured waits until after leaving the country to purchase insurance, but also if the purchase is made within Canada but outside the insured's home province. It is not unusual for travellers to consider making a purchase only after their trip is under way. Travel insurance is often a last-minute thought, and sometimes the

---

[2] Julie Appleby, "Hospital Bills Spin Out of Control", *USA Today*, April 13, 2004, http://www.usatoday.com/money/industries/health/2004-04-13-rising-hospital-costs_x.htm.

purchase is intentionally postponed because the traveller may see it as unimportant or as something that can be done en route. Cellphones and the Internet make mobile purchases easy; unfortunately, the buyer may not be aware of this limitation until it is too late.

Rate Calculations

The rate is based upon the exact number of days of the trip, including both the departure and return dates. Rates are calculated per day, and the insurer may have a minimum policy size (such as $25) or minimum number of days that must be covered (such as 10 days). This addresses the issue of administrative costs relative to the premium. Rates are banded by age and may also be based on the health status of the traveller. Rates do not vary by gender or smoker status. Discounted family rates are available for families travelling together. The insurer may have a maximum number of dependants that can be included in the fixed family rate, after which an additional charge will apply. To be covered under the family rate, children must meet the definition of "dependant" contained in the policy, and partners must meet the definition of "spouse". Most insurers have mandatory medical underwriting for older travellers above a given age.

Expiry of Coverage

Benefits expire on the earlier of the expiry date purchased (at midnight) or the return to the province of residence.

Pre-Existing Condition Limitation Period

Every travel insurance policy contains a pre-existing condition limitation period. This provision eliminates the insurer 's liability, throughout the full duration of the policy, for any expenses that relate to a condition that was present during the defined period prior to the policy's effective date. This generally pertains to any condition for which the traveller had symptoms, saw a physician, had treatment, took medication, or was referred for treatment yet to be completed, if any of these things occurred during a specified period of time, such as the 90- or 180-day period prior to the effective date of coverage. Note that it is the effective date of coverage, not the purchase date, that is relevant here. The insurer may make exceptions to this provision, as described below under "Stability Period Provision".

Under an annual plan, a new pre-existing condition limitation period begins with each departure from the insured's province of residence.

A policy does not cover an individual who is travelling against a doctor's order or whose travel is for the purpose of obtaining medical assistance.

Stability Period Provision

Some insurers will automatically cover an existing condition that has been continuously stable through the pre-existing condition limitation period (i.e., the 90- or 180-day period). Where available, the definition of the term "stability" must be reviewed, as each insurer has its own description. In general, "stability" means that the insured did not consult a physician or require a change in type or dosage of medication. Medical underwriting is required if the insured wishes to try to cover a condition that was not stable.

Medical Underwriting

Some insurers offer medical underwriting for travellers who have a pre-existing condition that they want covered. While not all conditions can be covered, many can. When deciding whether a condition can be covered, insurers consider such factors as how old the applicant is, how much time has passed since the condition appeared, whether the condition is stable, how many medications the applicant is taking, and whether other conditions are also present. The insurer determines a surcharge for coverage or advises if the condition cannot be covered. The cost of reports obtained from the traveller's physician may be charged to the traveller. In most cases, once coverage is approved and purchased, the insured must report changes in health that occur between the application date and the effective date of coverage.

Benefits Covered

Some plans provide an aggregate amount of up to $1 million, but many offer coverage as high as $5 million for only a nominal difference. Benefits cover fees not paid by the government health plan, and it is very important to ensure that the purchaser is covered by the government health plan prior to processing their request for coverage. Otherwise, most insurers limit reimbursement to a maximum of $3,000 only. The traveller must be covered by the provincial health plan not only at the time he or she purchases travel insurance, but for the entire duration of the period of coverage. A traveller who is leaving for an extended trip (such as eight or nine months) should be asked to first confirm with the provincial Ministry's office whether permission will be granted for coverage for an extended absence. If the traveller will not have continuous provincial health plan coverage, the more appropriate coverage for the traveller is an "expatriate plan", which provides global health insurance coverage and continues to protect the traveller when going from one country to another.

The benefits typically covered by a travel insurance plan are:

- Hospitalization and medical and paramedical services
- Medical equipment
- Physicians' fees

- Diagnostic tests
- Nursing care
- Prescriptions in conjunction with an emergency
- Dental care following an accident causing injury to the teeth
- Ambulance services
- Repatriation to the province of residence
- The cost of an escort to return a child home
- Transportation for the purpose of identifying a deceased covered person
- Return of a vehicle to the province of residence
- Cost of baggage return when a person is repatriated
- Return of a family pet travelling with the insured
- Repatriation of remains, or cremation or burial at the place of death
- Subsistence allowance covering meals and accommodation expenses when the insured must delay return due to illness or injury
- Non-medical assistance, such as translation services, aid replacing a lost passport, or assistance in contacting the local embassy or consulate.

Exclusions

While all travel insurance policies contain a list of exclusions, this list can vary widely among insurers. Some typical exclusions follow.

Pregnancy

The policy may exclude expenses or complications of pregnancy during the later stages, usually the last four to eight weeks. This limits the insurer's exposure to expenses that may arise for premature birth, delivery, or complications. Some policies also specify that expenses related to pregnancy that occur in the first 32 weeks are excluded if they are routine or elective. Generally, any expense related to a high-risk pregnancy is excluded regardless of when it occurs during the pregnancy.

Self-Inflicted Injury

Any loss resulting from attempted suicide or self-inflicted injury is excluded.

Emotional and Nervous Disorders

Any loss resulting from an emotional, mental, or nervous disorder, including but not limited to anxiety or depression, is excluded.

Acts of War

Expenses resulting from any act of war, including kidnapping, or act of terrorism, including but not limited to those caused by nuclear, chemical, or biological means, are excluded. This provision also excludes losses resulting from riot, strike, or civil commotion.

Travel Advisory Warning

Travel to a destination where the Canadian government has issued a travel advisory warning is excluded. Generally, when this exclusion is contained in the policy, it refers to situations where the travel warning was issued before the insured left his or her province of residence; it would not apply if the warning was issued after the insured arrived at the destination. The warning may be issued due to concerns about safety, health, natural disaster, or climate conditions. For example, in 2010, the volcanic eruptions in Iceland created an ash cloud that caused roughly 20 countries to close their airspace, affecting hundreds of thousands of travellers. In March 2011, a warning was issued for Canadians to avoid non-essential travel to northern Honshu, an area in Japan that was affected by an earthquake and subsequent tsunami, along with an "avoid all travel" warning to the Fukushima nuclear power plan area. Travel advisory warnings change frequently and may affect only specific regions of a country. They are published on the government's Web site at www.voyage.gc.ca. Advisers should be familiar with geographic areas that may be a concern if they are selling a travel insurance product that contains this restriction.

Participation in Military and Other Activities

Expenses relating to participation in the armed forces, any illegal activity, or protests are excluded.

Use of Alcohol

Any expense related to an injury or illness is excluded where evidence shows the insured was affected by the use of alcohol or prohibited drugs, or by the misuse of medication or other intoxicants.

Trips Undertaken for Medical Treatment

Any trip where the primary purpose was for a medical consultation or treatment is excluded.

Non-Emergency Treatment

Any expenses incurred for treatment that was not essential and could have been reasonably postponed until return to the province of residence, are excluded.

Travel Against a Physician's Advice

Any travel which is undertaken against the advice of a physician, or when the insured is terminally ill, is excluded.

Participation in Hazardous Sports, Sports for Profit, or Hazardous Activities

Policies exclude any expenses incurred while participating in events such as:

- Speed contests
- Professional sports activities or non-professional sports for remuneration or cash prize
- High-risk activities, such as mountain climbing, bungee jumping, skydiving, parasailing, or scuba diving below a specified depth.

Optional Benefits

Optional benefits are available for travellers who wish to enhance the protection provided by their travel insurance. Some of these options are described below.

Trip Cancellation Benefit

This provides for reimbursement of the non-refundable prepaid cost of the trip if it must be cancelled prior to departure for reasons unforeseen at the time the trip was purchased. The reason must really be one that is unforeseen. For instance, during the 2010 volcanic eruptions in Iceland, travellers affected by airspace closures caused by the ash cloud were protected if they purchased their cancellation insurance before the incidents began in April. However, those who purchased tickets and cancellation coverage between April and October were not covered because the situation was not unforeseen. Most insurers kept the public advised of their position regarding travel insurance and cancellation coverage during the Eyjafjallajokull eruptions in Iceland.

Trip Interruption Benefit

The trip interruption benefit provides for the cost of one-way transportation to the point of departure from Canada if the trip is interrupted for any of the specific reasons listed in the policy. These reasons may include illness of the insured traveller; illness or death of a close relative or business partner, necessitating the return of the insured traveller; and illness of the caregiver to the insured traveller's children. The event must be one that was unexpected. (If Uncle Johnny was on his deathbed before the insured left, for example, his passing was not unexpected and the benefit will not likely be paid.)

Baggage Benefit

This benefit protects insured travellers in the event of loss due to theft, burglary, vandalism, disappearance, or damage of their luggage, or delay of the luggage by more than 12 hours. The benefit is purchased in various amounts ranging from $500 to $2,000. The policy provides a maximum insured value per article (such as $300). An "article" includes a matched pair, a set, or a group of related articles. For example, "jewellery" would be considered one group, and the sum of all jewellery would not exceed $300. Similarly, "camera equipment" would be another category and might include several cameras (such as both a video camera and a still-shot camera) and all peripherals for them. When travelling with expensive equipment, it is best to insure it through one's house insurance as scheduled property and to confirm that it is still covered while travelling. Jewellery is best left at home, as it can be a target for thieves, threatening the safety of the traveller.

Flight Accident Benefit

This pays a benefit to the traveller for accidental injury caused by a flight accident. The principal amount is usually in the range of $100,000 to $500,000. The benefit schedule is similar to schedules under an AD&D policy, providing a breakdown of the percentage of the principal payable based on the nature of the loss incurred. In addition to being covered while flying, the traveller is often protected while in the airport and while travelling in an airport limousine to and from the airport. The insurer may protect itself against catastrophic loss caused by an injury simultaneously affecting many insured individuals travelling on the same flight by setting an aggregate maximum benefit per incident, such as $10 million.

Top-Up Insurance

A traveller who has coverage under group insurance at work may be planning a trip that is longer than the covered period contained in the policy. "Top-up insurance" refers to purchasing additional days of coverage to cover the traveller during the entire period of travel. For instance, if the trip will last 60 days, and the existing coverage provides for a maximum of 35 days per trip, the traveller would purchase 25 days of top-up insurance.

Not all insurers permit top-up insurance in conjunction with their coverage, so the traveller must first confirm if their existing insurer will recognize it. The insurer from whom the top-up insurance is being purchased must be made aware, as well, that the coverage is top-up insurance.

It is also important to advise the client to confirm with the existing insurer whether the policy contains exclusions, restrictions, or reductions, and the client must be made aware that the initial period of the trip is covered by the existing plan, with the top-up period following thereafter. The certificate issued by the insurer will identify the coverage as top-up insurance.

Annual Plans

A person who travels three or more times per year may be financially better off purchasing an annual travel plan. Annual plans protect the insured traveller for an unlimited number of trips throughout the year. The buyer selects a maximum duration per trip, with the range being as follows: 8 days, 15 days, 30 days, 60 days, 90 days, 120 days, 150 days, or 180 days.

This is particularly advantageous for a traveller who makes several short trips and is otherwise likely to incur the minimum policy size with each trip.

For example, let us say that Christine, a 32-year-old, is travelling for four days. She is likely to incur a minimum policy size of $25, and if she travels three times in a given year, she will have spent $75 in single-trip travel insurance fees. Alternatively, she could purchase an annual plan covering an unlimited number of trips of up to eight days each, for as little as $42. She would also have saved herself the time and energy of having to arrange the coverage before each trip, which is something she might forget to do if her trip is sudden and unexpected.

Advisers should explain to the client at the point of sale how the pre-existing condition limitation works on an annual plan. That is to say, it begins again with each departure from the province of residence.

If the insured is planning two short trips (of one week each) and one long trip (of three weeks) in a given year, the traveller can purchase an eight-day annual plan, which will be sufficient for two of the three trips, plus a 13-day top-up insurance plan to supplement the long trip. This will provide the best value.

Reporting a Claim

Insurers require immediate notification when a claim arises. Along with emergency telephone numbers, the traveller should be briefed concerning claims reporting requirements. Some insurers provide that a percentage of the proceeds will be withheld (such as 25%) if the traveller fails to report the claim when it happens, while others will deny the claim totally. Minor claims are not the issue; major claims are. Specifically, the traveller must call the emergency contact number immediately upon admission to a hospital and in advance of any surgery being performed. Some insurers have provider networks that travellers must go through, particularly in certain states in the United States. In these instances, the traveller is expected to call the emergency contact number for directions on where the nearest authorized health clinic or hospital is located. The insurers also want the opportunity to deal directly with the hospital to negotiate charges before the expenses are incurred.

VISITORS' MEDICAL INSURANCE

Visitors, new Canadians, and returning Canadians are not covered by the provincial health insurance plan. There is up to a three-month waiting period for returning Canadians and new Canadians. Visitors are not eligible for coverage under the provincial health insurance plan. Visitors' medical insurance addresses this need.

Coverage should be purchased prior to arrival in Canada; otherwise, a waiting period applies to benefits. The waiting period varies depending on the insurer's provisions, but it can be in the range of 48 to 72 hours, during which time the visitor is not covered. Furthermore, should an incident happen during the waiting period, it constitutes a pre-existing condition and is not covered by the plan.

Visitors' medical insurance protects the traveller throughout Canada and usually on short trips outside the country, provided the majority of the covered period is spent in Canada. However, if the traveller returns to his or her country of origin, coverage expires immediately.

Policies contain pre-existing condition limitations, exclusions, and other provisions similar to those found in individual emergency medical insurance. Partial refund provisions may differ from those found in individual emergency medical insurance. Some insurers offer medical underwriting to determine whether a pre-existing medical condition can be covered at an additional cost. Visitors' plans do not cover pregnancy-related expenses or complications.

Some visitors may be planning an extended stay, and the cost of insurance may feel onerous. The temptation may be to purchase a reduced period with the intention of renewing it, thereby staggering the expenditure. The adviser's role is to explain the issues that can arise with this method and to caution against it. Coverage should be purchased for the full duration of the trip, as the renewal is treated as a separate period and is subject to a new pre-existing condition limitation. If a claim arises in the initial period, it will constitute a pre-existing condition and a recurrence will not be covered during the additional period. If the claim is extensive, the insurer may refuse to renew the coverage altogether for a further period. There is also a risk that the traveller will forget to renew the coverage, and once it expires there will be a waiting period for new benefits, leaving the traveller uninsured.

The adviser should also explain provisions related to partial refunds in the event of an early return. If the insured has made any claims, no partial refund is available, because the amount insured is an aggregate benefit, and as a claim has been made against it, a partial refund cannot be made.

Coverage amounts vary, and range from $10,000 to $150,000. Some plans may require a small deductible to be paid at the time of a claim. While coverage should be purchased in advance of arrival, most insurers will still offer coverage after arrival in the country, subject to an appropriate waiting period (48 to 72 hours). Some insurers set a limited time following arrival in

Canada after which no coverage can be purchased, such as 30 days. Other insurers allow a purchase for up two years after arrival.

Some visitors make frequent trips to Canada, particularly between border cities for shopping excursions or visits to relatives. A few insurers offer multi-trip annual plans for visitors which parallel the annual plans available for Canadians. The insured is covered for an unlimited number of trips throughout the year provided each trip does not exceed the stated per trip maximum length, such as 30 days.

GLOBAL EXPATRIATE PLANS

A global expatriate plan is emergency medical coverage for a Canadian who is not covered by a provincial health insurance plan — for example, a Canadian living outside Canada for a temporary period or a returning Canadian who is fulfilling the three-month waiting period for provincial benefits. Some companies also offer their global expatriate plans to non-Canadian citizens residing outside Canada and their country of origin if they are working for a Canadian company, or if they are residing permanently in Canada while fulfilling the waiting period for provincial benefits.

These plans generally offer higher amounts of coverage than visitors' plans, such as $500,000 or $1 million, and they often require medical underwriting. The insured is covered for global travel with some exceptions.

The exclusions and conditions in global expatriate plans are similar to those found in other forms of travel insurance, with the exception of pregnancy. If the insured is pregnant at the time of purchasing coverage, pregnancy is excluded. When coverage is purchased for a period of longer than 10 months, it may include a pregnancy that began a month or more after the insurance became effective.

THE ADVISER'S RESPONSIBILITIES

Adding travel insurance to an adviser's range of services can bring new clients and additional revenue to the business, but it also brings additional responsibilities. Consider the following scenarios.

Case Studies

Case 1:

Jeffrey Ad Viser receives a call from Elizabeth, a returning Canadian who has been living in Buffalo. Elizabeth tells Jeffrey that she is entering Canada through Niagara Falls on March 1, and she will be driving through to Calgary, where she will reside. Jeffrey proceeds to insure Elizabeth for a 90-day period under the visitors' medical plan for $150,000 coverage, effective March 1, without asking Elizabeth whether she will be making any return trips to the United States during the coverage period.

Case 2:

Jeffrey Ad Viser receives a call from Andrew, who found Jeffrey's Web site on the Internet. Andrew advises Jeffrey that he needs travel insurance for his family, for a vacation in San Juan. Jeffrey proceeds to issue a travel insurance policy covering Jeffrey and his family for $5 million per person — ample insurance for eight days.

Case 3:

Jeffrey Ad Viser is on a roll. Later the same day, he receives a call from Bernardo, who was referred to Jeffrey by one of his clients. Bernardo asks Jeffrey for travel insurance for his business trip to Florida, after which he plans to stay for a few days of vacation — 10 days in total. Jeffrey issues the same $5 million plan to Bernardo and wishes him a happy and safe trip.

Case 4:

Jeffrey Ad Viser's brother-in-law, Tom, heard he was now offering travel insurance. He calls Jeffrey for insurance to cover his son's upcoming trip to Mexico, where he and several classmates are heading for the school break to celebrate the end of exams.

Jeffrey is proud of the research he did to find an insurer offering a $5 million plan that has reasonable rates and that offers visitors' plans up to $150,000. He is confident in his transactions.

Outcomes

Case 1:

It turns out that Elizabeth's route required her to cross the border twice en route to Alberta. During one of these points, she was in a car accident and contacted the emergency number for assistance, only to find out her coverage expired as soon as she crossed back into the United States, as this had been her "country of origin" prior to returning to Canada from living in New York. Her claim for benefits was denied. Her expenses were US$18,400. Her next phone call was to her adviser, Jeffrey.

Case 2:

It turns out that while in San Juan, Andrew's wife got sick with food poisoning. Andrew called the emergency telephone number to obtain assistance with his wife's medical care. The customer care operator asked Andrew for his wife's provincial health card number and learned that, while Andrew is a landed immigrant, his wife is not, and she has no provincial health insurance. Her medical expenses totalled $7,500. Despite buying $5 million of coverage, the insurance company covered only $3,000 — the maximum limit provided under the plan for an insured not covered by the provincial health plan. His next phone call was to his adviser, Jeffrey.

Case 3:

It turns out that while in Florida, Bernardo got chest pains and visited the emergency room, where he was admitted for observation for 24 hours and then released. He waited for his return home to file the claim for $3,800, having simply charged it to his credit card. Bernardo was thankful it was a false alarm. The insurer later advised Bernardo that his claim was being denied because he failed to contact them immediately upon admission to a hospital. His next phone call was to his adviser, Jeffrey.

Case 4:

It turns out that Jeffrey's nephew (whom the family always referred to as their "resident daredevil") met up with a bunch of local teenagers, went bungee jumping, and sustained a broken leg. When the hospital contacted his insurer to confirm coverage, he discovered the policy contained an exclusion for dangerous sports and he was not covered. His medical expenses totalled $5,250, for which Tom presented an invoice to his brother-in-law, Jeffrey, in person. Jeffrey decided not to sell travel insurance any more.

Adviser's Checklist

Finding the right insurer to use is the starting point. The adviser must then learn and fulfill his or her responsibility to provide the right coverage and the appropriate information. All information should be conveyed verbally to the insured and confirmed in writing.

- ❐ Be sure to quote the correct type of insurance.
- ❐ For outbound Canadians, confirm that all travellers are covered by the provincial health insurance plan.
- ❐ Explain the benefits covered.
- ❐ Ensure the traveller meets the insurer's eligibility criteria.
- ❐ Explain the pre-existing condition limitation verbally and confirm the information in writing.
- ❐ Ask about the insured's health, existing medications, chronic conditions, and other pre-existing conditions. If insuring a young couple or a female applicant of child-bearing age, explain the policy provisions regarding pregnancy.
- ❐ Offer medical underwriting as an option to cover a pre-existing condition.

- ❒ Explain other exclusions, such as participation in hazardous sports (such as rock climbing), and limitations for Canadians regarding travel to countries for which Canada has issued a Traver advisory warning.
- ❒ For visitors' coverage, ask about intended travel to thc United States, the country of origin, and other countries during the covered period, and explain whether insurance continues or ceases.
- ❒ Explain the refund provisions in writing.
- ❒ Explain the claims procedure, the emergency contact numbers, and any time limitations on reporting a claim.
- ❒ Explain the method of obtaining extended coverage if the return trip is delayed and any new waiting periods or pre-existing conditions that may apply under the extension.
- ❒ Confirm everything in writing and get your client's signature.

Chapter 18

Critical Illness Insurance

Life insurance has existed for over 250 years. Product development departments continue to tweak it, create varied versions of it, but the fundamentals have not changed. Actuarial departments continue to price it based on past experience; underwriting departments continue to evaluate the risk based on sound underwriting principles that reflect many years of accumulated knowledge; and advisers continue to advocate the need for it to thousands of Canadians each year, who buy it to protect their loved ones.

What has changed? People today are living longer lives than did generations before them. They do so while coping with chronic conditions that once were the chief causes of death. Physicians, surgeons, and other specialists can now diagnose and treat many conditions sooner and better, thanks to rapid progress in medical science and clinical procedures. We have traded mortality (death) for morbidity (disability). But the financial burden on those who are ill and their families can be extremely onerous, if not completely devastating. Many serious illnesses require expensive therapy and rehabilitation, and government programs and private health insurance do not always cover the costs. Disability insurance and life insurance, while helpful, have different focuses: disability insurance will help to replace lost income during periods of lost earnings, and this can be used to meet the daily costs of living; life insurance will help the family adjust financially after a loved one succumbs to illness. But while the loved one is still fighting illness, what will finance expensive drugs and treatment? What will protect the family's assets from depletion? Critical illness insurance has emerged to meet this need.

BACKGROUND

On December 3, 1967, a major world event occurred — a team of doctors in South Africa performed the first human-to-human heart transplant. The team was led by Dr. Christiaan Barnard and included his brother, Dr. Marius Barnard. Today, heart transplants are performed all around the world.

In his personal practice, Dr. Marius Barnard had to convey distressing news to patients on an almost daily basis. For some, it was cancer; for others, the permanent effects of a stroke. Their questions were always the same: Is it treatable? Will I be cured? What will the treatment cost?

Dr. Marius Barnard saw his clients regularly for checkups following major surgery, and they all complained of the same things. They talked about their lack of money and the effects it had on their families' lives. Businesses were affected, and life insurance, too. Some even lost their homes. This financial devastation that Dr. Barnard witnessed was repeated time and time again. While he was helping them to live longer, their quality of life had diminished because of the financial impact their illness had on their lives.

It was not a product department, a sales department, or a team of actuaries that provided the impetus for critical illness insurance; it was Dr. Marius Barnard, a cardiac surgeon, who recognized the need for "dread disease" insurance that would provide money to deal with expenses following a heart attack, a stroke, or a cancer diagnosis. He described to insurers the need for a special policy for people — not because they were going to die, but because they were going to live. This insurance would pay its benefit upon diagnosis of a dread disease, and it would enable them to avoid the financial death many of his clients personally experienced following their diagnosis.

On August 6, 1983, the first critical illness insurance policy emerged in South Africa, known as "dread disease insurance". By 1987, it had appeared in the United Kingdom. By 1991, it was being sold in the United States and Australia. In 1995, critical illness insurance as we know it today began to be sold in Canada. Different countries have used different labels — to be more "marketing friendly" and to reflect growth of this type of insurance beyond dread disease coverage.

Prior to 1983, policies covering certain types of cancer were being sold in the United States. The emergence of a policy covering a broader range of dread disease in Africa and the news of Dr. Barnard's story play an important role in how critical illness insurance has gained momentum worldwide.

The product has changed significantly in a short period of time. It began as coverage for four critical conditions — heart attack, stroke, cancer, and coronary bypass surgery — but today, it insures many more conditions. The "Big Four" remain the primary conditions and, together with multiple sclerosis, account for roughly 90% of all claims. One-upmanship among insurers has led to the expansion beyond these conditions to enhanced versions covering as many as 20 additional conditions. Each of these expanded conditions has a low probability of occurrence, some as low as 1%. Still, the primary purpose of critical illness insurance remains the same: to provide protection for life-threatening conditions. This coverage pays a lump-sum benefit if the insured is diagnosed with a covered condition as defined by the policy and survives a stipulated survival (waiting) period following diagnosis. Some policies additionally cover a listed non-life-threatening condition, for which they pay a smaller recovery assistance benefit, usually as a percentage of the principal amount.

Critical illness insurance is available as both individual and group insurance. In the individual markets, some companies offer guaranteed-issue programs whereby certain coverage amounts are issued without medical underwriting when sold in a business setting if certain conditions are met. These may include additional pre-existing condition limitations not found in medically underwritten plans. Creditor products are also sold through banks and lending institutions. This chapter focuses on medically underwritten individual coverage.

Buyers in Canada

A review of the typical policyholder in Canada shows that men and women between the ages of 35 to 55, with an average age of about 40, are purchasing it almost equally. The average policy has a face amount of about $100,000, and the average premium is roughly $1,000 annually.

THE NEED

Dr. Barnard saw first-hand the financial impact that critical illness had on his patients. They experienced financial difficulties due to increasing medical costs for their critical conditions, but they also experienced a decreasing ability to earn the money needed just to live. This affected their children's education, their ability to keep their homes, and their ability to avoid bankruptcy. He witnessed how their financial problems also impacted their physical health. In the words of Dr. Barnard, "You need critical illness insurance not because you're going to die, but because you're going to live".

The Financial Impact

Government health insurance plans do not cover all the expenses associated with treating a critical illness or resulting from having one.

Critical illness insurance can provide necessary funds to do the following:

- Pay medical expenses not covered by a governmental health insurance plan or group plan
- Hire a nurse, child care provider, or housekeeper
- Seek medical treatment outside Canada or in another province
- Purchase equipment, such as a wheelchair, scooter, or home care bed
- Pay for home alterations, such as widening doors or changing floor surfaces, or altering the bathroom, bedroom, kitchen, or front entrance
- Pay for vehicle modifications
- Pay off an outstanding mortgage
- Pay off an outstanding car loan
- Pay off outstanding credit cards
- Pay off other lines of credit and personal or business loans
- Preserve an RRSP
- Preserve a child's education fund
- Provide a source of cash to cover the time required to find a new job or retrain for a different job when the insured is ready to go back to work
- Cover a variety of business expenses, including hiring a replacement in the insured's absence
- Provide the insured with time free from financial worry that he or she can devote to loved ones.

Statistics

A growing number of Canadians will be diagnosed with a critical illness at an increasingly early age. With the advances in medical technology and the increase in life expectancy, people have a greater chance of experiencing a serious illness and surviving. Consider the following statistics:

- One out of two heart attack victims is under age 65; 95% survive their first attack.
- One out of three Canadians will develop some form of cancer; 65% will survive at least five years.

- One out of four Canadians will develop heart disease.
- One out of 20 Canadians will suffer a stroke before age 70; 75% will survive it.
- After age 55, the risk of stroke doubles every 10 years.
- 50,000 Canadians have multiple sclerosis.
- 70,000 Canadians each year suffer heart attacks.
- 750,000 Canadians or more are predicted to suffer from Alzheimer's disease by 2031.

A snapshot of industry claims provides insight into the causes for critical illness insurance claims:

- cancer: 65%–70%
- heart attack: 14%
- stroke: 5%
- other (e.g., brain tumour, Parkinson's, coronary angioplasty): 5%
- coronary bypass: 3%–4%
- multiple sclerosis: 2%–3%.

Not surprisingly, the majority of claims are due to cancer and heart attack, which together form roughly 80% to 85% of total claims. The claims are almost equally divided between men and women, and claimants range in age from 20 to 70.

Let's look individually at the profiles of some claimants (these are not their real names, but their profiles are representative of industry claims):

- Joe, a 44-year-old truck driver, purchased $100,000 of coverage. He needed coronary bypass surgery just 18 months after buying his policy.
- Elma, a 63-year-old teacher, was diagnosed with cancer. Fortunately, four years earlier, she had purchased $250,000 of coverage.
- Dr. Jamieson, a 50-year-old physician, bought $100,000 of coverage. He was diagnosed with cancer 4½ years later.
- Anita, a 35-year-old homemaker, purchased $100,000 of critical illness insurance. After her coverage had been in force for 1½ years, she was diagnosed with cancer.
- Maureen, a 29-year-old nurse, developed kidney failure just under three years after buying $25,000 of coverage.
- Ray, a 35-year-old construction worker, had had his policy for less than a year when he was diagnosed with cancer. He had purchased $25,000 of coverage.

- George, a 58-year-old finance manager, suffered a heart attack just four months after buying $100,000 of critical illness coverage.
- Nathan, a 54-year-old insurance agent, purchased $50,000 of coverage. He suffered a stroke after his policy had been in force for only one-and-a-half years.

Each of these individuals thought they would never need critical illness insurance, but as can be seen by the variety of ages, critical illnesses happen to people of all ages, and not just to older adults. Nor does it happen only after many years of paying premiums. It can happen much sooner than expected.

PLANS OFFERED

Just as life insurance is available with various premium and coverage durations, so is critical illness insurance. In fact, plan descriptions sound similar to those used to describe life insurance. There are permanent plans, renewable term plans, and limited-period level plans. A permanent plan provides a level amount of coverage at a guaranteed level rate through to age 100. A renewable term plan provides level coverage for a specified term, but rates increase at fixed intervals throughout the coverage period. A limited-period level plan provides a level coverage amount for a specified term and has level rates through the coverage period.

Following are examples of critical illness plans offered:

- Permanent level premium plan, paid up at age 100
- Ten-year renewable term to age 75, convertible to age 65
- Twenty-year renewable term to age 75
- Level premium term to age 75, paid up at age 65
- Level premium term to age 75.

As the names indicate, the plans offer a variety of coverage terms and payment durations. The term "convertible" means that clients can change the plan from temporary to permanent critical illness insurance coverage.

Plans can also be categorized by the breadth of conditions they cover. Some plans cover primary conditions only, while others cover an extensive list of up to 24 (or even more) conditions.

CRITICAL ILLNESS COVERAGE AS AN OPTIONAL BENEFIT

Many companies also offer critical illness insurance as a rider to a term or universal life insurance policy. This rider provides benefits similar to a stand-alone critical illness policy. The savings to the insured are usually in the form of a single policy fee.

ACCELERATED CRITICAL ILLNESS BENEFIT PLAN

Some life insurance policies provide an advance benefit if the insured has a limited time to live. This type of insurance is not considered to be critical illness insurance. These life policies began to appear in the United States during the late 1980s, when one life insurer began including an agreement to advance part of the death benefits if the insured had a life expectancy of less than 12 months. Accelerated critical illness benefits evolved from this, when later, some companies began to provide a specified amount of the death benefit, such as 25%, upon diagnosis of a listed critical illness. When the insured ultimately died, the life insurance proceeds would then be reduced by an equivalent amount.

Some banks have developed an accelerated policy as a form of mortgage insurance to cover the mortgage holder in the event of death or critical illness. This type of coverage pays the principal amount regardless of which event occurs first.

HYBRID PLANS

More recent changes have also seen hybrid versions appear in the market, whereby a critical illness policy gradually converts over time to long-term care insurance. As the need for critical illness insurance starts to diminish, the need for long-term care insurance rises. A hybrid plan may either automatically convert a certain percentage of coverage yearly at a predetermined time (e.g., starting at age 55 and finishing by age 65), or it may be an election contained in the policy providing simply "the right to convert".

One of the most recent developments in critical illness insurance is a multi-purpose/single-sum plan. This hybrid plan is really a form of accelerated benefits. It is a life insurance policy with a term to age 65 that pays an advance benefit for either a disability or a critical illness. During a disability lasting longer than 90 days, a stipulated amount of the death benefit, such as 0.5%, is payable monthly while disability continues. On the other hand, if the insured is diagnosed with a covered critical illness, 25% of the face amount is paid as a lump sum. Any advanced benefits reduce the remaining pool that would be paid upon death. When the insurance expires at age 65 (assuming all the funds have not been exhausted already), there is a conversion option for converting the remaining benefit to a permanent life insurance policy.

This type of coverage does not replace the need for regular disability and critical illness insurance, but it is useful as a supplement for mortgage and debt protection, since the disability benefit is not financially underwritten. As the underlying coverage is life insurance, the critical illness benefit is not subject to the usual rigours of underwriting family medical history.

PLANS FOR SPECIAL MARKETS

Some insurers offer plans for special markets such as those described below.

Critical Illness Insurance for Women

This plan provides protection primarily for women's cancer. It is a basic term product generally sold through direct marketing with guaranteed acceptance. Some of the features found in this type of insurance include:

- A maximum coverage limit in the range of $50,000
- A payment schedule based on type (location) of cancer
- A monthly benefit for six months when surgery is involved, or a monthly benefit upon diagnosis
- A cash hospital benefit
- In some plans, a lesser benefit for heart attack, stroke, or coronary artery surgery
- A return of premiums if no claim is made
- Access to the Best Doctors® program for a second opinion on a treatment plan.

As the coverage is offered on a guaranteed-acceptance basis, some limitations apply for the initial period following the effective date. Rates are generally graded, with increases every five years according to a schedule contained in the policy. Coverage terminates at a specified age, such as 65 or 70, depending upon the insurer.

With this type of coverage, the primary focus is on cancer affecting women.

Breast cancer incidence rose steadily from 1980 to the early 1990s, partly because of increased mammography screening, according to the Canadian Cancer Society. It is predicted that one in nine women will develop breast cancer. It is the most common cancer among Canadian women (excluding non-melanoma skin cancer). Breast cancer accounts for over a quarter (28%) of new cancer cases in women.

Heart disease is the number one cause of death for Canadian women over the age of 55, according to Statistics Canada. Experts believe this could be due to a reduction in estrogen levels occurring after this age.

Heart disease and stroke affect women differently from men. While men have a slightly higher risk of stroke, women are much more likely to die from it. Additional risk factors that affect women include the use of oral contraceptives combined with smoking. Women are more likely to live alone because of their longer life expectancy, and this contributes to longer stays in the hospital. For this reason, they are also more likely to be transferred to a chronic care facility rather than sent home.

Critical Illness Insurance for Children

The Need

While no one wants to consider the possibility that their child may have a critical illness, when this does happen, the emotional and financial impact on the family can be quite dramatic. Critical illness coverage for children can provide much-needed resources to enable a parent to take time off work to be with a sick child. Parents may need additional help with caring for other children. Some conditions may require treatment only available in a different city, resulting in increased living expenses.

Children's Plans

There are guaranteed-issue children's plans sold through direct marketing that cover a basic range of 8 to 10 critical conditions most likely to be of concern to parents. Their coverage amount and duration are usually very limited, and there may be a waiting period for some benefits. There are also fully underwritten plans that cover the typical comprehensive range of 21 to 24 conditions, plus several childhood-related conditions.

The childhood conditions that are usually included are:

- Cerebral palsy
- Congenital heart disease
- Cystic fibrosis
- Muscular dystrophy
- Type 1 diabetes mellitus.

Most of the underwritten plans can be converted to adult plans when the child reaches a stipulated age, such as 25.

Critical Conditions

Cerebral palsy is a condition in which brain damage affects muscle movements and posture. There is no cure, and it is not progressive, as brain damage does not increase over time. Treatment involves a team of specialists whose goal is to help maximize and coordinate movement, minimize discomfort and pain, and prevent long-term complications. Some of the symptoms can cause behavioural and emotional problems, and for this reason, children may benefit from counselling or behavioural therapy.

Cystic fibrosis is a condition characterized by difficulty breathing, respiratory tract problems, severe chronic lung infections, failure to grow or gain weight, and extreme difficulty digesting food. It was first described as a disease in the late 1930s. At that time, the disease was recognized only after the child had died, usually from malnutrition or pneumonia. Today, newborn screening programs are available. Despite this, mild cases are sometimes mistaken for asthma, chronic bronchitis, pneumonia, or celiac disease.

One in 25 Canadians carries a defective version of the gene responsible for cystic fibrosis, and one in every 3,600 children is born with cystic fibrosis. Approximately 60% are diagnosed in the first year of life, 90% by age 10. In the 1960s, most children with cystic fibrosis did not live long enough to attend kindergarten; today half of all Canadians with cystic fibrosis are expected to live into their 40s and beyond.[1] Some provinces provide full coverage for the required medications through special programs, while other provinces provide partial or no coverage. There is often a deductible for those that do provide coverage. Other medical expenses that may be incurred include the cost of equipment, nutritional supplements, and enzymes.

Muscular dystrophy is a group of neuromuscular disorders that, over time, may cause the person to lose the ability to walk, speak, and ultimately breathe. There is no cure, and it can be fatal. Some forms are passed from generation to generation, and others can occur spontaneously in a single individual as the result of a mutation of a particular gene. While it is often considered a childhood disorder, anyone can be affected.

CONDITIONS COVERED IN POLICIES FOR ADULTS

In addition to the primary conditions (cancer, heart attack, stroke, coronary artery bypass), other conditions that may be covered include multiple sclerosis, conditions that affect major organs (kidney failure, major organ transplant), cardiovascular conditions (heart valve replacement, aortic surgery), degenerative conditions (motor neuron disease, Parkinson's, Alzheimer's), brain conditions (coma, benign brain tumor), sensory conditions (blindness, deafness, loss of speech), and other conditions affecting the body (paraplegia, quadriplegia, major burns, occupational HIV). A few companies may include aplastic anemia and bacterial meningitis. Some also include a provision for loss of independent existence (i.e., the inability to perform activities of daily living).

POLICY PROVISIONS

Rate Guarantee

Most insurers in Canada offer fully guaranteed premiums for critical illness insurance. By contrast, in many other countries, coverage is guaranteed renewable but the insurer reserves the right to change the premium for a block of business if this is deemed necessary based on experience. This point has received much discussion. It is believed that Canadian insurers will one day cease to offer non-cancellable (fully rate-guaranteed) coverage. Critical illness insurance is a relatively young product, so insurers do not

[1] Cystic Fibrosis Canada Web site, www.cysticfibrosis.ca, accessed September 20, 2011.

have much Canadian experience to use in preparing rates. Some Canadian insurers have already begun to offer guaranteed renewable plans as an alternative to higher-priced non-cancellable plans. There is a fear that the margin added to non-cancellable rates will not be sufficient to deal with unpredictable trends. Rates for new coverage under non-cancellable plans have been increasing from the time the original plans were launched. Factors that have affected this include the availability of more sensitive diagnostic testing tools, enabling earlier diagnosis; expansion of the number of critical illness conditions covered; product enrichment, such as third-party assistance programs; and reduced payments for conditions that are not life threatening. All of these factors have increased claims. The future claims experience is likely to change with new diagnostic procedures and improved surgical methods. Television advertising campaigns encourage regular cancer examinations, which could eventually increase cancer claims due to earlier detection and reduced mortality. Perhaps, to go even a step beyond education and awareness, what if governments or employment legislation allowed for mandatory screening for cancer, heart disease, and diabetes? There are many unpredictable changes that could happen in the future, and these could make critical illness experience different from what was expected when rates were first struck for non-cancellable policies.

Regardless of whether coverage is non-cancellable or guaranteed renewable, both offer the promise that once the policy has been issued, the insurer cannot cancel or change the benefits in any way.

Conversion Feature

Some companies provide the insured with the right to convert from a renewable term plan to a level premium plan prior to age 65. As with conversion provisions in renewable term life insurance, this provision offers the insured the right to do so without evidence of insurability up to a certain age. However, the insured cannot be disabled at the time of conversion. Rates under the new plan will be based on current rates in force at the time of conversion for the insured's attained age.

Third-Party Assistance

Some insurers make available additional assistance through third-party providers that help the insured locate the best treatment for the condition and get a second opinion. These services are available without cost to the insured. The insurer is charged a premium rate by the third-party provider, which is in turn factored into the premium for the critical illness insurance.

Reduced Benefits

Some policies may also cover several illnesses generally not considered to be life threatening if caught in the early stages. The benefit payable for these conditions is a smaller recovery assistance benefit, such as 10% or 25% of the principal amount up to a stated maximum, such as $25,000 or

$50,000. These conditions may include coronary angioplasty, ductal breast cancer, stage A prostate cancer, HIV-related cancer, and superficial malignant melanoma. This benefit is usually a one-time lump-sum benefit, which does not terminate the policy but does affect the return of a premium option if it is also included in the policy.

Claiming for Benefits

As provided under statutory conditions, the insurer sets a time within which a claim must be reported, after which it may be denied. The insured must report the claim within the initial period stated (such as 30 days) and provide proof of claim before another stipulated deadline (such as 90 days). If an insured can prove that there was a valid reason for not meeting the stipulated deadlines, the claim will still be honoured provided a year has not expired. The following is an example of what the policy wording might look like for this provision:

> Any claim for benefits must be made in writing to our principal head office. We must receive notice of claim within 30 days of the date that the claim arises.
>
> Within 90 days we must receive reasonable proof of the event for which you are claiming, the resulting loss, the right of the claimant to receive payment, and proof of his or her age.
>
> Failure to provide us with such notice or proof will not invalidate your claim if you do so as soon as reasonably possible and if you can provide reasons why it was not possible to make a claim within the prescribed time. In any event, you must provide proof of claim within one year of the date a claim arises under this policy.

The policy will also indicate the insurer's promise to provide claim forms within a period of time (such as 15 days) upon receiving notice of claim, and a promise to pay all benefits within a certain period of time (such as 60 days) after all outstanding claim forms have been received.

The stipulated deadlines should be taken seriously; otherwise, insured individuals may find themselves without payment for otherwise eligible claims. Most insurers are not flexible on this issue, so advisers should take time, upon delivery of critical illness insurance policies, to review the process of what happens if they need to claim and impress upon them the importance of promptly notifying the insurer.

Claims that occur during the two-year incontestable period are specifically evaluated for non-disclosure of material facts, since there can be a greater incentive to withhold material medical information in living benefits policies. A claim can be denied for non-disclosure of a material fact if the underwriter would have reached a different decision given knowledge of the fact, even if it is not relevant to the event being claimed under. After the two-year incontestable period has passed, the insurer must prove fraudulent intent.

General Exclusions and Limitations

Critical illness policies contain exclusions and limitations that are similar to disability insurance. The most standard of these are:

- Intentionally self-inflicted injuries
- Intentional use or abuse of drugs, poisonous substances, intoxicants, or narcotics other than as prescribed by a physician or, in the case of a non-prescribed medication, by the manufacturer
- Committing or attempting to commit a criminal offence
- Operating a motor vehicle while intoxicated
- War, declared or undeclared; hostile action of the armed forces.

This section also describes the standard waiting period that applies to various conditions, as described in more detail below, under "When Benefits Are Payable". Some policies refer to this as the "survival period", since it is the period of time the insured must survive following the date of diagnosis or surgery before a critical illness benefit will be paid.

OPTIONAL BENEFITS

Insurers offer several different optional benefits that can be added to critical illness insurance. Some of the more popular options follow.

Second Event Option

This optional benefit provides for a second payout of a lesser amount for certain conditions. If the first claim is for a heart attack or stroke, then it will cover a later occurrence of cancer. If the first claim is for cancer, then the second event covered is for a heart attack. The amount payable is a percentage up to a stated maximum, such as 50% of the original amount up to $50,000. In order for the second event to be covered, there may be a passage of time requirement, such as 12 months or more, from the first payout. The rider does not require premiums to be paid after the first event has occurred. Even though this rider is being added to a non-cancellable policy, the rider itself may not contain a guaranteed premium. Some companies reserve the right to change the premium for this option on in-force policies on any anniversary date.

Options for Return of Premium

There are three different return options made available on critical illness policies:

- Return of premium on death
- Return of premium on surrender
- Return of premium on expiry.

Some companies bundle the return of premium on death as part of their core benefits without additional charge, while others make it available as an optional benefit. Taxation issues may arise related to return-of-premium features, and consequently, many insurers no longer build this feature into their core benefits. Under the return-at-death feature, all premiums are refunded to the insured's beneficiary if the insured dies without having collected a benefit. It addresses a common concern: "What if I die during the waiting period and don't qualify for a benefit?"

The option for return of premium on surrender provides the insured with a percentage (up to 100%) return of premiums paid if the policy is surrendered after a period of time. The policy contains a schedule of surrender values related to how long the policy was in force. If the policy is cancelled before 10 years, for instance, there may be no return, whereas if the policy has been kept in force for at least 20 years, there may be a full return.

The option for return of premium at expiry provides for a full return of premiums paid if the insured maintains it through to the expiry date (such as age 75). It addresses the issue, "What if I pay premiums all those years and never need it?"

For each version of the refund benefit, the policy will outline the adjustments to be made to any refund based upon claims for smaller recovery assistance benefits paid out, and whether premiums paid for other riders will be included in the refund calculation.

The question that arises is, how can insurers afford to return the premiums paid? There are three considerations. A premium is charged for this feature, interest is earned on its investment, and actuaries make certain lapse assumptions knowing that not all policyholders will continue the policy and qualify for the premium return.

Promises of premium return can be attractive, but the insured should consider if it is the best use of premium dollars. Perhaps it would be wiser to purchase a higher amount of coverage.

Waiver of Premium

Unlike with disability insurance, an insured who wishes to have a waiver of premium in the event of disability must add the option at an additional cost, as would be the case with life insurance. Some companies make variations available, recognizing there may be a third party paying the premiums ("payer waiver of premium"). Third-party waivers may cover disability only or, additionally, death of the premium payer.

Automatic Benefit Increase Option

This option automatically increases coverage by a specified amount at a given interval as a means of inflation protection. The additional coverage is not optional (the increase takes place automatically). If the insured no longer wishes to have coverage increase, he or she can have the option removed. Increases are subject to financial underwriting maximums and the overall maximum issue limits. Any exclusion(s) contained in the original contract will apply to the increases in coverage.

Loss of Functional Independence

Some severely debilitating health issues can arise that do not fall under one of the listed critical illness conditions. These can eventually result in the person's inability to perform some of the normal activities associated with daily tasks, such as dressing and eating. For this reason, some insurers offer an optional benefit, which pays a percentage of the lump-sum benefit in the form of a monthly income not to exceed the total critical illness benefit purchased. A waiting period must be satisfied (such as 60 days), during which the insured is unable to perform two or more activities of daily living without significant help from another person. The benefit is not payable if the activities can be performed with the use of assistive devices, equipment, or home modifications. The activities include bathing, toileting, continence, dressing, transferring, and eating. Alternatively, the insured may qualify for the benefit if he or she suffers a cognitive impairment. This is a form of advance payment, and once the sum of benefits paid equals the total principal critical illness benefit, payments cease and the policy terminates. If, during the time benefits are received, the person satisfies the definition for payout under one of the listed critical illness conditions, a lump sum will be paid minus the benefits already paid out as a monthly income.

DEFINING CONDITIONS

When Benefits Are Payable

Benefits are payable under the policy after the insured has acquired a covered condition (as defined by the policy), survived the waiting period, and met any other terms of the policy contract.

The Waiting Period

The insured must survive the waiting period following the occurrence, as stated either in the general exclusions and limitations or as indicated in the condition's definition.

Example of Policy Wording: Waiting Period

> No covered Condition will be paid unless the insured survives the waiting period. It is the longer of: (a) 30 days following the first diagnosis of a covered Condition; and (b) the period of time stipulated for a specific Condition.

Diagnosis

In the definition of each covered condition, the insurer describes what the covered risk is and what tests the diagnosis must be based on. If there are any exclusions specific to the particular condition (different from the general limitations), they will also be stated.

Following are examples of policy wording for the four primary conditions.

Heart Attack

A heart attack is the death of heart muscle caused by the lack of oxygenated blood supply to the heart. During this process, the heart muscle releases cardiac enzymes. Elevated levels of these enzymes in the blood indicate that a heart attack has occurred. One specific type of cardiac protein, called troponin, may be present in the blood even though other cardiac enzymes are not. Due to its greater sensitivity in measuring whether damage has occurred, it has become the biomarker of choice. Prior to this, many patients seen in emergency departments for chest pain were incorrectly diagnosed with unstable angina, when in fact they had had heart attacks. The good news is that cardiac troponin testing will allow for better treatment sooner, through more accurate diagnosis. The sooner blood flow is re-established, the more heart muscle is saved. The flip side for insurers is that the number of patients diagnosed with acute myocardial infarction (heart attack) has doubled due to the availability of more sensitive testing methods, and this may lead to a significant increase in claims under critical illness policies. Critical illness insurance is intended to provide money to deal with the devastating after-effects that occur following a significant critical illness — in other words, life-changing events, not non-events. Insurers will no doubt re-examine policy wording contained in critical illness contracts to maintain this focus.

Example of Policy Wording: Heart Attack

Heart Attack (Myocardial Infarction)

The death of a portion of heart muscle as a result of inadequate blood supply to the relevant area. The diagnosis must be based upon visible new changes in an electrocardiogram indicative of a myocardial infarction, and elevation of biochemical cardiac markers to levels considered diagnostic for infarction. Exclusion: we will not pay a benefit if it is diagnosed by any other method, unless the diagnosis is confirmed as described above.

Some policies may specifically state that a heart attack which occurs during coronary angioplasty is covered provided new Q waves develop during or immediately following the procedure, as evidenced by an ECG, and provided there is an elevation of cardiac markers.

Some policies specifically exclude a heart attack discovered through an incidental finding of ECG changes, if it is discovered in the absence of an "event". This is known as a "silent heart attack", because it occurs without the person realizing that such an event has happened. Months may pass and it may only come to light during a routine ECG.

Stroke

A stroke is a type of brain injury resulting either from a sudden interruption in the blood supply to part of the brain or from a blood vessel bursting. How a stroke affects a person depends upon the part of the brain that is injured. Following a stroke, a person may have weakness on one side of the body or trouble moving, talking, or thinking. Stroke is the third leading cause of death (following heart disease and cancer) and a major cause of long-term disability.

There is a strong connection between high blood pressure and stroke: between 40% and 90% of all stroke patients had high blood pressure prior to having a stroke. That is why it is so important for those with high blood pressure to take their prescribed medication without fail and to monitor their blood pressure regularly.

In defining a stroke, the policy requires that there be evidence of a measurable objective neurological deficit that has lasted longer than 30 days. It specifically excludes transient ischemic attacks (TIAs), which are often erroneously referred to as "mini-strokes". They start out like regular strokes but then resolve themselves, leaving no symptoms or damage. As no brain damage has occurred, TIAs are actually not strokes at all.

Example of Policy Wording: Stroke

Cerebrovascular Incident

> Any cerebrovascular event producing neurological sequelae lasting more than 30 days and caused by intracranial thrombosis or hemorrhage, or embolism from an extra-cranial source. There must be evidence of measurable, objective neurological deficit lasting longer than 30 days. Exclusion: transient ischemic attacks.

This wording points out that there are three types of strokes and that all three are covered. A "thrombosis" is an injury to the brain caused by a blood clot formed in one of the arteries that supplies blood to a portion of the brain. A "brain hemorrhage" is a leak in a blood vessel that hemorrhages into the brain tissue. An "embolus" is a blood clot that does not originate in the brain, which plugs an artery to the brain causing brain damage.

An example of a "neurological sequela" is partial paralysis.

Coronary Artery Bypass Graft Surgery

Coronary artery bypass graft surgery is used to treat heart disease when coronary arteries are blocked. A blood vessel is removed from one area and placed around the blocked area to "bypass" it and allow blood flow to be restored.

In defining this, the policy specifically excludes the use of any non-surgical techniques, such as coronary angioplasty or laser relief of an obstruction. The policy may, however, provide a lesser benefit for angioplasty.

Cancer

Cancer is the leading cause of premature death in Canada. Cancer risk increases with age; however, it can occur at all ages. Lung, prostate, breast, and colorectal cancer are the four most common cancer types in Canada and account for over 50% of all new cancer cases.[2]

Survival rates differ based on the type of cancer. The Canadian Cancer Society indicates that survival rates range from poor (for cancers such as lung and pancreas), to average (for colorectal cancer), to good (for cancers such as prostate and thyroid).

Cancer is not just one disease, but many diseases. The term "cancer" refers to diseases wherein abnormal cells divide without control and invade other tissues. Cancer cells can spread to other parts of the body through the blood and lymph systems. There are more than 100 different types of cancer, and they are usually named for the organ in which they start (e.g., colon cancer, breast cancer). There are broader categories used to group different types of cancer, such as:

- **Carcinoma** — cancer that begins in the skin or tissues that line or cover organs
- **Sarcoma** — cancer that begins in bone, cartilage, fat, muscle, blood vessels, or other connective tissue
- **Leukemia** — cancer that starts in the blood-forming tissue such as the bone marrow
- **Lymphoma** — cancer that begins in the cells of the immune system
- **Central nervous system cancers** — cancers that begin in the tissues of the brain and spinal cord.

Tumours can be either "benign" (meaning non-cancerous) or "malignant" (meaning cancerous). Benign tumours do not spread, whereas malignant tumours can. When cancer spreads from one part of the body to another, it is called "metastasis". Not all cancers form tumours. For instance, leukemia spreads through the blood and invades the bone marrow. Lymphoma is a cancer of the lymphatic system, which is the system that carries lymph fluid and white blood cells throughout the body to fight infections. While lymphoma cells are sometimes found in the blood, they more often form solid tumours in the lymph system or in organs. "Carcinoma *in situ*" refers to cancer that is superficial and has not penetrated the organ involved.

---

[2] Canadian Cancer Society Web site, www.cancer.ca, accessed September 20, 2011.

Critical illness insurance is intended to cover cancers that are life threatening. The policy wording will specify those that are not covered because they are usually not life threatening when caught in the early stages. An example is a cancerous mole less than 0.75 mm in size.

Example of Policy Wording: Cancer

Cancer (Life Threatening)

> A tumour characterized by the uncontrolled growth and spread of malignant cells and the invasion of tissue. This includes leukemia, Hodgkin's disease, and non-melanoma skin cancer that has metastasized to distant organs. The following cancers are excluded from coverage: carcinoma *in situ*; stage 1A malignant melanoma (melanoma less than or equal to 1 mm in thickness, not ulcerated, and without level IV or V invasion); any non-melanoma skin cancer that has not become metastatic; stage A (T1a or T1b) prostate cancer; any tumour in the presence of any HIV.

To protect the company against the risk of anti-selection, the policy will also specify that no benefit is payable for a diagnosis of cancer within 90 days of the effective coverage date, or if symptoms were present during the 90-day period prior to the effective date of coverage.

Some policies provide a smaller benefit payable for prostate or breast cancer caught in the early stages, which is otherwise excluded under the policy.

SELLING CRITICAL ILLNESS INSURANCE

Critical illness insurance helps to protect against the high costs that can arise in connection with a serious illness. Even in Canada, where we have a meaningful level of social security in place, costs can arise that make it difficult for people to focus on getting well. Some costs are not medical. For instance, some parts of the home may need to be redesigned to accommodate a wheelchair, or supports may be required to help a person get in and out of the shower or use the toilet. A ramp may have to be installed at the entrance of the home. A car may have to be adapted. Even with a plan of disability insurance or long-term disability in place, the need does not disappear. Income benefits help to meet the daily living costs, such as food, clothing, and household expenses, including hydro, heat, water, and property taxes. But disability income benefits do not continue 100% of earnings, and the shortfall may mean the insured cannot pay mortgage payments and other loans.

Some needs may be for daily living supports. There may be a need for assistance with caring for the home, or for personal activities, such as bathing and dressing.

The chances of having and surviving a critical illness are quite high. Governments face the challenge of providing health care to an aging population. The money provided by critical illness insurance can be used in any way the insured sees fit; the funds are not limited to reimbursement or proof of medical expenses being incurred. Critical illness insurance speaks to the needs of the four great motivators: greed, fear, love, and obligation.

There are many reasons why people become concerned:

- Fear of not meeting mortgage payments
- Fear of facing a significant, permanent change in lifestyle
- Fear of the financial costs associated with a major illness
- Fear that the government will not cover the cost of expensive and necessary medication
- Knowing a friend or relative who has just been diagnosed with a critical illness
- Desire for peace of mind.

Who Should Buy Critical Illness Insurance

Young singles may not feel the need for life insurance as much as they do critical illness insurance. When purchased at a young age, the cost is relatively small as compared to purchase at an older age.

Young families are often concerned with being able to make mortgage payments. Debt is common and may include car loans and credit card debt as well. There is an increase in the number of young couples living together and jointly buying a home. Whereas a married couple may be more likely to remain together after a critical illness, unmarried couples may not feel the same responsibility.

Mature couples may be at a life stage in which they are focused on accumulating retirement savings. In the event of a critical illness, they need a safety net that will help to prevent the depletion of their savings. Some may be caregivers to aging parents. If the caregiver were to take ill, not only would he or she need adjustment funds for his or her own personal health, but there would be an additional need to replace the assistance he or she gives as caregiver to the older adult, similar to the concept of key person insurance. Some may have children in, or about to start, university. There is a need to protect education funds from erosion.

Older couples may be more focused on investments or may be aware of their greater statistical risk of having a critical illness. Critical illness insurance helps to protect their investments and provide funds to deal with the critical illness and getting well. As the maximum age for purchasing critical illness insurance may be approaching, their need is all the more time sensitive.

Divorced singles may be even more aware of the need to protect against a critical illness. "Illness" is not the only focus of critical illness insurance; a car accident could leave a person paraplegic and in need of medical assistance. Now on their own, they may have a heightened awareness of the need to be able to provide for themselves "in sickness and in health".

In a business setting, there may be a need for key person, creditor, or partnership insurance. Just as the need for life insurance exists, so there is a financial concern to the business in the event that a key person or partner acquires a critical illness. Self-employed individuals are affected in terms of needing to meet business expenses when a critical illness prevents them from generating the income that runs the business.

Insurance for Protecting Lifestyle Issues

Critical illness insurance is about coming to grips with a complete change of lifestyle, whereas most other forms of insurance are about maintaining a lifestyle.

Sharing statistics can help your client see the *chance* of a critical illness happening, but discussing lifestyle issues can help the client to see the *impact* of a critical illness. Having critical illness insurance can bring peace of mind. There are three main areas to consider in protecting one's lifestyle:

- Maintaining quality of life
- Adapting one's lifestyle
- Being able to meet continuing financial commitments.

A critical illness not only brings about financial issues, but the impact is also felt as a psychological blow, as the person begins to accept their new reality. Retaining dignity after a serious illness is important to both the physical and emotional recovery.

Clients deal with making decisions about many forms of insurance. Ask them to consider their degree of personal concern and the degree to which they have protected themselves from the following events:

- Repairing a car following an accident
- Recovering from bypass surgery
- Replacing stolen household items following a break-in
- Recovering from cancer treatment
- Replacing a computer after the hard drive crashes
- Recovering following a heart attack.

This form of questioning may help to put into perspective the many tangible things we protect, relative to the bigger events with life-threatening consequences that would certainly be more devastating.

The Importance of Explaining the Definitions

Clients need to understand what they are and are not covered for. This includes explaining many features, such as:

- The waiting period (survival period) following a diagnosis
- The definition that must be satisfied to claim for benefits under a listed condition (what constitutes a myocardial infarction, a stroke, and so on)
- What diagnostic tests will be used to confirm the diagnosis
- The claims process and the need to adhere to submission deadlines when notifying the insurer
- The initial 90-day qualifying period for cancer
- Conditions that are eligible for partial benefits as opposed to full benefits.

Planners may recall the adverse circumstances surrounding the denial in the 1990s of some disability insurance claims because insured individuals' disabilities did not meet the "occupation" definition contained in their policy. ("What do you mean *you* don't consider me disabled? My doctor does!") Just as the definition of disability needs to be explained to the disability insurance client, so should the definitions for each critical illness condition be reviewed with the critical illness insurance client.

When presenting the critical illness solution, be cautious about presenting too high a benefit amount, which will make the plan unaffordable. Clients may simply decide to purchase a totally different product form as a substitute — one that may not suit their needs.

Evaluating Different Critical Illness Policies

When deciding which critical illness policy to show a client, consider the following:

❐ Is the policy true critical illness insurance or a life policy with "accelerated" payment?

❐ Does the policy guarantee that the rate will never change ("non-cancellable") or does the insurer have the right to change rates for a block of business in the future ("guaranteed renewable")?

❐ Are the covered critical illnesses important events or events that are unlikely to happen?

❐ What survival period is required for each covered condition?

❐ How must a diagnosis be determined for each condition in order for the insured to qualify for benefits?

❐ Are benefits payable if the insured is residing outside Canada?

- ❒ Can the policy be later reduced to cover "primary conditions" only, if affordability becomes an issue?
- ❒ Are multiple claims permitted?
- ❒ Does the coverage expire at age 65? age 75? age 100?
- ❒ Does the coverage provide for conversion to another form of insurance, such as long-term care insurance?
- ❒ What are the exclusions listed in the policy?
- ❒ Which listed conditions are covered at a reduced percentage of the principal?
- ❒ Is the insurer financially sound based on independent rating agencies, and is it a member of Assuris?

Planning Considerations

People with critical illnesses may not be able to make medical decisions on their own behalf and may also need someone to manage their financial affairs. Therefore, during the planning process, it is wise to include arrangements for a "power of attorney for personal care" and a "power of attorney for property".

A power of attorney for personal care, also known as a "living will", ensures that loved ones will know the person's wishes regarding care and treatment if he or she is no longer able to express those wishes personally.

A power of attorney for property can be structured so that it springs to life only in the event of incapacity. This may occur as a result of a critical illness, such as following a stroke. In this instance, it would be wise to have someone appointed to take care of assets and finances.

It may also be worth considering whether the proceeds should be paid to a third party at the time of claim. While life insurance provides for a beneficiary designation, critical illness insurance does not (except in Quebec). Most insurers will recognize a "direction to pay", which is a written request from the policyholder to pay the benefits to a third party at the time of a claim. Some companies accommodate such a designation on the application form itself (e.g., "benefit recipient"). This type of designation does not protect the funds from creditors as it does with life insurance. Additionally, consideration must first be given as to whether the policy contains a "return of premium on death benefit", as this will impact the options available.

A direction to pay does not take into consideration the current state of the person's health and could result in proceeds being paid to a third party, even though the insured is capable of making personal decisions and handling his or her own finances. There is no guarantee that the funds will be used in accordance with the insured's wishes.

UNDERWRITING

In some ways, critical illness insurance mirrors life insurance in its product design. A lump sum is purchased, and coverage may be renewable or level to age 100. The underwriting requirements for critical illness applications are similar to the requirements for preferred term life insurance.

There are also ways in which critical illness insurance is similar to disability insurance. As the saying goes, "the insured does not have to die to collect; they only have to get sick" (or in the case of critical illness, "they only have to be diagnosed"). Because the person insured is still around to benefit personally from the proceeds, the chance of anti-selection is greater than it is with life insurance. This is not to suggest that people would intentionally do something to contract a critical illness in order to receive the benefit, but they might conveniently "forget to mention" symptoms they have been ignoring until after they have purchased their critical illness insurance. This appears to be borne out by the fact that the population insured against critical illness has a substantially higher incidence of multiple sclerosis than the general population. The underwriting process takes this into consideration. The company must assess the *risk of diagnosis*, not the *risk of dying*, and the company must be thorough in its approach to obtain all pertinent information. Having said that, underwriting of critical illness insurance is unique: some conditions warrant a stricter approach than they would with disability insurance, while others are of lesser concern. The same is true when comparing its underwriting with the underwriting of life insurance. The examples that follow illustrate this difference.

Some conditions that affect critical illness underwriting *more* than they do disability insurance underwriting:

- High blood pressure
- Physical build
- Non-insulin-dependent diabetes
- Heart disease
- Smoking
- Family history.

Some conditions that affect critical illness underwriting *less* than they do disability insurance underwriting:

- Asthma
- COPD (chronic obstructive pulmonary disease) in non-smokers
- Mental illness
- Musculoskeletal disorders
- Rheumatoid arthritis (without steroid medication)
- Soft-tissue injuries.

Some conditions that affect critical illness underwriting *more* than they do life underwriting:

- High blood pressure
- Physical build
- Ulcerative colitis
- Non-insulin-dependent diabetes
- Epilepsy
- Family history
- Heart disease.

Some conditions that affect critical illness underwriting *less* than they do life underwriting:

- Asthma
- Mental illness
- COPD in non-smokers
- Rheumatoid arthritis (without steroid medication).

Family History

Some chronic illnesses tend to run in families. Because of the strong genetic factor linked with certain conditions, family history plays an important role in medical underwriting of critical illness insurance. The significance of family history varies based on the specific condition, the age of initial onset, the age of the applicant, and other health factors present for the applicant. The following are some examples of conditions where family history may be particularly pertinent:

- Cardiovascular conditions with early onset
- Diabetes with early onset
- Some types of cancer with early onset
- Alzheimer's with early onset
- Any motor neuron disease.

Age of onset is more important in the family member's medical history than is age at death, as the underwriter is assessing the probability of diagnosis, not the probability of death. Family members of interest include biological parents and siblings, referred to as "first-degree" relatives. The underwriter is concerned with early onset (prior to age 60) where there are two or more occurrences of the same condition (conditions where genetic factors play a particularly strong role, such as a heart attack at a very young age and certain types of cancer, may be of concern with only one occurrence).

The significance of family history varies depending on the age and gender of the applicant. For example, a 42-year-old female applicant whose mother was diagnosed with breast cancer at age 65 will likely be subject to a premium rating such as 25%. Any applicant, regardless of age, who has two first-degree relatives diagnosed with Alzheimer's disease is likely to be declined. An applicant whose mother had a stroke at age 56 and whose father has had type 2 diabetes since age 40 is likely to be approved at standard rates because each condition is considered separately.

Standardizing the Risk

As with disability insurance, the underwriter uses several methods to standardize the risk. The insurer may do one or more of the following:

- Exclude the condition
- Increase the premium (25% to 150% extra)
- Amend the plan design (reduce coverage and/or delete optional benefits).

Some conditions do not lend themselves to exclusion, and in this instance, if an increase in premium would not be sufficient to standardize the risk, the underwriter must decline the application. For example, the risk of blindness can be excluded, but the risks of diabetes cannot, since diabetes can lead to other conditions such as blindness, kidney failure, major organ transplant, or even loss of limbs.

In the past, most insurers excluded whole categories of conditions, such as cancer, that the insured had an increased risk of incurring. In this instance, the policy would cover all listed conditions except any form of cancer. Today, insurers have more experience with the product and are often able to exclude subcategories, such as breast cancer.

About 15% of critical illness cases are amended or ultimately declined. This rate is higher than the rate for life insurance, which is 7–8%, but lower than the rate for disability insurance, which is about 25%. Inexperienced advisers usually have a higher rate, which reduces as their knowledge and experience with the product increases.

Underwriters follow an underwriting guide that has been developed through their reinsurer and reflects sound practices based on the collective experiences of the reinsurer. The reinsurer's book of business is larger than that of any individual insurer, and they are at risk for the amount of benefit above the insurer's retention limit. For this reason, large cases will be sent to the reinsurer for approval, as will smaller cases that fall outside the macro guidelines set by the reinsurer.

Field Underwriting

Advisers play an important role in the overall underwriting process as they can gather first-hand knowledge of the insured's situation. Insurers provide "pre-qualifying checklists", which the adviser uses to screen out any applications that are outright declines. The adviser's role is to develop full information through open-ended questions, so that occurrences of non-disclosure and misrepresentation are reduced. Non-disclosure discovered during the underwriting process calls the applicant's credibility into question, and usually leads to a decline even in cases where the applicant might otherwise have been insurable on some basis. When non-disclosure is discovered in the claims process, the policy is usually rescinded, again leaving the client unprotected. Non-disclosure is not always intentional, and through skilful questioning techniques the adviser can help the client to recall important facts. In addition, advisers can help to avoid intentional non-disclosure by explaining the ramifications to the applicant.

Maximum Coverage Limits

The maximum coverage available through most insurers is $2 million. This limit takes into consideration coverage in force through all insurers, not just the coverage applied for. The maximum age for purchase is usually age 65. The medical requirements for coverage vary based on age and amount purchased. The coverage amount is also subject to an individual maximum based on financial underwriting, as described below.

Financial Underwriting

Insurers set maximum issue limits for critical illness insurance based on earnings. This is usually expressed as a multiple of the applicant's net earned income (i.e., income after expenses but before taxes) based on various age brackets. To this amount, insurers add the amount of any outstanding personal mortgage if there is one. The multiple may range from 5 times to 9 or 10 times. A different formula applies to a non-working spouse and to critical illness coverage sold as business insurance (e.g., key person, buy-sell, business loan coverage). As with disability insurance, new professionals in certain high-income-potential occupations may have special issue limits. A person with no earnings may still be able to purchase a limited amount of coverage, such as $100,000.

Sports, Avocations, and Occupations

Participation in some sports or avocations is associated with greater risk of injury and is considered during the underwriting process. Some sports can cause traumatic injuries that include loss of limbs, paralysis, coma, burns, deafness, and blindness, which would result in payment of benefits under the listed critical illness conditions. Consequently, insurers will add an extra premium and/or an exclusion for a claim arising from the particular event, such as boxing, mountain climbing, diving, or car racing.

For similar reasons, a person with a poor driving record may be given a rating.

Some occupations have increased risk of injury associated with them, and others may have an increased risk of illness, such as cancer developed from exposure to toxic substances. Applicants in these occupations may be declined altogether or offered coverage with an extra premium rating.

FUTURE INDUSTRY CHALLENGES

Insurers constantly strive to ensure that their products remain competitive and unique in the market. As the number of critical illness insurance policies sold continues to increase, this will create a larger base from which to draw statistical experience — or will it? The rapid progress being made in medical technology and diagnostic procedures may render historical experience outdated and irrelevant. Consider the change in the medical community regarding the use of troponin as the marker of choice in diagnosing a heart attack.

Similarly, there may be new methods of diagnosis and treatment of cancer in the future that lead to higher incidences of diagnosis, and earlier treatment may mean that some forms of cancer considered life threatening today will be treatable with routine procedures in the future.

The bottom line is that pricing critical illness insurance appropriately for the long term can be an issue for non-cancellable policies that prevent companies from making future rate adjustments or changes to the definitions of covered conditions. Many believe it is only a matter of time until the Canadian industry follows other countries in moving away from non-cancellable critical illness policies, in favour of five-year renewable policies. One thing is certain: rates will continue to increase for newly insured individuals as improvements in diagnostic procedures and treatments evolve. Products will also evolve, and some conditions may continue to be insured but at a reduced percentage of the face amount, as in charts contained in AD&D policies, where less financially impacting events pay only a percentage of the face amount. For instance, technology may one day render a coronary bypass a minor surgery.

The risk of anti-selection remains a concern, particularly given that consumers today are better informed, and informed buyers may be more likely to buy coverage, armed with the personal knowledge that they are at greater risk based on undiagnosed symptoms or family history.

Taxation of benefits and premiums remains something of a grey area. In some respects, critical illness insurance mirrors life insurance, while in other ways it resembles accident and sickness insurance. And some policies contain refund provisions for death, others for early surrender, and still others at maturity. While the Canada Revenue Agency has confirmed that it views critical illness insurance policies providing no return of premium benefits as accident and sickness insurance, it has not confirmed this view for policies containing return of premium on death benefits outside Quebec.[3]

---

[3] *Understanding Taxation of CI Insurance*, Manulife Financial (April 2007).

Chapter 19

Long-Term Care Insurance

Long-term care insurance is coverage that helps provide for the cost of care associated with loss of independence. Over time, the needs of the person being cared for will change, ranging from light assistance with daily tasks, such as eating, bathing, toileting, dressing, and transferring (known as "activities of daily living", or ADLs), through to 24-hour supervision by trained staff.

THE NEED FOR CARE

People can lose their independence in a short period, even hours or days (acute loss), or the loss may be gradual, occurring over a period of weeks or months (subacute or chronic loss). An acute loss may occur from a heart attack, a stroke, or even a complex surgery. Loss of independence associated with a sub-acute or chronic condition may be brought on by deterioration from an illness such as Alzheimer's, Parkinson's, heart failure, or advanced forms of cancer.

"Subacute care" refers to a level of care for someone who needs services such as skilled therapy, rehabilitation, or nursing care on a short-term basis to regain function and return home. This may be needed following surgery, cancer treatment, cardiac care, or joint replacement. It is about time-limited intervention involving assessing and managing complex conditions and maximizing independence and quality of life. This range of services is sometimes called "intermediate care". "Chronic care" refers to treatment for conditions that are ongoing. Almost half of all people with chronic illness have multiple conditions.

Initially, care is often provided in a person's home, through a plan of home care. In this stage, the need may be temporary, following release from the hospital, or partial, requiring help with activities that can be scheduled on a weekly basis, such as taking a bath. Eventually, it may be necessary for the person to move to a facility equipped to provide a higher level of ongoing care, such as a nursing home, also called a "long-term care centre" or a "home for the aged". This type of care is referred to as "facility care".

Some long-term care (LTC) insurance policies describe different features for home care benefits versus facility care benefits, while others do not distinguish based on where care is being received. As not all policies automatically include home care coverage, advisers should review policies carefully to determine the extent of protection.

THE COST OF CARE

The cost of care varies depending upon what service is performed and who provides the service. Costs can vary considerably by province, but the following guide will help the planner have a general idea of the cost of care.

Community Services	
• Skilled nursing care (post-surgical care, changing dressings, administering IVs, arranging dosette boxes, instructional assistance to families, administering injections)	$40 to $50 per hour
• Companion services (friendly visits, medication reminders, reading and writing letters)	$18 to $20 per hour
• Home helper services (light housekeeping, laundry, ironing, accompaniment to appointments, help with meal preparation, grocery purchase)	$20 to $25 per hour
• Personal care services (feeding, assistance with bathing, incontinence care, washroom assistance)	$25 to $35 per hour
• Foot care	$25 to $30 per treatment
• Community volunteer services (Meals-on-Wheels)	No charge or small charge depending upon the province
• Adult day support centres	$16 to $20 per day or $300 to $400 per month, based on a five-day week
Residential Facilities	
• Respite care (short stay)	$30 to $40 per day
• Nursing home basic (ward)	$45 to $55 per day or $1,500 to $1,700 per month
• Nursing home preferred (semi-private)	$60 to $70 per day or $1,800 to $2,100 per month
• Nursing home preferred (private)	$70 to $80 per day or $2,100 to $2,400 per month
• Retirement homes	$1,600 to $6,000 per month

The cost of nursing homes represents the accommodation fee or copayment required by the resident. The government pays the health care component in most provinces. Income and asset testing is still in place in

Newfoundland and Labrador, and the cost of facility care can run higher for those who do not have low incomes and for those who have assets.

POLICY STRUCTURES

Long-term care insurance policies can be classified into three fundamental structures, although hybrid versions are appearing that have evolved from these fundamentals. They are:

- Reimbursement-based models
- Indemnity-based models
- Income-based models.

Fundamental Policy Structures

Reimbursement-Based Model

Reimbursement-based contracts require the insured to submit receipts for expenses incurred, and then the insurer reimburses the amount paid, up to a stipulated daily maximum. To qualify for reimbursement, the expense must be considered an "eligible expense" within the terms of the policy. This type of policy is primarily associated with home care benefits, not facility care benefits. However, not all home care benefits are reimbursement-based. Most companies that provide separate home care benefits offer it only as an optional rider under a facility care contract, not as a stand-alone policy. The base policy is normally an indemnity-based contract.

As the expense incurred is sometimes less than the daily benefit amount purchased, the policy carries forward any unused benefit, which in effect extends benefits beyond the maximum benefit period purchased. Sometimes for ease of administration, and since the benefit payments are issued monthly anyway on a daily benefit plan, the insurer will simply overlook the daily benefit maximum and calculate the monthly equivalent, against which incurred expenses are then measured. This procedure enables the insured to schedule multiple services on the same day without exceeding that day's maximum, instead of scheduling individual services on separate days. Of course, procedures that are not contractual can later be changed to a more literal interpretation of the contract.

A licensed care agency must provide the services, not an informal caregiver or a relative of the insured (such as the spouse), regardless of whether the relative is a licensed professional, such as a registered nurse.

Consequently, the policy stipulates both *where* care can be received and *who* can provide the care.

Indemnity-Based Model

Indemnity contracts pay the entire predetermined benefit on a daily or monthly basis and are found in both home care benefits and facility care benefits. The insurer may request receipts to validate that a covered service has been performed; once verified, the insured receives a payment equal to the benefit amount purchased (which may be more or less than the actual expense incurred). Under this model, there is no "lengthening" at the back end if the actual expense is less, since the full amount is paid out anyway. The difference may help to defray other non-covered expenses, such as the cost of medication or equipment.

As with a reimbursement-based contract, a licensed care agency must provide the services.

Consequently, indemnity contracts also stipulate both *where* care can be received and *who* can provide the care.

Income-Based Model

The most significant difference with income-based contracts is that they do not stipulate where care can be received or who can provide the care. The policy functions similarly to a disability income policy, insofar as the insured purchases a stipulated monthly benefit, which is paid regardless of the actual level of expenses incurred. The insured can use the benefits in any manner, similar to a paycheque. Of course, the insured must satisfy a definition of dependence and certain other triggers.

Hybrids and Variations

Conversion Model

A conversion policy starts out as some other form of insurance (such as disability, critical illness, or term life insurance) and then eventually converts to long-term care facility coverage. The transition may be gradual over several years, or the policy may simply "spring" to its new form when the insured reaches a given age, such as age 65. Generally, the policy covers only facility care but may allow for the addition of a home care benefit option. Once the coverage converts to long-term care, the policy format follows one of the fundamental models above.

Conversion policies offer an excellent method of covering a current need that will diminish with time, while providing for a future need that will increase with time.

Pooled Benefits Model

A "pooled benefit" policy is a hybrid of the income-based and indemnity-based models. As with other income-based plans, the policy does not stipulate *who* can provide care; consequently, an informal caregiver, such as the spouse, can provide care. As with the indemnity-based model, benefit payment is determined based on *where* care is received (home versus facility). Benefits double once the insured transitions from home care to facility care.

The insurance is purchased as a lump sum (such as $500,000), from which a predetermined monthly amount is drawn (such as 2%), until such time as the pool is exhausted. The pool may be established for a single individual, or a couple can draw from a common pool. For this reason, it is also referred to as a "shared benefits" plan.

The benefit automatically increases to a higher amount if the insured is being cared for in a facility. The overall pool of benefits remains the same and, thus, is depleted faster.

DEFINITION OF DEPENDENCE

Every LTC policy specifies the changes in functional dependence that entitle the insured to receive benefits. There are two categories:

- ADL-based definitions, which describe functional limitations
- Cognitive impairment definitions.

Policies also have other criteria that must be met, such as the need to be under the care and supervision of a physician.

ADL-Based Definitions

ADL-based definitions relate to the insured's ability to perform two or more activities of daily living. The focus is on functional limitation, which, as it can be determined by tests, is an objective measure.

Activities of Daily Living

There are six ADLs that are commonly measured:

- **Bathing** — the ability to wash oneself in a tub or shower, or by a sponge bath
- **Eating** — the ability to feed oneself
- **Dressing** — the ability to put on and take off clothes or fasten and unfasten them
- **Toileting** — the ability to get to and from the toilet
- **Transferring** — the ability to move in and out of a chair, wheelchair, or bed with or without the aid of a cane or other supporting device
- **Continence** — the ability to maintain bladder control.

Studies conducted show a strong relationship between deterioration in these functional areas and the use of acute, subacute, and chronic care services. An American physician, Dr. Sidney Katz, originally developed the scale. LTC policies indicate that there must be a loss of two or more of these activities.

Measuring the Functional Loss

People pass through three stages of functional loss. In the first stage, they can continue to cope well with the use of assistive devices, such as canes or adaptive cutlery, or special devices for reaching and grabbing. In the second stage, they begin to need a higher level of support, called "standby assistance", where another person must stay within arm's reach for them to safely perform a particular task, such as stepping out of a tub. In the third stage, they need one-on-one assistance, where another person must provide hands-on help in performing a particular task, such as moving from a bed to a chair.

Not all companies measure functional loss the same way in policy provisions that serve as payment triggers. Consequently, one policy may pay benefits sooner than another. Consider the following examples of different measures:

- Needs standby or partial assistance from another individual
- Needs one-on-one assistance such that the person is completely dependent upon another individual
- Cannot perform the task unaided or aided with the assistance of another individual or the use of a device.

The definition most easily satisfied is one that defines functional limitation as one where the person requires standby or partial assistance from another individual, while the most stringent definition will be one indicating that the person must not be able to perform the task aided or unaided with the assistance of another individual or the use of a device. Some policies may consider the use of a feeding tube as a "device", in which case it would be very difficult to satisfy the ADL of "inability to feed oneself".

The loss of activities tends to occur in the reverse order that these skills are acquired as infants, and this is believed to be due to the mental complexity associated with performing the task. This means that the first ability to go is often the ability to bathe oneself, followed by dressing, then transferring, then toileting, and finally, feeding oneself. So a stricter definition related to feeding, the last ability to go, would be of lesser concern than one related to the first activity likely to go, bathing.

Cognitive Impairment Definitions

Benefits can also be triggered if the insured suffers a cognitive impairment. Most LTC policies provide that the insured qualifies for benefits if he or she is unable to perform two or more ADLs or suffers a cognitive impairment. To qualify under this trigger, the cognitive impairment must be due to an organic cause, such as Alzheimer's or Parkinson's disease, or severe brain injury, such as stroke or trauma. Cognitive inefficiencies associated with normal aging are not cognitive impairment. LTC policies generally do not cover a cognitive impairment that is caused by alcoholism or a non-prescription drug disorder or addiction. Diagnoses can be confirmed using standardized tests that measure reductions in short- and long-term memory and general orientation.

Defining "Cognitive Impairment"

Some LTC policies recognize the need for verbal cueing as a cognitive impairment that qualifies for payment of benefits. "Verbal cueing" refers to when the person can perform tasks but requires a verbal cue first. For example, dressing oneself may require a cue such as "put your arm in here" or "put your socks on first, then your shoes".

Some LTC policies require a higher level of functional deficit than verbal cueing, such as requiring the insured to be in need of 24-hour supervision by another person, to protect the insured from personal injury, for a sustained period, such as 90 days. Some companies may simply apply an administrative practice instead of a defined time period. When the measure is not stated in the policy, it is a good idea to explore this with the insurer, as some may provide a longer period, such as six months.

Wandering is a common problem with Alzheimer's, and the insured may require substantial supervision for safety to be ensured.

INSTRUMENTAL ACTIVITIES OF DAILY LIVING

While the loss of ability to perform instrumental activities of daily living (IADLs) cannot be reliably used as a predictor of whether someone will eventually suffer the loss of ADLs, it is of interest to insurers, because it does place the person at higher risk. IADLs are less complex tasks, such as cooking, grocery shopping, doing laundry, paying bills, taking medicine, telephoning, and housekeeping. Not everyone who experiences difficulties with instrumental activities continues on to experience loss of ADLs. However, almost everyone who has a loss of ADLs first has difficulties with instrumental activities. During the underwriting process, the underwriter may probe further for signs of deficits in ADLs if it is apparent that the person is currently having difficulties with some instrumental activities. There is a cultural issue associated with IADLs, and measurement of loss tends to be more subjective than objective. For example, in some cultures, men do not cook or purchase groceries, so the applicant's inability to perform these activities could be due to never having performed them, not due to a deficit.

IADLs are evaluated when assessing the care and assistance a person needs when developing a plan of care. One solution may be to use an adult day support centre while the primary caregiver is at work.

PLAN DESIGN OPTIONS

There are several things to consider when preparing an LTC insurance recommendation. How soon should benefits begin following evidence of deficits? How much should be payable? What is the maximum time during which benefits should be payable? Ideally, everyone would like benefits indefinitely, but cost is a consideration.

The Elimination Period

The elimination period is the number of days of functional dependence that must pass before the insurer begins to pay benefits. It is a form of deductible, or a period of self-insurance. Two different elimination periods may be found in one policy: one that applies to home care benefits and one that applies to facility care benefits. As with disability insurance, the variations may include 0 days, 30 days, 60 days, and 90 days, with a corresponding reduction in premium for longer elimination periods.

Care Days Versus Calendar Days

When counting days to satisfy the elimination period, some insurers may refer to "care days" while others may refer to "calendar days". When care days are counted, only days in which a covered service is received get counted towards satisfying the elimination period. When calendar days are counted, all days are counted from the measurement date. It takes longer to satisfy the elimination period when only care days are counted.

The Measurement Date

How does one determine the date that functional dependence occurred? This is important, because this date is the point from which the elimination period will begin to be counted. The "measurement date" in the policy may begin with any of the following occurrences:

- The date of physician certification
- The date that covered-care services are first received
- The date a care assessment has been conducted
- The documented date of a major event (such as a severe stroke) that documents dependence
- The date that a plan of care is approved.

The policy will specify which of these methods will be used.

Continuous Periods of Care

A continuous period of care is usually required to satisfy the elimination period. This means that the individual has been continuously receiving home care or has been continuously confined to a facility throughout the elimination period. The policy will indicate whether periods of home care and facility care can be added together to satisfy the elimination period or whether separate periods must satisfy each. This can be an important issue.

Recurrent Periods of Care

Two or more recurrent periods of functional dependence may be considered as one period if they are separated by less than a stipulated period of time, such as 180 days. The benefit to the insured is that he or she does not have to satisfy a new elimination period for benefits to resume; however, the maximum benefit period will be reached sooner. LTC policies do not generally allow the individual, however, to accumulate separate periods of care to satisfy the elimination period.

Plan of Care

Some companies offer the services of a care adviser as a value-added benefit. The care adviser's role is to work with the insured and his or her caregivers to develop a plan of care. The use of this service is generally voluntary at claim time. Some older policies used the services of an independent care adviser as part of the initial assessment in determining eligibility for benefits during a claim. The recommended plan of care required approval of both the insurer and the care recipient; however, if the latter refused an approved plan of care, it could result in no benefit being paid. This method helped to ensure that the person was using the most cost-effective means for obtaining the right services. Today, these services are made available at the insured's option and perform an important service of helping both the insured and the informal caregivers to navigate the complex health care system and to obtain valuable care assistance in the community and through government programs.

Selecting the Elimination Period

Benefits are paid at the end of the month following the fulfillment of the elimination period. Therefore, if the elimination period is 60 days, the first payment that the insured receives is actually disbursed three months from the triggering event. The best rule of thumb is to consider the amount of out-of-pocket expenses that can be covered personally prior to beginning benefit payments. Using an average of $3,500 per month in expenses, then, a side fund of $14,000 would be required if the insured were to select a 90-day elimination period.

The Benefit Amount

The amount payable during a claim may be calculated as a daily amount, a weekly amount, or a monthly amount, depending upon the insurer. It represents the maximum payable for the calculated period. Daily amounts, for instance, are purchased in increments of $10 and range from $10 to $350 per day. Integrated home care and facility care policies provide the same amount for each portion of coverage, while policies that have separate home care benefits allow the purchase of different coverage amounts for each benefit.

Maximum Benefits

The "maximum benefit" refers to the overall maximum time period that the policy will cover or the overall dollar amount that can be claimed under it. It is sometimes referred to as a "benefit period" or the "maximum benefit limit". Purchasers have a wide range to choose from, including plans that offer 1 year, 2 years, 5 years, 10 years, and even lifetime benefits. Sometimes, the benefit period for home care benefits is calculated in days, such as 730, instead of years.

Policies sometimes use a multiple of the daily rate to determine the overall maximum benefit limit, such as 2,000 times the daily rate. Using that multiple and $100 as the basic daily rate, the overall maximum would be equal to 2,000 × $100 = $200,000. This method recognizes that when care days (instead of calendar days) are used to calculate benefits, the number of years is less relevant than is the overall dollar amount covered by the plan. It is sometimes used in an integrated policy of home and facility care, because both share the pool of available benefits. That is, in the above example, the individual can receive up to $200,000 of home care, facility care, or a combination of both.

The "benefit period method" places more specific limits on each type of care. For example, an individual might purchase 730 days of home care benefits plus 1,825 care days (i.e., five years) of facility care benefits. This method may be found in policies that add home care benefits as a rider to a base of facility care benefits. In this instance, the individual could claim up to 730 days of home care. Some plans will then subtract the amount collected from the available benefit period for facility care, which in this example would leave a remainder of three years as the maximum for facility care. The elimination period is not counted in this calculation, and as the actual benefits are per day, only the cumulative total of days on which home care was actually received is deducted from the duration for facility care. Consequently, the elapsed calendar time may be longer than five years. However, not all plans that treat home care benefits as a rider work in this fashion (i.e., some do not reduce the period of coverage for facility care), and the method used should be clearly explained by the adviser to the client.

Under a "pooled benefit plan", the amount of insurance is selected at the time of purchase as a lump sum, similar to how one might purchase life insurance or critical illness insurance. The monthly benefit amount paid out during a claim is a pre-selected percentage, such as 1%, which reduces the size of the remaining pool dollar for dollar. The percentage selected determines how quickly the pool is exhausted. The care setting also impacts how quickly the pool is depleted, since the benefit increases for facility care and, therefore, reduces the remaining pool sooner. The pool is a finite amount and is not replenished.

Premium Payment Term

Some insurers offer the choice of making premium payments for a limited time, such as 20 years, or to a specified age, such as age 70. This offers younger buyers the tremendous advantage of being able to pay for coverage during their working years and having their plan fully paid up by retirement. It protects the policyholder from further rate adjustments, because once coverage is fully paid up, the exposure to rate change is eliminated. The risk of lapse is also eliminated, since no premiums are payable now that the insured is likely on a reduced fixed pension.

OTHER POLICY PROVISIONS

Exclusions and Limitations

As with other forms of health insurance, LTC policies list risks not covered. This makes coverage more affordable and protects the company from significant loss. They vary slightly from one company to another and are unlikely to be of concern to the client. The following are examples of typical exclusions:

- Intentionally self-inflicted injury
- Occurrences while in the military
- Alcoholism
- Drug addiction from chemicals not prescribed by a physician
- Commission of a criminal offence
- Mental and nervous conditions that do not have an organic cause.

Some policies also limit a pre-existing condition. For example, the policy might provide that the individual must have been free from treatment for a continuous period of time, such as the preceding six months, before a period of care for which the individual is claiming. Although prior and existing conditions are generally dealt with during the underwriting process, this provision helps to protect the company against anything that was missed or that may only surface after issue of the policy but relates to a pre-purchase condition.

Exclusions and limitations should always be reviewed by the adviser prior to making a recommendation to a client, and they should be fully explained at the time of purchase.

Coordination of Benefits

The "coordination of benefits" provision eliminates the duplication of payment for the same expense. It enables the insurer to be a second payer when the insured is eligible for benefits from another source, for example, government benefits. Some policies require evidence at the time of claim that the insured has applied for any government benefits to which he or she is entitled, after which the policy will then cover expenses not paid by the government. The wording of such provisions is important, as some may indicate that proof of application is required, while others may indicate that proof of receipt or approval of benefits is required, thereby lengthening the time until benefits will commence under the LTC policy.

Some policies go a step further and protect against overinsurance by including an offset provision against other sources of coverage, both private and public. Overinsurance occurs when an individual has a total amount of insurance that exceeds the insurance company's maximum issue limits. This is a concern, because there is a fear that it can lead to an increased tendency to claim for benefits, which ultimately affects rates for everyone.

Policy Series and Rate Guarantees

Guaranteed Renewable

The majority of LTC policies available today are sold as guaranteed renewable plans. This means that the policy cannot be cancelled if the insured pays the premium on time or within the defined grace period. However, the insurer reserves the right, if necessary, to change the premium in the future for a class of insured individuals based on the experience of the entire block of business. The insurer cannot single out one particular client, so a personal claim has no bearing on the likelihood of that client facing a rate increase down the road for having claimed on a policy.

Some insurers sell plans with "level rates". This means that the insurer has calculated rates with the expectation that they will remain level; however, such plans are still subject to an adjustment by the insurer based on the experience of the entire block for a class of individuals. Insurers who offer the option of level rates also offer the alternative of "attained age" rates. This latter method is a pay-as-you-go calculation, which "steps up" as the insured crosses certain age bands.

While every effort is made to strike conservative pricing assumptions, the fact remains that LTC insurance is still a relatively young product in the market and companies do not have lengthy historical claims experience on which to base their rates. Offering coverage as guaranteed renewable insurance provides insurers with a safeguard.

In order to give the public some peace of mind regarding the stability of rates, insurers have used various methods of providing the insured with a limited guarantee. For example, some have guaranteed that during the first five years, the rate will not be changed. Some older policies contain a provision stating that, should a rate increase become necessary, it will not exceed a percentage maximum overall, such as 50% above the original base premium. Few, if any, new policies today provide this valuable guarantee; however, some do promise that rates will not be increased after a period of time, such as 20 years, or after age 75. These features provide the insured with some protection against escalating prices at the time that they may be most likely to need the protection.

Waiver of Premium

The waiver of premium benefit is a standard provision that does not require an additional cost. The normal period stipulated in most policies is 90 days, but contracts may differ regarding whether the insured must be continuously confined during this period or whether the individual must have simply received a covered treatment for a continuous period of 90 days. This may impact whether benefits will be received during a period of home care treatment.

Some contracts provide that the premium will be waived as it falls due. In this case, an annual premium would only be waived if it fell due during the period of confinement. Some contracts provide that if the premium is not currently being paid monthly, the frequency will be changed to monthly and waived for as long as the insured continues to receive benefits. This relieves the company of having to pay the full annual premium for a coverage period lasting less than a year.

As with other forms of insurance, the premiums paid during the 90-day waiting period are reimbursed upon qualifying for a waiver, but they initially must be paid throughout, as coverage will otherwise lapse for non-payment.

Grace Period and Extensions

All LTC policies contain a 30-day grace period for the payment of premiums after the due date. Some even provide guarantees that go beyond this. For instance, one company offers, at its discretion, to extend the grace period for up to six months upon submission of satisfactory evidence that a cognitive impairment or a mental-nervous disorder has contributed to the unintentional oversight of paying the premium. This is a valuable provision.

Some companies provide a special reinstatement offer that waives medical evidence and restores lapsed protection if the outstanding premium is received within a specified time following lapse, such as 10 or 14 days.

Finally, some companies allow the insured to name an alternate contact for notification in the event a premium remains outstanding following its due date. This helps to guard against unintentional lapsing of coverage. The onus is on the insured, however, to keep the insurance company's records updated regarding changes in this contact information.

Non-Forfeiture Provisions

While LTC policies are purchased as long-term coverage, insurers recognize that not everyone will continue coverage in force. This lapse assumption is a critical part of how insurers develop prices for premiums. Some take the approach that the premiums paid from policies lapsed belong to the insurance company, and rates are set with this assumption in mind. Others may take the approach that the premiums paid by a particular individual should belong in part to that person if the coverage is later cancelled or lapses. Non-forfeiture provisions provide a method for dealing with the cash build-up that occurs in the policy and for returning it to the insured at a later date. Two methods are used: reduced paid-up insurance and extended term insurance.

The reduced paid-up insurance method provides the insured with a paid-up benefit for a smaller amount, the size of which depends upon how long premiums have been paid at the time of discontinuance. The policy contains a scale of values. Insurers who utilize this method believe that it is better to have some coverage than none at all.

The extended term insurance method provides the insured with continuing benefits for the same amount for as long as the cash build-up will allow, based on the cost of pure term insurance. The policy contains a scale of values. Insurers who utilize this method believe that it is better to have the right amount of coverage for as long as it will last than to have a policy too small to be of any value.

Not all insurers offer non-forfeiture provisions in their LTC policy, and those that do provide a valuable feature to the insured.

Indexing Benefits While on Claim

Some policies provide for benefits to increase once the insured has been on claim for 12 months. This helps to deal with rising costs due to inflation. Some insurers build this feature into their plans with the cost already factored in the base premium, while others offer it as an optional benefit coupled with "pre-claim indexing". It is important to determine what will happen to the benefit level once the benefit ends in a temporary claim. Can the insured "buy up" the additional coverage, or will the amount revert to the original benefit amount?

OPTIONAL BENEFITS

Optional riders are benefits made available at an additional cost. While there is not a wide range of optional riders for LTC policies, the three most popular options are shown below.

Return of Premium at Death

This option provides for a return of a portion of the premium if the insured dies while the plan is in force. The benefit is graded upward based on how long the premiums have been paid. For example, it may return 10% (or as much as 50%) of premiums once 10 years of premiums have been paid, but 100% if premiums have been paid for 20 or more years at the time of death. Some versions may require that no claims have been made, while others may simply deduct claims paid from the premium refund due. The schedule of entitlement is contained in the policy listing the refund due for various durations of premium payment. The cost of this rider can range from 25% to as high as 60% more than the regular cost of the coverage.

Inflation Protection Benefit

The erosive effects of inflation can diminish the value of coverage over time. The inflation protection benefit helps to guard against this. For an additional premium, the individual can have the daily and maximum benefit limits increase at a fixed annual rate, such as 2% or 3%. Generally, there is no corresponding increase in the annual premium related to this increased coverage, as it has been factored into the cost of the rider. This form of predisability adjustment helps maintain the purchase power of the benefit.

Future Purchase Option

This offers another method of increasing coverage during the life of the policy prior to a claim. The insured has the right to purchase additional coverage at specified option dates in the future without providing evidence of continued good health. For example, the period options may occur in three-year intervals up to a specified age, such as age 80. The amount that can be purchased is limited to a "per option" amount, such as 2% or 3%, or it may be calculated based on the Consumer Price Index, up to a stipulated maximum. There will also be an overall maximum beyond which coverage cannot increase. The increased coverage requires an increase in premium related to the new benefit amount and is based on the insured's attained age. The benefit must be applied for, as the adjustment in coverage is not automatic. The insured may lose the right to future increases by "passing up" the right on two consecutive option dates. This helps to protect the insurer against anti-selection.

UNDERWRITING

The Application

In many respects, the application form for LTC insurance is similar to the application forms for other types of coverage. It gathers personal information, as well as details concerning the insured's health and the coverage applied for. Thorough and accurate completion is important to ensure that the insured will not be denied benefits because of a misrepresentation. In addition to the application, the process also involves paramedicals and attending physician statements.

Applicants for LTC insurance will most likely rely on their informal caregiver to handle their claim when the time comes, and the caregiver, in arranging for the insured's care, will use the policy proceeds. For this reason, whenever possible, it is wise to include the person who is likely to be the informal caregiver in the interviews and the application process. This is often an adult son or daughter, or the son or daughter's spouse. The same person may also be granted power of attorney for personal care to act on the insured's behalf.

Most insurers ask for the name of the individual who has power of attorney for personal care on the application form. Insurers are interested to know that there is someone who can act on the individual's behalf if the insured cannot act on his or her own behalf at a later date.

In-depth financial information is not required for LTC insurance, as it is for disability insurance, because income is not being insured. However, it is nevertheless important to ensure that the client has the financial ability to maintain the coverage over many years. A few companies have established maximum policy amounts using earnings of the person being insured and may, for this reason, ask for related details on the application.

Adviser's Cover Letter

Providing a cover letter can help the underwriter get a complete picture of the applicant, particularly his or her abilities and limitations today. Great emphasis is placed on the individual's current activity level, mental acumen, and general lifestyle. In this respect, the adviser's letter should include detailed information about the insured in the following areas:

- **Physical Activity Level of the Insured.** Comment on whether the person participates in activities such as daily walks, gardening, and sports, such as golf or tennis. Build the visual image for the underwriter of the person's mobility skills.
- **Community Activities Involvement.** Comment on how involved the person is in community activities. For example, does the person belong to a social centre, play cards, or provide volunteer assistance to others or organizations? Build the visual image of a mentally healthy lifestyle.
- **Current Caregiver Responsibilities.** Comment on whether the person is providing help to someone else, such as a spouse. Describe his or her role, how much time is involved, and the relationship to the individual being cared for. There may be stresses in the person's life, and it is important to outline how the person is coping with them.
- **Travel and Vacations.** Comment on the frequency that the person travels, the mode, the distance, and the length of stay. The underwriter is interested to know how active and mobile the person is.
- **Hobbies.** Comment on any hobbies the person participates in regularly, how often the person performs them, and what is involved. These not only help to show the activity level of the person, but may also give some insight into the person's mental acuity.
- **Mastering New Tasks.** Comment on the person's undertakings with new tasks that give insight into his or her mental ability. For example, perhaps the person routinely uses a computer, learns new software programs, takes music lessons, or gives lectures.

- **Other Activities.** Comment on any other activities the person performs routinely that involve planning, organizing, or abstract thinking.
- **Physical Limitations.** Comment on any physical limitations the person may already have and any aids that the person may use, such as a single- or multi-pronged cane. Comment on whether any such aids are related to a temporary condition, such as an accident or illness. Indicate whether the person has fallen without the aid and whether it is used in the home as well as outside the home. The use of a single-prong cane outside the home does not necessarily mean that the person is uninsurable, but requiring a multi-pronged cane is usually considered an uninsurable risk.
- **Support Network.** Comment on the person's support network. Does the person live alone or with a spouse? Are there adult children in town? Describe the spouse's state of health. The support network is a major underwriting factor and affects a person's ability to remain living in the home with the assistance of a caregiver.
- **Disposition and Outlook.** Comment on the person's overall disposition and outlook. A person who goes through life "seeing the glass half-empty" tends to have more health issues and less ability to cope.
- **Year-over-Year Changes.** Comment on the person's abilities and overall health this year relative to the previous year. Are there things that the person could do last year but can now no longer do? Paint a picture of the stability of his or her abilities.

Pre-Screening the Applicant

Most insurers provide pre-screening tools to help advisers with field underwriting. This helps to prevent putting someone through the process of applying for coverage only to be turned down, when there was a clear indication up front that the person would not meet submission criteria. For instance, a person who clearly has problems dressing or walking without assistance is not an insurable risk for LTC insurance. The key indicators of an uninsurable risk are:

- Current inability to independently perform an activity of daily living (eating, dressing, walking, transferring, toileting, continence)
- Exhibiting signs of memory loss, confusion, disorientation, or unusual inhibition.

Lifestyle Interview

A lifestyle interview is usually conducted as part of the underwriting process and may involve either a telephone call or a face-to-face interview with the applicant. This interview is a key source for the underwriter to evaluate mental acuity through a series of questions designed to evaluate the person's cognitive thinking abilities. The interviewer also probes to evaluate whether there are currently any deficits with the individual's ability to perform instrumental activities (grocery shopping, meal preparation, homemaking tasks, etc.) and ADLs.

The decision regarding whether the lifestyle interview will be conducted by telephone or in person is based on the amount of coverage applied for and the age of the insured. In some cases, the underwriter may request a person-to-person lifestyle interview for other reasons. During a face-to-face meeting, the interviewer will also be observing the environment the insured lives in and the person's gait and general appearance. An abnormal gait may be visible, such as a tendency to take small, slow steps, swaying, shuffling, or hesitation in walking. These may be indicators of an underlying condition, such as Parkinson's disease, stroke, or another neurological disease. Non-neurological conditions, such as arthritis, heart disease, or breathing problems, can also cause a noticeably unusual gait.

Underwriting Factors

Family history plays a significant role in the underwriting process, as some illnesses are passed on from one generation to the next. Other areas that are significant include cognitive testing and the infrastructure and support network that the applicant has available.

The main underwriting factors include the following:

- Age
- Gender
- Smoking habits
- Medical history
- Physical build
- Physical condition
- Mental acuity
- Home environment
- Current abilities with ADLs
- Current abilities with IADLs.

Even when insurers do not have separate rates for smokers and non-smokers, the underwriter is interested in knowing the smoking habits of the applicant, as this may impact other conditions, such as asthma.

Although LTC insurance relates to a person's health, the underwriting is different in many ways from the underwriting for disability insurance. While there are many conditions that would render the applicant uninsurable for LTC, there are some that are insurable and worth pursuing, at least in the form of an informal inquiry. The underwriter looks for indications of full recovery from a previous condition, a satisfactory passage of time since recovery, and other positive factors, such as a strong family network, good cognitive skills, and a healthy lifestyle overall.

Underwriting LTC insurance is unique for many reasons. For instance, older adults often have co-morbid conditions (i.e., secondary conditions that affect the primary condition). Some conditions that occur independent of others may be of little concern, but when they occur in combination with another, there is an increase in morbidity. Older adults have a higher rate of chronic conditions that often lead to eventual physical dependence. There is an increased incidence of conditions that affect cognition, such as Alzheimer's. Some seniors are physiologically older than their chronological age. This can be thought of as the visual effects of wear and tear on the body, which may be caused by a sedentary lifestyle, poor nutritional habits, chronic illness, or surgery. There is a tendency for women to get osteoporosis, and decreased bone mass places them at higher risk of fractures and institutionalization. Many older adults take multiple medications and have more than one doctor (such as when several specialists are treating various conditions). Social connection has a positive impact on the independence of older adults, so it, too, is significant in this aspect of underwriting LTC insurance. Weight changes place older adults at increased risk. For instance, obesity can create complications, such as excess wear and tear on joints, leading to the need for hip or knee replacement surgery. There is also an increased risk of type 2 diabetes, heart disease, obstructive sleep apnea, arthritis, and some forms of cancer. Being underweight can be just as dangerous, as frailty often occurs in older adults and places them at increased risk of institutionalization.

Adjusting for Increases in Risk

Some applicants are insurable but have a condition that increases their likelihood to claim. In such a case, the policy may be offered with the following adjustments:

- Increase in premium ("rated policy")
- Exclusion for the condition ("exclusion")
- Reduction in the amount applied ("benefit reduction")
- Altered plan design.

An altered plan design may involve a change in the elimination period offered or the maximum benefit period. Most companies do not offer policies with an exclusion, because it creates a situation where the insured has paid premiums for many years and may not be able to claim. It also ineffectively deals with secondary conditions, so the insurer is not adequately protected either.

Some applicants will be found uninsurable on any basis. The rate of decline for LTC insurance is lower than that of other insurance products, such as disability insurance. This is due, in part, to the pre-screening role of the financial adviser and the tools that insurers provide for this purpose.

GETTING STARTED

People ranging in age from 30 to 80 can purchase LTC insurance, but buyers tend to range in age from 60 to 65. Perhaps this is a reflection of the target market chosen by advisers; more likely, it reflects people's ability to identify with the need to plan today for coverage not likely to be used for another 20 or 30 years. Advisers can help to change this by educating their 40- and 50-year-old clients about the importance of planning during the working years for health care in the senior years. Some plans provide the option for coverage to be fully paid up in 20 years, so that when the person retires, coverage can be "sitting on the shelf", waiting for the day it is needed.

People are candidates for LTC insurance if they have assets to protect, can afford the premiums, are not suffering from an uninsurable condition, and want to retain control in the future over their health care. Long-term care insurance can provide freedom in choice, flexibility in care options, and dignity to the insured in his or her final years.

People should begin by educating themselves on the costs of care in their area and what the government provides today. Keep in mind that the cost of care will go up not just due to inflation; rather, technology will change the way illness is treated in the future in ways we cannot imagine today. The government will not cover everything.

Remember that healthy clients have the greatest need. The healthy mature client who stays physically active will live through the heart attack or stroke that the unhealthy client will not survive.

Boomer Reality

Our population is aging, and people are living longer lives. Families no longer live close together, and adult children often live at a distance. Divorce rates have risen, and many people, particularly women, will face their senior years living on their own. Every day, 600 people turn age 65. Current estimates indicate that almost 50% of people over age 65 will need some kind of home care at some point.

In 1966, there were seven workers in the workforce for every retiree, but by 2015, this ratio will drop to three workers per retiree. This affects social programs, because they are funded on a pay-as-you-go basis, with current workers funding benefits for current retirees. But the cost of health care is increasing due to many factors beyond the aging of the population. For instance, the cost of drugs is rising, there are advancements in technology, and the health-seeking behaviour of people is also changing. Baby boomers are expected to demand a higher level of wellness. To this end, they will seek more therapies, surgeries, and treatments, and this will further contribute to a higher demand on the health care system.

Many changes are taking place in the structure of our health care system, and more change is yet to come. This change has resulted in care being downloaded from hospitals to nursing homes and home care agencies.

Better surgical techniques, such as lasers, cut down recovery times, because smaller incisions heal faster so less time is being spent in the hospital. Care is being pushed out into the community, with more and more emphasis on aging at home. Despite the fact that people are living longer lives, they are doing so with chronic conditions that were once the chief causes of death. In this respect, we have traded death for living with chronic illness. The annual health care cost for treating chronic disease is $39 billion nationally.

Another area of concern is the rate of increase expected in the number of people who will be diagnosed with Alzheimer's disease. Currently, there are roughly 316,000 people in Canada living with Alzheimer's, but this will increase to 750,000 people by 2031.

There are frequently stories in the media about the state of nursing homes and lack of adequate home care. This situation exists today, so concerns are not just restricted to the future and whether down the road there might be a problem fulfilling the health care needs of the aging public. The evidence confirming the need for personal planning is already visible.

People have three options in dealing with this challenge:

- Continue to rely on the government as provider
- Rely on personal savings
- Turn to private programs, such as LTC insurance.

The concept of using "discount dollars" has always been a key rationale favouring the use of insurance over personal assets. Even people who have savings today may find that their dollars quickly diminish with the cost of care. Selling the home is not a viable option if one spouse continues to live there while the other is in need of long-term care. The reality is that it could take a lifetime to save, without a guarantee that time will be on your side.

Planning for health care in the senior years is an important part of retirement planning. Long-term care insurance offers a solution that meets this need. It is not intended to replace other forms of care, but to build upon it by providing informal caregivers, such as the spouse and adult children, with valuable resources to bring in the right kind of support at the right time, whether the setting is in the home or in a care centre. It lessens the stress the family feels over whether the government is going to approve the much-needed care services and, if so, for how long. Despite the social safety net that exists, there are still substantial out-of-pocket costs associated with a serious illness.

As the saying goes, when people fail to plan in advance of changing health, they plan to fail. Their choices in the moment of need become very limited. Planning in advance includes gathering information, evaluating options, and putting a strategy in place, such as LTC insurance, as a funding mechanism.

Chapter 20

Putting It All Together

The following case studies illustrate some considerations regarding disability income and health benefits planning. They show various product solutions that may be incorporated into a client's personal security plan.

CASE STUDY 1

Employee, No Benefits, Single

Personal Profile

Our client is Joe Werner, a single, 32-year-old sales manager and a non-smoker. Joe's province of residence is Ontario, but he travels extensively to British Columbia, Manitoba, and Nova Scotia, where the company has principal clients. He has been working for ACE Incorporated for a full year now, and he is paid a salary of $110,000. As of next year, he will be entitled to a sales bonus of up to $10,000 based on the prior year's results. The company provides him with a car, and he owns a condo in Toronto.

Health Status

Joe's health is good. He does not take prescription medication routinely, nor has he taken any in the past five years. He does not have a chronic condition. He has no personal history of illness or accident, but he does mention that his father had a heart attack at the age of 52 and a second one at the age of 57. This is a concern to Joe for his own future, as he has heard that heart problems run in his father's family, although he has no symptoms himself at this time. His mother is alive and well, and his parents live in Prince Edward Island.

Existing Benefits

Joe's status with ACE is "employee", and he confirms that he has EI and WC. The company he works for is a small, privately owned family business, and in lieu of group benefits, each manager is given $1,500 for a health spending account (HSA). Joe gets three weeks of vacation annually. Each year, he spends one week at his friend's condo in Jamaica, and every other year, he also spends two weeks in July sailing off the coast of Florida.

Existing Financial Status

Joe's mortgage payment for his condo, including interest and taxes, is $1,200. He currently has just over $30,000 saved, which he has invested in GICs. He is contributing $300 per month to an RRSP, which is deducted automatically from his bank each month. He does not believe in debt, so he pays his credit cards off each month, a total of about $800. His average monthly spending on food, entertainment, and other necessities is $1,000 per month. He sets aside $290 a month for vacations.

Analysis of Situation

Joe's net monthly income is about $4,583 per month. His monthly expenses total $3,590. This leaves $993 of disposable income, of which Joe indicates he is comfortable committing up to $400 per month to insurance (about 4% of his gross income).

His areas of need include a benefit plan, disability income coverage, mortgage protection, travel insurance, and critical illness insurance. As he lives alone, he should also consider long-term care insurance. Given that his mother is the primary caregiver for his father, Joe prefers not to be in a position where he might be a burden to her if he was ever in a severe car accident or incurred a catastrophic illness. Some consideration should also be given to Joe's mother. Joe's father has serious health problems and will likely predecease his mother. After Joe's father passes on, his mother wants to remain living in PEI. The cost of facility care is based on income and assets, and given her current financial circumstances, she would be required to pay the maximum for personal care. She is currently in good health and can qualify for long-term care insurance; however, she is not the focus of today's planning session with Joe.

His employer provides $1,500 in the form of an HSA, which will assist with costs related to benefits and travel insurance. He will have to personally cover any shortfall (if there is one), plus he must fund his coverage for the remaining benefits with after-tax dollars.

As he has a family history that will impact the underwriting of critical illness insurance with most insurers, he will need an insurer who underwrites critical illness insurance without regard to family history. This will mean using a guaranteed issue plan, which will have a lower maximum benefit and will limit a claim related to a pre-existing condition if it occurs in the first 24 months (the amount paid will be a return of premiums). However, the lump sum, even though it is relatively small (about $25,000), will help to deal with immediate adjustment expenses upon diagnosis. As Joe presently has no signs of illness, the 24-month limitation is of lesser concern. Because the coverage amount is limited, Joe also needs long-term care insurance to deal with the care needs that may result from a critical illness.

Joe has not indicated for how long his business trips take him out of the province. Upon further investigation, it is determined that each business trip lasts less than a week. Therefore, his need for travel insurance annually is for covering trips of up to one week, and every other year, his need for travel insurance is for one trip of up to two weeks, plus unlimited additional trips of up to one week. Although his business travel does not take him outside the country, he does travel outside the province, and this means exposure to non-health-related expenses, such as the return of his vehicle and the possible need to fly a companion to be at his bedside in the event of a severe medical condition.

He has expressed concern with catastrophic illness, and his benefits coverage should concentrate on protecting against unexpected catastrophic expenses. His dental expenses are predictable and he can use his HSA to cover these as incurred; therefore, the insurance should de-emphasize dental. As most benefit plans also include life insurance, and given that this cannot be run through the HSA without adverse tax consequences, he is better off to look at buying life insurance with after-tax dollars. A term survey can be conducted to find the best cost for long-term coverage.

Joe has demonstrated that he is disciplined with budgeting. He has EI benefits that he can collect during the initial period of disability; however, they will not protect him in the event of a partial disability. His ability to systematically save could mean that Joe is a good candidate for self-insuring an initial period of disability (by setting up a reserve for this purpose), and by utilizing a longer elimination period on his disability insurance (DI) coverage, he can include a cost-of-living rider to maintain the focus of his plan on the long term, rather than on the short term. As Joe expects to have a substantial increase in his earnings in the near future, he should also include a future purchase option on his DI plan. While he cannot include the future bonus in his insurable earnings today, once he has established a three-year predictable pattern, he will be able to adjust his coverage by exercising the future purchase option.

Joe should also look at mortgage DI to cover his mortgage payment. This will ease any cash flow challenges during a disability, as proceeds from the income policy can be used to meet other living costs.

Joe's RRSP contributions will cease if he becomes disabled. He can continue to save for retirement by including a retirement savings rider on his DI policy.

Legal considerations that should also be addressed include implementing a power of attorney for property and a power of attorney for personal care. A similar review should take place for Joe's parents, so that Joe will have legal authority to assist his parents.

Coverage Recommendation

COVERAGE #1

The Benefit Plan

Coverage Objective:	To provide protection against catastrophic loss, particularly related to the cost of drugs and nursing care.
Premium Allocation:	$64.80 per month.
Plan Structure:	Premiums are paid through the HSA and are not a taxable benefit to the client.
Benefits Provided:	Prescription Drugs 85% of the cost of drugs (generic) to $4,000, then a deductible of $400 must be paid, after which his catastrophic drug plan will pay 100%. Unlimited maximum. Extended Health Care Home care and nursing, prosthetic appliances, and medical equipment (e.g., wheelchair) covered 100% up to $35,000 per year (lifetime maximum of $100,000). Paramedical specialists up to $750 combined per year. Ambulance, accidental dental ($3,000), hearing aids ($500), vision care ($100/2 years). Travel $5 million, maximum seven days.
Notes:	Joe has chosen not to include semi-private or private hospitalization as a means of keeping the cost of the benefit plan down. His government health plan will provide basic hospital accommodation, and Joe acknowledges that given the limited number of beds in hospitals today, the reality is that he must take any room that is available, which could mean paying premiums for benefits that he might not be able to receive. This saves Joe about $10 per month. He will submit a receipt for premiums on his benefit plan to his HSA plan administrator for reimbursement. This leaves $722 in his HSA for other qualified medical expenses, such as dental care, travel insurance premiums, or drugs not covered by his medical plan.

COVERAGE #2

Travel Insurance

Coverage Objective:	To provide protection during trips outside the province or country.
Notes:	Joe's basic plan covers trips of up to seven days. He has checked with his provider, and the pre-existing condition limitation is nine months. The coverage is part of a bundled benefit plan and cannot be deleted. However, Joe decides to purchase a separate annual travel plan with more comprehensive provisions. He will supplement it with top-up insurance every other year when he takes his two-week vacation.
Premium Allocation:	$42 per year. $16 every other year for top-up insurance.
Plan Structure:	Annual plan covering an unlimited number of trips of up to eight days. Top-up single-trip coverage every other year for an additional seven days. A receipt for premiums will be remitted to his HSA plan administrator.
Benefits Provided:	$5 million emergency medical protection.

COVERAGE #3

The Disability Income Plan

Coverage Objective:	To provide income during a disability. The focus of coverage is on the long term. The plan must provide the right to purchase additional coverage without medical evidence as earnings rise. The plan must also provide inflation protection during a disability. Finally, the plan must protect retirement savings contributions during a disability. Joe plans to establish an emergency reserve of $10,000, sufficient to cover three months of fixed expenses.
Notes:	Joe's income for the current year is $110,000, and in the prior two years he made $100,000 and $90,000. He does not yet have tax forms for the current year, as he is just finishing his 12th month. While he will be entitled to a bonus starting next year, it cannot be included as insurable earnings this year. After a preliminary inquiry, the insurer agrees to base insurance upon $105,000, giving consideration to a letter from his employer confirming this year's income and the fact that he will be entitled to the bonus next year (so his income will continue to show a pattern of increase), and subject to his prior year's tax form, confirming $100,000 earnings. While Joe has been with his existing employer for only one year, his prior work was in the same field. A preliminary inquiry has also confirmed that the insurer will consider Joe as a Class 3A.
Premium Allocation:	$198.25 per month.
Plan Structure:	Personally owned and personally paid for. Premiums are not deductible, and benefits are tax-free during a claim.
Benefits Provided:	Disability Income Commencing on the 90th day, $3,700 per month to age 65; plus Commencing on the 120th day, $1,150 per month to age 65. Benefits payable for total and reduced disability.

Additional Benefits

Future insurance option of $1,000 per option, overall maximum of $5,150.

Cost-of-living option — compound indexing tied to CPI up to an annual maximum of 10%.

Retirement protector option — commencing on the 90th day of disability, $1,500 per month to age 65 deposited to a locked-in trust account.

COVERAGE #4

The Mortgage Disability Plan

Coverage Objective:	To cover the mortgage payments in the event of disability.
Premium Allocation:	$30 per month.
Plan Structure:	The benefit amount is $1,200 per month. Premiums are paid with personal dollars and are not deductible for income tax. Benefits during a claim are tax-free. The proceeds during a claim will be paid to the loan institution by the insurance company. This method is more cost effective than individual DI by about $20 per month and offers a stand-alone policy. Benefits will be paid after 90 days, retroactive to the 30th day of total disability. Benefits are payable up to age 65 if required.

COVERAGE #5

The Critical Illness Benefit

Coverage Objective:	To provide a lump-sum benefit that will assist with adjustment expenses related to a critical illness.
Premium Allocation:	$20.60 per month.
Plan Structure:	Premiums are paid personally with after-tax dollars and benefits are tax-free during a claim.
Notes:	As this is a guaranteed issue plan, it contains a 24-month pre-existing condition limitation. If a claim arises during this period, it provides for a return of premiums. Due to family history, Joe does not qualify for medically underwritten critical illness insurance. This coverage is supplemented with Joe's extended health care benefits, which provide up to $35,000 for nursing and durable medical equipment such as wheelchairs, as well as long-term care insurance to cover expenses associated with the cost of care.
Benefits Provided:	$25,000. Conditions covered Cancer, heart attack, coronary artery bypass, stroke, blindness, major burns, major organ failure requiring transplant, multiple sclerosis, coma, kidney failure, benign brain tumour, paraplegia, quadriplegia, hemiplegia, dismemberment, loss of speech, Lou Gehrig's disease, deafness.

COVERAGE #6

Long-Term Care Insurance

Coverage Objective:	To provide funds to cover the cost of care if Joe is unable to perform activities of daily living related to caring for himself. To cover Joe for both home care and facility care.
Premium Allocation:	$163.85 per month.
Plan Structure:	Premiums are paid with after-tax dollars, and benefits during a claim are tax-free. Joe's plan will be fully paid up in 20 years, and no further premiums will be due.
Benefits Provided:	Home care and facility care $250 per day after 90 days, payable for life. Benefits are indexed during a claim by an amount equal to the CPI index up to 4%, based on the original amount.

Summary of Coverage

The total monthly cost of Joe's plan is as follows:

Disability Income:	$193.91
Disability Mortgage Plan:	$ 30.00
Critical Illness:	$ 20.60
Long-Term Care:	$163.85
Total:	$408.36

Plus premiums submitted through his HSA:

Benefits Plan:	$ 64.80

Travel Insurance: $42 (annual) plus $16 (annual) every other year.

Joe's adviser will conduct a review of his coverage in a year to adjust the amount of disability income. His adviser has also urged him to meet with his lawyer for completing a power of attorney for property and a power of attorney for personal care.

CASE STUDY 2

Small Private Canadian Company

Corporate Profile

Our client, ZEUS Inc., is an advertising firm consisting of three unrelated shareholder-employees, a silent partner, two non-shareholder executives, and five full-time employees. The current shareholders have owned the business for three years, but the company had been established five years earlier by the silent partner, who retained 10% of the shares. Each of the active shareholders owns 30% of the business. The two executives and five staff have been with the business since its inception.

The three active shareholders own the office building, which has a monthly mortgage payment of $30,000 through the bank. A holding company has been set up in the name of the three active shareholders for this purpose.

Personal Profiles

The Shareholders

George Duffrey, MBA, is 52 years old and married, and he has one son still in university. His salary from the business is $110,000. His portion of net profits from the business is $250,000. He is president of the company, and he is responsible for overall operations. He is in good health and does not smoke. Prior to purchasing shares in ZEUS, George was an advertising executive for Aardvark Advertising, one of ZEUS's competitors. George's personal net worth is $3.2 million, and he has annual unearned income of $12,500.

Emma Rigby, CA, is 42 years old and divorced, with one daughter (age 11) and one son (age 9). Her salary is also $110,000. Her portion of net profits from the business is $250,000. She is chief financial officer, and she is responsible for all financial aspects of the business. She is in good health and does not smoke. Prior to purchasing shares in ZEUS, she worked with George as Aardvark's finance director. It was Emma who heard about the opportunity at ZEUS and approached George to go into business with her. Emma's personal net worth is $2.2 million, and she has annual unearned income of $6,200.

Normand Francois, B.Sc., is 41 years old and married, with twin eight-year-old sons. His salary from the business is $110,000. His portion of net profits from the business is $250,000. He is vice-president, marketing and sales. Prior to purchasing shares in ZEUS, Normand headed the marketing division of a large pharmaceutical firm. George knew Normand for several years through a sports and fitness centre they both belong to, and George recruited Normand for his knowledge and connections in the pharmaceutical industry. George realizes that with the increasing number of seniors and the growing rate of chronic illness, the pharmaceutical industry will grow significantly, and he and Normand want to position the firm to capture the advertising dollars of this growth industry. Normand's personal net worth is $2.8 million and he has annual unearned income of $10,400.

Anthony Bennett is 72 years old, and he is married with no children. He is the founder of ZEUS, but he suffered a heart attack three years ago, which led to his decision to sell the business. Anthony and Emma are neighbours and have crossed paths many times at industry events. With no family members to pass the business along to, Anthony thought of Emma as a candidate for buying the business when he decided to retire. Anthony retained 10% of the shares as a silent partner and acts informally as a mentor to George, Emma, and Normand whenever they have questions or simply want a sounding board. Other than that, Anthony is not active in the operations.

The Executives

Rhonda Jacks is 32 years old, single, and a non-smoker. She has been with the business since its inception. Rhonda is known for her edgy, creative style, and her originality in advertising has attracted many high-end accounts to the firm. Rhonda is paid $90,000 in salary, plus a substantial bonus based on fees generated from accounts that she handles. Her total earnings have averaged $180,000 for each of the last three years. Rhonda's personal net worth is $720,000, and she has annual unearned income of $3,500.

Dan Silverman is 38 years old, married, and a non-smoker. He was the first person hired by Anthony and has been a loyal employee. He has worked his way up through the organization to become an account executive with ZEUS. He is now in his fifth year. Dan's parents live in the Middle East, and he flies back to visit each year. Dan is paid $70,000 in salary, plus a bonus based on fees generated from accounts that he handles. His total earnings have averaged $85,000 for each of the last three years. Dan's personal net worth is $450,000, and he has annual unearned income of $2,400.

Health Status

None of the above people have any known health issues, except for Anthony, who suffered a heart attack three years ago. However, he is not active in the business, so this is of no consequence.

Existing Coverage

The business has an established group plan, which includes an HSA and long-term disability for everyone (except the silent partner). The shareholders have stated no product changes are required at this time, rates are stable, and the existing insurer is providing excellent service.

All employees' salaries are fully covered under the LTD plan. The LTD plan provides 60% of earnings to a maximum of $5,000, non-taxable, with an 85% all-source maximum and primary offsets only. The plan uses a two-year "own-occupation and not working" definition of disability. The LTD plan does not provide partial benefits if the employee is able to work part-time. A corporate-owned wage loss replacement plan has been set up to top up the coverage for the three shareholder-employees and Rhonda (Dan is fully covered under the limits of the group LTD plan).

Issues

1. There is a buy-sell agreement in place covering death of one of the partners, but no provision has been made for permanent disability. This area needs to be addressed.
2. There is a substantial business loan outstanding. If one of the active shareholders became disabled, the ongoing payments would put a strain on the business. This area needs to be addressed.
3. Rhonda Jacks is considered to be a key person whose absence from the business would severely impact the company financially. This potential for financial loss to the business needs to be addressed, as well as a review of others who may be considered key, and whose sudden and lengthy absence would cause a financial impact to ZEUS.
4. Although a wage loss replacement plan has been established, it only addresses the gap in the amount of coverage, not the need for residual benefits if the employee is able to work part-time. This area should be addressed. A discussion should also take place regarding the definition of disability.
5. Dan Silverman has family in the Middle East, and his group LTD plan contains a travel exclusion for disability that occurs outside North America. If he has a disability while visiting back home, he will have no disability benefits. This area needs to be addressed.

Analysis and Solutions

Buy-Sell Funding

Analysis of Situation

If Anthony were to suffer a further disability, it would be of no consequence to the operation of the business as he is not active in it. He is, therefore, not a party to the disability buy-out agreement.

A cross-purchase arrangement would be advantageous if the business partners planned to sell the business following the buy-out of a disabled partner's share. In this instance, the remaining partners would be able to adjust (increase) the cost base in the business when computing their income taxes and, therefore, pay a smaller capital gains tax on the difference between their investment and the final selling price.

Our clients, however, have discussed this scenario and are confident the remaining two would continue the business if this were to happen. There is also the issue of a significant age difference between the two younger shareholders and the oldest shareholder (10 and 11 years, respectively). A cross-purchase would require the younger shareholders to make a larger commitment in terms of insurance premiums.

They could take the money out of the business as compensation and then use it to pay the premiums. However, these funds would be taxable at the individual level. This tax disadvantage represents a near-term certainty, while the adjustment to the cost base upon acquiring the disabled partner's shares is a distant, less likely outcome (they have already indicated that they are unlikely to sell following a shareholder's disability). All three have children, and there is a possibility that their offspring may decide to enter the business in the future.

The advantage of a corporate share redemption is the equalization of premium costs to the individuals. From the healthy shareholders' point of view, it will be the company, using company resources, that buys out the disabled shareholder's share and thereby increases the remaining shareholders' ownership. Since the business is paying for the program, everyone will share the burden of the program equally.

Administratively, too, it is simpler because there will be a total of only three policies required (one per shareholder) instead of a total of six policies (two per shareholder).

The disadvantage of a corporate share redemption is that the remaining shareholders would not get an adjustment (increase) in the cost base, as would happen under a cross-purchase arrangement. This would mean a larger capital gains tax if the business is sold in the future by the remaining shareholders.

ZEUS has decided in favour of using the corporate share redemption method.

Product Solution

ZEUS is classified as a personal service business. Based on the insurer's method of valuation for advertising agencies for disability buy-sell insurance purposes, the company's insurable business value is $2.62 million. As each active shareholder owns 30% of the shares, the amount of buy-sell insurance required is $786,000 for each shareholder.

The shareholders have decided upon a 365-day trigger in the agreement and want a clean break thereafter. As such, a lump-sum payment method has been chosen.

The cost of the policies to be purchased is:

George:	$ 740
Emma:	$ 450
Normand:	$ 360
Total Monthly Premium:	$ 1,550

Business Loan Protection

Analysis of Situation

ZEUS decided to purchase the building it operates from and convert the second floor of the building into four units, which are rented to other businesses. The mortgage payments total $30,000 monthly. The shareholders agree that it is wise for ZEUS to insure each shareholder for his or her portion of this mortgage, using a business loan protection policy. To keep the cost down, they are comfortable with the idea of self-insuring the initial 60-day period.

Product Solution

Coverage will be purchased based on a $10,000 monthly benefit, commencing after 60 days of disability, payable for up to 24 months. The cost of the policies to be purchased is:

George:	$ 220
Emma:	$ 150
Normand:	$ 120
Total Monthly Premium:	$ 490

Key Person Protection

Analysis of Situation

George has worked in the industry the longest and has the best understanding of how to identify trends that affect their industry. His business acumen is unique, as demonstrated by his consistently successful track record of finding opportunities ahead of his competitors. This has resulted in ZEUS winning a prestigious industry award for three consecutive years since he took over the helm. The firm would suffer financially if George had an extended absence from the business.

Normand knows the pharmaceutical industry, has key contacts within it, and has proven his ability to tap the potential in this growth industry. As much as 40% of ZEUS's new sales in the last three years have been directly due to his work in this industry sector. The firm would suffer financially if Normand had an extended absence from the business.

Rhonda is the glue that has held the existing accounts together since the new owners took over the business from Anthony, the former owner. They expected that some accounts might be lost when Anthony was no longer directly involved, but they soon discovered that the true relationship was with Rhonda, their account executive. Rhonda's edgy style and unique creativity have also been instrumental in closing many new accounts since George, Normand, and Emma took over. They are considering promoting her next year to be a vice-president and, perhaps, giving her some shares, to lessen the possibility of losing her to a competitor.

Emma is very knowledgeable on financial matters and strong in administration. Despite this, the skills she brings to their business are not unique, and George, Normand, and Emma herself agree that if she were absent from the business for any period of time, someone could be brought in to handle financial matters. Emma's involvement in ZEUS was largely the result of being in the right place at the right time.

Dan, while very loyal, is not seen as a mover and shaker. He handles most of the smaller accounts for ZEUS. If he were absent from the business for an extended period of time, the partners agree that a suitable replacement could be found with minimal financial impact on the business.

It is agreed that ZEUS should protect itself from the financial impact that would occur due to a lengthy and sudden absence of George, Normand, or Rhonda by means of purchasing key person DI on each of them.

Product Solution

ZEUS will apply for key person policies, which will be owned by ZEUS. Benefits during a claim are payable to ZEUS on a tax-free basis. The premiums are not a tax-deductible expense. The coverage will commence on the 60th day of total disability and pay for up to 12 months. The policies will include a replacement expense benefit of four times salary, to cover the recruiting costs associated with finding a replacement.

Insured	Benefit Amount	Monthly Premium
George:	$9,000	$ 250
Normand:	$9,000	$ 130
Rhonda:	$7,500	$ 150
Total Monthly Premium:		$ 530

Wage-Loss Replacement Plan

Analysis of Situation

Although a wage loss replacement plan has been established, it only addresses the gap in the amount of coverage, not the need for residual benefits if an employee is only able to work part-time. During the first 24 months of total disability, benefits are payable under the group plan if the employee cannot work at his or her regular occupation, provided that he or she is not working at any other occupation. After 24 months, benefits continue only if the employee is unable to work at any gainful occupation and cannot be expected to do so within the next six months. A "gainful occupation" is defined in the contract to mean one that can be expected to generate earnings equal to or greater than the scheduled monthly benefit.

Although the shareholders felt that no changes were required to their group LTD plan, some options should be brought to their attention, so that they can decide whether they want to address certain limitations through changes to the LTD plan or by means of the wage loss replacement plan.

For instance, the "scheduled benefit" method of defining gainful income means that the owners and Rhonda would have their group benefits cease after being on claim for 24 months if they are deemed to be able to earn at least $5,000 per month in another occupation for which they are qualified. Using Rhonda as an example, this is only one-third of what she earns. If ZEUS changed the gainful definition to one based on 60% of prior earnings, the termination of benefits would not occur until she was deemed to be able to earn at least $9,000. The current definition is more beneficial to the lower-paid staff, whose benefits fall below the cap of $5,000. In effect, it discriminates against the higher-paid executives.

Another possibility is to divide the group into two classes — Class 1 being management and account executives, and Class 2 being all other employees. This would enable ZEUS to enhance the LTD plan without necessarily extending the same features to regular staff. The shareholders believe that the 24-month own-occupation period serves to discourage staff from malingering, and that if the individual is able to work elsewhere, he or she should be required to do so. Their philosophy for management and account executives is quite different. In this case, their objective is to use the benefit plan as one means of attracting and retaining top-notch people. ZEUS could amend the LTD definitions for Class 1 to include a longer own-occupation period, residual benefits when able to work part-time, and a more liberal gainful definition following the end of the own-occupation period.

The definition of income already goes beyond salary, and includes bonuses and profit sharing. But the cap of $5,000 could be raised to cover a higher limit of earnings. Some insurers may be willing to go as high as $8,000.

Another possibility is to continue to offer LTD for staff only (Class 2), and remove LTD benefits for Class 1 altogether, replacing it with a full wage loss replacement plan. This could cause problems, however, for existing staff. Eliminating the higher-income earners would lower the maximum LTD that can be offered in the plan. Also, if ZEUS decided to hire another account executive and this executive happened to have a small health condition, this would necessitate exclusions, ratings, or possibly even a decline under the medically underwritten wage loss replacement plan. The LTD plan offers the security of knowing that at least some level of LTD is available non-medically.

Currently, Dan is not included in the wage loss replacement plan. But if he were disabled, the benefit payable under his group LTD plan would be only $3,144, based on the following calculation:

The group LTD plan pays the lesser of:

(a) stipulated percentage of earnings: 60% ($85,000/12) less direct CPP of $1,106 = $3,144

(b) stated maximum benefit: $5,000 less direct CPP of $1,106 = $3,894

(c) all-source maximum: 85% ($85,000/12) less direct CPP of $1,106 = $4,915

After much discussion, the decision was made to leave the group LTD plan in place, without any changes made to it. The wage loss replacement plan will be changed from top-up coverage to a full second payer plan, and Dan will be added to it.

This will be done by means of additional personal policies, not replacement coverage. This will preserve the nature of the existing DI plans, which are currently free of second payer provisions, and recognize that the policies are now beyond the two-year incontestability period.

Product Solution

ZEUS will own and pay for the coverage, and benefits during a claim will go directly to the disabled insured. The premiums being paid by ZEUS will not be an add-back to the T4 earnings of the person being covered. A second payer amendment will be inserted by the insurer, whereby the group will be considered first payer. Consequently, if the group LTD plan does not pay a benefit (or ceases to pay a benefit following the expiry of the own-occupation period), the individual policy will pay benefits. The policies selected are non-cancellable residual policies containing an own-occupation (to age 65) rider. Benefits begin on the 90th day of disability and are payable to age 65. A cost-of-living option has been added. The insurer has provided a 10% reduction as a small group, plus a 5% reduction for inclusion of a second payer provision for a total discount of 15%.

ZEUS is happy with the more comprehensive nature of the plan and feels it will serve the company well.

The benefits have taken into consideration the existing wage loss replacement plans, and the rates for the new coverage are as follows:

Insured	Existing Coverage	New Benefit Amount	Premium on New Coverage
George:	$13,825	$5,000	$ 250
Emma:	$13,825	$5,000	$ 245
Normand:	$13,825	$5,000	$ 150
Rhonda:	$ 6,550	$5,000	$ 160
Dan:	0	$5,650	$ 200
Total Monthly Premium:			$ 1,005

Dan Silverman and the Travel Exclusion

Analysis of Situation

Dan Silverman has family in the Middle East, and his group LTD contains a travel exclusion for disability that occurs outside North America. If he has a disability while visiting back home, he will have no disability benefits. This situation has been brought to the attention of the shareholders, and after much discussion, it was agreed that since Dan is not required to travel on company business to the Middle East, this is not a business consideration. But it does present a risk from a personal planning viewpoint that should be brought to Dan's attention. Now that Dan will be included in the wage loss replacement plan, this may still be an issue, depending upon the nature of any travel exclusion that may be added to the individual disability plan.

Product Solution

Dan can purchase special risk disability coverage each time he travels to the Middle East, the cost of which will vary depending upon his circumstances at the time of purchase.

Summary of Coverage

The total monthly cost of ZEUS's new coverage is as follows:

Buy-Sell Funding:	$1,550
Business Loan Protection:	$ 490
Key Person Protection:	$ 530
Wage Loss Replacement Plan:	$1,005
Total:	$3,575

ZEUS's adviser will conduct a follow-up in six months to ensure that the disability buy-sell agreement has been put in place. At the annual review, ZEUS's adviser will inquire about whether plans have moved forward to appoint Rhonda as a vice-president and whether there has been a change in the share ownership. This is in addition to reviewing changes in earnings and business valuation, and inquiring whether any additional account executives have been brought into the company.

EPILOGUE

Three Decades of Change

In 2001, the Canadian life and health insurance industry consisted of roughly 117 firms, down from 168 in 1990. During the period between 1990 and 2001, the market share of Canadian-controlled companies increased from 69% to 72% of total premium income. Much of the industry consolidation has involved foreign insurers selling their operations to Canadian insurance companies.[1] Industry consolidation and the convergence of service offerings have led to the virtual disappearance of the "niche marketer" DI insurer and the evolution towards financial supermarkets. On the rise is a redefined adviser specialist with access to a fuller spectrum of product offerings, a development that has transformed the living benefits arena from simply offering disability insurance (DI) to offering a broader continuum of health insurance solutions, which now also includes critical illness insurance, long-term care insurance, health and dental insurance, and travel insurance.

How Did We Get to This Point?

During the 1980s, disability insurers focused on increasing their market share by introducing discounts that did not ultimately support their experience. This included practices such as limited time offers for target occupation groups and gender-blended rates. It was also a time when high replacement ratios were introduced, resulting in a significant increase in the average insured benefit per person. Narrowing the gap between earned income and disability benefits, coupled with increasing the average insured benefit per person, opened the door to potential abuse. The resulting financial trouble came to a head in the 1990s.

[1] Department of Finance, *Canada's Life and Health Insurers*, www.collectionscanada.gc.ca/webarchives/20071119214059/http://www.fin.gc.ca/toce/2001/health_e.html (accessed February 23, 2012).

During the 1990s, emerging sociological trends surpassed the downward turn in the economic cycle as the chief driver of claims. Mental and nervous disorders became a primary concern among disability insurers, who undertook major re-engineering efforts to transform claims processing departments into proactive benefits management centres.

By the mid-1990s, policy rescissions were on the rise, and disability insurers discovered that a predominant number of the rescissions that occurred at the time of claim resulted from misstatements of earnings at the time of underwriting. This discovery led insurers to require that applicants submit Canada Revenue Agency tax forms when applying for disability insurance (DI). Companies focused upon educating underwriters in the area of financial accounting, and more conservative practices were adopted in calculating the client's earned income, so as to avoid the trend towards overinsurance that had arisen during the previous decade.

What Lies Ahead?

The previous decades laid the groundwork for the products and services offered in the industry today and those that will emerge in the decades ahead. Insurers continue their paradigm shift to more appropriate ways of delivering meaningful solutions to a diverse and changing customer base. Job creation is no longer prevalent in the sectors that purchased disability insurance in the past. Instead, the growth is now in part-time workers, home-based workers, and contract workers. New illnesses will continue to affect the design of products, as well as the shift in the nature of the work performed. The products developed in the 1980s were designed to fit the era of high interest rates and low claims incidence. Disability insurance designed in the 1990s focused on rectifying the misalignment that resulted between product provisions and evolving economic and social conditions. The 21st-century industry recognizes Canada's changing demographics, such as increased immigration, aging of the population, and new work patterns. Insurers have looked through fresh eyes and found new ways to approach the DI risk. New forms of coverage have found their place alongside conventional products, enabling the adviser to respond to our changing society.

It is not just the design of products that is changing. Technology is vital to the future of the industry, and it will impact how companies do business in the decades ahead. Currently, the industry is largely process-oriented. Harnessing technology can transform every area of insurance operations, from product development to distribution, underwriting, and claims approval. Today, on average, it takes four to eight weeks, from the time the decision is made to proceed, to put a DI policy into the buyer's hands. The availability of electronic health records (a major health delivery objective of all provincial governments) could change this almost overnight. With appropriate authorization to tap into a central "warehouse" of health data on an applicant, underwriting could be completed in hours or days, not weeks. Claims approval time could similarly be reduced. Technology can enable companies to operate more efficiently by driving down costs and simultaneously increasing service. It is also likely to change the way that service is provided and client interactions occur.

Insurance is an infrequently purchased product bought at various life stages, then not thought about again until it is needed to claim benefits. The consumer engages in self-education only at these infrequent intervals, with only about 15% to 20% being information seekers;[2] the remainder must be reached by knowledgeable specialists at the right moment in the life cycle, when the consumer is open-minded and ready to discuss the topic, or what is sometimes referred to as "teachable moments". Many insurance products, such as disability, critical illness, and long-term care, can be complex to understand and difficult to compare. The specialist adviser can help to simplify and guide the consumer through the decision-making process.

Future delivery models are likely to make greater use of evolving technology to give consumers what they want. A study conducted by TEAMmakers Inc. for CIBC Insurance, which looked at consumers and their insurance perspectives, concluded that "consumers want to buy at their own convenience, when and where they please, and want to talk to a live person, not a message machine".[3] These consumer wishes and technology will no doubt impact both product design and distribution in the decades to come.

While no one can predict with certainty exactly what lies ahead, history has shown that the industry always finds a way to reinvent itself to respond to the external forces driving the change.

---

[2] TEAMmakers Inc., *Bridging the Gap Between the Insurance Industry and Its Consumers*, http://www.insurance-canada.ca/consinfogeneral/marketpl.php (July 1996).

[3] *Ibid.*

Topical Index